COMPUTER SCIENCE, TECHNOLOGY AND APPLICATIONS

Additional books in this series can be found on Nova's website
under the Series tab.

Additional E-books in this series can be found on Nova's website
under the E-book tab.

COMPUTER SCIENCE, TECHNOLOGY AND APPLICATIONS

COMPUTER SCIENCE RESEARCH AND THE INTERNET

JACLYN E. MORRIS
EDITOR

Nova Science Publishers, Inc.
New York

For permission to use material from this book please contact us:
Telephone 631-231-7269; Fax 631-231-8175
Web Site: http://www.novapublishers.com

NOTICE TO THE READER

The Publisher has taken reasonable care in the preparation of this book, but makes no expressed or implied warranty of any kind and assumes no responsibility for any errors or omissions. No liability is assumed for incidental or consequential damages in connection with or arising out of information contained in this book. The Publisher shall not be liable for any special, consequential, or exemplary damages resulting, in whole or in part, from the readers' use of, or reliance upon, this material. Any parts of this book based on government reports are so indicated and copyright is claimed for those parts to the extent applicable to compilations of such works.

Independent verification should be sought for any data, advice or recommendations contained in this book. In addition, no responsibility is assumed by the publisher for any injury and/or damage to persons or property arising from any methods, products, instructions, ideas or otherwise contained in this publication.

This publication is designed to provide accurate and authoritative information with regard to the subject matter covered herein. It is sold with the clear understanding that the Publisher is not engaged in rendering legal or any other professional services. If legal or any other expert assistance is required, the services of a competent person should be sought. FROM A DECLARATION OF PARTICIPANTS JOINTLY ADOPTED BY A COMMITTEE OF THE AMERICAN BAR ASSOCIATION AND A COMMITTEE OF PUBLISHERS.

Additional color graphics may be available in the e-book version of this book.

LIBRARY OF CONGRESS CATALOGING-IN-PUBLICATION DATA

Computer science research and the internet / editors, Jaclyn E. Morris.
    p. cm.
  Includes index.
  ISBN 978-1-61728-730-5 (hardcover)
  1. Computer science--Research. 2. Internet. I. Morris, Jaclyn E.
  QA76.27.C6735 2010
  004--dc22
                        2010025442

Published by Nova Science Publishers, Inc. † New York

CONTENTS

PREFACE

This book presents leading-edge research from across the globe in the field of computer science research, technology, the internet and applications. Each contribution has been carefully selected for inclusion based on the significance of the research to this fast-moving and diverse field. Some topics included are virtual applications in ENT medicine and for teaching surgery; genome web-browsers as critical bioinformatics tools; Ethernet networks; routers and networks with near-zero buffers; and augmented reality systems using 3D fiducial markers.

In Chapter 1, prokaryotic (T4 phage) and eukaryotic (human) molecular genetic data demonstrating quantum information processing of coherent DNA states by transcriptase measurements (BioSystems 2009, 97, 73-89) are reviewed and possible contributions to quantum computing are suggested. Coherent states – within decoherence-free base pair sites – are introduced as consequences of interstrand hydrogen bond arrangement, *keto-amino* $\rightarrow$ *enol-imine*, where product protons are shared between two sets of indistinguishable electron lone-pairs, and thus, participate in coupled quantum oscillations at frequencies of $\sim 10^{13}$ s^{-1}. This quantum mixing of proton energy states introduces stability enhancements of ~ 0.25 to 7 Kcal/mole. Transcriptase genetic specificity is determined by hydrogen bond components *contributing to* the formation of complementary hydrogen bonds which, in these cases, are variable due to coupled quantum oscillations of coherent enol-imine protons. The transcriptase deciphers and executes genetic specificity instructions by implementing measurements on superposition proton states at G'-C', *G-*C & *A-*T sites in an interval Δt $<< 10^{-13}$ s. Transcriptase measurement on a coherent G' site can yield observable specification for 3 of the 4 quantum G' states where – just before transcriptase measurement – the ket for the two G' quantum protons is $|\psi> = \alpha|+ +> + \beta|+ -> + \gamma|- +> + \delta|- ->$. Data demonstrating entanglement between coherent protons and transcriptase components are identified. After initiation of transcriptase measurement, model calculations indicate proton decoherence time, τ_D, satisfies the relation $\Delta t < \tau_D < 10^{-13}$ s. Decohered isomers participate in *accurate* Topal-Fresco replication to introduce base substitutions G' $\rightarrow$ T, G' $\rightarrow$ C, *C $\rightarrow$ T & *G $\rightarrow$ A, but coherent state *A-*T sites are evolutionarily deleted. Quantum uncertainty limits on amino protons drive the *keto-amino* $\rightarrow$ *enol-imine* arrangement. A 'rate constant' expression for introducing coherent states into duplex DNA is obtained. This allows an analytical expression for consequences of coherent states populating unstable $(CAG)_n$ repeats in human genomes. Measurements of 37^0 C lifetimes of the metastable keto-amino DNA hydrogen bond indicate a range of ~ 3000 to 60000 yrs. These results imply that natural selection at the quantum level has generated effective schemes (*a*) for introducing superposition proton states – at rates appropriate for DNA evolution – in decoherence-free subspaces and (*b*) for creating entanglement states that augment (*i*) transcriptase quantum processing and (*ii*) effective decoherence for complete (~100%) participation in Topal-Fresco replication of decohered isomers. In this scenario, the evolutionarily generated quantum information processing system has implemented coupled quantum proton oscillation in decoherence-free subspaces for 'low error' entangled qubits, which may provide insight into improved designs for room temperature quantum processing.

Chapter 2 discusses two applications which were developed to allow an instructor to guide and teach a medical student in a surgical training scenario. The most interesting feature of these applications is that both participants can simultaneously interact within the scene with haptic (force) feedback, allowing them to co-operatively touch and manipulate the virtual body organs. As well as this, the instructor can effectively grasp the student's hand and haptically guide it in a task within the scene. The first application was designed to teach the procedural aspects of a cholecystectomy (removal of the gall bladder), and incorporated several pliable body organs. The second application focused on temporal bone surgery, a procedure that involves drilling away part of the skull behind the ear to gain access to the middle and inner ear. Both applications allow instructor and student to be located in different places connected by the Internet. The first application was used for distance trials to determine the maximum geographical distance that was feasible between the two participants. Results showed that interaction between Australia and the USA was excellent and between Australia and Europe was adequate. The second application was used in a clinical trial with ear surgeons and their students. The results of these trials showed improved learning times over traditional methods. It was also discovered that there were unexpected benefits of having a networked system even when the two networked workstations were side-by-side.

A quantum algorithm is implemented using a quantum logic circuit that uses quantum mechanical phenomena to solve the problem. The quantum logic circuit is constructed with quantum gates using reversible logic synthesis techniques. Most of the quantum algorithms are binary algorithms. However, there are ample possibilities to develop multiple-valued quantum algorithms. The reasons are (i) multiple-valued quantum gates are realizable using existing quantum technologies, (ii) multiple-valued reversible logic synthesis is now possible, and (iii) multiple-valued quantum logic circuit is more compact and manageable than binary quantum logic circuit. The quaternary quantum logic circuit has additional advantage that qubits can be very easily encoded into quaternary qudits by grouping two qubits together. This advantage opens an avenue for using quaternary quantum logic circuit internally in binary quantum algorithms. Though there are other approaches of multiple-valued reversible/quantum logic circuit synthesis, the most promising and practical approach is to synthesize multiple-valued reversible/quantum logic circuit as Galois field sum of products (GFSOP) circuit. The advantage of this approach is that any multiple-valued non-reversible logic function with many input variables can be expressed as minimized GFSOP expression and the GFSOP expression can be realized as cascade of 1-qudit, M-S, Feynman, and Toffoli gates. Moreover, macro-level Feynman and Toffoli gates can be realized on the top of 1-qudit and M-S gates without using any ancilla input constant. In Chapter 3 the authors have developed effective method for synthesis of ternary and quaternary multiple-output logic functions as GFSOP circuit. For this purpose, the authors have introduced the concept of Galois filed (GF) with example of GF(3) and GF(4) and discussed the notion of GFSOP expression. The authors have developed Galois field expansions (GFE) for ternary and quaternary cases and have proposed heuristic algorithm for GFSOP minimization by application of these GFEs. For synthesizing quantum logic circuits with lesser width, the authors have developed method of realizing macro-level ternary and quaternary Feynman and Toffoli gates on the top of 1-qudit and M-S gates without use of any ancilla input. Finally, the authors have proposed method for multiple-output GFSOP realization as cascade of 1-qudit, M-S, Feynman, and Toffoli gates, which minimizes both the gate count and the width of the synthesized quantum circuit. The authors have established effectiveness of the GFSOP minimization algorithm with sufficient experimental results. The very important feature of the proposed synthesis method is that the method inherently converts a non-reversible function into a reversible one for GFSOP based realization using quantum gates.

In the last decades quantum theory – a theory based on quantum mechanical principles – has appeared in space research. Quantum theory based communication offers answers for some of nowadays' technical questions in satellite communication. In the authors' point of view, the quantum computing algorithms can be used to affirm their free-space communication in the following four ways: open-air communication, earth-satellite communications, satellite broadcast and inter-satellite communication. Quantum cryptography – cryptography based on quantum theory principles – gives better solutions for communication problems e.g. key distribution than the classical cryptographic methods, which have been found to have vulnerabilities in wired and wireless systems as well. The long distance quantum communication technologies in the future will far exceed the processing capabilities of current silicon-based devices. In current network technology, in order to spread quantum cryptography, interfaces able to manage together the quantum and classical channel must be implemented. Currently, the quantum cryptographic key generation systems (QKD) have been realized in metro-area networks over couple of ten kilometers The QKD can be used in wired or wireless (free-space) environment as well. The free-space based QKD solutions can achieve megabit-per-sec data rate communication. Long-distance open-air and satellite quantum communication experiments have been demonstrated the feasibility of extending quantum channel from ground to satellite, and in between satellites in free-space. The satellite based single photon links already allow QKD on global scale. In Chapter 4 the authors introduce how the quantum principles will affect the world of space communication. The authors summarize the ideas from the past until present and show solutions to set up an efficient quantum channel for the quantum based satellite communication.

Recently, virtual reality systems have been presented for simulation of machining processes, aiming at the determination of specific machining parameters, such as the required fixtures and the machining environment, the cutting tool dynamics, the chip shape and volume, and the shape of the cutting tool.

A methodology is presented in Chapter 5 for the development of a virtual environment for 3 axis milling process simulation. The technological and research challenges involved in this methodology are described.

The operation of a new system developed by the authors for machining-process simulation in a virtual environment is presented. This system integrates a virtual reality environment with computational and graphical models for the simulation of three axis milling processes. A computational model has been developed for the visualization of the milling process in the virtual environment and graphical model has been developed for the calculation of quantitative data related to surface roughness of machined surfaces.

Chapter 6 presents a review of some of the most common virtual environments to the neural simulation and a technological approach to make feasible the visualization of the simulation of neuron birth, growth and death, at the neural tissue level. This is called Distributed Environment to Neural Simulation (DENS).

As discussed in Chapter 7, analysis of the architecture and organization of protein structures is a major challenge to better understand protein flexibility, folding, functions and interactions with their partners and to design new drugs.

Protein structures are often described as series of α-helices and β-sheets, or at a higher level as an arrangement of protein domains. Due to the lack of an intermediate vision which could give a good understanding and description of protein structure architecture, the authors have proposed a novel intermediate view, the Protein Units (PUs). They are novel level of protein structure description between secondary structures and domains. A PU is defined as a compact sub-region of the 3D structure corresponding to one sequence fragment, defined by a high number of intra-PU contacts and a low number of inter-PU contacts. The methodology to obtain PUs from the protein structures is named Protein Peeling (PP). For the algorithm, the protein structures are described as a succession of Cα. The distances between Cα are translated into contact probabilities using a logistic function. Protein Peeling only uses this contact probability matrix. An optimization procedure, based on the Matthews' coefficient correlation (MCC) between contacts probability sub matrices, defines optimal cutting points that separate the region examined into two or three PUs. The process is iterated until the compactness of the resulting PUs reaches a given limit. An index assesses the compactness quality and relative independence of each PU.

Protein Peeling is a tool to better understand and analyze the organization of protein structures. The authors have developed a dedicated bioinformatic web server: Protein Peeling 2 (PP2). Given the 3D coordinates of a protein, it proposes an automatic identification of protein units (PUs). The interface component consists of a web page (HTML) and common gateway interface (CGI). The user can set many parameters and upload a given structure in PDB file format to a perl core instance. This last component is a module that embeds all the information necessary for two others softwares (mainly coded in C to perform most of the computation tasks and R for the analysis). Results are given both textually and graphically using JMol applet and PyMol software. The server can be accessed from http://www.dsimb.inserm.fr/dsimb_tools/peeling/. Only one equivalent on line methodology is available.

With the increasing amount of data being produced by radiological imaging modalities such as Magnetic Resonance Imaging (MRI) and especially Multi Detector Computed Tomography (MDCT) with datasets ranging up to over 1000 individual slices of half a millimeter thickness the demand for other visualization methods than just paging through all these slices in a stack is also growing rapidly. Traditionally, the evaluation of such datasets would be performed on dedicated workstation, powerful enough to handle the large amounts of data at acceptable speed using more advanced visualization techniques such as maximum intensity projection (MIP), Multi Planar Reformation (MPR) and three-dimensional volume rendering (VR). Although the need certainly existed, the more widespread use of these advanced visualization techniques was hampered by the fact that these tools were expensive and only available at a limited number of locations in the hospital. However, higher availability of advanced visualization has nowadays grown into a requirement to keep up with the growing data production. To meet this requirement, server based strategies for advanced visualization have found their way in to the clinical practice in radiology. In Chapter 8 the different levels of "thickness" of the server-client combinations will be covered as well as the current state-of-the-art both for the intranet of the hospital and for tele-medicine on the internet. Next implementation requirements will be covered that are obligatory to provide the conditions under which a server based advanced visualization system can strive within radiological practice. Besides this description of past and present the authors will also try to provide a view into the future and discuss where the server based advanced visualization could lead us.

Genome browsers are critical bioinformatics tools for biologists to visualize genome annotations and the other sequence features along a reference sequence. GBrowse is one of the most popular genome browsers used by the research community. However, its installation and configuration prove to be difficult for many biologists. The authors have developed a web server, WebGBrowse, which takes a user-supplied annotation file in GFF3 format, guides users through the configuration of the display of each genomic feature, and allows them to visualize the genome annotation information via the GBrowse software. Chapter 9 describes an upgraded WebGBrowse server, WebGBrowse 2.0, which provides users with a choice to display their genome annotation with different versions of the GBrowse software. The modular design of WebGBrowse 2.0 allows easy integration of future GBrowse upgrades. The authors have also developed a web-based GFF3 template generator to facilitate the preparation of the required annotation file in the correct format. The entire WebGBrowse 2.0 package is portable and can be freely downloaded and installed locally.

Virtual three-dimensional (3D) models of the individual human anatomy support the understanding in ENT (ear, nose, throat) medicine significantly. The interdisciplinary coactions of medicine and engineering enabled encompassing developments in reconstructing complex anatomies. Different fields of application can benefit from virtual models such as pre-surgery planning, medical education, and postoperative planning and patient information. To date, various visualization systems are available but according processes are not compatible and lead to time consuming efforts by veering away from medical needs. To overcome that limitations standardization is necessary to realize. Therefore, Chapter 10 intends to state the substantial needs of ENT medicine on virtual environments.

In Chapter 11 the authors analyze, through simulations, the performance of *Spanning Tree Protocol* (STP)-based Ethernet networks with ring and double ring topologies. In particular, the authors consider both the presence and the absence of *Virtual Local Area Networks* (VLANs), and they derive the optimized STP parameters which minimize the STP convergence time and maximize the network stability. Two possible techniques for STP internal timers management are evaluated. The presence of failures (either broken links or nodes) is also taken into account, in order to determine the proper STP parameters which guarantee connectivity recovery and convergence in all possible network scenarios. Some of the simulation results are also verified through an experimental testbed. Finally, the use of "transparent" switches is proposed as a solution to (i) accelerate the STP convergence, (ii) increase the reaction capability to failures, and (iii) overcome the limitations, imposed by the STP, on the maximum sustainable number of nodes. In particular, this approach allows to extend the number of nodes in the network, still guaranteeing the possibility of incorporating VLANs. In order to evaluate the impact of failures in a realistic network, the Open Shortest Path First (OSPF) protocol and the Hot Standby Router Protocol (HSRP) are introduced in an STP-based network. This analysis shows that the use of OSPF protocol and the HSRP does not affect the STP performance, even if a longer delay is required in order to start the transmission of ping messages and a reduced reaction capability to node/link failures must be accounted for.

All routers have buffers to store packets during periods of congestion. However, as Internet link speeds reach hundreds of Gigabits-per-second and beyond, it is becoming increasingly difficult to equip high-speed routers with large buffers, especially as switching moves into the all-optical domain. In Chapter 12 the authors first trace the evolution in thinking over recent years on how much buffering is required at Internet routers, focusing specifically on the push towards smaller buffers, from Gigabyte down to Kilobyte sizes, making them amenable for all-optical realisation. The authors then highlight some of the implications of the move towards such small buffers, such as end-to-end performance for real-time and TCP traffic, the reaction of TCP to reduced buffer availability in the network, and the unexpected interactions between TCP and open-loop traffic. Finally, the authors propose mechanisms ranging from edge traffic conditioning to packet-level forward error correction within the network as means of overcoming the limitations posed by small buffers in the network, and speculate on the feasibility of a zero-buffer Internet core in the future.

Augmented reality (AR) often makes use of a 2D fiducial marker to render computer graphics onto a video frame so that the computer-generated object appears aligned with the scene. In Chapter 13 the authors extend this idea to 3D where real-world objects are used as fiducial markers and propose a distributed AR system that utilizes geographically located resources to meet high computing demand, enable sustained remote operations, and support collaborative efforts. Within the distributed AR system, the authors present technical solutions to several key modules in AR that form a linear computing pipeline. The authors generalize and formulate the pipeline network mapping as optimization problems under different mapping constraints and develop heuristic algorithms that maximize the frame rate to achieve smooth data flow. Extensive simulation-based results show that the proposed mapping heuristics outperform the existing methods.

Multi-Processors System on Chip (MPSoCs) and Massively Parallel Processors (MPPs) architectures are conceived to efficiently implement Thread Level Parallelism, a common characteristic of modern software applications targeted by embedded systems. Each core in a MPP environment is designed to execute a particular instructions flow, known as thread, in a completely self-sufficient manner, being able to communicate with the other cores in order to exchange shared data. The demand of parallelism in MPPs and MPSoCs entails the design of an efficient communication layer able to sustain it. This means that the interconnection medium has to be both scalable, to allow multiple accesses of the different cores to the shared resources, and optimized in terms of wiring. These are all native characteristics of Networks on Chip (NoCs).

In MPSoCs and MPPs, it is necessary to provide:

- quick resolution of the interdependencies among different threads, single scalar data or even vectors. Interdependencies are responsible of completion time delay because prevent a thread from completion when not resolved;
- load balancing support techniques to avoid hot spots and to efficiently exploit all the cores available on chip. When threads migration occurs, a regular and continuous traffic is generated, made up of long streams of data;
- management of end-to-end small control data.

Circuit Switching (CS) technique is the method by which a dedicated path, or circuit, is established prior the sending of the sensitive data. Circuit switched networks are suitable for guaranteed throughput applications, especially in case of real time communications.

In Packet Switching (PS) methodologies the intermediate routers are responsible for routing the individual packets through the network, neither following a predefined nor a reserved path. Packet switched networks are suitable for best-effort services or for soft-timing constrained communications. In Chapter 14 the authors will look at the possibility of combining CS and PS in order to support the heterogeneous traffic patterns coexisting in a MPP environment. Hybrid switching networks are designed to guarantee the benefits of both CS and PS consisting in a better usage of the available bandwidth and in a global increase of the overall throughput, at the price of a more complex hardware implementation. In this scope, the latest approaches in literature are presented, together with a particular NoC model able to provide dual-mode hybrid switching in a non-exclusive way, intended as the possibility of co-sharing the amount of available bandwidth between CS and PS communications.

In: Computer Science Research and the Internet   ISBN: 978-1-61728-730-5
Editor: Jaclyn E. Morris, pp. 1-41   © 2011 Nova Science Publishers, Inc.

Chapter 1

Evolutionarily Designed Quantum Information Processing of Coherent States in Prokaryotic and Eukaryotic DNA Systems[*]

W. Grant Cooper[*]

International Physics Health & Energy, Inc.,
Lubbock, Texas

Abstract

Prokaryotic (T4 phage) and eukaryotic (human) molecular genetic data demonstrating quantum information processing of coherent DNA states by transcriptase measurements (BioSystems 2009, 97, 73-89) are reviewed and possible contributions to quantum computing are suggested. Coherent states – within decoherence-free base pair sites – are introduced as consequences of interstrand hydrogen bond arrangement, *keto-amino → enol-imine*, where product protons are shared between two sets of indistinguishable electron lone-pairs, and thus, participate in coupled quantum oscillations at frequencies of $\sim 10^{13}$ s^{-1}. This quantum mixing of proton energy states introduces stability enhancements of ~ 0.25 to 7 Kcal/mole. Transcriptase genetic specificity is determined by hydrogen bond components *contributing to* the formation of complementary hydrogen bonds which, in these cases, are variable due to coupled quantum oscillations of coherent enol-imine protons. The transcriptase deciphers and executes genetic specificity instructions by implementing measurements on superposition proton states at G'-C', *G-*C & *A-*T sites in an interval $\Delta t \ll 10^{-13}$ s. Transcriptase measurement on a coherent G' site can yield observable specification for 3 of the 4 quantum G' states where – just before transcriptase measurement – the ket for the two G' quantum protons is $\left| \psi \right> = \alpha \left| + +\right> + \beta \left| + -\right> + \gamma \left| - +\right> + \delta \left| - -\right>$. Data demonstrating entanglement between coherent protons and transcriptase components are identified. After initiation of transcriptase measurement, model calculations indicate proton decoherence time, τ_D, satisfies the relation $\Delta t < \tau_D < 10^{-13}$ s. Decohered isomers participate in *accurate* Topal-Fresco replication to introduce base substitutions G' → T, G' → C, *C → T & *G → A, but coherent state *A-*T sites are evolutionarily deleted. Quantum uncertainty limits on amino protons drive the *keto-amino → enol-imine* arrangement. A 'rate constant' expression for introducing coherent states into duplex DNA is obtained. This allows an analytical expression for consequences of coherent states

---
[*] E-mail address: cooperwg@sbcglobal.net.

populating unstable $(CAG)_n$ repeats in human genomes. Measurements of 37^0 C lifetimes of the metastable keto-amino DNA hydrogen bond indicate a range of ~ 3000 to 60000 yrs. These results imply that natural selection at the quantum level has generated effective schemes (*a*) for introducing superposition proton states – at rates appropriate for DNA evolution – in decoherence-free subspaces and (*b*) for creating entanglement states that augment (*i*) transcriptase quantum processing and (*ii*) effective decoherence for complete (~100%) participation in Topal-Fresco replication of decohered isomers. In this scenario, the evolutionarily generated quantum information processing system has implemented coupled quantum proton oscillation in decoherence-free subspaces for 'low error' entangled qubits, which may provide insight into improved designs for room temperature quantum processing.

Keywords: Quantum information storage; Quantum information transfer; Coupled quantum oscillation; Decoherence-free subspaces; Transcriptase quantum processing; 'Stable' entanglement; Transcriptase-assisted decoherence; Coherent proton bonds; Quantum uncertainty limits; Quantum biology

I. Introduction

Quantum information science (Vedral, 2007; Leon, J., Martin-Martinez, E., 2009; Appel et al., 2009) is an extremely active endeavor where current designs of quantum computers (e.g., Kim et al., 2009; Herskind et al., 2009; Roloff et al., 2009; Devitt et al., 2009) employ different quantum systems – electrons (Tsai et al., 2009), atoms (Gaetan et al., 2009), ions (Feng et al., 2009) and molecules (Mishima et al., 2009) – as single and multiple qubits (Fedichkin et al., 2009) that participate in entanglement (Goold et al., 2009) to implement quantum computing. This activity in quantum information science is motivated by the potential to exploit applications of quantum theory to significantly enhance the versatility of acquiring, transmitting and processing information, using a quantum mechanical basis for information codes (Nielson and Chuang, 2000; Rezakhani, et al., 2009). Consistent with the notion that quantum information science could benefit from direct evidence of quantum information processing by living cells (Vedral, 2003), this chapter reviews recent studies (Cooper, 2009a, b, 2010) and presents new evidence that genetic specificity information residing within time-dependent coherent states in duplex DNA is routinely measured and deciphered by transcriptase quantum processing. Although the initial assessments were on bacteriophage T4 DNA systems (Cooper, 1994), the introduction of coherent states and subsequent transcriptase quantum processing are also exhibited by human DNA systems (Sec. V). In an effort to connect molecular genetic observations of quantum information processing to concepts utilized in quantum computing, this chapter identifies (*a*) the quantum model for DNA instability, (*b*) the origin of coupled coherent states (e.g., Fedichkin et al., 2009) in decoherence-free subspaces (Bell et al., 2002; Oreshkov et al., 2008; Poccia et al., 2009; Mei et al., 2009) of duplex DNA and (*c*) the necessity of quantum coherence to explain molecular genetic observations, including (*i*) multiple genetic specificities exhibited by transcriptase measurements on coherent states within individual G' and *C genetic sites (see Figure 2 for notation) and (*ii*) entanglement between coherent protons and transcriptase components.

Genetic sites capable of exhibiting coherence, and thus transcriptase quantum processing, are time-dependent 'point' lesions in mammalian genomes (Hwang and Green, 2004; Beerenwinkel et al., 2007; Elango et al., 2008) and in bacteriophage T4 DNA (Kricker & Drake, 1990; Cooper, 1994, 2009a, b). The time-dependent molecular clock (Bromham and Penny, 2003) event, CpG → TpG, is the most frequent point mutation observed in the human genome and the rate is ~ 15-fold greater when cytosine is methylated (Elango et al., 2008). Since this form of time-dependent substitution, C → *C → T, is one of four related substitutions, i.e., also G' → T, G' → C & *G → A, exhibited by T4 phage DNA, this chapter and other studies (Cooper, 1994, 2009a, b) assume a general mechanism is responsible for time-dependent substitutions (hereafter, *ts*) and time-dependent deletions (hereafter, *td*) in all duplex DNA systems. Phage T4 DNA systems are particularly susceptible to an examination of *ts* and *td* since their origin and consequences of transcription and replication can be evaluated in terms of fine scale genetic mapping (Benzer, 1961), reversion analysis (Baltz et al., 1976) and strand analysis (Cooper, 1994, 2009b). The latter can specify the particular isomer of a complementary G'-C' or *G-*C pair responsible for a *ts*. Consequently the two classes of time-dependent point lesion accumulated in extracellular T4 phage DNA (Ripley, 1988), G-C → G'-C' and G-C → *G-*C (Figs 1-2), can be assayed genetically at the resolution of an individual G', C', *G or *C isomer within a G'-C' or *G-*C genetic site (Benzer, 1961; Kricker and Drake, 1990). In an attempt to provide insight into "room temperature" quantum information processing, this chapter illustrates how evolutionarily designed coherent state genetic specificities are created, and subsequently – measured, deciphered and decohered – at biological temperatures by transcriptase quantum processing, which is the purpose of this (Figure 1a) article. The resulting quantum model of intrinsic DNA instability is consistent with observation (Cooper, 1994, 2009a, b) and quantum theory (Merzbacher, 1997; Zurek, 1991; Bell et al., 2002; Ghosh et al., 2003; Vedral, 2003; Chen et al., 2009).

The next section summarizes the quantum model for introducing time-dependent coherent states into duplex DNA and identifies the rationale for transcriptase quantum processing. The quantum system for transcriptase processing of two interacting two-level proton states on G' is outlined in Sec. III. Reactive proton states within duplex DNA are treated in Sec. IV. Quantum uncertainty limits on –NH$_2$ protons drive the *keto-amino* → *enol-imine* arrangement, which introduces enol-imine protons that participate in coupled quantum oscillations at frequencies of ~10^{13} s^{-1}. Based on experiment, lifetimes of 37^0 C keto-amino hydrogen bonds are the order of ~ 3000 to ~ 60000 years. Approximate quantum methods are used to obtain a 'rate constant' expression for introducing coherent states via the *keto-amino* → *enol-imine* arrangement. Section V develops a polynomial model (quantum + classical) for phenotypic expression of a (CAG)$_n$ repeat human disease as a function of a (CAG)$_n$ "genetic threshold" becoming populated beyond its evolutionarily allowed limit by time-dependent coherent states. The Conclusion is presented in Section VI.

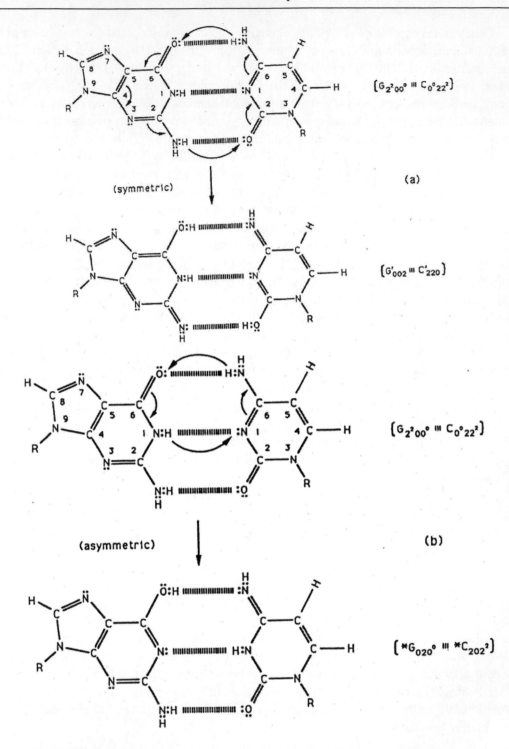

(a)

(b)

Figure 1. (a) Symmetric channel for proton exchange tunneling electron rearrangement, yielding two enol-imine hydrogen bonds between complementary G-C. (b) The asymmetric exchange tunneling channel, yielding the G-C hybrid state containing one enol-imine and one keto-amino hydrogen bond. An annulus of reaction is identified by arrows within each G-C reactant duplex. Electron lone-pairs are represented by double dots, :.

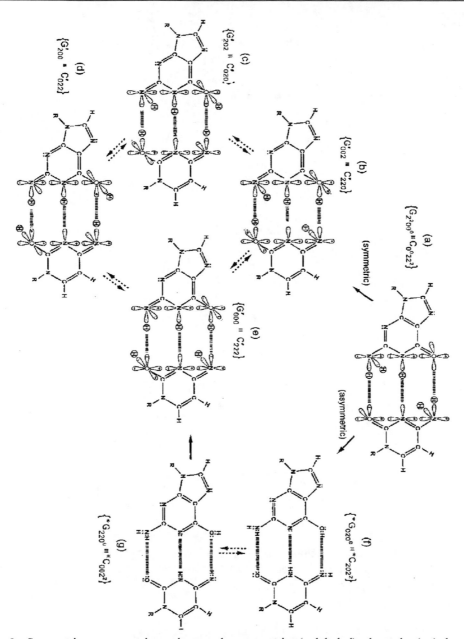

Figure 2. Symmetric, asymmetric and second asymmetric (unlabeled) channels ($\rightarrow$) by which metastable keto-amino G-C protons populate enol-imine states. Dashed arrows identify pathways for quantum mechanical flip-flop of enol-imine protons. Approximate electronic structures for hydrogen bond end groups and corresponding proton positions are shown for the metastable keto-amino duplex (a) and for enol-imine G'-C' coherent states (b-e). The asymmetric channel introduces the hybrid state super position, *G-*C (f, g). Electron lone-pairs are represented by double dots, :, and a proton by a circled H. Proton states are specified by a compact notation, using letters G, C, A, T for DNA bases with 2's and 0's identifying electron lone-pairs and protons, respectively, donated to the hydrogen bond by – from left to right – the 6-carbon side chain (see Figure 1 for numbering of atom positions), the ring nitrogen and the 2-carbon side chain. Superscripts identify the component at the outside position (in major and minor groves) as either an amino group proton, designated by 0^0, or a keto group electron lone-pair, indicated by 2^2. Superscripts are suppressed for enol and imine groups.

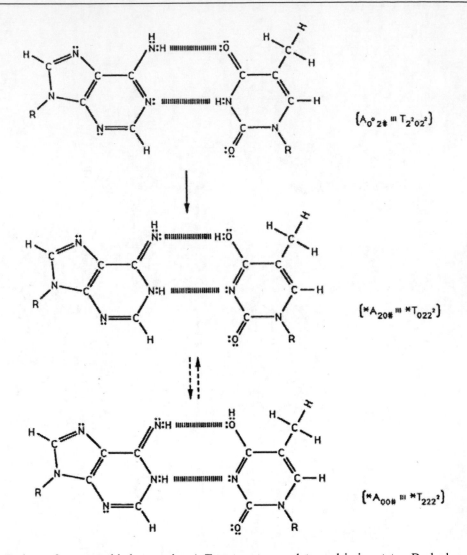

Figure 3. Pathway for metastable keto-amino A-T protons to populate enol-imine states. Dashed arrows indicate proton flip-flop pathway between coherent enol-imine *A-*T states. Notation is given in Figure 2 legend. The # symbol indicates the position is occupied by ordinary hydrogen unsuitable for hydrogen bonding.

II. Summary of the Quantum Model of Time-Dependent DNA Instability

A. Time-Dependent Creation of Coherent States and Consequences

Consistent with molecular genetic observables (Cooper, 1994, 2009a, b, 2010), the quantum model of DNA specificity assumes the replicase generates complementary duplex DNA in terms of metastable hydrogen-bonded keto-amino protons that satisfy the criteria for a noninteracting isolated system (Reif, 1965), which is not at equilibrium. Based on compatibility between observation (Cooper, 1994, 2009a, b), chemistry (Löwdin, 1965;

Scheiner, 1997) and physics (Zurek, 1991; Bell et al., 2002; Ghosh et al., 2003; Vedral, 2003; Chen et al., 2009), the metastable keto-amino state populates accessible enol-imine states as consequences of hydrogen bond arrangement, *keto-amino* → *enol-imine* by symmetric and asymmetric channels (Figures 1– 3), designated by G-C → *G-*C, G-C → G'-C' and A-T → *A-*T. Product enol and imine protons are shared between two sets of indistinguishable electron lone pairs, and therefore, participate in coupled quantum oscillation between near symmetric double minima at frequencies of ~ 10^{13} s^{-1} (Tables 5-8). The asymmetric channel yields two superposition *G-*C states and the symmetric channel creates a superposition of four quantum G'-C' states (Figure 2). Genetic specificity at a coherent superposition site, G'-C', *G-*C (Figure 2) or *A-*T (Figure 3), is stored as an input qubit. Before decoherence or replication, the informational content within a coherent superposition is deciphered and processed by the transcriptase as an output qubit in an interval $\Delta t \ll 10^{-13}$ s. In the case of a *C site on the template strand (T-strand), the transcriptase distinguishes genetic specificities of quantum states, *C2 0 2^2 ⇌*C0 0 2^2 (Figure 2f-g), on the basis of measurements on the cytosine carbon-6 imine proton, which participates in coupled quantum oscillation. Similarly in the G' case, genetic specificities residing within quantum states, G'2 0 2 (Figure 4b) ⇌ G'0 0 2 (Figure 4d), are deciphered by coherent state measurements on the guanine carbon-6 enol proton. Figure 4 illustrates that normal thymine, T2^2 0 2^2, and enol and imine quantum states, G'2 0 2 and *C2 0 2^2, contribute identical proton and electron lone-pair components in their formation of complementary hydrogen bonds. If transcriptase specificity of a base were exclusively determined by protons and electron lone-pairs contributing to the formation of complementary hydrogen bonds, transcriptase measurements on G'-C' and *G-*C sites (Figure 2) would decipher quantum states, G'2 0 2 & *C2 0 2^2, as normal T2^2 0 2^2, and consequently, substitutions G'2 0 2 → T and *C2 0 2^2 → T would be phenotypically expressed by transcription before replication incorporates T2^2 0 2^2, which in fact is observed (Baltz et al., 1976; Bingham et al., 1976; Cooper, 1994, 2009b). Data are therefore consistent with transcriptase specificity governed by the configuration of protons and electron lone-pairs *contributed to* the formation of complementary hydrogen bonds when the transcriptase implements its measurement. Transcriptase measurement creates an entanglement state (Vedral, 2003) – which is also a superposition – between coherent protons and transcriptase components. Entanglement is implied by the fact that mutation frequencies, *C2 0 2^2 → T & G'2 0 2 → T, phenotypically expressed by transcription – before replication – are identical to the subsequent frequencies, *C2 0 2^2 → T & G'2 0 2 → T, exhibited by genotypic incorporation at replication (Cooper, 2009b). Therefore after transcription and before replication, template quantum states, *C2 0 2^2 and G'2 0 2, were protected from exposure to H_2O (Topal and Fresco, 1976) due to entanglement between coherent protons and transcriptase components. The entanglement state ultimately causes a rapid decoherent transition from quantum to classical, yielding a statistical ensemble of enol and imine isomers suitable for Topal-Fresco replication (Table 1). Decoherence is governed by the dynamics of the coherent quantum system and its interaction with the transcriptase environment as a measurement is implemented. Nevertheless, data (Cooper, 2009b) show that *all* (~ 100%) decohered *C2 0 2^2 and G'2 0 2 isomers participate in the formation of complementary mispairs, *C2 0 2^2–A0^0 2 # and G'2 0 2–syn-A0^0 2 # (Table 1), required for substitutions, *C2 0 2^2 → T & G'2 0 2 → T, introduced by Topal-Fresco replication. Therefore before the initial replication after decoherence, these decohered isomers are also protected from exposure to H_2O. In the next round of replication, entanglement is absent and ~ 20% of *C2 0 2^2 exhibits reequilibration, *C2 0 $2^2 \rightarrow C0^0$ 0 2^2 (Cooper, 2009b). Replication of decohered isomers introduces *ts* transversions, G'2 0 2 $\rightarrow$ T & G'0 0 2 $\rightarrow$ C, and *ts* transitions, *G0 2 0^0 $\rightarrow$ A & *C2 0 $2^2 \rightarrow$ T; however, coherent states within *A-*T sites (Figure 3) cause deletion, *td* (Cooper, 2009b). Explanations other than "entanglement protection" are not obvious. This mode of determining specificity by the transcriptase (Table 1) is independent of the proton or electron lone-pair at the "outside" position (in the major and minor groves) on keto, enol and imine groups (Figure 4). Otherwise, enol and imine groups on quantum states G' 2 0 2 and *C2 0 2^2 could *not* simulate keto groups on normal $T2^2$ 0 2^2 at transcription as observed. Also, this method of determining specificity is tolerant of gross structural dissimilarities between the dual ring purine, G'2 0 2, and single ring pyrimidines, *C2 0 2^2 & $T2^2$ 0 2^2, as observed.

Table 1. Transcribed messages of coherent states, decohered isomers and formation of complementary mispairs for Topal-Fresco replication. Normal tautomers (top row) and coherent quantum flip-flop states/decohered tautomers (left column) are listed in terms of the compact notation for hydrogen-bonding configurations identified in Figure 2 Legend. Consistent with Topal-Fresco (1976), base pair substitution notation at the respective row-column juncture identifies decohered tautomers that will form a complementary mispair with a normal base, including syn-purines. Transcribed messages obtained from a coherent quantum state are identified in the right hand column

Quantum flip flop States	Allowable Pair Formation at Replication						Transcription Message
	NORMAL BASES				Syn-Purines		
	$G_2^2 00^0$	$C_0^0 22^2$	$A_0^0 2\#$	$T_2^2 02^2$	$G_2^2 2\#$	$A_0^0 2\#$	
G'_{002}					G-C → C-G		$U^{\mp}$
G'_{202}						G-C → T-A	$T_{2^2 02^2}$
G'_{200}		not detectable					$G_{2^2 00^0}$
G'_{000}							U
$*G_{020^0}$			G-C → A-T				U
$*G_{220^0}$							U
C'_{220}							U
C'_{020}							U
C'_{022}	not detectable						$C_{0^0 22^2}$
C'_{222}							U
$*C_{202^2}$		G-C → A-T					$T_{2^2 02^2}$
$*C_{002^2}$							U
$*A_{20\#}$		A-T → G-C				A-T → T-A	U
$*A_{00\#}$					A-T → C-G		U
$*T_{022^2}$	A-T → G-C						$C_{0^0 22^2}$
$*T_{222^2}$							U

$\mp$ Undefined

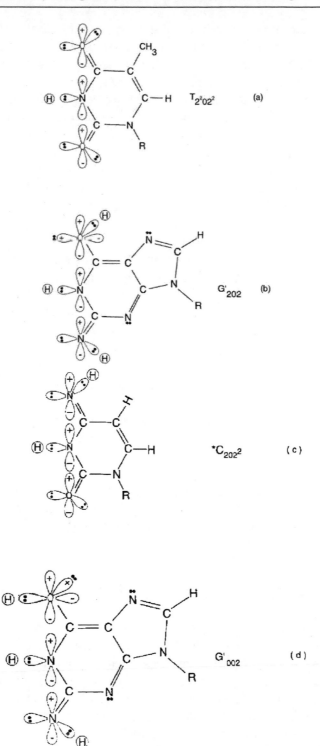

Figure 4. Approximate proton electron hydrogen bonding structure "seen by" transcriptase systems when encountering (a) normal thymine, $T2^2 0 2^2$, (b) coherent enol-imine G'2 0 2, (c) coherent imino cytosine, *C2 0 2^2, and (d) coherent enol-imine G'0 0 2.

Although decoherent process could be expected to disallow coherent states from accumulating in duplex DNA, Bell et al. (2002) have shown that strong interactions with an external thermal bath can cause an out of phase quantum system to become re-synchronized, and thus, maintain a form of coherence. Also if the system is in an entangled state of left and right well locations, this entanglement can be preserved by environmental interactions. These properties exhibited by a quantum neutrino system in dense media are general and thus provide rationale for coherent states to accumulate in duplex DNA. Analogous to the neutrino system studied by Bell et al. (2002), coupled coherent proton states may – through certain degrees of freedom – have identical interactions with their environment, and consequently, occupy decoherence-free subspaces (Grace et al., 2007; Mei et al., 2009; Chen et al., 2009). Also strand separation caused by DNA breathing (Alberts et al., 2002) could reequilibrate unusual tautomers. However, base pairs consisting of superposition proton states are stabilized by ~ 0.25 to 7 Kcal/mole (Table 9), and thus, could impede lower levels of strand separation since this disruptive energy would be the order of ~ ½ to a few kT (Metzler and Ambjörnsson, 2005). Consequently time-dependent point mutations are introduced at the DNA level as observed (Hwang and Green, 2004; Beerenwinkel et al., 2007; Elango et al., 2008). Recent data (Cooper, 2009a, b) and this chapter imply that evolutionary pressures have implemented effective schemes for (*a*) introducing coherent proton states – at rates appropriate for DNA evolution – which occupy decoherence-free subspaces (Bell et al., 2002; Grace et al., 2007; Oreshkov et al., 2008; Mei et al., 2009; Chen et al., 2009) at G'-C', *G-*C and *A-*T sites in duplex DNA and (*b*) using entanglement states to augment transcriptase quantum processing and subsequent transcriptase-assisted decoherence at biological temperature. This model of DNA instability is a combination of the Löwdin (1965) and Topal-Fresco (1976) models, referred to as the LTF model. Thus an additional venue is presented for studying the relationship between superposition protons states (Karlsson, 2003; Fillaux et al., 2008), entanglement (Ghosh et al., 2003; Vedral, 2003), and the resulting statistical ensemble of decohered isomers (Zurek, 1991, 2003; Table 10), using data from (*i*) time-dependent DNA lesions exhibited by bacteriophage T4 (Cooper, 1994, 2009a, b) and (*ii*) microsatellite evolution data exhibited by human $(CAG)_n$ repeats responsible for heritable human diseases, i.e., Eq (38).

B. A 'Point' Mutation at a G' Site Exhibits Multiple Genetic Specificities

In the case of time-dependent rUV74 *rII* → r^+ transversion revertants, G' is on the T-strand (Cooper, 1994, 2009 b). The transcriptase implements a measurement on coherent states at the G' site and deciphers genetic specificities originating from quantum states G'0 0 2, G'2 0 2, G'2 0 0 & G'0 0 0, using Figure 2 notation. Data demonstrate that 350 of the 460 (76%) revertants detected express G'2 0 2 →T as a consequence of transcription *before* replication was initiated, but 110 of the 460 (24%) revertants required replication (passage) to express G'0 0 2 → C. In this case, genetic specificities originating within quantum states, G'2 0 2 (Figure 4b) ⇌ G'0 0 2 (Figure 4d), are deciphered by the transcriptase on the basis of different coherent states for the guanine carbon-6 enol proton, which participates in coupled quantum oscillation. State G'0 0 2 communicates that it is *not* a transcription analog of $C0^0$ 2 2^2 or $T2^2$ 0 2^2; so, passage (replication) is required for expression of the G'0 0 2 → C substitution, which involves Topal-Fresco replication of the complementary mispair, G'0 0 2–

syn-$G2^2$ 2 # (Figure 5), to insert normal $C0^0$ 2 2^2. Compared to state G'0 0 2, expression of state G'2 0 2 was enhanced by a single round of transcription *before* replication was initiated. After transcription and before replication, the template quantum state, G'2 0 2, was *not* subjected to H_2O and reequilibration, but was preserved by entanglement between coherent protons and transcriptase components. Additionally, *all* decohered G'2 0 2 isomers formed complementary mispairs, G'2 0 2–syn-$A0^0$ 2 # (Table 1; Figure 5), required for the G'2 0 2 → T substitution resulting from Topal-Fresco replication. Given these two conditions, straightforward analysis predicts the number of G'2 0 2 → T events should be ~ 2-fold greater (after passage) than the number of G'0 0 2 → C events. However observation shows G'2 0 2 → T (76%) is ~ 3-fold more numerous than G'0 0 2 → C (24%). Since the quantum state G'2 0 2 is "preferred" compared to state G'0 0 2 (Figure 6; Sec. II C), this would cause an enhanced availability of quantum G'2 0 2 at transcription and a corresponding increased yield of the decohered G'2 0 2 isomer at replication, which would explain the greater than expected yield, i.e., 3-fold rather than 2-fold, of G'2 0 2 → T compared to G'0 0 2 → C.

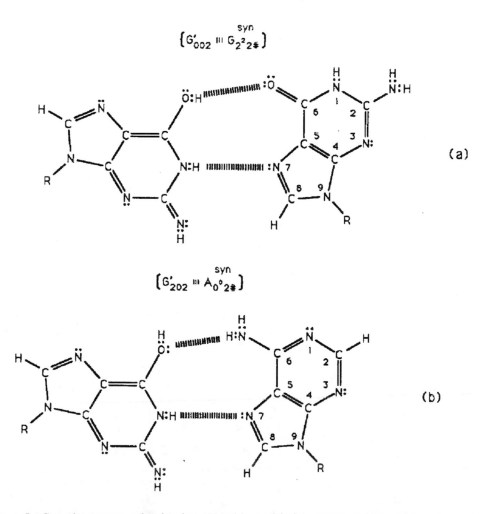

Figure 5. Complementary mispairs between (a) enol-imine G'002 (Figure 2b) and syn-guanine (syn-$G2^2$2#) and (b) enol-imine G'202 (Figure 2c) and syn-adenine (syn-$A0^0$2#). The # symbol indicates the position is occupied by ordinary hydrogen unsuitable for hydrogen bonding.

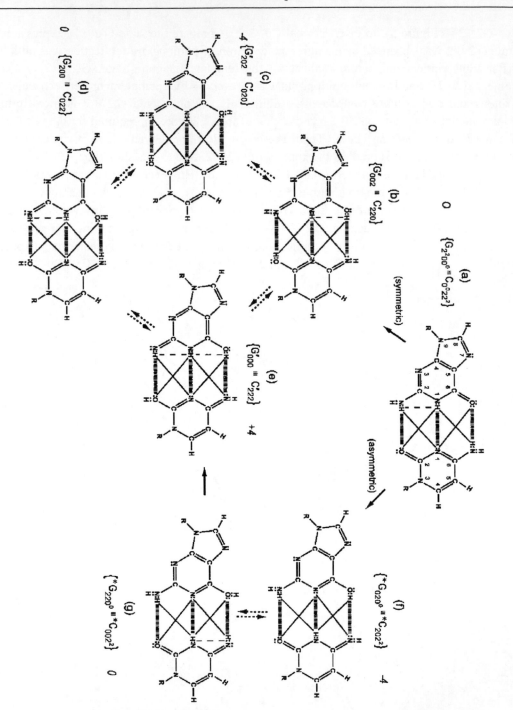

Figure 6. Secondary interaction model (Pranata et al., 1991) applied to coherent superposition G'-C' and *G-*C states for purposes of identifying relative base pairing energies. A +1 is assigned to each secondary interaction between opposite charges and a –1 for an interaction between same sign charges, yielding a +4 for state (e) and a – 4 for flip-flop states (c) and (f). The remaining four states – (a), (b), (d), (g) – are intermediate with base pairing energy values of 0. The dashed lines identify intramolecular proton-proton repulsion.

C. "Favored Status" of the G'2 0 2 Quantum State in Terms of Secondary Electrostatic Interactions

Time-dependent transversions originate at G'-C' sites (Cooper, 1994, 2009b) where a complementary duplex contains a superposition of four quantum states illustrated in Figure 2b-e. In the case of rUV74 $rII \rightarrow r^+$ transversion revertants, G' is on the T-strand. Section II B noted that, compared to state G'0 0 2, expression of state G'2 0 2 was enhanced by a single round of transcription *before* replication was initiated. Under conditions of entanglement and all decohered G'2 0 2 states forming the complementary mispair, G'2 0 2–syn-A0^0 2 #, the number of G'2 0 2 $\rightarrow$ T events should be ~ 2-fold greater (after passage) than the number of G'0 0 2 $\rightarrow$ C events. However observation shows G'2 0 2 $\rightarrow$ T (76%) is ~ 3-fold more numerous than G'0 0 2 $\rightarrow$ C (24%). Although quantum proton oscillations are the order of ~ 10^{13} s^{-1}, the relative distribution of quantum duplex G'-C' states can be qualitatively estimated, using Jorgensen's model (Jorgensen and Pranata, 1990; Pranata et al., 1991) for secondary electrostatic interactions within a superposition of complementary duplex states. This is illustrated in Figure 6 where the duplex state G'000 – C'222 (Figure 6e) exhibits the maximum *intramolecular* proton-proton repulsion and thus is the least preferred configuration. This state is identified by an energy pairing value of +4. The preferred states exhibit the minimum intrabase proton-proton repulsion interactions and are identified in Figures 6c,f. These preferred configurations yield energy pairing values of – 4. Since the G'2 0 2– C'0 2 0 duplex (Figure 6c) is a favored "relaxed" configuration compared to G'0 0 2–C'2 2 0 (Figure 6b), this would cause an enhanced availability of quantum G'2 0 2 at transcription and a corresponding increased yield of the decohered G'2 0 2 isomer at replication, which would explain the greater than expected yield, i.e., 3-fold rather than 2-fold, of G'2 0 2 $\rightarrow$ T compared to G'0 0 2 $\rightarrow$ C. Curiously both G'2 0 2 and *C2 0 2^2 are transcribed as normal T2^2 0 2^2 and are therefore responsible for "transcription enhancement" of mutation, G'2 0 2 $\rightarrow$ T and *C2 0 2^2 $\rightarrow$ T, and further, quantum duplex states G'2 0 2– C'0 2 0 (Figure 6c) and *G0 2 0^0–*C2 0 2^2 (Figure 6f) are the only "preferred" configurations in Figure 6. Evidently this is part of the time-dependent evolutionary scheme favoring A-T richness (Cooper, 2009b).

III. Outline for Transcriptase Measurement of Coherent G' Protons

Coherent enol and imine G'-protons are identified here as p_1 and p_2, respectively, and constitute two subspaces, $\varepsilon_x(1)$ and $\varepsilon_x(2)$, of the combined space, ε_x. A coherent G' proton is in state $| + >$ when it is in position to participate in interstrand hydrogen bonding and is in state $| - >$ when it is "outside", in the major or minor grove. These two states form a computational basis for each proton, p_1 and p_2, and obey the relation $< + | - > = \delta_{+ -}$. Other pure states of the proton system can be expressed as a superposition, $\alpha | + > + \beta | - >$, for some α and β where $|\alpha|^2 + |\beta|^2 = 1$. Each coherent proton of this G'-state is a superposition of "in" (interstrand H-bond) and "out" (outside, groove position) states. The position states of proton p_1 form a two-dimensional subspace $\varepsilon_x(1)$, and likewise, the position state of proton p_2 is defined by a ket belonging to a two-dimensional state space, $\varepsilon_x(2)$. The position observables of p_1 and p_2 are designated by x_1 and x_2, respectively. In $\varepsilon_x(1)$ and $\varepsilon_x(2)$, the basis eigenkets of x_1 and x_2 are designated by $|1:+>$, $|1:->$ and $|2:+>$, $|2:->$. The general ket of $\varepsilon_x(1)$ can be written as

$$|\chi(1)> = \alpha_1 |1:+> + \beta_1 |1:-> \tag{1}$$

and that of $\varepsilon_x(2)$ is given by

$$|\zeta(2)> = \alpha_2 |2:+> + \beta_2 |2:-> \tag{2}$$

where α_1, β_1, α_2, β_2 are arbitrary complex numbers. The proton systems, p_1 and p_2, can be coalesced into a four-dimensional state space, ε_x, by expressing the tensor products of $\varepsilon_x(1)$ and $\varepsilon_x(2)$ as

$$\varepsilon_x = \varepsilon_x(1) \otimes \varepsilon_x(2). \tag{3}$$

This yields the following ket notation as

$$|++> = |1:+> |2:+> \tag{4}$$

$$|+-> = |1:+> |2:->$$

$$|-+> = |1:-> |2:+>$$

$$|--> = |1:-> |2:->.$$

Here $<+-|$ is the conjugate bra of the ket $|+->$ where the first symbol is associated with p_1 and the second with p_2. Since the bases $\{|1:\pm>\}$ and $\{|2:\pm>\}$ are orthonormal in $\varepsilon_x(1)$ and $\varepsilon_x(2)$ respectively, the basis given by Eq (4) is orthonormal in ε_x, expressed as

$$< \varepsilon_1\, \varepsilon_2 \,|\, \acute{\varepsilon}_1\, \acute{\varepsilon}_2 > = \delta_{\varepsilon_1 \acute{\varepsilon}_1}\, \delta_{\varepsilon_2 \acute{\varepsilon}_2} . \tag{5}$$

Also the system of vectors in Eq (4) satisfy a closure relation in ε_x given by

$$\Sigma_{\varepsilon_1 \varepsilon_2} \,|\, \varepsilon_1\, \varepsilon_2 ><\varepsilon_1\, \varepsilon_2\,| \;=\; |++><++| \;+\; |+-><+-| \;+ \tag{6}$$

$$|-+><-+| \;+\; |--><--| \;=\; \mathbf{1}.$$

A ket of ε_x can be constructed in terms of an arbitrary ket of $\varepsilon_x(1)$ and an arbitrary ket of $\varepsilon_x(2)$, given by

$$|\chi(1)> |\zeta(2)> = \alpha_1\alpha_2 |++> + \alpha_1\beta_2 |+-> \tag{7}$$

$$+ \alpha_2\beta_1 |-+> + \beta_1\beta_2 |-->.$$

The components of Eq (7) in the basis of Eq (4) are the products of $|\chi(1)>$ and $|\zeta(2)>$ in the bases of $\varepsilon_x(1)$ and $\varepsilon_x(2)$, which were used to construct Eq (4). However, not all kets of ε_x can be expressed as tensor products. The most general ket of ε_x is an arbitrary linear combination of the basis vectors given by

$$|\psi> = \alpha |++> + \beta |+-> + \gamma |-+> + \delta |-->, \tag{8}$$

where for normalization, $|\alpha|^2 + |\beta|^2 + |\gamma|^2 + |\delta|^2 = 1$. Equation (8) can not generally be expressed as a tensor product of $|\chi(1)>$ and $|\zeta(2)>$, in which case Eq (8) would be the form for an entangled state. In order for Eq (8) to be the form of Eq (7), the condition, $\alpha/\beta = \gamma/\delta$, is required, which is not necessarily satisfied. The symmetric *keto-amino* → *enol-imine* arrangement channel generates G' states in terms of two coherent protons, p_1 and p_2, each of which constitutes a qubit. The transcriptase implements its measurement which, according to data, is in terms of proton flip-flop states, $|+>$ and $|->$. The superposition at G'-C' sites consist of two sets of coupled two-level coherent proton states that interact with a quantum reader, the transcriptase, which deciphers the four quantum states within the superposition and transforms this information into observable biochemical instruction. Given Eq (8) describes the four-state G'-C' (Figure 2b-e) superposition system just before transcriptase measurement, one can express the probability of finding the system in each of its states. For example, the probability of the system being in state G'0 0 0–C'2 2 2 as assayed by transcriptase measurement is expressed as

$$|<++|\psi>|^2 = |\alpha|^2. \tag{9}$$

Similarly, the probabilities of the system being in states G'0 0 2–C'2 2 0, G'2 0 0–C'0 2 2 and G'2 0 2–C'0 2 0 are given respectively by

$$|<+-|\psi>|^2 = |\beta|^2, \tag{10}$$

$$|<-+|\psi>|^2 = |\gamma|^2, \tag{11}$$

$$|<--|\psi>|^2 = |\delta|^2. \tag{12}$$

Values for $|\delta|^2$ and $|\beta|^2$ can be determined from straightforward observables – G'2 0 2 → T and G'0 0 2 → C, respectively. Since the transcriptase reads G'2 0 0 as normal G2^2 0 0^0, the value of $|\gamma|^2$ could be determined from clonal analysis (Ripley, 1988). The value of $|\alpha|^2$ would be determined from normalization. These observables are, of course, expressed in terms of decohered states. Observables yielded by transcriptase measurements, e.g., $|<--|\psi>|^2 = |\delta|^2$ and $|<+-|\psi>|^2 = |\beta|^2$, are in qualitative agreement with the distribution of G'–C' states predicted by Jorgensen's model shown in Figure 6. In particular, the relative contribution of the "preferred" state, G'2 0 2, is quantified by $|\delta|^2$, which is observed as the no. of G'2 0 2 → T events. Observation shows that $|\delta|^2$ is ~ 3-fold, rather than 2-fold, > $|\beta|^2$ which is consistent with Figure 6 This observation is consistent with decohered observable results of transcriptase measurements yielding the relative distribution of quantum duplex G'-C' states at time of measurement.

Enol and imine protons oscillate through intervening barriers between coherent states, $|+>$ and $|->$, but the ring proton does not exhibit coherence. Evidently the ring proton on G' and *C states may serve as a type of "transcriptase anchor" between, or adjacent to, protons that oscillate between states $|+>$ and $|->$. After transcriptase measurement, the ensuing entanglement between coherent protons and transcriptase components ultimately causes the rapid decoherence of quantum states into a statistical ensemble of enol-imine isomers suitable for Topal-Fresco replication. However after transcription and before replication, these coherent G' states – G'0 0 2, G'2 0 2, G'2 0 0, G'0 0 0 (Figure 2) – are protected by entanglement from the usual reequilibration interactions with H_2O. Additionally, the corresponding decohered isomers are prevented from H_2O reequilibration since ~ 100% of the decohered G'2 0 2 and G'0 0 2 isomers (Table 1) participate in the formation complementary Topal-Fresco mispairs (Figure 5) that subsequently implement the substitutions, G'2 0 2 → T and G'0 0 2 → C (Cooper, 1994, 2009a, b). Therefore entanglement between coherent protons and transcriptase components plays a central role in forming complementary mispairs (Table 1) responsible for genotypic substitutions via the Topal-Fresco mechanism. This biological system of two coupled G' qubits is an evolutionarily designed processing system consisting of interacting two-level coupled protons that – through entanglement interaction with the transcriptase – execute quantum information processing at biological temperature. Further study of this evolved qubit system may provide insight into the dynamics of avoiding decoherence (Grace et al., 2007; Chen et al., 2009; Mei et al., 2009) and an improved understanding of entanglement (Rezakhani et al., 2009) and quantum error corrections (Oreshkov et al., 2008).

IV. Reactive Proton States in Duplex Dna

A. Origin of Coherent States: Mechanism for *keto-amino* → *enol-imine* Hydrogen Bond Arrangement by Symmetric and Asymmetric Channels

Coherent proton states at G'-C' and *G-*C sites are introduced as consequences of hydrogen bond arrangement, *keto-amino* → *enol-imine* via symmetric and asymmetric channels (Figure 1), where product enol and imine protons are shared between two sets of indistinguishable electron lone pairs. Consequently, these protons participate in coupled quantum oscillations through intervening barriers between near symmetric double minima (Figure 2). In addition to satisfying previously 'inexplicable' molecular genetic observations (Cooper, 1994, 2009a, b), this model must also agree with the basic tenets of quantum theory (Löwdin, 1965; Zurek, 1991; Bell et al., 2002; Vedral, 2003). Molecular genetic data (Cooper, 2009a,b) and quantum uncertainty arguments imply coherent enol-imine states in duplex DNA are energetically accessible by hydrogen bonded amino ($-NH_2$) protons. The four $-NH_2$ G-C protons are localized on the two amino end groups (Figure 1) and are thus confined to a relatively small space, Δx, compared to the four redistributed enol-imine protons (Figure 2). The uncertainty relation, $\Delta x\, \Delta p_x \geq \frac{1}{2}\,\hbar$, expresses the product of uncertainties, Δx and Δp_x, introduced by quantum effects in any attempt at a simultaneous specification of a position x and corresponding momentum p_x of a particle. In the approximation that $p \approx \hbar/\Delta x$, proton kinetic energy may be approximated by $mv^2/2 = p^2/2m = \hbar^2/[2m\,(\Delta x)^2]$. This illustrates how uncertainty limits on the four $-NH_2$ protons between normal G-C pairs can increase proton momentum and kinetic energy. Enhanced proton energy could be dissipated through collisional de-excitations, thereby increasing the energy density of local chemical bonds in DNA. More energetic vibrational modes would introduce smaller $a_0\, V_0^{\frac{1}{2}}$ values in Eq (15) and would also introduce larger γ_ρ values in Eq (31). This would increase *keto-amino* → *enol-amine* reaction rates and cause smaller lifetimes, τ, for metastable protons. Equation (31) illustrates how those rates of populating superposition proton states in duplex DNA are driven by quantum uncertainty limits on the four $-NH_2$ G-C protons. On the other hand, redistributed enol-imine protons oscillate back and forth over larger Δx without the possibility of proton-proton interaction causing proton confinement, implying deeper energy wells for enol-imine quantum protons.

This argument implies an energetic amino proton on carbon-2 guanine initiates exchange tunneling by the symmetric channel. Proton departure causes a reorganization of π and σ electrons in guanine. Proton arrival at carbon-2 keto on cytosine induces proton departure at carbon-6 amino cytosine and a reorganization of π and σ electrons, including double bond shifts, $C = N\text{:}_{ring} \rightarrow C = N\text{:}H_{side\ chain}$ at carbon-2 guanine and carbon-6 cytosine, illustrated in Figure 1a. The asymmetric channel is instigated by an energetic amino proton on carbon–6 cytosine. Proton arrival on guanine carbon-6 keto induces proton transfer at the ring nitrogen position, from G to C, which facilitates a double bond shift into the ring and a reorientation of the cytosine carbon-6 double bond, i.e., $C = N\text{:}_{ring} \rightarrow C = N\text{:}H_{side\ chain}$, illustrated in Figure 1b. This "sequence of events" description assumes a coupling between the motion of the two protons and the reorganization of π and σ electrons (Sekiya and Sakota, 2006). Quantum uncertainty limits on the four $-NH_2$ protons between keto-amino G-C thus determines the symmetric or asymmetric channel (Figure 1a, b) for the *keto-amino* $\rightarrow$ *enol-imine* arrangement. Thus as opposed to a "simultaneous tunneling" of two hydrogen bonded protons at their instantaneous energy levels, the time-dependence of *keto-amino* $\rightarrow$ *enol-imine* arrangement may be simulated in terms of an initially energetic amino proton with the second proton transfer during electron reorganization, which could cause reductions in barrier height for the second proton. This model treats exchange tunneling time-dependence in terms of a single regular proton and a "composite proton", of mass equal two protons. A discussion of the energetics and dynamics of proton exchange tunneling in normal G-C is given by Zoete and Meuwly (2004). Also, Smedarchina et al. (2007) discuss double proton transfer along two identical hydrogen bonds. Matsui et al. (2009) discuss proton transfer in stacked G-C pairs, whereas Ceron-Carrasco et al. (2009) discuss double proton transfer between monohydrated G-C pairs.

B. Approximate Lifetimes of Metastable *keto-amino* Protons and Corresponding Energy Surface Parameters

According to the LTF model and uncertainty considerations, replicase systems create a DNA double helix containing metastable hydrogen-bonded protons that satisfy the criteria for a noninteracting isolated system (Reif, 1965), which is not at equilibrium. Consequently, keto-amino protons populate accessible enol-imine states by "synchronized" proton exchange tunneling (Löwdin, 1965) electron rearrangement pathways discussed above and illustrated in illustrated in Figures 1-3. These exchange tunneling reactions imply energy conservation along reactant and product coordinates (Cooper, 1979) and intramolecular charge conservation, thereby avoiding energetically unstable ionic states. Since unperturbed quantum oscillations of duplex enol-imine states will not repopulate the original keto-amino state, an approximate relationship between the characteristic lifetime, τ, of the metastable state and the total transition rate, Γ, out of the unstable state can be expressed as (Merzbacher, 1997)

$$\Gamma = \Sigma_f W_{if} = 1/\tau, \qquad (13)$$

where W_{if} is the transition rate out of the unstable state and the sum Σ_f is over all final enol-imine states. Based on experimental measurements, order of magnitude estimates are listed in Table 2 for *ts* events per G-C (and *td* events per A-T) at 37^0 C. Equation (13) is solved for τ to yield the mean lifetime of metastable protons for each Γ value in Table 2. The value, $\Gamma = 9.76 \times 10^{-12}$ *ts*/GC/s, is obtained from the study by Baltz et al. (1976) where forward, $r^+ \to r$, *ts* rates were measured as a function of temperature in T4 phage (Cooper, 2009a). Kricker and Drake (1990) reported a 37^0C *ts* transversion rate of 4×10^{-9} events per G-C per hr, which is 9.6×10^{-8} per 24 hr. However a value of 1.92×10^{-7} per 24 hr [$=2 \times (9.6 \times 10^{-8})$] would include both time-dependent transversions and transitions since their average rates are approximately equal (Baltz et al., 1976; Drake and Baltz, 1976). This yields a Γ value of 2.22×10^{-12} s^{-1}, listed in Table 2. Drake and Baltz (1976) have estimated *ts*/GC/day to be $\sim 4 \times 10^{-8}$ or 4.63×10^{-13} *ts*/GC/s at 37^0 C. The Γ value for time-dependent deletions at *A-*T sites is, $\Gamma = 5.32 \times 10^{-12}$ *td*/AT/s (Cooper, 2009b), which is in order of magnitude agreement with two of the three values in Table 2. Data yielding Γ values in Table 2 include experimental contributions from both symmetric and asymmetric channels (Figures 2-3) for populating coherent states at G'-C', *G-*C and *A-*T sites. In this order of magnitude treatment, no distinction is made between the symmetric and asymmetric channels for generating coherent proton states.

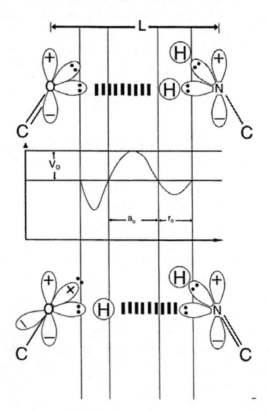

Figure 7. Schematic display of keto-amino and enol-imine hydrogen bonds. The asymmetric double well potential represents an energy surface for the metastable hydrogen bonded proton.

Table 2. Relationship between events per G-C or A-T per 24 hrs, <k>, events per sec, Γ, and mean lifetimes,τ, of metastable keto-amino Hydrogen-bonded protons

<k> (events/24 hrs)	Γ (sec^{-1})	τ (yrs)
8.43x10^{-7}	9.76x10^{-12}	3246
1.92x10^{-7}	2.22x10^{-12}	14273
4x10^{-8}	4.63x10^{-13}	68436
†4.60x10^{-7}	5.32x10^{-12}	5956

†Deletions at *A-*T sites

Table 3. Mean lifetimes, τ (yrs), of a metastable regular proton (m = 1.67252×10^{-24} g) before penetrating potential energy barrier heights, V_0 (eV), of 4.25, 4.50, 4.75, 5.00 and 5.25 eV where the one dimensional tunneling distance, a_0 (Å) is varied from 0.74 to 0.8 Å in increments of 0.01 Å. Mean lifetime calculations use Eq (15) where proton frequency is ν = 5×10^{13} s^{-1}. Approximate lines of constant τ are indicated for τ = 3200, 6000, 14000, 68000 yrs

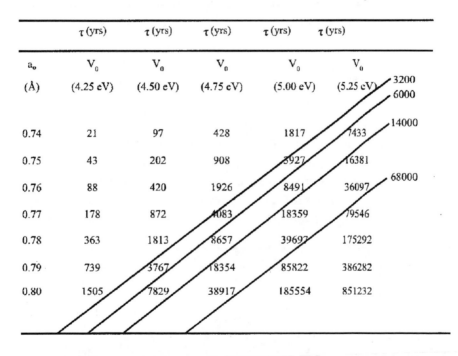

a_0 (Å)	τ (yrs) V_0 (4.25 eV)	τ (yrs) V_0 (4.50 eV)	τ (yrs) V_0 (4.75 eV)	τ (yrs) V_0 (5.00 eV)	τ (yrs) V_0 (5.25 eV)	
0.74	21	97	428	1817	7433	3200 / 6000 / 14000
0.75	43	202	908	3927	16381	
0.76	88	420	1926	8491	36097	68000
0.77	178	872	4083	18359	79546	
0.78	363	1813	8657	39697	175292	
0.79	739	3767	18354	85822	386282	
0.80	1505	7829	38917	185554	851232	

In an effort to include mass effects in exchange tunneling of two protons, the present chapter evaluates exchange tunneling time-dependence in terms of a regular proton, of mass m = 1.67252×10^{-24} g, and a composite proton of mass m = 3.34×10^{-24} g. Accordingly at t = 0, the regular proton is in the metastable energy well, illustrated in Figure 7, which is separated from the deeper enol-imine energy well by a parabolic barrier of height (V− E) eV and width a_0 angstroms (Å). The characteristic lifetime, τ, of the proton in an initial energy well can be estimated in terms of the Gurney and Condon (1929) approximation given by

$$\tau \approx r_0 \, (m/2E)^{\frac{1}{2}} \exp\{a_0 \, \pi \, /2\hbar[2m(V-E)]^{\frac{1}{2}} \}, \tag{14}$$

where $r_o = 0.6$ Å, width of the classical energy well, and $m = 1.67252 \times 10^{-24}$ g, mass of the regular proton. Since interstrand hydrogen bonded protons in duplex DNA oscillate at frequencies the order of 10^{13} to 10^{14} s^{-1}, this report uses $\nu = 5 \times 10^{13}$ s^{-1} as the frequency (Löwdin, 1965). Ground level keto-amino proton energy is $E = h\nu = 0.206$ eV where Planck's constant h is 6.625×10^{-27} erg-sec. Equation (14) can be rewritten as

$$\tau = 0.95 \times 10^{-14 + 14.976 a_o V_o^{1/2}} \tag{15}$$

In order to include mass effects on time-dependence of exchange tunneling, the regular proton is replaced by a composite proton, of mass $m = 2$ protons (3.34×10^{-24} g). The corresponding form of Eq (14) is rewritten as

$$\tau = 1.35 \times 10^{-14 + 21.179 a_o V_o^{1/2}} \tag{16}$$

where $(V - E)$ is defined as V_0 in units of eV. Equation (16) is used to calculate lifetimes of metastable composite protons in Table 4. Here potential energy barrier heights, V_0, vary from 2.10 to 2.60 eV, and tunneling distances, a_o, vary from 0.700 to 0.800 Å in increments of 0.010 Å. This range of a_o and V_0 values is selected to be compatible with dimensions of hydrogen bonds and also generate metastable proton lifetimes, τ, that approximate experimentally determined values in Table 2. Calculations in Table 4 indicate lifetimes of ~ 3200 yrs could be expected for a_o and V_0 values along the line from $a_o \approx 0.784$ Å with $V_0 = 2.25$ eV to $a_o \approx 0.727$ Å with $V_0 = 2.6$ eV. Lines of constant τ are identified in Table 4 for $\tau = 3200$, 6000, 14000, and 68000 yrs.

Table 4. Mean lifetimes, τ (yrs), of a metastable composite proton ($m = 3.34 \times 10^{-24}$ g) before penetrating potential energy barrier heights, V_o (eV), of 2.10, 2.25, 2.35, 2.50 and 2.60 eV where the one dimensional tunneling distance, a_o (Å) is varied from 0.70 to 0.8 Å in increments of 0.01 Å. Mean lifetime calculations use Eq (16) where composite proton frequency is $\nu = 5 \times 10^{13}$ s^{-1}. Lines of constant τ are shown, approximately, for $\tau = 3200$, 6000, 14000, 68000 yrs

a_o (Å)	τ (yrs) V_0 (2.10 eV)	τ (yrs) V_0 (2.25 eV)	τ (yrs) V_0 (2.35 eV)	τ (yrs) V_0 (2.50 eV)	τ (yrs) V_0 (2.60 eV)	
0.70	1	7	23	118	344	
0.71	3	15	48	255	755	
0.72	5	32	102	552	1657	3200
0.73	11	66	215	1193	3637	6000
0.74	22	138	454	2579	7985	14000
0.75	45	287	958	5577	17530	
0.76	90	596	2023	12058	38484	68000
0.77	183	1239	4272	26070	84486	
0.78	372	2574	9022	56365	185474	
0.79	754	5349	19053	121865	407178	
0.80	1528	11117	40237	263480	893894	

C. Rate Expression for Hydrogen Bond Arrangement, *keto-amino* → *enol-imine*, Using Approximate Quantum Methods.

For purposes of discussing consequences of coherent states populating G'-C' and *G-*C sites within duplex triplet repeats, an expression is obtained for the quantum mechanical "rate constant" associated with hydrogen bond arrangement, *keto-amino* → *enol-imine* via symmetric and asymmetric channels (Figure 2). This result allows a polynomial description of triplet repeat disease incidence, i.e., phenotypic expression, as a function of genotypic alterations of genetic specificities due to coherent states populating $(CAG)_n$ tracts. Time-dependence for the reactive five proton system of metastable G-C to populate complementary enol-imine states is modeled in terms of a composite proton, of mass equal two protons, in an appropriate asymmetric three-well potential illustrated in Figure 8. Here the motion of two tunneling-exchange protons, using the symmetric and asymmetric channels (Figure 2), is simulated in terms of a composite proton model. Secondary contributions by the 2nd asymmetric pathway (unlabeled) are neglected. At t = 0 the composite proton is replicated into the metastable state $|3>$ at energy E_3 which, according to data (Cooper, 2009a) and shown in Figure 8, is separated from the enol-imine ground state, $|1>$, and hybrid state, $|2>$, by approximately equal energy barriers. The relationship $E_1 < E_2 < E_3$ for the ground state, hybrid state and metastable state, respectively, is displayed in Figure 8. Enol-imine product states are designated by a general arrangement state $|\rho>$ where the energy E_ρ would equal E_1 or E_2 as appropriate. Time-dependence of an eigenstate, $|\Psi>$, is expressed by $|\Psi> = |\phi_I>$ exp(- i E_i t/ ℏ), so $|\Psi> = |\phi_I>$ at t = 0 (Merzbacher, 1997). The relationship $|\Psi> = \Sigma_i |i><i|\Psi>$ is used to express an eigenstate $|\Psi>$ in terms of base states $|i>$ and amplitudes C_i as

$$|\Psi> = |1><1|\Psi> + |2><2|\Psi> = |1>C_1 + |2>C_2, \qquad (17)$$

where base states satisfy $<i|j> = \delta_{ij}$. The eigenstate is normalized, $<\Psi|\Psi> = 1$, and an eigenstate and eigenvalue E are related to the Hamiltonian matrix, $\Sigma_{ij} <i|H|j>$, by $\Sigma_j <i|H|j><j|\Psi> = E<i|\Psi>$, which can be rewritten as

$$\Sigma_j (H_{ij} - E^k \delta_{ij}) C^k_j = 0 \qquad (18)$$

for an expression to solve for amplitudes, $\{C^k_j|_{i=1,2; j=1,2}\}$. A nonzero solution to Eq (18) is available if the determinant of $\Sigma_j (H_{ij} - E \delta_{ij}) = 0$.

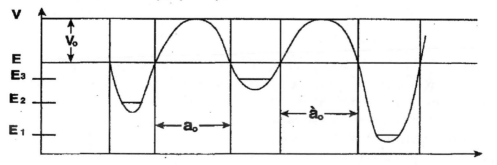

Figure 8. Asymmetric three-well potential to simulate metastable keto-amino protons populating accessible enol-imine states in terms of a "composite" proton originating in the metastable E_3 energy well at t = 0 where $E_1 < E_2 < E_3$.

A two-level Hamiltonian that will allow a composite proton to tunnel from the metastable state $|3>$ at energy E_3 to an arrangement state $|\rho>$ at energy E_ρ can be written as

$$H = \begin{pmatrix} E_3 & -\alpha_\rho \\ -\alpha_\rho & E_\rho \end{pmatrix} = \begin{pmatrix} H_{11} & H_{12} \\ H_{21} & H_{22} \end{pmatrix} \tag{19}$$

where α_ρ is the quantum mechanical coupling between states $|3>$ and $|\rho>$. The resulting upper and lower eigenvalues, E_{Ap} and E_{Bp}, are found as

$$E_{Ap} = \xi_\rho + \gamma_\rho \tag{20}$$

and

$$E_{Bp} = \xi_\rho - \gamma_\rho \tag{21}$$

where $\xi_\rho = (E_3 + E_\rho)/2$, $\gamma_\rho = [(E_3 - E_\rho)^2/4 + \alpha_\rho^2]^{1/2}$ and $\rho = 1, 2$ for the symmetric and asymmetric channels, respectively. The time-dependent wave function $|\Psi(t)>$ of the composite proton in the asymmetric three well potential can be expressed in terms of the corresponding eigenstates as

$$|\Psi(t)>= |\Psi_{A1}> \exp(-i E_{A1} t/\hbar) + |\Psi_{A2}> \exp(-i E_{A2} t/\hbar) \tag{22}$$

$$+ |\Psi_{B1}> \exp(-i E_{B1} t/\hbar) + |\Psi_{B2}> \exp(-i E_{B2} t/\hbar),$$

which can be expressed in terms of physical base states $|3>$, $|2>$, $|1>$ as (Cooper and Kouri, 1971)

$$|\Psi(t)> = \exp(-i \xi_1 t/\hbar) \{ |3> \exp(-i \gamma_1 t/\hbar) + |1'> \exp[-i(\gamma_1 t/\hbar + \delta)]\} \tag{23}$$

$$+ \exp(-i \xi_1 t/\hbar) \{ |3> \exp(+i \gamma_1 t/\hbar) + |1'> \exp[+i(\gamma_1 t/\hbar + \delta)]\}$$

$$+ \exp(-i \xi_2 t/\hbar) \{ |3> \exp(-i \gamma_2 t/\hbar) + |2'> \exp[-i(\gamma_2 t/\hbar + \delta)]\}$$

$$+ \exp(-i \xi_2 t/\hbar) \{ |3> \exp(+i \gamma_2 t/\hbar) + |2'> \exp[+i(\gamma_2 t/\hbar + \delta)]\}.$$

This can be written more succinctly as

$$|\Psi(t)> = (0.5)^{1/2} \exp(-i \xi_1 t/\hbar) \{ |3> \cos(\gamma_1 t/\hbar) + |1'> \sin(\gamma_1 t/\hbar)\} \tag{24}$$

$$+ (0.5)^{1/2} \exp(-i \xi_2 t/\hbar) \{ |3> \cos(\gamma_2 t/\hbar) + |2'> \sin(\gamma_2 t/\hbar)\}$$

where $|1> = |1'>e^{i\delta}$, $|2> = |2'>e^{i\delta}$ and δ of the arbitrary phase factor $e^{i\delta}$ is $-\pi/2$ and the relation $\cos(\theta - \pi/2) = \sin(\theta)$ is used. Data show that *ts* rates are approximately equal for transversions and transitions (Baltz et al., 1976; Bingham et al., 1976); so, quantum mechanical "rate constants" for hydrogen bond arrangements, *keto-amino* → *enol-imine* via symmetric and asymmetric channels, are approximately equal (Figure 8). Since the lifetimes, τ, for 37^0 C keto-amino G-C protons are the order of ~ 3200 yrs (Table 2), the wave function expression in Eq (24) would be applicable in the interval, $0 < t < \sim 3200$ yrs.

At $t = 0$, the composite proton was in the metastable state $|3>$ at energy E_3. The probability, $P_1(t)$, that the proton is in the ground state $|1>$ at a later time t is given by

$$P_1(t) = |<1'|\Psi(t)>|^2 \tag{25}$$

$$= 0.5 \sin^2(\gamma_1 t/\hbar),$$

which identifies $P_1(t)$ in terms of contributions by the symmetric channel. The probability of the proton being in the hybrid state $|2>$ at a later time is given as

$$P_2(t) = |<2'|\Psi(t)>|^2 \tag{26}$$

$$= 0.5 \sin^2(\gamma_2 t/\hbar),$$

which is the contribution by the asymmetric channel. The probability that the proton is in metastable state $|3>$ at time t is given by

$$P_3(t) = |<3|\Psi(t)>|^2 \tag{27}$$

$$= 0.5[\cos^2(\gamma_1 t/\hbar) + \cos^2(\gamma_2 t/\hbar)],$$

which is the sum of contributions for protons exiting state $|3>$ by the symmetric and asymmetric channels. The sum of Eqs (25-27), given by

$$\Sigma^3_{i=1} P_i(t) = (0.5)[\sin^2(\gamma_1 t/\hbar) + \cos^2(\gamma_1 t/\hbar)]$$

$$+ (0.5)[\sin^2(\gamma_2 t/\hbar) + \cos^2(\gamma_2 t/\hbar)] = 1, \tag{28}$$

is consistent with the requirement that the composite proton be confined to its set of base states, $|3>$, $|2>$, $|1>$. The time derivative of $P_\rho(t)$, Eqs (25 & 26), can be expressed as

$$dP_\rho/dt = (\gamma_\rho/\hbar)\sin(\gamma_\rho t/\hbar)\cos(\gamma_\rho t/\hbar) \tag{29}$$

where $P_\rho(t)$ represents either $P_1(t)$ or $P_2(t)$ and the 0.5 normalization factor is omitted. A Taylor series expansion of Eq (29) is given by

$$dP_\rho/dt \approx (\gamma_\rho/\hbar)^2 t - 4/3 (\gamma_\rho/\hbar)^4 t^3 + 4/15 (\gamma_\rho/\hbar)^6 t^5 + \ldots \tag{30}$$

where the first three terms are given. The experimental lifetime of metastable keto-amino hydrogen bonded G-C protons is the order of ~ 3200 yrs, which is large compared to human lifetimes of, say, ~ 100 yrs. For times $t \ll 3200$ yrs (e.g., $t < 100$ yrs), one could employ a small t approximation to express the probability of metastable protons populating enol-imine states $|1>$ or $|2>$ as

$$P_\rho(t) = \tfrac{1}{2}(\gamma_\rho/h)^2 t^2, \tag{31}$$

indicating a *nonlinear* time dependence. This is consistent with exponential increases in base substitutions and deletions as a function of age (Kadenbach et al., 1995) observed in human mitochondria DNA. Equation (31) is instrumental in developing the polynomial model in Sec. V for phenotypic expression of a triplet repeat disease as a function of coherent states introducing genotypic changes in genetic specificities.

D. Model Calculations of Coupled Quantum Oscillation Frequencies, Using a Double Minimum Symmetric Potential and an Asymmetric Double Minimum Potential

Figure 2a-e illustrates the tunneling exchange creation of a G'-C' pair (symmetric channel) where genetic specificity is in terms of a superposition of four coherent proton states. The asymmetric channel – Figure 2a,f,g – illustrates exchange tunneling where genetic specificity is in terms of two coherent proton states. The energy surfaces "seen by" enol and imine protons are near symmetric since significant components are contributed by two sets of indistinguishable electron lone-pairs located at each hydrogen-bond end group. In these cases, enol and imine protons will participate in coupled quantum oscillation through intervening barriers between near symmetric double-minima (Hameka and de la Vega, 1984). Order of magnitude estimates of flip-flop frequencies use both a regular proton (m = 1.67252×10^{-24} g) and the composite proton (m = 3.34×10^{-24} g) on a one-dimensional model double-minimum symmetric energy surface illustrated in Figure 9. An estimate for the interminimal distance, θ, can be given by specifying distances identified in Fig. 7. The distance L between the enol O and imine N is taken as L = 2.8775 Å for the symmetric channel (Fig. 1a) and L = 2.9135 Å for the asymmetric channel (Fig.1b). These values are obtained from an average of the reactant state G-C distances given by Zote and Meuwly (2004), i.e., from their Fig. 1, (2.901+ 2.854)/2 = 2.8775 Å and (2.854 + 2.973)/2 = 2.9135 Å. The central energy barrier, a_o, is initially assigned a width of 0.775 Å with r_o = 0.6 Å. From these approximations, interminimal distances, θ in Fig. 9, can be estimated by defining ℓ as $\ell = L - (r_o + r_o + a_o)$ so that θ is given by $\theta^2 = (\ell/2)^2 + (\ell/2)^2$, illustrated in Fig.10.

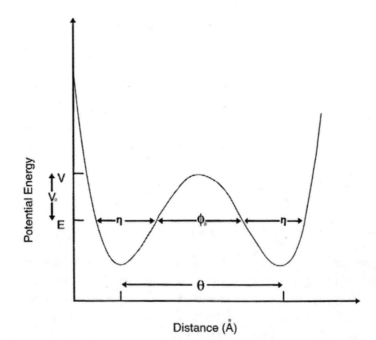

Figure 9. Double minimum symmetric potential energy surface for regular and composite coherent enol and imine protons.

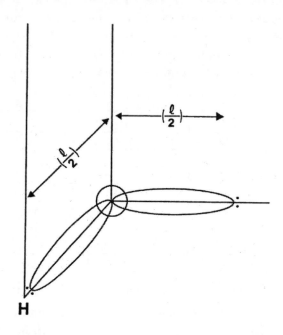

Figure 10. Schematic representation of dimensions for determining the interminimal flip-flop distance, θ, listed in Tables 5-6 for coherent enol-imine protons.

Table 5. Flip-flop frequencies, ν_θ (s^{-1}), for the regular enol-imine proton – oscillating in its classically allowed energy well at a frequency $\nu = 5 \times 10^{13}$ s^{-1} – to tunnel back and forth between the symmetric double minimum potential illustrated in Figure 9. Energy barriers, V_0, vary from 0.10 to 0.30 eV in increments of 0.05 eV, and the one-dimensional tunneling distance, ϕ_0, varies from (a) 0.0382 to 0.0736 Å for the symmetric channel (Figure 2) and (b) from 0.0636 to 0.0990 Å for the asymmetric channel. Interminimal distances, θ, vary from (a) 0.6382 to 0.6736 Å for the symmetric channel and from (b) 0.6636 to 0.6990 Å for the asymmetric channel

ϕ_0 (Å)	θ (Å)	ν_θ (s^{-1}) V_0 (0.10 eV)	ν_θ (s^{-1}) V_0 (0.15 eV)	ν_θ (s^{-1}) V_0 (0.20 eV)	ν_θ (s^{-1}) V_0 (0.25 eV)	ν_θ (s^{-1}) V_0 (0.30 eV)
		(a)				
0.0382	0.6382	3.47×10^{13}	3.16×10^{13}	2.92×10^{13}	2.72×10^{13}	2.56×10^{13}
0.0558	0.6558	2.86×10^{13}	2.50×10^{13}	2.23×10^{13}	2.01×10^{13}	1.83×10^{13}
0.0736	0.6736	2.36×10^{13}	1.97×10^{13}	1.69×10^{13}	1.48×10^{13}	1.31×10^{13}
		(b)				
0.0636	0.6636	2.63×10^{13}	2.25×10^{13}	1.97×10^{13}	1.76×10^{13}	1.58×10^{13}
0.0813	0.6813	2.17×10^{13}	1.78×10^{13}	1.50×10^{13}	1.30×10^{13}	1.13×10^{13}
0.0990	0.6990	1.79×10^{13}	1.40×10^{13}	1.14×10^{13}	9.55×10^{12}	8.11×10^{12}

Table 6. Flip-flop frequencies, v_θ (s^{-1}), for the composite enol-imine proton – oscillating in its classically allowed energy well at a frequency $v = 5\times10^{13}$ s^{-1} – to tunnel back and forth between the symmetric double minimum potential illustrated in Figure 9. Energy surface parameters are identical to those for the regular proton given in Table 5.

ϕ_o (Å)	θ (Å)	v_θ (s^{-1}) V_0 (0.10 eV)	v_θ (s^{-1}) V_0 (0.15 eV)	v_θ (s^{-1}) V_0 (0.20 eV)	v_θ (s^{-1}) V_0 (0.25 eV)	v_θ (s^{-1}) V_0 (0.30 eV)
				(a)		
0.0382	0.6382	2.05×10^{13}	1.80×10^{13}	1.61×10^{13}	1.46×10^{13}	1.34×10^{13}
0.0558	0.6558	1.57×10^{13}	1.29×10^{13}	1.10×10^{13}	9.50×10^{12}	8.34×10^{12}
0.0736	0.6736	1.19×10^{13}	9.22×10^{12}	7.44×10^{12}	6.16×10^{12}	5.19×10^{12}
				(b)		
0.0636	0.6636	1.36×10^{13}	1.11×10^{13}	9.25×10^{12}	7.85×10^{12}	6.77×10^{12}
0.0813	0.6813	1.06×10^{13}	7.98×10^{12}	6.29×10^{12}	5.10×10^{12}	4.22×10^{12}
0.0990	0.6990	8.05×10^{12}	5.71×10^{12}	4.28×10^{12}	3.31×10^{12}	2.63×10^{12}

Table 7. Flip-flop frequencies, v_θ (s^{-1}), for the regular enol-imine proton of Table 5 to tunnel back and forth between a near symmetric double minimum potential. In this case, the one dimensional tunneling distance, ϕ_o (Å), and the energy barrier, V_o (eV), are each reduced by 20% for the left-hand well. This is indicated by ratios, ϕ/Φ_o (e.g., 0.0306/0.0382) for tunneling distances and v/V_o (e.g., 0.08/0.1) for energy barriers

ϕ/Φ_0 Å	v_θ s^{-1} v/V_0 (0.08/0.1)	v_θ s^{-1} v/V_0 (0.12/0.15)	v_θ s^{-1} v/V_0 (0.16/0.20)	v_θ s^{-1} v/V_0 (0.20/0.25)	v_θ s^{-1} v/V_0 (0.24/0.30)
			(a)		
0.0306/0.0382	3.68×10^{13}	3.39×10^{13}	3.16×10^{13}	2.98×10^{13}	2.82×10^{13}
0.0446/0.0558	3.11×10^{13}	2.76×10^{13}	2.50×10^{13}	2.29×10^{13}	2.11×10^{13}
0.0589/0.0736	2.63×10^{13}	2.24×10^{13}	1.96×10^{13}	1.74×10^{13}	1.57×10^{13}
			(b)		
0.0509/0.0636	2.89×10^{13}	2.52×10^{13}	2.25×10^{13}	2.03×10^{13}	1.85×10^{13}
0.0650/0.0831	2.44×10^{13}	2.05×10^{13}	1.77×10^{13}	1.55×10^{13}	1.38×10^{13}
0.0792/0.0990	2.06×10^{13}	1.66×10^{13}	1.34×10^{13}	1.18×10^{13}	1.02×10^{13}

For the symmetric channel, one obtains $\ell_s = 2.8775 - (0.6 + 0.6 + 0.775) = 0.9025$ Å and the expression for the asymmetric channel is $\ell_a = 2.9135 - (0.6 + 0.6 + 0.775) = 0.9385$ Å. The corresponding θ relations are $_s\theta^2 = (0.9025/2)^2 + (0.9025/2)^2$ and $_a\theta^2 = (0.9385/2)^2 + (0.9385/2)^2$, yielding $\theta_s = 0.6382$ Å (Table 5a) and $\theta_a = 0.6636$ Å (Table 5b). Additional a_o values (Figure7) of $a_o = 0.750$ Å and $a_o = 0.725$ Å are considered, yielding corresponding θ values of $\theta_s = 0.6558$ Å & $\theta_s = 0.6736$ Å (Table 5a) and $\theta_a = 0.6813$ Å & $\theta_a = 0.6990$ Å (Table 5b). The interminimal tunneling barrier, ϕ_o (Figure 9), is given by $\phi_o = \theta - (\eta/2 + \eta/2)$ where, in the symmetric double well, the classically allowed energy wells, η, are parabolic of width 0.6 Å. The intervening energy barriers, ϕ_o, for the symmetric channel are $_s\phi_o = 0.0382$, 0.0558, 0.0736 Å (Table 5a) and for the asymmetric channel, $_a\phi_o = 0.0636$, 0.0813, 0.0990 Å, listed in Table 5b. The proton frequency along the θ-axis is taken as $v = 5\times10^{13}$ s^{-1}. On the symmetric energy surface of Figure 9, the time interval for the proton in each energy well is equal. Thus the escape time, τ, from the left well equals that from the right well; so, flip-flop tunneling frequencies in Tables 5-6 are given by $\nu_\theta = 1/2\tau$. Escape times, τ, for regular protons use Eq (15) for flip-flop frequency calculations, ν_θ, listed in Table 5. Potential energy barrier heights, ν_o, vary from 0.10 eV to 0.30 eV in increments of 0.05 eV and flip-flop frequencies, ν_θ, vary from 8.11×10^{12} to 3.47×10^{13} s^{-1} for regular protons in Table 5. Similar flip-flop frequency calculations for composite protons oscillating at 5×10^{13} s^{-1} are listed in Table 6, using Eq (16). In this case, flip-flop tunneling frequencies vary from 2.63×10^{12} to 2.05×10^{13} s^{-1}.

Table 8. Flip-flop frequencies, ν_θ (s^{-1}), for the composite enol-imine proton of Table 6 to tunnel back and forth between a near symmetric double minimum potential. Energy surface parameters are identical to those for the regular proton given in Table 7.

ϕ/Φ_0	ν_θ s^{-1} v/V_0	ν_θ s^{-1} v/V_0	ν_θ s^{-1} v/V_0	ν_θ s^{-1} v/V_0	ν_θ s^{-1} v/V_0
Å	(0.08/0.1)	(0.12/0.15)	(0.16/0.20)	(0.20/0.25)	(0.24/0.30)
(a)					
0.0306/0.0382	2.23×10^{13}	2.02×10^{13}	1.84×10^{13}	1.69×10^{13}	1.57×10^{13}
0.0446/0.0558	1.76×10^{13}	1.51×10^{13}	1.31×10^{13}	1.16×10^{13}	1.04×10^{13}
0.0589/0.0736	1.38×10^{13}	1.05×10^{13}	8.57×10^{12}	7.17×10^{12}	6.10×10^{12}
(b)					
0.0509/0.0636	1.58×10^{13}	1.36×10^{13}	1.16×10^{13}	1.01×10^{13}	8.93×10^{12}
0.0650/0.0831	1.24×10^{13}	1.01×10^{13}	8.26×10^{12}	6.90×10^{12}	5.86×10^{12}
0.0792/0.0990	9.77×10^{12}	7.53×10^{12}	5.86×10^{12}	4.69×10^{12}	3.83×10^{12}

In an effort to simulate tunneling frequencies of a regular proton on a near symmetric energy surface, V_0 (eV) and ϕ_o (Å) values in Table 5 are reduced by 20% each for one of the two energy wells displayed in Figure 9. The resulting flip-flop frequency calculations are shown in Table 7 where the asymmetric energy barriers are designated by v/V_0 (e.g., 0.08/0.1 in 2nd column) and asymmetric tunneling distances are identified by ϕ/Φ_0, e.g., 0.0306/0.0382 in the first row. Since the symmetric surface of Figure 9 (calculations in Table 5) was rendered asymmetric by reducing both V_0 and ϕ_o by 20% each, the proton will spend less time in the more shallow energy well with a reduced classical barrier. Consequently compared to the symmetric surface (Table 5), flip-flop frequencies on this asymmetric surface will be slightly enhanced as illustrated in Table 7. Here the frequency ν_θ is calculated from $\nu_\theta = 1/(\tau + \tau_{0.8})$ where $\tau_{0.8}$ is the escape time from the shallow energy well and the calculated frequency range is from 1.02×10^{13} to 3.68×10^{13} s^{-1}. A similar consideration of the composite proton on this asymmetric energy surface uses Eq (16) to calculate flip-flop tunneling frequencies, given by $\nu_\theta = 1/(\tau + \tau_{0.8})$ and listed in Table 8. Here the frequency range for the composite proton is from 3.83×10^{12} to 2.23×10^{13} s^{-1}.

Enhanced stability of coherent enol-imine hydrogen bonds can be estimated by including effects of quantum proton oscillations. This quantum mixing of proton energy states introduces the quantum mechanical energy splitting term, Ω, such that the average energy, E_o, is split by $\pm \Omega$. In the approximation that each enol and imine proton would contribute $E_o - \Omega$

to the energy, stability enhancements can be estimated by $2\Omega = h\nu_\theta$ where h is Planck's constant and ν_θ is the flip-flop frequency. Flip-flop frequency calculations for regular protons (Tables 5 & 7) and for composite protons (Tables 6 & 8) identify a frequency range of 2.63×10^{12} to 3.68×10^{13} s^{-1}. Stability enhancements in Kcal/mole with corresponding frequencies are given in Table 9. Duplex states with four coherent protons (Figure 2b-e) would be stabilized by 4Ω, whereas reduced energy states with only two coherent protons would be stabilized by 2Ω. Although other quantum chemical studies (e.g., Gullar et al., 1999; McFadden and Al-Khalili, 1999; Li et al., 2001; Kryacho and Sabin, 2003; Podolyan et al., 2003; Zote and Meuwly, 2004; Matsui et al. 2009; Ceron-Carrasco et al., 2009) of Watson-Crick base pairs did not conclude that enol-imine duplex states are stable, those investigations neglected effects resulting from a quantum mixing of proton energy states at G'-C' and *G-*C sites. Protons exhibiting quantum oscillation frequencies listed in Table 9 would emit infrared and stability enhancements would vary, approximately, from 0.25 to 7.15 Kcal/mole.

E. Model for Decoherence Time Estimates

According to the present discussion, genetic specificities within a G'-C' or *G-*C site are determined by transcriptase measurements on coherent proton states in duplex DNA. The transcriptase executes several very specific and precise tasks that include identifying the particular genetic specificity of each quantum state, processing and transferring this information, which communicates specific biochemical instruction. Additionally, the transcriptase is implementing a proper decoherent transition from coherent superposition states into a statistical ensemble of decohered classical isomers – which are protected against H_2O reequilibration – and participate in base substitutions according to Topal-Fresco replication. Thus operations performed by the transcriptase imply the entanglement state between coherent protons and transcriptase components, which is also a superposition, may be allowed more "quantum versatility" than if the entanglement state and resulting decoherence were due to an ordinary thermal bath or "quantum friction". In fact, data herein discussed imply an entanglement state between quantum transcriptase components and coherent protons plays a major role in creating "proper" complementary mispairs after transcription, thereby insuring a very high percentage (~ 100%) of the 'original' decohered isomers participates in Topal-Fresco base substitution.

The time scale over which quantum coherence is lost by superposition states of hydrogen bond protons in duplex DNA can be estimated in terms of the treatment by Zurek (1991). Accordingly, off-diagonal terms in the density matrix will decay at a rate τ_D^{-1} where decoherence time, τ_D, is given, approximately, by

$$\tau_D \approx \gamma^{-1}(\lambda_T/\Delta x)^2. \tag{32}$$

Here λ_T is the thermal de Broglie wavelength for a quantum proton with two degrees of freedom and Δx is the interminimal distance, θ, displayed in Figure 9. A relaxation time, $\tau_R = \gamma^{-1}$, is the time for energy dissipation between coherent states and is a measure of the speed of energy dissipation due to a coherent proton interacting with its immediate environment. The thermal de Broglie wavelength for a single proton is $\lambda_T = \hbar/(2mkT)^{1/2} = 4.91/(T)^{1/2} = 0.28$ Å for

T= 310 K, 37 ^{0} C. In the case of a composite proton, $\lambda_T = 0.197$ Å, whereas if m is mass of four protons, $\lambda_T = 0.139$ Å. Coherent protons in duplex DNA can occupy decoherence-free subspaces and, through certain degrees of freedom, may avoid decoherence until "processed by" the transcriptase. After initiation of transcriptase processing, Eq (32) allows an estimate of the ratio, $\tau_D/\tau_R = (\lambda_T/\Delta x)^2$, which is given in Table 10 for mass m = 1 proton, 2 protons and 4 protons. Consistent with Tables 5-8, the interminimal distance, Δx (θ of Figure 9), is varied from 0.5 to 0.7 Å. The first entry in Table 10, $\Delta x = 0.5$ Å, indicates that a quantum proton would remain coherent for ~ 30% of the relaxation time, τ_R, i.e., $\tau_D/\tau_R = 0.31$. In the case of a composite proton where $\Delta x = 0.5$ Å, $\tau_D/\tau_R = 0.16$; so, the composite proton would maintain coherence for about 16% of the relaxation time. The bottom row in Table 10 gives the corresponding τ_D/τ_R ratios when the mass m = 4 protons.

Table 9. Stability enhancements (Kcal/mole) for duplex enol-imine states calculated from $\Delta E = h\nu_\theta = 2\Omega$ for flip-flop frequencies, ν_θ, in the range of 2.6×10^{12} to 3.7×10^{13} s^{-1}. Each enol-imine hydrogen bond is assumed to provide an enhancement of 2Ω

ν_θ (10^{13} s^{-1})	2Ω (Kcal/mole)	4Ω (Kcal/mole)
3.7	3.56	7.15
3.5	3.38	6.76
3.0	2.90	5.80
2.2	2.16	4.25
1.5	1.45	2.90
0.93	0.90	1.80
0.43	0.42	0.84
0.26	0.25	0.50

Table 10. Ratios, $\tau_D/\tau_R = (\lambda_T/\Delta x)^2$, where Δx (Å) is varied from 0.5 to 0.7 Å and mass m, in $\lambda_T = \hbar/(2mkT)^{\frac{1}{2}}$, equals 1, 2 and 4 protons

No. Protons	τ_D/τ_R	τ_D/τ_R	τ_D/τ_R	τ_D/τ_R	τ_D/τ_R	τ_D/τ_R
	Δx	Δx	Δx	Δx	Δx	Δx
	0.50	0.55	0.60	0.64	0.68	0.70
1	0.31	0.26	0.22	0.19	0.17	0.16
2	0.16	0.13	0.11	0.10	0.09	0.08
4	0.08	0.06	0.05	0.05	0.04	0.04

Flip-flop tunneling frequency calculations (Tables 5-8) imply the transcriptase must implement its genetic specificity reading of coherent proton states in a time $\Delta t \ll 10^{-13}$ s. This quantum measurement determines the genetic specificity of all participating superposition states. According to Table 10, a quantum proton would retain coherence for about 16 to 30% of the relaxation time, τ_R. Evidently, this approximately 16 to 30% availability of τ_R is sufficient for the transcriptase to implement its reading before energy dissipation between coherent states introduces decoherence, which would interfere with quantum processing. Consistent with evolutionary design, quantum processing by the transcriptase is completed within an interval, Δt, before decoherence could interfere. However at or near the "end" of Δt, an entanglement state is created between coherent protons and transcriptase components which ultimately yields decohered isomers suitable for Topal-Fresco replication. Entanglement is thus instrumental in selecting complementary mispairs for Topal-Fresco replication (Table 1). This explanation implies $\Delta t < \sim 0.2\tau_R$ and $\Delta t < \tau_D$. Since $\Delta t << 10^{-13}$s, an order of magnitude estimate of decoherence time can be given as $\Delta t < \tau_D < 10^{-13}$ s. This "ballpark" estimate is in order of magnitude agreement with more rigorous calculations (Tegmark, 2000) of proton decoherence times.

V. Consequences of Coherent States Populating Unstable $(CAG)_N$ Repeats In Human Genomes

Expandable DNA microsatellite repeats are responsible for approximately 30 heritable human genetic diseases (Mirkin, 2007). Heritable repeat diseases are expressed early in life as consequences of expanded DNA repeats (Wells and Ashizawa, 2006), e.g., Huntington's disease due to expanded $(CAG)_n$ repeats illustrated in Figure 11. According to the expansion/contraction hypothesis (Cooper, 1995), microsatellite repeat instabilities originate as consequences of time-dependent coherent states (Hwang and Green, 2004; Elango et al., 2008; Cooper, 2009a, b) populating G'-C' and *G-*C sites within repeat microsatellite, which subsequently can be expressed as initiation codons – UUG, CUG, AUG, GUG – and/or stop codons – UAA, UAG, UGA (Alberts et al., 2002). An unstable microsatellite repeat, e.g., 5'-CAG-3', achieves "expanded status" in successive generations as consequences of implementing information provided by newly acquired initiation codons, i.e., dynamic mutations (Cooper, 1995; Richards, 2001), which cause the addition of more metastable G-C and A-T sites (Cooper, 2009a, b) within expanded repeat tracts. This enhances the probability for future coherent state expansions, thereby increasing gene fitness advantage (Beerenwinkel et al., 2007; Wolf and Krug, 2009). Since coherent state mutations are selected by an expanded gene environment *and* the evolved gene function – phenotypic expression of repeat disease – is driven by subsequent coherent state mutations, these mutations are *adaptive* (Rosenberg, 2001). Coherent state expansion of the $(CAG)_n$ tract is thus consistent with "driver" mutation behavior (Greenman et al., 2007). Each expansion represents incremental progress in achieving the ultimate "expanded status", and therefore, confers an incremental increase in fitness advantage on the gene. As the expanded repeat becomes larger in successive generations and accumulates a significant selective fitness advantage, the probability increases for an earlier age at onset of an associated genetic disease, a phenomenon identified as genetic *anticipation* (Pearson et al., 2005). If expansion and phenotypic expression of a repeat disease have common origins (Cooper, 1995), the present chapter implies that alterations in genetic specificities caused by coherent states populating G'-C', *G-*C and *A-*T sites in unstable repeats may play a role in (a) genetic anticipation and (b) phenotypic expression of a repeat disease. In this scenario, expanded repeat tracts provide enlarged targets of metastable G-C and A-T sites which enhance probabilities for coherent states to introduce time-dependent substitutions, *ts,* at G'-C' and *G-*C sites and time-dependent deletions, *td,* at *A-*T sites, which are *stochastic* mutations (Kadenbach et al., 1995; Beerenwinkel et al., 2007). Since mechanisms responsible for phenotypic expression of disease are unclear (Wells et al., 2005; Gatchel and Zogbhi, 2005; Wells and Ashizawa, 2006; Mirkin, 2007), this section identifies possible insight into molecular genetic processes responsible for *anticipation* (Figure 11) by evaluating phenotypic expression of a $(CAG)_n$ repeat disease as a function of time-dependent changes in genetic specificities in an unstable repeat, using a – quantum + classical – polynomial model.

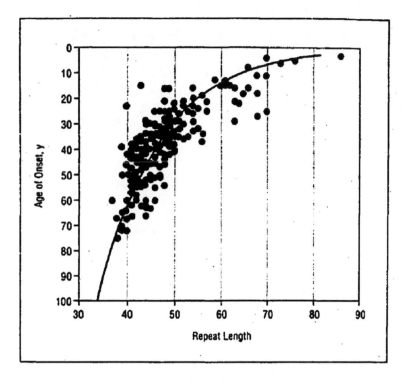

Figure 11. $(CAG)_n$ repeat length versus age-of-onset of Huntington's disease [adapted from Figure 3 of Gusella et al. (1993)].

For purposes of investigating gene product participation in processes responsible for phenotypic expression of a repeat disease, a mathematical relationship is proposed for phenotypic expression as a function of genotypic alteration of genetic specificities in a target gene, g, containing a potentially unstable triplet repeat $(CAG)_n$ tract. This model considers M individuals – the population – who have inherited a $(CAG)_n$ repeat of length $£$ inserted in the coding region of a conserved gene, g (Cooper, 1995; Mirkin, 2007). According to Eq (31), the probability, P(t), of hydrogen bond arrangement – *keto-amino* → *enol imine* by symmetric and asymmetric channels – can be simulated, approximately, by $P(t) = \frac{1}{2}(\gamma/\hbar)^2 t^2$ where γ is the energy shift between states and $\hbar$ is Planck's constant divided by 2π. The time derivative of biological noise, dN/dt, accumulating in the particular gene, g, can be expressed as

$$dN/dt = \lambda + \beta t .$$ (33)

Here λ is the classical constant mutational load discussed by Muller (1950) and $\beta = (\gamma/\hbar)^2$, which is the proportionality constant for the *keto-amino* → *enol imine* arrangement. A general expression for the total biological noise, N(t), in all M individual genes, g, in the population at age t is given by

$$N(t) = M\{ N_o + \sum_{i=1}^{m} \lambda_i t + \sum_{j=1}^{k} (\beta_j/2) t^2 \}$$

$$(34)$$

where N_o is the average number of mutations per gene g in the population of M at t = 0. The sum $\sum_{i=1}^{m}$ is over all m G-C + A-T pairs in the gene – excluding the $(CAG)_n$ repeat – and $\sum_{j=1}^{k}$ is over the k CAG repeats in the $(CAG)_n$ tract of length £, which exhibits expansion. Note that *keto-amino* → *enol imine* arrangement at A-T, i.e., A-T → *A-*T, causes deletion (Cooper, 2009b) and outside of the $(CAG)_n$ sequence, time-dependent substitutions, *ts*, generally do not contribute to expansion and are thus treated as conventional 'point'substitutions, which would be included in the $\sum_i \lambda_i t$ terms of Eq (34).

This model assumes that target gene g can – as a consequence of accumulating effective alterations in genetic specificities – be "converted" into a disease producing mode, including expansion to disease length. The time rate of change of converted target genes, dg(t)/dt, is proportional to the total number of *ts* + *td* plus generation dependent mutations contained in all M genes, g(t), in the population at age t. This is given by

$$d/dt\ g(t) = 1/K\ N(t)$$

$$(35)$$

where the proportionality constant is 1/K and N(t) is the noise defined in Eq (34). The number of converted target genes, g(t), in the population of M at age t is given by

$$g(t) = g_o + M/K \{ N_o t + \sum_{i=1}^{m} (\lambda_i/2) t^2 + \sum_{j=1}^{k} (\beta_j/6) t^3 \}$$

$$(36)$$

where g_o is the number of converted genes in the population at t = 0. Generally Eq (36) implies the condition *k > normal copy no.* for the particular repeat (Pearson et al., 2005). Phenotypic expression incidence, E(t), in the population of age t would change at a rate, dE/dt, which is proportional to the total number of converted genes, g(t), in the population. This relationship is expressed as

$$d/dt\ E(t) = 1/B\ g(t)$$

$$(37)$$

where 1/B is the proportionality constant. The incidence of phenotypic expression, E(t), in the population at age t is given as

$$E(t) = E_o + (g_o/B)\ t + M/2KB \{ N_o t^2 + \sum_{i=1}^{m} (\lambda_i/3) t^3 + \sum_{j=1}^{k} (\beta_j/12) t^4 \}$$

$$(38)$$

where E_o is the incidence at t = 0. Here time t = 0 when the egg is fertilized; so, at t = 0, E_o = *ts* = 0. In this case, N_o is the average number of inherited mutations per gene, and zero coherent states are designated by *ts* = 0. Initial conditions (observation) determine the value of g_0, which generally is $g_0 = 0$. Phenotypic expression, E(t), of a repeat tract disease is a consequence of transcription ultimately yielding mutant disease protein, which can occur without replication (Cooper, 2009a, b).

Anticipation – the decreasing age of phenotypic expression in successive generations containing larger expansions – is displayed in Figure 11 (Duyano et al., 1993; Gusella et al., 1993) and is mathematically expressed in Eq (38). The classical terms, $\Sigma^m_{i=1} \lambda_i t^3$, are over all m base pairs of the gene – excluding the $(CAG)_n$ tract – which, generally, is significantly longer than the $(CAG)_n$ insert. An increase in length of an inherited $(CAG)_n$ repeat is represented in Eq (38) by an appropriate increase of the upper limit, k, in the expression, $\Sigma^k_{j=1}\beta_j t^4$. Time-dependent contributions to E(t) in Eq (38) by quantum mechanical terms, $\Sigma^k_{j=1}\beta_j t^4$, would be greater for large upper limit, k, corresponding to longer $(CAG)_n$ sequences versus a smaller k value for short repeat tracts. Since quantum contributions to E(t) are coefficients of t^4 terms, as the upper limit k increases for longer $(CAG)_n$ sequences, these contribution will increase nonlinearly, consistent with Figure 11. Phenotypic expression displayed in Figure 11 is simulated by $\Sigma^k_{j=1}\beta_j t^4$ terms in Eq (38). Since E(t) = 0 from birth to ages ~ 6 to 70 yrs or more (Figure 11) and unperturbed β is small (~ 2×10^{-23} s^{-2}; Cooper, unpublished result), Eq (38) illustrates that coherent state contributions, $\Sigma^k_{j=1}\beta_j t^4$, could remain "sub-threshold", i.e., $\Sigma^k_{j=1}\beta_j t^4$ < threshold, for long time periods if the upper limit k is small. This would disallow sufficient coherent state events, *ts* + *td,* from populating the requisite "genetic threshold". Data in terms of the model are consistent with phenotypic expression as a consequence of coherent states populating G'-C', *G-*C and *A-*T sites within $(CAG)_n$ sequences such that the "genetic threshold" is populated beyond its evolutionarily allowed limit. In this case, phenotypic expression is due to $\Sigma^k_{j=1}\beta_j t^4$ > threshold. The disease-free "incubation time," i.e., time when $\Sigma^k_{j=1}\beta_j t^4$ < threshold, between conception (birth) and age at onset – time when $\Sigma^k_{j=1}\beta_j t^4 \geq$ threshold – is the time required for coherent states to populate the genetic threshold and is a function of $(CAG)_n$ length. Large $(CAG)_n$ targets provide enhanced 'cross sections' for coherent states to populate the requisite G'-C', *G-*C and *A-*T sites causing phenotypic expression, whereas small $(CAG)_n$ tracts present a reduced 'cross section' which requires longer times to populate. The disease-free copy number, k, is identified by the normal $(CAG)_n$ copy number such that, $\Sigma^k_{j=1}\beta_j t^4$ < threshold for a normal life time. If life expectancy were to significantly increase, the disease-free repeat copy number requirement, $\Sigma^k_{j=1}\beta_j t^4$ < threshold, implies a smaller upper limit k value. By simulating Figure 11 data in terms of Eq (38), one could obtain experimental estimates of the "rate constant", β, for phenotypic expression due to *keto-amino* → *enol-imine* arrangements in human $(CAG)_n$ tracts.

VI. Conclusion

Transcriptase quantum processing of time-dependent coherent states is manifested by bacteriophage T4 DNA systems and by expanded $(CAG)_n$ repeats inherited by human genomes. Time-dependent coherent states, designated by G-C → G'-C', G-C → *G-*C and A-T → *A-*T, are consequences of hydrogen bond arrangement, *keto-amino* → *enol-imine*, by symmetric and asymmetric channels (Figures 1-3). For times t < 100 y, approximate quantum methods yield the probability, P(t), of *keto-amino* → *enol-imine* arrangement is P(t) = ½$(\gamma/\hbar)^2 t^2$ where γ is the energy shift between states, Eq (31). These reaction rates are driven by quantum uncertainty limits on amino ($-NH_2$) protons. The four G-C amino protons are localized within two different hydrogen bond, $-NH_2$ end groups, and consequently, are confined to a relatively small space, Δx, compared to the four redistributed enol-imine coherent protons. From the uncertainty relation, $\Delta x \, \Delta p_x \geq \frac{1}{2} \hbar$, amino proton momentum can be expressed, approximately, as $p \approx \hbar / \Delta x$; so, proton kinetic energy can be approximated by $mv^2/2 = p^2/2m = \hbar^2 / [2m(\Delta x)^2]$. Self interaction between amino protons on carbon-2 guanine can cause proton confinement to too small of space, Δx, thereby enhancing reactivity of guanine amino protons, which initiate exchange tunneling by the symmetric channel (Figure 1a). The asymmetric channel is initiated by energetic amino protons on carbon-6 cytosine (Figure 1b). This introduces coherent proton states at G'-C', *G-*C & *A-*T sites, where product enol and imine hydrogen bonded protons are shared between two sets of indistinguishable electron lone pairs. Consequently, these protons participate in coupled quantum oscillations between near symmetric double minima at frequencies of $\sim 10^{13}$ s^{-1} (Tables 5-8). Genetic specificity at a superposition site, G'-C', *G-*C, or *A-*T, is stored as an input qubit, the quantum counterpart to the classical information bit. Before decoherence or replication, the informational content within a superposition is deciphered and processed by the transcriptase as an output qubit in an interval $\Delta t \ll 10^{-13}$ s. The delay in phenotypic expression of an inherited $(CAG)_n$ repeat disease (Figure 11) is the time required for coherent states, i.e., contributions by $\Sigma^k_{j=1} \beta_j \, t^4$ terms in Eq (38), to populate the inherited $(CAG)_n$ repeat.

Consistent with molecular genetic transcription data, as a consequence of the transcriptase measuring superposition proton states at G'-C' and *G-*C sites within an interval $\Delta t \ll 10^{-13}$ s, genetic specificities are determined and executed before an entanglement is created between coherent protons and quantum components of the transcriptase. This causes a decoherent transition from quantum to classical, yielding a statistical ensemble of decohered enol and imine isomers – G', C', *G, *C – subsequently replicated via the Topal-Fresco mechanism. This chapter and recent studies (Cooper, 2009a, b, 2010) are consistent with transcriptase quantum processing evolving with duplex DNA. Consequently natural selection at the quantum level has generated effective schemes for introducing coherent proton states – at rates appropriate for evolving DNA systems (Kadenbach et al., 1995; Hwang and Green, 2004; Beerenwinkel et al., 2007; Elango et al., 2008) – within decoherence-free subspaces, using entanglement states (Ghosh et al., 2003; Vedral, 2003) to augment transcriptase quantum processing at biological temperature. The evolutionarily selected quantum information processing system has utilized coupled proton qubits which may enhance error reduction (Oreshkov et al., 2008; Fedichkin et al., 2009) and may also provide a basis for decoherence-free subspaces (Bell et al., 2002; Grace et al., 2007; Mie et al., 2009; Chen et al., 2009; Poccia et al., 2009). Hence, further experimental and theoretical study of this evolutionarily generated qubit system and its transcriptase-assisted decoherence may provide new insight into quantum information processing and entanglement states at elevated temperature.

Evidence of entanglement is demonstrated by quantum transcription of coherent states and subsequent replication of decohered G' and *C sites. When G' or *C is on the T-strand, substitutions G'2 0 2 $\rightarrow$ T and *C2 0 2^2 $\rightarrow$ T are phenotypically expressed by transcription *before* replication is initiated. In these cases, phenotypic expression is a consequence of the transcriptase reading quantum states G'2 0 2 and *C2 0 2^2 – as normal T2^2 0 2^2 (Figure 4) – before the wild-type base, T2^2 0 2^2, is genotypically replicated into G' and *C sites of T4 DNA. In fact the mutation frequencies, G'2 0 2 $\rightarrow$ T and *C2 0 2^2 $\rightarrow$ T, phenotypically expressed via transcription are identical to subsequent substitution frequencies, G'2 0 2 $\rightarrow$ T and *C2 0 2^2 → T, expressed as a consequence of Topal-Fresco replication (Cooper, 1994, 2009a, b). Therefore after transcription and before replication, quantum states G'2 0 2 and *C2 0 2^2 on T-strands were preserved by entanglement (Ghosh et al., 2003; Vedral, 2003) between coherent protons and transcriptase quantum components. Otherwise quantum states, G'2 0 2 and *C2 0 2^2, would be subjected to H_2O, causing decoherence and reequilibration. In this case, mutation frequencies for G'2 0 2 → T and *C2 0 2^2 → T expressed by replication would be less than G'2 0 2 → T and *C2 0 2^2 → T frequencies expressed phenotypically by transcription, which is inconsistent with data. However, in the next round of replication, entanglement is absent and ~ 20% of *C2 0 2^2 exhibits reequilibration, *C2 0 2^2 → $C0^0$ 0 2^2. This explains how time-dependent G'2 0 2 → T and *C2 0 2^2 → T mutations are "transcriptionally enhanced" by a factor of two (Cooper, 2009b). Other explanations are not obvious.

Transcriptase quantum processing is required to explain multiple genetic specificities exhibited a single G' site. When the transcriptase encounters a G' on the T-strand, the transcriptase deciphers genetic specificities originating from quantum states G'0 0 2, G'2 0 2, G'2 0 0 & G'0 0 0, using Figure 2 notation. Data from rUV74 revertants demonstrate that 350 of the 460 (76%) revertants detected express G'2 0 2 →T as a consequence of transcription *before* replication was initiated, but 110 of the 460 (24%) revertants required replication (passage) to express G'0 0 2 → C. In this case, the transcriptase deciphers and processes genetic specificities originating within quantum states, G'2 0 2 (Figure 4b) ⇌ G'0 0 2 (Figure 4d), on the basis of coherent proton states, $|+>$ and $|->$, for the guanine carbon-6 enol proton. When this proton is in state $|->$, the "outside" position, the guanine quantum state is G'2 0 2, which is transcribed as normal $T2^2$ 0 2^2. However when this proton state is $|+>$, the quantum guanine state is G'0 0 2, which is not a transcription analog of $C0^0$ 0 2^2 or $T2^2$ 0 2^2. Therefore expression of the substitution G'0 0 2 → C requires passage, a round of replication. This requires (i) transcriptase measurement on G' states which results in an entangled state, (ii) decoherence of G' states, (iii) Topal-Fresco replication of the complementary mispair, G'0 0 2–syn-$G2^2$ 2 #, to insert normal $C0^0$ 2 2^2 and (iv) transcription of normal $C0^0$ 2 2^2. Compared to state G'0 0 2, expression of state G'2 0 2 was enhanced by a single round of transcription *before* replication was initiated. Straightforward analysis predicts the number of G'2 0 2 → T events should be ~ 2-fold greater (after passage) than the number of G'0 0 2 → C events. But observation shows G'2 0 2 → T (76%) is ~ 3-fold more numerous than G'0 0 2 → C (24%). Since the quantum state G'2 0 2 is "preferred" compared to state G'0 0 2 (Figure 6), this would cause an enhanced availability of quantum G'2 0 2 at transcription and a corresponding increased yield of the decohered G'2 0 2 isomer at replication, which would explain the 3-fold rather than 2-fold yield of G'2 0 2 → T compared to G'0 0 2 → C. These observations can not be simulated by classical models.

Transcriptase quantum processing explains the reason the no. of time-dependent *C → T mutants is generally two-fold > the no. of *G → A mutants. When the transcriptase encounters a *C site, it implements a measurement on superposition states, *C2 0 2^2 ⇌*C0 0 2^2 (Figure 2 f-g), which is governed by coherent proton states, $|+>$ and $|->$, at the cytosine carbon-6 imine proton position (Figure 4c). When this proton is in state $|->$, the quantum cytosine state is *C2 0 2^2, which is transcribed as normal $T2^2$ 0 2^2. This allows phenotypic expression of the substitution, *C2 0 2^2 → $T2^2$ 0 2^2, by transcription before replication is initiated. The complementary quantum state, *G0 2 0^0, is on the C-strand; so passage (replication) is required for expression of the substitution, *G0 2 0^0 → A0^0 2 # (Cooper, 2009b). This requires (i) transcriptase measurement on superposition *C states which results in an entangled state, (ii) decoherence of *G0 2 0^0 (and *C2 0 2^2), (iii) Topal-Fresco replication of the complementary mispair, *G0 2 0^0–T2^2 0 2^2, yielding A0^0 2 # – T2^2 0 2^2, and (iv) transcription of the incorporated normal A0^0 2 #. As a result, the no. of *C → T mutants due to time-dependent lesions on the T-strand is generally two-fold > the no. of *G → A mutants due to lesions on C-strand.

The transcriptase is a 'quantum reader' that can yield observable specification of the relative distribution of coherent states measured in duplex DNA. Just before transcriptase measurement, the quantum distribution of G'-states is described by Eq (8). As a result of transcriptase measurement of the G' superposition, three of the four G'-states yield the corresponding decohered molecular genetic observables. For example, Sec. III illustrates that the probability of G' being in state G'2 0 2 is given by $|<--|\psi>|^2 = |\delta|^2$ where $|\delta|^2$ is determined from transcriptase measurement yielding a particular molecular genetic observable, G' → T. Values for the forth G'-state would be determined by normalization. Transcriptase measurements on coherent states at a G' or *C site also specify quantum states, $|+>$ or $|->$, for the guanine carbon-6 enol proton and the cytosine carbon-6 imine proton.

The coupled flip-flop "proton dance" exhibited by enol-imine protons in duplex DNA is a coupled proton analog to the π-electron "dance" in benzene. Approximate quantum calculations identify a frequency range of 2.6×10^{12} to 3.68×10^{13} s^{-1} for coupled quantum oscillations of enol-imine protons. Tables 5-8 illustrate that the flip-flop frequency, ν_θ, for the regular proton is 2-fold greater than that for the composite proton for given values of V_0 and ϕ_0 (Figure 9). This quantum mixing of proton energy states enhances the stability of coherent enol-imine hydrogen bonds by, approximately, 0.25 to 7 Kcal/mole (Table 9). Since coupled proton oscillations in duplex DNA have evolved consistent with laws of physics and biology, difficulties associated with decoherence-avoidance (e.g., Grace et al., 2007; Poccia et al., 2009; Chen et al., 2009; Mie et al., 2009) and high temperature (37^0 C) entanglement appear to have been evolutionarily resolved. Coupled qubits may yield reductions in error (Oreshkov et al., 2008; Fedichkin et al., 2009). Also symmetry considerations imply coupled quantum oscillations involving two protons may provide a degree of "synergistic stability" against decoherence compared to flip-flop tunneling of a single less massive particle. Evidently, through certain degrees of freedom, coupled coherent proton states have identical interactions with their environment analogous to the neutrino system in dense media studied by Bell et al. (2002). The present chapter implies superposition proton states occupy decoherent-free subspaces that generally allow coupled quantum oscillations until the transcriptase implements its measurement within an interval $\Delta t \ll 10^{-13}$ s. After initiation of transcriptase measurement, an order of magnitude estimate for proton decoherence time, τ_D, is $\Delta t < \tau_D < 10^{-13}$ s, which is in agreement with more rigorous model calculations (Tegmark, 2000). A quantum proton would retain coherence for ~ 20% of the relaxation time, τ_R (Table 10), which is sufficient time for transcriptase processing of coherent states. The ensuing entanglement state plays a significant role in bestowing well defined three-dimensional structure on decohered isomers – G', C', *G, *C – which is a requirement for efficient Topal-Fresco replication. Otherwise decohered states could be ill defined ghostly structures (Davies, 2004).

Quantum uncertainty arguments are consistent with the observation that time-dependent CpG → TpG is ~ 15-fold greater when cytosine is methylated (Elango et al., 2008; Moser et al., 2009). A consequence of $-CH_3$ attached to cytosine carbon-5 is additional proton-proton interaction for cytosine amino protons, i.e., $-NH_2$ - - H_3C-. This causes further proton confinement to too small of space, Δx, thereby increasing proton kinetic energy which would enhance *keto-amino* $\rightarrow$ *enol-imine* rates by the asymmetric channel (Figure 1b), consistent with observation. Additionally, *C2 0 2^2 $\rightarrow$ T mutations exhibit "transcription enhancement" (Cooper, 2009b).

Acknowledgement

This investigation has benefited from insight provided by Professor Jacques Fresco on catalytic site specificities of replicase and transcriptase systems, for which the author is grateful. Informative discussions and questions by Nikolay Sarychcv and Altonie Barber are appreciated.

References

Alberts, B., Johnson, A., Lewis, J., Raff, M., Roberts, K. & Walter, P. (2002). *Molecular Biology of the Cell,* 4th edition. Garland, New York.

Appel, J., Windpassinger, P. J., Oblak, D. et al. (2009). Mesocopic atomic entanglement for precision measurements beyond the standard quantum limit. *Proc. Natl. Acad. Sci. US,* **106**, 10960-10965.

Baltz, R. H., Bingham, P. M. & Drake, J. W. (1976). Heat mutagenesis in bacteriophage T4: The transition pathway. *Proc. Natl. Acad. Sci., USA,* **73**, 1269-1273.

Beerenwinkel, N., Antal, T., Dingli, D., Traulsen, A., Kinzler, K. W. et al. (2007). Genetic progression and the waiting time to cancer. *PLoS Comput. Biol.* **3**(11), e225. doi:10.1371/journal.pcbi.0030225.

Bell, N. F., Sawyer, R. F. & Volkas, R. R. (2002). Entanglement and quantal coherence: Study of two limiting cases of rapid system-bath interactions. *Phys. Rev., A***65**, 052105-1-052105-12.

Benzer, S. (1961). On the topography of the genetic fine structure. *Proc. Natl. Acad. Sci., USA* **47**, 403-415.

Bingham, P. M., Baltz, R. H., Ripley, L. S. & Drake, J. W. (1976). Heat mutagenesis in bacteriophage T4: The transversion pathway. *Proc. Natl. Acad. Sci., USA,* **73**, 4159-4163.

Bromham, L. & Penny, D. (2003). The modern molecular clock, *Nat. Rev. Genet.,* **4**, 216-224.

Ceron-Carrasco, J. P., Requena, A., Zuniga, J., et al. (2009). Intermolecular proton transfer in microhydrated guanine-cytosine base pairs: A new mechanism for spontaneous mutation in DNA. *J Phys. Chem. A* **113**, 10549-10556. DOI: 10.1021/jp906551f.

Chen, J. M., Liang, L. M., Li, C. Z., et al. (2009). Distributed quantum computing in decoherence-free subspace via adiabatic passage. Opt. *Commun.,* **282**, 3181-3184. DOI: 10.1016/j.optcom.2009.04.040.

Cooper, W. G. (1979). Proton transitions in hydrogen bonds of DNA: A first order perturbation model. Int. *J. Quantum Chem. Quantum Biol. Symp.,* **6**, 171-188.

Cooper, W. G. (1994). T4 phage evolution data in terms of a time-dependent Topal-Fresco mechanism. *Biochem. Genet.,* **32**, 383-395.

Cooper, W. G. (1995). Evolutionary origin of expandable G-C rich triplet repeat DNA sequences. *Biochem. Genet.*, **33**, 173-181.

Cooper, W. G. (1996). Hypothesis on a causal link between EMF and an evolutionary class of cancer and spontaneous abortion. *Cancer Biochem. Biophys.*, **15**, 151-170.

Cooper, W. G. (2009a). Evidence for transcriptase quantum processing implies entanglement and decoherence of superposition proton states. *BioSystems*, **97**, 73-89. DOI: 10.1016/j.biosystems.04.010.

Cooper, W. G. (2009b). Necessity of quantum coherence to account for the spectrum of time-dependent mutations exhibited by bacteriophage T4. *Biochem. Genet.*, **47**, 892-410. DOI: 10.1007/s10528-009-9293-8.

Cooper, W. G. (2010). Coherent states as consequences of *keto-amino* → *enol-imine* hydrogen bond arrangements driven by quantum uncertainty limits on on amino DNA protons. *Int. J. Quantum Chem.* (in press).

Cooper, W. G. & Kouri, D. J. (1971). N-particle noninteracting Green's function. *J. Math. Phys.*, **13**, 809-812.

Davies, P. C. W. (2004). Does quantum mechanics play a non-trivial role in life? *BioSystems*, **78**, 69-79.

Devitt, S. J., Fowler, A. G. & Stephens et al. (2009). Architectural design for a topological cluster state quantum computer. *New J. Phys.*, **11**, 083032. DOI 10.1088/1367-2630/11/8/083032.

Drake, J. W. & Baltz, R. H. (1976). The biochemistry of mutagenesis. *Ann. Rev. Biochem.*, **45**, 11-37.

Drake, J. W., Charlesworth, B., Charlesworth, D. & Crow, J. F. (1998). Rates of spontaneous mutation. *Genetics*, **148**, 1667-1686.

Drake, J. W. & McGuire, J. (1967). Characteristics of mutations appearing spontaneously in extracellular particles of bacteriophage T4. *Genetics,* **55**, 387-398.

Drake, J. W. & Ripley, L. S. (1994). Mutagenesis. In: Karam, J.D. (ed.) *Molecular Biology of Bacteriophage T4*, pp. 98-124. American Society for Microbiology, Washington, D.C.

Duyano, M., Ambrose, C., Meyers, R., Novelletto, A., Persichette, F., Frontali, M., Folstein, S., Ross, C., Franz, M., Abbott, M., Gray, J., Conneally, P., Young, A., Penney, J., Hollingsworth, Z., Shoulson, I., Lazzarini, A., Falek, A., Koroshetz, W., Sax, D., Bird, E., Vonsattel, J., Bonilla, E., Alvir, J., Conde, J., Cha, J. H., Dure, L., Gomez, F., Ramos, M., Sanchez-Ramos, J., Snodgrass, S., de Yong, M., Wexler, N., Moscowitz, C., Penchaszadeh, G., MacFarlane, H., Anderson, M., Jenkins, B., Srinidhi, J., Barnes, G., Gusella, J. & MacDonald, M. (1993). Trinucleotide repeat length instability and age of onset in Huntington's disease. *Nat. Genet.*, **4**, 387-392.

Elango, N., Kim, S. H., NICS Program, Vigoda, E. & Yi, S. V. (2008). Mutations of different molecular origins exhibit contrasting patterns of regional substitution rate variation, *PLoS Comput. Biol.* **4**, e1000015. doi: 10.1371/journal.pcbi.1000015.

Fedichkin, L., Sharpiro, M. & Dykman, M. I. (2009). Quantum measurements of coupled systems. *Phys. Rev. A* **80**, 012114. DOI: 10.1103/PhysRevA.80.012114.

Feng, M., Xu, Y. Y., Zhou, F. & Suter, D. (2009). Nuclear spin qubits in a trapped-ion quantum computer. *Phys. Rev. A.*, **79**, 052331. DOI: 10.1103/PhysRevA.79.052331.

Fillaux, F., Cousson, A. & Gutmann, M. J. (2008). A neutron diffraction study of macroscopically entangled proton states in the high temperature phase of the $KHCO_3$

crystal at 340 K. *J. Phys.-Condes. Matter* **20**, 015225. DOI: 10.1088/0953-8984/20/01/015225.

Gaetan, A., Miroshnychenko, Y., Wilk, T. et al. (2009). Observation of collective excitation of two individual atoms in the Rydberg blockade refime. *Nat. Phys.*, **5**, 115-118.

Gatchel, J. R. & Zoghbi, H. Y. (2005). Diseases of unstable repeat expansion: Mechanisms and common principles. *Nat. Rev. Genet.*, **6**, 743-755.

Garcia-Viloca, M., Gao, J., Karplus, M. & Truhlar, D. C. (2004). How enzymes work: analysis by modern rate theory and computer simulations. *Science*, **303**, 186-195.

Ghosh, S., Rosenbaum, T. F., Aeppll, G. & Coppersmith, S. N. (2003). Entangled quantum states of magnetic dipoles. *Nature*, **425**, 48-51.

Goold, J., Heaney, L., Busch, T. & Vedral, V. (2009). Detection and engineering of spatial mode entanglement with ultracold bosons. *Phys. Rev. A* **80**, 022338. DOI: 10.1103/ PhysRevA.80.022338.

Grace, M., Brif, C., Rabitz, H., Walmsley, I. L., Kosut, R. L. & Lidar, D. A. (2007). Optimal control of quantum gates and suppression of decoherence in a system of interacting two-level particles. *J. Phys. B: At. Mol. Opt. Phys.*, **40**, S103-S125.

Greenman, C., Stephens, P., Smith, R., Dalgliesh, G. L., Hunter, C. et al., (2007). Patterns of somatic mutation in human cancer genomes. *Nature*, **446**, 153-158.

Guallar, V., Douhal, A., Moreno, M. & Lluch, J. (1999). DNA mutations induced by proton and charge transfer in the low-lying excited singlet electronic states of the DNA base pairs: A theoretical insight. *J. Phys. Chem. A*, **103**, 6251-6256.

Gurney, R. W. & Condon, E. U. (1929). Quantum mechanics and radioactive disintegration. *Phys. Rev.*, **33**, 127-140.

Gusella, J. F., MacDonald, M. E., Ambrose, C. M. & Duyao, M. P. (1993). Molecular genetics of Huntington's disease. *Arch. Neurol.*, **50**, 1157-1163.

Hameka, H. F. & de la Vega, J. (1984). Intramolecular proton exchange in near symmetric cases. *J. Am. Chem. Soc.*, **106**, 7703-7705.

Herskind, P. F., Datan, A., Marler, J. et al., (2009). Realization of collective strong coupling with ion Coulomb crystals in an optical cavity. *Nat. Phys.*, **5**, 494-498.

Hwang, D. G. & Green, P. (2004). Bayesian Markov chain Monte Carlo sequence analysis reveals varying neutral substitution patterns in mammalian evolution. *Proc. Natl. Acad. Sci.*, USA, **101**, 13994-14001.

Jorgensen, W. L. & Pranata, J. (1990). The importance of secondary interactions in triply hydrogen-bonded complexes: guanine–cytosine vs uracil – diaminopyridine. *J. Am. Chem. Soc.*, **112**, 2008-2010.

Kadengbach, B., Munscher, C., Frank, V., Muller-Hocker, J. & Napiwotzki, J. (1995). Human aging is associated with stochastic somatic mutations of mitochondrial DNA, *Mutation Res.*, **338**, 161-172.

Karlsson, E. B. (2003). Quantum coherence and decoherence of protons and muons in condensed matter. Eur. Phys. *J. D At. Mol. Opt. Phys.*, **22**, 393-400.

Kim, K., Chang, M. S., Islam, R. et al., (2009). Entanglement and tunable spin-spin coupling between trapped ions using multiple transverse modes. *Phys. Rev. Lett.*, **103**, 120502; doi: 10.1103/PhysRevLett.103.120502.

Kricker, M. & Drake, J. W. (1990). Heat mutagenesis in bacteriophage T4: Another walk down the transversion pathway. *J. Bacteriol.*, **172**, 3037-3039.

Kryachko, E. S. & Sabin, J. R. (2003). Quantum chemical study of the hydrogen-bonded patterns in A-T base pairs of DNA: Origins of tautomeric mispairs, base flipping and Watson-Crick → Hoogsteen conversion. Int. *J. Quantum Chem.*, **91**, 695-710.

Leon, J. & Martin-Martinez, E. (2009). Physical qubits from charged particles: Infrared divergences in quantum information. *Phys. Rev. A* **79**, 052309. DOI: 10.1103/ PhysRevA.79.052309.

Li, X., Cai, Z. & Sevilla, D. (2001). Investigation of proton transfer within DNA base pair anion and cation radicals by density function theory (DFT). *J. Phys. Chem.* B, **105**, 10115-10123.

Löwdin, P. O. (1965). Quantum genetics and the aperiodic solid: Some aspects on the biological problems of heredity, mutations, aging and tumors in view of the quantum theory of the DNA molecule. In: Löwdin, P.O. (Ed.), Adv. *Quantum Chem.*, **2**, 213-359.

McFadden, J. & Al-Khalili, J. (1999). A quantum mechanical model of adaptive mutations. *BioSystems*, **50**, 203-211.

Mei, F., Yu, Y. F. & Zhang, Z. M. (2009). Decoherence-free quantum memory for photonic state using atomic ensembles. *Int. J. Quantum Info.*, **7**, 811-820.

Merzbacher, E. (1997). *Quantum Mechanics*, 3rd edition. John Wiley & Sons, New York.

Metzler, R. & Ambjörnsson, T. (2005). Dynamic approach to DNA breathing. *J. Biol. Phys.*, **31**, 339-350.

Mirkin, S. M. (2007). Expandable DNA repeats and human diseases. *Nature* **447**, 932-940. doi: 10.1038/nature05977.

Mishima, K. & Yamashita, K. (2009). Quantum computing using rotational modes of two polar molecules. *Chem. Phys.*, **361**, 106-117.

Moser, A., Guza, R., Tretyakova, N. et al., (2009). Density functional study of the influence of C-5 cytosine substitution in base pairs with guanine. *Theoret. Chem. Acc.*, **122**, 179-188. DOI: 10.1007/s00214-008-0497-5.

Muller, H. J. (1950). Our load of mutations. *Am. J. Hum. Genet.*, **2**, 111-176.

Nielson, M. A. & Chuang, I. L. (2000). *Quantum computation and quantum information.* Cambridge University Press, Cambridge, UK.

Oreshkov, O., Lidar, D. A. & Brun, T. A. (2008). Operator error correction for continuous dynamics. *Phys. Rev. A,* **78**, 022333. DOI: 10.1103/PhysRevA.78.022333.

Pearson, C. E., Edamura, K. N. & Cleary, J. D. (2005). Repeat instability: Mechanisms of dynamic mutation. *Nat. Rev. Genet.*, **6**, 729-742.

Poccia, N., Ricci, A., Innocenti, D. & Bianconi, A. (2009). A possible mechanism for evading temperature quantum decoherence in living matter by Feshbach resonance. *Int. J. Mol. Sci.*, **10**, 2084-2106.

Podolyan, Y., Gorb, L. & Leszczynski, J. (2003). *Ab Initio* study of the prototropic tautomerism of cytosine and guanine and their contribution to spontaneous point mutations. *Int. J. Mol. Sci.*, **4**, 410-421.

Pranata, J., Wierschke, S. G. & Jorgensen, W. L. (1991). OPLS potential functions for nucleotide bases. Relative association constants of hydrogen bonded base pairs in chloroform. *J. Am. Chem. Soc.*, **113**, 2810-2819.

Reif, F. (1965). *Fundamentals of Statistical and Thermal Physics*. McGraw Hill, New York.

Rezakhani, A. T., Kuo, W. J., Hamma, A. et al., (2009). Quantum adiabatic brachistochrone. *Phys. Rev. Lett.* **108**, 080502. DOI: 10.1103/PhysRevLett.103.080502.

Richards, R. I. (2001). Dynamic mutations: a decade of unstable expanded repeats in human genetic disease. *Mol. Hum. Genet.*, **10**, 2187-2194.

Ripley, L. S. (1988). Estimation of *in-vivo* miscoding rates. Quantitative behavior of two classes of heat-induced DNA lesions. *J. Mol. Biol.*, **202**, 17-34.

Roloff, R., Wenin, M. & Potz, W. (2009). Optial control for open quantum systems: Qubits and quantum gates. *J. Comp. Theoret. Nanosci.*, **6**, 1837-1863. DOI: 10.1166/jctn.2009.1246.

Rosenberg, S. M. (2001). Evolving responsively: adaptive mutations. *Nature Rev. Genet.*, **2**, 504-515.

Scheiner, S. (1997). *Hydrogen Bonding. A Theoretical Perspective*. Oxford University Press, New York.

Sekiya, H. & Sakota, K. (2006). Excited-state double proton transfer in the 7-azaindole dimer in the gas phase. Resolution of the stepwise versus concerted mechanism controversy and a new paradigm. *Bull. Chem. Soc. Jpn.* , **79**, 373-385.

Smedarchina, Z., Siebrand, W. & Fernández-Ramos, A. (2007). Correlated double-proton transfer. I. Theory. *J. Chem. Phys.*, **127**, 174513-174525.

Tegmark, M. (2000). The importance of quantum decoherence in brain processes. *Phys. Rev.* E61, 4194-4206.

Topal, M. D. & Fresco, J. R. (1976). Complementary base pairing and the origin of base substitutions. *Nature,* **263**, 285-289.

Tsai, D. B., Chen, P. W. & Goan, H. S. (2009). Optimal control of the silicon-based donor-electron-spin quantum computing. *Phys. Rev. A* **79**, 060306. DOI: 10.1103/PhysRevA.79.060306.

Vedral, V. (2003). Entanglements hit the big time. *Nature*, **425**, 28-29.

Vedral, V. (2007). *Introduction to Quantum Information Science*. Oxford University Press, Oxford, UK.

Wells, R. D. & Ashizawa, T. (2006). *Genetic instabilities and neurological diseases*. Elsevier, San Diego.

Wells, R. D., Dere, R., Hebert, M. L., Napierala, M. & Son, L. (2005). Advances in mechanisms of genetic instability related to hereditary neurological diseases. *Nucleic Acids Res.*, **33**, 3785-3798.

Wolff, A. & Krug, J. (2009). Robustness and epistasis in mutation-selection models. *Physical Biol.*, 6, 036007. doi: 10.1088/1478-3975/6/3/036007.

Zoete, V. & Meuwly, M. (2004). Double proton transfer in the isolated and DNA-embedded guanine-cytosine base pair. *J. Chem. Phys.* **121***, 4377-4388.

Zurek, W. H. (1991). Decoherence and the transition from quantum to classical, *Phys. Today,* **44**, 36-44.

Zurek, W. H. (2003). Decoherence, einselection and the quantum origins of the classical. *Rev. Mod. Phys.*, **75**, 715-775.

In: Computer Science Research and the Internet
Editor: Jaclyn E. Morris, pp. 43-71

ISBN: 978-1-61728-730-5
© 2011 Nova Science Publishers, Inc.

Chapter 2

A NETWORKED VIRTUAL ENVIRONMENT FOR TEACHING SURGERY

Chris Gunn

Commonwealth Scientific Industrial Research
Organisation (CSIRO), Australia

Abstract

This chapter discusses two applications which were developed to allow an instructor to guide and teach a medical student in a surgical training scenario. The most interesting feature of these applications is that both participants can simultaneously interact within the scene with haptic (force) feedback, allowing them to co-operatively touch and manipulate the virtual body organs. As well as this, the instructor can effectively grasp the student's hand and haptically guide it in a task within the scene. The first application was designed to teach the procedural aspects of a cholecystectomy (removal of the gall bladder), and incorporated several pliable body organs. The second application focused on temporal bone surgery, a procedure that involves drilling away part of the skull behind the ear to gain access to the middle and inner ear. Both applications allow instructor and student to be located in different places connected by the Internet. The first application was used for distance trials to determine the maximum geographical distance that was feasible between the two participants. Results showed that interaction between Australia and the USA was excellent and between Australia and Europe was adequate. The second application was used in a clinical trial with ear surgeons and their students. The results of these trials showed improved learning times over traditional methods. It was also discovered that there were unexpected benefits of having a networked system even when the two networked workstations were side-by-side.

Introduction

Traditionally, surgery has been taught using the apprenticeship model, along with intensive study of diagrams and textbooks. Surgeons would pass on their practical skills to students during a real surgical procedure. Another training method is to practice surgery on a cadaver. This has the disadvantage that the body does not react in the same way that live tissue would. It has been described by surgeons as 'flat'. Cadarvic material can also be difficult to acquire and costly to store and prepare. A third method is to practice surgery on live animals. There is a growing movement against this practice, on ethical grounds. It also suffers from the fact that the anatomy of each animal is considerably different to a human. Surgical training methods such as these also have the disadvantage of destroying the material during practice, so that a procedure cannot be repeated frequently. More recently, sophisticated artificial plastic models have been manufactured, with the ability to provide movement, vital signs and a reaction to drugs and injections [21]. However, they also cannot undergo most surgical procedures without being damaged or destroyed.

Virtual environments have been increasingly filling the need for the practical components of training courses for surgeons. While most of these lack the realism of interacting with flesh and body organs, they have several compensating advantages. Firstly, the three dimensional (3D) view presented to the user can be enhanced with annotations, in the style of text, animations or diagrams. Components of the scene can be made transparent or translucent to reveal underlying structure. Different, perhaps rare, conditions can be drawn from a library of cases and represented within the model. The 3D model can be rotated during inspection, allowing a student to gain a better understanding of the shapes, sizes and inter-connecting features of the anatomy. The ability to zoom and fly-through can also assist in understanding. Graphical overlays which appear and disappear at appropriate times are another aid to memory and understanding. Haptic feedback can also provide an experience to the student that approximates the forces felt by a surgeon through the surgical instruments.

2. Cholecystectomy Simulator

One of the training systems we have developed at CSIRO [4] addresses the cholecystectomy procedure; a fairly common procedure of removing the gall bladder. It involves accessing the site, separating the gall bladder from its attaching tissue, applying clips to the cystic duct and cutting that duct, between the applied clips. The training system has been designed with the philosophy of supporting discussion between the instructor and student. It allows an instructor to teach the relevant anatomy and lead the student through the procedural steps required for the operation. It has several views, which can be visited by users individually or in unison. The primary view is of a 3D model of body organs such as liver, stomach and kidneys, obtained by segmenting data from CT[1] scans. Other views contain a shared whiteboard, a shared image viewer and shared video player for viewing pre-recorded video of real surgery, all modeled within the 3D environment. Users can jump back and forth between the views.

Virtual surgical training environments have several components that can be combined in a number of ways. Since surgery involves three dimensional dexterous actions, most of these components aim to present a 3D scene in a way that allows a student to concentrate on the task being learned, rather than the skills required to run the system. To be successful, the interface to the system needs to be simple and intuitive enough to allow the student to concentrate on the learning task. Ideally, a student should be able to see an instrument, pick it up and use it in a fairly natural way. Objects in their view (such as tissue) should react to the instrument in an expected way. There should be little difference between the instrument and

---

[1] computed tomography

tissue being in the real world or a virtual world. Using a mouse and cursor along with a 2D computer screen may be sufficient for the theoretical aspects of a surgery course, but do not provide sufficient realism to prepare a student for the challenges of the practical tasks ahead.

Surgical training systems often use stereo vision, proprioception[2], haptics and 3D modeling to provide an immersive experience in a virtual world. A further component, less often found in surgical training systems, is the ability for more than one participant to help and guide another, via networking.

3. Surgical Training Needs

There are several aspects to training in a surgical environment. A student needs to learn the anatomy of the body, the functions of the body organs, as well as physiology and chemistry. The practical skills of cutting, suturing, drilling, swabbing and clipping need to also be conveyed from an expert (the instructor) to the student. The procedural aspects of the surgery are also important. They include knowledge of the steps that are required, and the order of those steps, the dangers to be aware of at each stage and the signs to look out for, indicating the patient's condition. Also, common errors need to be demonstrated and explained, along with tips on how to avoid them. Students also need to be exposed to variations in anatomical and medical conditions.

Once the student can perform a procedure, there needs to be some way of providing feedback to the student and their instructor on the skill they are displaying. At some stage the student needs to be certified as proficient to undertake surgery on live patients, and some means of assessing their level of expertise needs to exist.

It is possible to provide some anatomical learning and the procedural components of surgical training with even a rudimentary model of the body. Any improvement in realism over this, can be considered a bonus, and may help in learning the practical, dexterous skills as well. If tissue can deform and spring back, and if organs can react to the surgical instruments to stretch, tear, cut and bleed, the learning process can be undertaken in a more experiential way. It has been shown [5] that practical experience, especially with a multi-modal interface [17], can provide the student with an improved knowledge of the subject over text based learning. This is especially true in surgical training, in both real and virtual environments and a combination of text and virtual reality training, followed by real surgical practice is probably the best compromise.

3.1. Stereo Vision and Proprioception

Some virtual environments are presented to the user in stereoscopic 3D [12], via stereo glasses or auto-stereoscopic screens [11 13]. Typically, the stereoscopic eye-convergence is adjusted so that the objects appear in a workspace behind the screen, or partly behind and partly in front of the screen.

The disadvantage in having objects behind the screen is that users cannot place their hands on the objects. If the eye-convergence of the model is adjusted to present the objects as if they were floating in front of the screen, the student can place their hands (or instruments)

---

[2] The ability to sense the position and orientation of the body and its parts without seeing them.

on the virtual objects themselves, as if they were actually there (Figure 1). This adds to the naturalness of interaction with the model and more closely represents the real world.

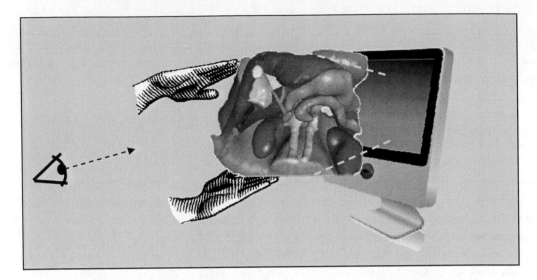

Figure 1. Stereo vision allows co-location of user's hands and model.

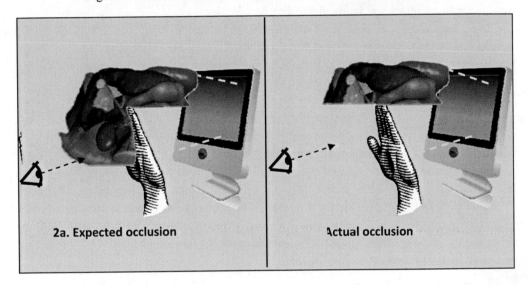

Figure 2. Expected occlusion. b) Actual occlusion, destroys illusion of 3D.

However, since the virtual objects are being projected from a computer screen facing the user, if the user places a hand in amongst the virtual objects, the hand will occlude part of the screen, and those 3D objects emanating from that position will disappear.

This would be expected for objects which should appear beyond the user's hands (between the hand and the screen) (fig 2a), but those objects being represented closer to the user's eyes, in front of their hands, would also disappear, due to the fact that all 3D objects are originally emanating from the screen (fig 2b). This can create a logical inconsistency, destroying the illusion of reality.

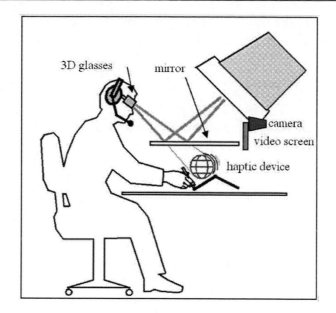

Figure 3. CSIRO Haptic Workbench.

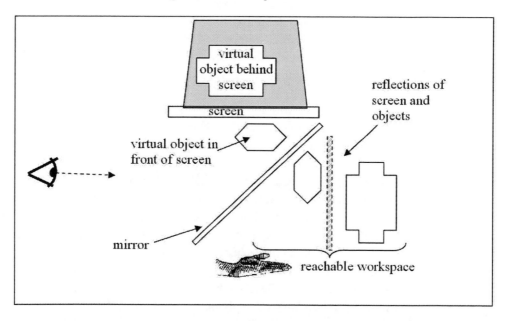

Figure 4. Reflected 3D scene allows a doubling of the reachable workspace.

The cholecystectomy simulator uses the CSIRO haptic workbench [23] shown in Figure 3 to overcome this problem by providing a workspace for the user's hands, hidden from the user's line of site by a mirror. In this way, the user can have their hands in the same location as the 3D model, but they do not see their own hands at all. Instead they see the virtual model and perhaps some avatar-like representation of their hands or instruments. This representation can then be computationally integrated into the 3D scene, so that it can move in and amongst the individual model parts and keep the occlusions of instruments and objects consistent. The user's proprioceptive knowledge of their hand position matches their visual understanding of the model and the virtual hand or instrument representations. The consistency of these components assists the user in understanding and interaction with the model.

A second advantage of the mirrored workbench is that the 3D objects can now be placed both in front of *and behind* the display screen, and still allow the user to place their hands or instruments at the location of *all* the virtual objects. This is because the screen plane is now a reflection in the mirror, at a depth equaling the distance of the real screen from the mirror. Being a reflection at some depth, the user's hand position can pass through that plane, from in front to behind it, unlike the case with a physical screen. This effectively allows a doubling of the reachable work area, over that allowed by using a 3D display directly from a screen.

3.2. Haptics

The word haptics describes the technique of providing a computer generated force to a user's hands, via a haptic device, such as the SensAble Phantom [20]. The cholecystectomy trainer uses haptics extensively to enhance the experience of instructor and student. The virtual anatomical models have organs that can be touched via haptic instruments, providing a force response proportionate to their deformation. When organs connected with ducts and tissue are moved, the ducts and tissue move and stretch, but in doing so contribute to the force being returned to the surgeon's hand. The ability to feel surfaces within the model helps in manipulating the objects. An instrument can be pushed forward until it makes contact with an object, at which point the surgeon may decide to activate the graspers. Without haptics, the surgeon would be relying on vision alone to decide if they are at the correct depth to contact the surface.

Haptic feedback also assists in portraying the safe limits of tissue stretch. If a student stretches a duct until it ruptures, they gain some feedback, haptically, of the point at which that rupture occurred, and may have a better understanding of this limit in the future. For this to be useful, the force threshold of rupture must match that found in the real world. This can be achieved either through laboratory measurement of real tissue properties, or by trialing the virtual system with surgical experts and iteratively improving the model to their satisfaction.

Another novel area of haptic use in the cholecystectomy system is the ability to allow an instructor to effectively hold the student's hand and guide them within the scene. Because the system is networked, the position of both the instructor's and student's instruments can be transmitted across the network, to provide a force to each user, proportional to their hands' separation. In this way the student's instrument (and hand) is attracted towards the instructor's, and vice versa. If the student is compliant, they can allow their hand to be guided by the instructor in this manner. Of course, if they so wish, they can resist the instructor's pull, and break free, just as they could in the real world with a guiding hand on their wrist.

3.3. Drawing and Indication

A teaching task involving anatomy benefits from the ability to draw diagrams, arrows and circles to direct attention to a particular position or feature. The simulator has a shared whiteboard, where users can draw diagrams and sketches. This is represented as a solid, haptic surface which is drawn on as soon as the virtual tool tip (in this mode, a pen) touches it. The interface is intuitive and no instruction is required. The haptic surface makes the drawing action just the same as real-world drawing on a whiteboard with a marker. Both users can draw simultaneously in a choice of colors. This ability to draw-on-touch is achieved by detecting the pen's position and notifying the drawing algorithm as soon as the pen intersects the surface of the virtual object (in this case a whiteboard). The algorithm then modifies a texture that is currently mapped to the surface, coloring the relevant pixels at the point of touch and also in the immediate vicinity (depending on the chosen pen width). Since the algorithm can be applied to any touchable surface, the user can also draw on body organs in the 3D model. The drawing ability has also been added to the screens of the image viewer and video player. This allows users to sketch on the screens as they discuss the content.

Another mode of drawing allows the pen to draw in free space, by pressing the haptic tool's button. This is convenient when the instructor wants to draw an arrow or circle around a virtual object. An eraser mode permits removal of these annotations at any time.

3.4. Networking

Surgical training environments can be made more useful by allowing an instructor to join a student inside the virtual world, to help with their training. This help can take the form of pointing at objects while describing issues of anatomy, drawing diagrams, drawing annotations, such as arrows, within the 3D model, demonstrating surgical techniques, leading the student's viewpoint to new areas and physically holding the student's hand, via haptics, to guide them in an action.

If an intuitive interface to these features is desired, it is important to allow asynchronous access to anything in the model. The instructor or student should be able to touch and interact with any object at any time, perhaps simultaneously, and those objects should react in an expected way when more than one user interacts with them. To allow this, a system of combining the user's forces and moving the objects appropriately is required. All forces acting on the objects need to be collected and combined in one algorithm, and the resulting movements of those objects need to be displayed on both systems (instructor and student). The possible forces acting on an object comprise:

- both users' interactions on it,
- any stretching forces along connecting tissue,
- gravity and
- collisions with other objects.
- viscous forces for objects within fluid may also be considered.

One way to do this is with a master-slave arrangement. One of the two networked machines is nominated as a 'master' machine running some physics engine software. The other system can be considered as a 'slave' to this. All of the forces, except those of interaction by the slave machine's user, can be calculated from the model parameters already on the master machine. The slave user's interaction forces are transmitted over the network to the master, to also be incorporated into that calculation. The physics engine then determines the new position of each of the objects involved, and displays that new position in its own 3D display. It also sends those new positions back across the network to the slave machine, to be displayed there.

Using this scheme, there is a network delay to consider. Any significant delay can cause instability in the displayed objects' positions.. This can range from slight jittering to wild gyrations of the objects, depending on the physics and delay involved. If the users are haptically holding the objects, these unexpected motions can be relayed to their hands, producing a very disconcerting, if not alarming, effect! Fortunately, much of surgical training involves soft tissue, which inherently has a damping effect in its surfaces as it tends to deform slowly compared to typical network delays (~50-300mSec). This can alleviate any feedback effect in the physics response. Other compensating mechanisms are described later, in section 4.3.

An alternate networking scheme involves allocating an object to be manipulated by only one user at a time. A user needs to indicate that they are starting to interact with an object and from that point on, the object will be 'locked' and only respond to the one user's actions. Once finished, the user can relinquish control. This method avoids the issue of network delay but imposes unrealistic constraints on the user's actions. It is not suitable for surgical training, as anatomical objects are often interconnected, and moving one object will result in several others also moving. All interconnected objects would therefore need to be locked for the duration of the interaction, severely limiting the ability of both users to work together.

4. Developing a Virtual Surgical Training System

There are several platforms on which to develop a haptic virtual 3D environment. They typically provide the ability to create graphical representations of objects and, via haptics, the ability to touch and interact with those objects. The cholecystectomy trainer was implemented using a scene-graph API[3]. Examples of haptically enabled scene-graph API's are H3D [10] and ReachinAPI [19]. These platforms provide a scene-graph architecture, an object-oriented interface to OpenGL graphics functions, a haptic interface integrated with the graphical objects and an event propagation mechanism. They have programming interfaces of X3D, VRML, Python and C++.

4.1. Scene-Graph Architecture

A scene-graph is a description of a three dimensional scene and the way in which the objects in that scene inter-relate. It consists of nodes which are associated in a parent-child hierarchy (e.g. a Group node has a number of children and a Shape node has an Appearance and a Geometry node). Geometry primitives include Sphere, Box, Cone, IndexedFaceSct, Cylinder etc. One of the most important nodes is a Transform, which is a group with the knowledge of its position and orientation. A Transform can be moved and rotated, bringing its children (and perhaps its children's children) along with it. This is the basis of building a model that can have moving parts. Early in the design task, the programmer needs to decide which nodes will be needed to represent the body organs, surgical instruments and any other scene objects, such as buttons and widgets.

---

[3] Application Programming Interface

Nodes have attributes, called fields (e.g. a Material node has the fields of diffuseColor, shininess etc). The fields of nodes can be connected to each other via routes. (Note that this is a different, and orthogonal, connection to the parent-child relationship.) Using routes, if one field is changed by some user-interaction, an event can be sent along a route to some other field (usually in another node) which can also then change if necessary. Chains of routes can propagate events through the scene-graph. When a developer builds a scene-graph s/he inserts and connects together the parent child associations of nodes and also connects routes between fields. The former, results in the visual appearance of the model and the latter results in its behaviour.

Often the programmer needs to develop a new node specifically for a certain purpose. This is done by inheriting from another node, and adding extra geometry or behaviour to it. Examples of this in the gall bladder simulator are a duct node, a tissue node, a diathermy tool, and a whiteboard. Such custom made nodes are often necessary because there is no existing node in the system that has behaviour to satisfy the requirements (e.g. the diathermy tool). Another reason to create a custom node occurs when a group of existing nodes can be associated together and encapsulated within a single node to aid in modularizing the system (e.g. the arrow node – which is a cylinder and cone, with the cone automatically repositioning itself at the end of the cylinder when the arrow length is supplied).

4.2. Graphic and Haptic Thread

A haptic virtual environment needs to display changes graphically and also present forces to the user haptically. The tissue response of a human hand has sufficient sensitivity to detect vibrations not far below 1000 Hz. If a computer system is portraying the sensation of touching a solid, stationary surface, the calculation of the haptic force needs to happen at around 1000Hz (or more) to avoid the sensation of vibration. The graphic representation, however, does not need to be updated at anywhere near this frequency. This is because the human visual system integrates between discrete images and can interpret them as a continuously moving scene (the concept behind motion pictures). Because of this, the graphics frame rate needs to be only 20-30 Hz to be acceptable to most users.

These differing requirements, result in the need for two program threads to be used for a haptic virtual environment; one running a loop refreshing the graphics components and the other loop refreshing the haptics (often locked at 1000Hz). Because the graphics requirement is less restrictive, any extra program algorithms and logic are usually added to the graphics thread, unless they directly affect the force being felt, in which case they are put into the haptics thread. Since the haptics loop refresh rate is the most restrictive, sometimes gross-level haptics calculations can be performed in the graphics thread instead, allowing only refinements of those calculations to be carried out in the haptics thread.

4.3. Connecting Model Components across a Network

For the surgical training system, we developed a reusable collaboration toolkit which hides much of the complexity of handling the communications between two machines. Haptic applications require a constant streaming of data between the machines as the users interact with the virtual objects and each other. In our systems, we nominate one of the machines as a *server*, which waits for a connection from another machine, the *client*. It doesn't matter which machine is the client or server, as it is only in the initial connection that they differ. The difference is that the server must be 'listening' for a connection from *any* client, whereas the client must be told the specific name of the server that it needs to connect to. Care must be taken to circumvent any firewalls on the machines that may prevent a successful connection.

It is assumed that the model on both server and client are in an identical state at connection time. (This restriction could be avoided by transmitting the anatomical model from the server machine to the client at connection time.) From connection point onwards, any changes to the model, such as movements, cutting, and stretching, are transmitted between machines so that consistency between the users' views is maintained.

The two machines communicate via a port, which is identified by a port number. It is convenient to think of a port as the termination of a communications wire from one machine to another. While this is obviously not correct, since a computer can have a large number of ports open simultaneously with only one physical communications cable, logically this can be assumed. A port is often associated with a socket. The socket and port can both refer to the same communications line termination. A socket is a term for software providing the low level code that handles the communications protocol. The port is a reference the operating system uses for the line termination, regardless of the socket code using it.

The collaboration toolkit makes available two socket types: TCP/IP and UDP/IP [22], which can be used simultaneously in the same scene, for different purposes (i.e. connecting different fields). TCP is slower than UDP, but guarantees that each and every message gets through. For this reason UDP is preferred for any data that *directly* affects the haptic forces felt at each end while TCP is better for all graphical data or data that only indirectly affects the haptics.

The collaboration toolkit extends the scene-graph concept of 'routes between fields' to a network, so that a field in a scene-graph on one machine can effectively be routed to a field in a corresponding scene-graph on another machine (Figure 5). Within the toolkit, these are referred to as *remote routes* between *remote fields*. They allow linkage between a field of a node on one machine to a similarly typed field of any node on another machine, such that they keep each other informed of their current values. Once in place, these remote routes enable a user's interaction with objects in a scene to be reproduced across a network in another scene running on a different system.

Remote fields are typed. For example there are specialized remote fields for integers, floats, strings, positions, orientations and other types. There are also remote fields handling arrays of those types. The *array* remote fields can be set to transmit all the array values whenever there is a change, or alternatively to send only the array values that have changed, along with the indices of those values.

The remote routes are bi-directional, so that two users can simultaneously and co-operatively interact with scene-graph objects. The interaction involves both graphic and haptic effects, with the proviso that once haptics are involved, care needs to be taken to avoid feedback and instability issues when the latency of the network becomes significant, as these can easily make a system unusable. Components of the toolkit have been developed to directly address these issues and accommodate considerable latency under certain constraints. Using these components, it has been possible to have dual haptic interaction with scene objects over a network with latencies up to 170 mS in each direction [7]. As an example, this has allowed a haptic scene to be shared between a computer in Australia and one in the U.S. (using the Internet2 network [15]). The same software has also been run between Australia and Sweden.

Examples of simultaneous interaction are two users grasping a simulated body organ, such as a liver, and stretching it between themselves, or one user haptically 'holding the hand' of the other, to guide them within the scene. Networking also makes it possible to draw and point in the scene and have those annotations appear on the another system, as described in section 3.3.

It is important to note that creating a useful and efficient collaborative application may involve the careful selection of the particular nodes and fields within a scene that it makes sense to connect across a network, and how that connection is made. It may be wasteful to connect every possible field of every node to its equivalent across a network. Instead, it may be more suitable to do local processing on each connected machine for some behaviours, while limiting the network transmission to only those events that need to be synchronized between systems. For example, a field of grass waving in the breeze would not need the motion of each blade transmitted and reproduced. Instead, a single wind vector could be sent and the grass motion reproduced locally on the other machine. The cholecystectomy trainer applies this philosophy in the smoke that is generated by the diathermy tool. Only the position and intensity of the smoke generation is transmitted, with the local machines independently applying their particle generation algorithms to produce the effect.

The design of the networking toolkit allows this selective network routing. As such, the toolkit is NOT a utility that will automatically find all fields and hook up two complete scenes without developer input. The ability to pick and choose what is connected to what, gives the developer the flexibility to introduce interesting behaviours, because fields on one machine do not necessarily need to be routed to the identical field or node on the remote scene. Using this, a developer can create a 'master-slave' system where actions are not exactly symmetrical. An example of this in the gall bladder simulator is where one of the two connected systems receives all the forces from both systems, does the physics calculations and relays object positions back, as mentioned in section 3.40 and discussed further in section 4.3.

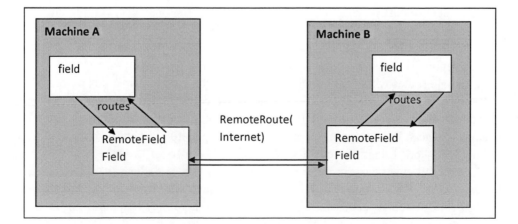

Figure 5. Remote field connected via remote route.

Another example of asymmetric connection is another system we developed, which allows a user to sculpt clay spinning on a virtual potter's wheel. A networked user can simultaneously work on the same clay, but can choose to have the clay stationary, make it spin at a different speed or even spin around a different axis. The clay deformations are transmitted and synchronized, but the rotation axis and speed are not.

As well as the nodes directly related to networking, the toolkit also contains other nodes that promote collaboration. The nodes can be described in four categories:

1. Networking nodes – performing the network messaging
2. Drawing Tool nodes – these assist teaching across a network by allowing lines and arrows to be drawn to help in adding annotation to discussion.
3. Object Movement nodes – allowing objects to be manipulated either individually or in collaboration between the users, whilst accommodating network latency.
4. Hand Guiding nodes – allowing one user to hold and guide another user's hand (actually their haptic tool). These nodes also enable tele-operation of one haptic tool from a user using another haptic tool elsewhere on a network.

The toolkit was developed to connect two machines together. However, since the networking has been encapsulated into a scene-graph node, it is possible to add the node multiple times in the scene-graph. It therefore should be possible to build a connection to more than one machine, thus allowing three-way (or even N-way) systems, although this has not been tested.

Circular Feedback

Because the remote routes are bi-directional, there needs to be a mechanism in place to prevent circular feedback of events. Circular feedback occurs when an event, initiated by a user on one machine, causes a change in an object in the model and this change is transmitted to the corresponding object in the model on the remote machine. This causes the remote machine's event mechanism to detect the change. Since the remote machine does not know whether the change was caused by data from the network or separate interaction by its own user, it may unnecessarily transmit the change back to the first machine, completing the cycle. This cycle can then continue endlessly, producing instability. This problem will occur if two separate remote routes are put in place; one in the forward direction and the other in the reverse direction.

The remote routes within the collaboration toolkit can guard against this problem because each RemoteField node handles both sending and receiving of events across the network. Each remote field checks a timestamp on any event received across the network. This timestamp is placed in all ongoing event messages propagating within its own field network. If the field network brings the event back to the remote route to be sent back across the network, and that event has the same time stamp as a *received* event, it ignores the request and does nothing, With this mechanism in place, the developer does not need to worry about guarding against circular feedback, except in the case where they may have introduced logic which circumvents the scene-graph field network connections.

Graphic and Haptic Fields

As a user interacts with a model, they typically change fields in the system. For example they may change the position and orientation of an object, or its color or transparency. In some cases the display of this change need only be in the graphical representation, while in others it may affect the haptics, via forces felt by another user. These forces can be felt either indirectly or directly. Indirect forces are transmitted through some intermediate object, such as when two users are both grasping and pulling on the liver, stomach or gall bladder. In this case the physical behaviour of the intermediate object(s) can be modeled in such a way as to damp out any instability effects introduced by the network latency (see section on Physics, below). Direct forces are those that go directly from one user's haptic tool to that of the other user. The simulator's hand-guiding feature is an example of this type of force.

Experimentation has shown [9] that fields which directly connect haptic forces require a transmission rate of 400 Hz or above. Depending on the strength of the attraction, this may need to be increased up to 1000Hz. This update range is considerably faster than the graphics loop can provide. To implement this, a position detector was inserted into the 1000 Hz haptic loop and this was connected to a UDP remote field. On the receiving machine, the corresponding UDP remote field transmits the positional information to a force field (operating within the other machine's haptics thread) which attracts the other user's haptic device to the new position. This mechanism is implemented bi-directionally, allowing both users to feel each other's actions. UDP/IP is required in such connections because it does not suffer the delays and jitter experienced by TCP/IP [7 22]. Although, UDP may lose packets, if we are connecting forces on the two machines, it is more important for a user to experience the most recent force than it is to get each and every force value transmitted while ramping up to that force. However, UDP also does not guarantee that packets will be received in the order sent. The consequence of this is that it could be possible for an old force value to arrive after a newer one, potentially resulting in a sudden jolt felt by the user. A sequence number inserted into each packet can allow any offending packets to be thrown away. The collaboration toolkit hides these details from the developer, but the developer needs to know when it is appropriate to choose the nodes implementing this UDP method.

Other fields need not use this network-intensive method of transmission, and can send their update data at around 30 Hz using TCP/IP, which guarantees delivery of all packets in order. This method is usually used for fields handled within the graphics thread.

Care must also be taken to make the code thread-safe. The networking code requires a separate thread for reading data from the socket, as it 'blocks', awaiting data arrival. This code sets the value of its own output field. However, that field may be routed to scene-graph fields being used in either the graphics thread or the haptics thread. A program crash is likely if two threads are accessing the data at the same time. The collaboration toolkit locks the data temporarily while it is accessed to avoid this, but the developer needs to specify whether the remote field will be accessed by either the graphics or haptics thread.

Buffering & Consistency

Some fields involve Boolean values. These can be connected in the same way as other remote field types but the developer needs to consider what should happen if a value change was missed by one of the systems. While TCP/IP does not lose packets, if the receiving computer is running at a speed slower than the sending computer, the receiving computer may not be retrieving packets from the communications socket as fast as new ones arrive. For most fields this does not matter, as the most recent value is all that is required and if a new value arrives and over-writes an older one that has not yet been used, it does not matter. However, in cases of Boolean values, this may not be the case.

For example, consider a system with a modeled pair of scissors which can cut a blood vessel in an anatomical model. Assume also that the developer has implemented a Boolean remote field that transmits a 'true' value if the scissors are closed and a 'false' value if they are open, allowing both machines to individually implement the animation of the 'snip' of the scissors and the consequence on the blood vessel. If one machine is running at a slower speed than the other, and if the transmitted true-false switch of the scissors is quick enough, the momentary 'true' value may get missed by the receiving machine, as the following 'false' value may over-write it before it has been handled. The consequence of this can be that the blood vessel is cut (and perhaps bleeding), on one user's display and still intact on the other.

The collaboration toolkit allows the developer to specify certain fields to buffer, to prevent this condition. With buffering switched on, all values received at the socket are immediately removed and added to a list. They are then used, one at a time in the update loop, by the rest of the system. Using this, in the case above, the 'true' value would be fully acted upon before the following 'false' value is processed. This again is a case where the developer needs to carefully choose the most appropriate nodes and attributes for networking each part of the model.

Physics

A haptic device provides a direct exchange of energy with the user holding the device. There is a feedback loop involving the user's hand, arm, muscles and voluntary and involuntary reactions as well as the robotic force feedback device, network and software involved in the user interface (figure 6a). Robotic systems with a feedback component can become difficult to control when there is a delay (i.e. latency) in the feedback loop [3]. Fortunately, in stand-alone (i.e. non collaborative systems), the latency is usually so small that the effect is controllable.

In a haptic-enabled, networked virtual environment, the latency can be much greater, and its effects can therefore be much more significant. The feedback loop, involves the physiology of each human holding the haptic device at each end of the network, as well as the network itself and the hardware. Tissue resilience and muscle response of each user plays a part, as does their sub-conscious reaction to a sudden force input on their hand [1]. These can combine to create *un-intended* force reflections, before the user has had time to respond with an *intended* movement. Hence, the system is susceptible to instability when these effects are combined with any significant latency.

Some fields affect the position of objects. Because a remote user has the ability to touch those objects these motions may indirectly affect the haptic feedback that the user feels. The feedback loop in figure 6b, combined with network latency has the potential to drive a system into instability. The collaboration toolkit has an embedded mechanism to work against this. It uses the master slave system described in section 3.4 to ensure that only one machine performs the physics calculation. It also replaces true solid body physics with a surrogate that does not strictly obey the Newtonian laws, but still allows objects to be moved smoothly, by ignoring any momentum in moving objects. For each moveable object, all forces are collected into an algorithm running on the master machine. The object's change in position is then calculated as a proportion of the resultant force. This causes motion under a force while that force is applied but also causes the motion to stop immediately when the force is removed. An object does not continue along the path of motion under its own momentum for a distance as a real object might. However, when moving objects in a viscous fluid or even moving objects contacting a frictional surface, this scheme is sufficiently close to the real world to be quite usable and believable in those circumstances. Obviously this would be unsuitable for some applications (such as anything that requires throwing or launching an object), but experimentation has shown [8] that for surgical training applications, it is sufficient. The pliability of body organs and the fact that they are typically embedded in a fluid-like environment also helps in keeping the physics stable, as it provides an inherent damping on the motion.

As well as the forces from the user's instruments, body organs have elastic tissue connecting them to surrounding body parts, as well as collision forces and gravity working on them. When the users cease to apply forces to them, these other forces are still present, so that the objects do continue to move until all of the forces reach equilibrium at which point they stop.

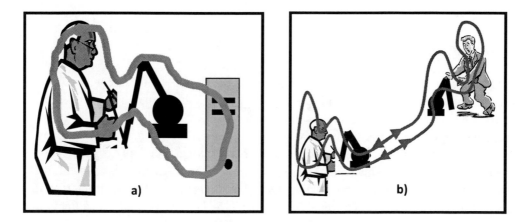

Figure 6. Single user feedback loop Feedback loop between two users in network. b) Feedback loop between two users in network.

5. Modelling

The anatomical models created in these virtual environments are often generated from medical scans of the human body, via a semi-automatic segmentation process.

Medical scans (such as CT scans), produce slices of data across the body. Each data slice is in the form of an image, with light or dark areas (or sometimes colors) representing different density tissue. The process of segmentation involves identifying which of these areas in each successive slice, is associated with which ones in the next slice, and therefore represents a single organ. The outline of the sequence of these 2D shapes comprises points on the outer surface of the organ and can be collected and triangulated to produce a three dimensional geometric shape.

Some segmentation can be performed computationally, but typically, the process requires a tedious manual stage, with an expert making decisions between ambiguous alternatives on the image slices. While scanning and segmentation is satisfactory for the larger organs, small and vascular objects sometimes need to be created artistically. This is because the density of the scanning that can be done is not sufficient to uniquely identify small or thin objects.

However, research is progressing on software that will be able to achieve a fully automated segmentation. With this, it would then be feasible to create a 3D model of a patient shortly before they are due for surgery, allowing the surgeons to have a discussion and walk through of the procedure using the model of the patient on which they are about to operate. Currently the process takes far too long for such patient-specific models to be possible. However, when the models are used for training they can be used over and over again, and the time and effort required to produce each model can be justified.

Another issue with using medical scans for this purpose is that the density of scan slices has to be kept low on live patients, for safety reasons. Cadavers can be scanned at much higher densities, and therefore produce more accurate models. However, cadarvic material does not exactly match the features of live tissue, because the blood pressure is absent and the tissue may have deteriorated.

5.1. Instruments

Both users hold a haptic device, which can be chosen to represent several different instruments within the virtual world. Each choice changes the virtual instrument's appearance and its behaviour when it comes into contact with objects within the scene. One instrument is a marker pen, which can draw on the whiteboard, video player screen or image viewer, and can also draw free lines, circles and arrows in space amongst the body organs. Another is a grasper that can grip and manipulate tissue. There is also a diathermy instrument, a clipping instrument, scissors and a hand guiding tool. The latter allows the instructor to drag the student's hand around in the scene. The student feels this as a haptic attraction to the instructor's virtual tool. The system is bi-directional, so that the instructor can also feel any force of resistance that the student presents. In fact it can be equally applied in the reverse direction, with the student guiding the instructor, if desired.

The action of the instrument on an object is encoded into the logic of the object, not the instrument. For example, when the clipping tool is activated on a duct, the duct creates the clip, attaches it to the relevant segment of itself, and keeps it aligned with that section as it moves around under elastic and user forces acting on it. If the clipping action is performed on another organ, nothing happens as no reaction to that particular tool has been coded into that organ's behaviour.

Similarly, if the diathermy tool interacts with tissue, the tissue displays a burnt cut by calling its own algorithms that affect its graphical representation. Those cuts move along with the tissue. In the simulator, the diathermy tool has no effect on bone. These behaviours can be changed if it was seen to be necessary for the training scenario.

5.2. Organs

Most organs in the model are deformable, simultaneously by both instructor and student (figure 7), allowing either participant to push, grasp and stretch the body organs. The pliability of each organ can be set differently. For example, the liver is configured to be stiffer than the stomach. Organs can also be connected to each other, and therefore apply forces on each other and move in unison.

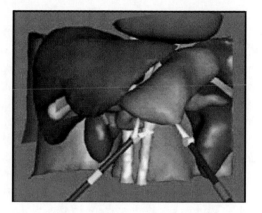

Figure 7. Deforming the stomach.

Deformation

Due to processing power limitations, all organs were built using a surface mesh. No volumetric calculations are performed during manipulation. This concession was not perceived as a problem by the medical professionals who took part in trials. The organ shape is stored in two meshes, the first holding the original organ geometry and the second holding its deformed shape during interaction by the user. The second shape is the one that is graphically rendered to the screen. The force feedback is proportional to the extent of deformation of the point of contact below the original surface (or above it, if grasped and pulled), so the original surface is the one used for haptic calculations. As well as providing a force to the user, this movement is used to calculate an offset for each of the other coordinates of the surface, depending on stiffness parameters and distance from the contact. The deformed coordinates are each placed at these offsets from the original coordinates and are used for rendering the shape graphically.

The deformation behaves in two different ways depending on the requirements of each organ. Some organs can be assumed to have an elastic surface which returns to its original shape when the deforming force is removed. Other organs are set to be permanently deformable to some degree and so are set to have some plasticity. This means that the longer that they are held in their deformed shape, the closer to that shape they will be when released. In this case the original coordinates are incrementally repositioned towards the deformed coordinates over time. Since the distance moved in each iteration is proportional to the distance between each original coordinate and its corresponding deformed coordinate, the plastic deformation achieved is proportional to the integral of the instantaneous deformation over time, approximately matching the behaviour of many real-world materials. The plasticity factor is introduced via a scaling on this incremental deformation.

When a networked, remote machine is introduced, the haptic 'touch' should not occur until the user's tool collides with the *already-deformed* shape, i.e. the one used for graphic rendering on the local machine. This allows the remote user to grasp the shape in its deformed state. It is those coordinates that need to be transmitted and used on the other machine.

Position

As well as having their surfaces deformed, organs can be movable to some degree, limited by their connection to other organs and body tissue. Some organs, such as the liver, are considered to be anchored to a position but with the ability to be moved temporarily from that position. The simulator utilizes two ways of implementing this behaviour. The first is used when only a rough approximation is required. It is done with a simulated spring-damper from the organ's centre to the default position. Under a user's force, the organ can move, but after the force is removed, the organ returns smoothly to its default position via the spring action. However, to maintain stability under different network latencies, the spring-damper physics is implemented using the method described in section 4.30.

The second behaviour is needed when a more accurate simulation is required, such as the movement of the gall bladder and cystic duct system in the cholecystectomy simulator. The gall bladder is connected to the cystic duct, which then bifurcates into two ducts .– the common bile duct and hepatic duct. The hepatic duct then splits in two before joining the liver at two places and the common bile ends at the duodenum [6]. Since the procedure focuses on this structure, with one surgeon extending the cystic duct while another applies clips and cuts it, it is important to model this part of the system more precisely. As the surgeon manipulates the ducts or gall bladder, the ducts stretch and slide according to axial linear forces (figure 8).

Figure 8. Two instruments manipulating the gall bladder.

To simulate this, the system was modeled as a series of elastic segments with hinges at the junction points. The number of segments and 'ball-joint' hinges is configurable with a parameter, allowing the visual smoothness of the duct to be tuned against the computing power of the machine on which it is running. Once a segment is grasped, a virtual spring is put in place between the tool and the nearest hinge. The spring extension or compression forces are transferred to the hinge which transfers the forces to adjacent hinges, by extending or compressing virtual spring-dampers within the connecting segments. These connecting springs have a natural, 'at rest' length. Forces applied to each end of the segment either stretch the segment or compress it. In this way, each hinge has knowledge of all the forces acting on it and can reposition itself depending on those forces. The extension or compression of the *grasping* virtual spring provides force, back to the haptic tool. When a user grasps the duct, the force from the connection to the gall bladder is the result of a sequence of interrelated movements of duct segments and that resultant force moves the gall bladder. The duct segments are graphically represented by a visible tapered cylinder and each hinge by a sphere of matching radius.

The movements are sequentially calculated, segment by segment, along the duct, taking into account any bifurcations, until the point being grasped is calculated. This last calculation also takes into account the invisible, grasping spring connected to the user's tool. Using this method, the repositioning of each segment in this system depends on the forces applied to it from any connecting segment, as well as any possible tool-grasping forces and collisions with other body organs. As with the organ repositioning, described in section 4.3, the movement of the duct segments also does not incorporate momentum, resulting in a smooth, controlled motion in a networked system. As each resultant force at each node is calculated the node is repositioned marginally in the direction of the force. Since each node handles its own force resolution and repositioning, the complexity of the interconnected system is reduced to a simple iteration through the interconnected chain of segments. Each node's position is calculated from only its neighbors' positions, and the force onto the users' haptic tools depends only on the positions of the immediate connections and collisions (figure 9).

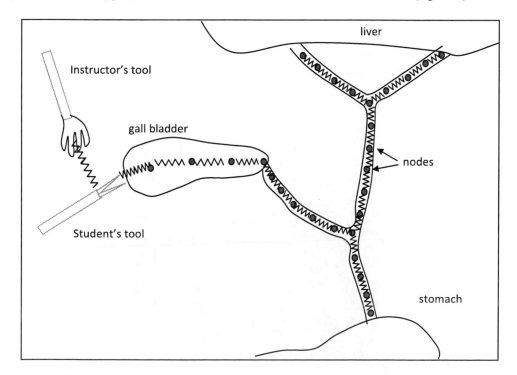

Figure 9. Force model of cystic duct system connected to a user's tool and 'hand-guided' from a remote user's tool.

Since the user's tool is connected to the grasp point on the gall bladder or duct by a simulated (invisible) spring, there can be a visual discrepancy when a large amount of tension is applied to the spring – a gap appears between the user's tool and the tissue. The user still feels the force of the stretched tissue, and the duct system behaves as if it is still grasped and being manipulated, but visually the tool does not appear to be in contact with the tissue because the simulated spring has stretched enough to allow the tool to emerge from the tissue surface. This problem can be solved by modifying the graphic representation of the surface to always deform towards the grasping tool tip. The underlying physics model and haptic behaviour do not need to change, as only the graphics rendering needs to be adjusted to provide a more believable representation.

5.3. Tissue Cutting

The gall bladder is connected to the liver with a webbing of elastic tissue. This is modeled as a 'web-strip', comprising a triangulated membrane surface with specialized behaviour along its long edges which allows it to be attached to both the gall bladder and liver. Such a configuration enables it to stretch and move when those organs are moved, as well as flex and deform when the user's tool interacts with it. The webbing is designed for use where the length of the membrane is greater by a factor of two or more than the width. It consists of a grid of rectangles, each sub-divided into two triangles across the diagonal. The rows of rectangles form bands, each stretching across the width of the strip. The strip can have a series of attachment points along its long edges, where routes from other attached object positions can be directed. These vector positions typically would be selected vertices of the liver or gall bladder, allowing their movement to affect the web strip. As the particular vertex moves, the route ensures that the corresponding point on the web strip also moves. These attachment points need not be on every web strip band. Unattached band points interpolate their positions between the attached ones. As an attached point moves, the bands surrounding it reposition themselves and the triangles across the band also interpolate to reposition themselves evenly.

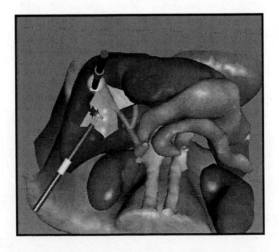

Figure 10. One grasper holds gall bladder, the other uses diathermy to cut attached tissue.

Initial trials showed that although this scheme worked satisfactorily, the resulting smoothness of the strip lacked the organic appearance of tissue, even when rendered with an appropriate texture. By adding a randomizing factor to the interpolation algorithm, a more irregular surface was achieved, providing a much more believable appearance. The graphical rendering of the strip was also modified to give the tissue some thickness, although it could still be specified as a single surface, but with a thickness parameter. The haptic behaviour did not have to take the thickness into account as the tissue was thin enough for the mismatch with the graphical rendering to be imperceptible [2].

The web strip also has the capacity to be cut. In the application this occurs when the diathermy tool comes into contact with it. When the tool touches the surface, it triggers an algorithm which increments a counter stored for that particular triangle of the web strip. For each successive graphics cycle that the contact occurs, the counter is again incremented. When the counter for a particular triangle reaches a certain number (specified by a 'toughness' parameter) the triangle is removed from the web, and the user sees a small hole in its place (figure 10). When at least one triangle has been removed from a band of the web strip, the band no longer has connectivity from one side of the strip to the other. Therefore, movement of any attachment point at one side will have an effect up to the cut point, but no further. The interpolation algorithm takes this into account, only interpolating left hand side movements on the left hand part of any cut band, and right hand movements on the right hand part. When the web strip has been cut along its entire length, all bands have been cut and the attached gall bladder can be removed, along with its attached half of the web strip, leaving the other half attached to the liver.

5.4. Clipping and Cutting

During a cholecystectomy, the gall bladder/duct system is freed from the liver and then put under tension to facilitate the application of clips and eventual cutting of the cystic duct (figure 11). Too much tension can result in rupture of the duct and escape of bile fluid or blood. The organs should be manipulated to allow the surgeon a clear view of the area for diathermy and clipping. If the duct is cut correctly between two clips, the gall bladder and its attached duct segment is detached from surrounding objects and can be removed. If the cut is made in a place that is not bordered by clips 'upstream' and 'downstream' on the duct, either bile or blood droplets are released. Tension should be applied to the duct to facilitate the clipping and cutting process, but a common mistake is to apply too much tension in this stage, which may result in a rupture. The simulator has the capability for the duct to rupture, emit fluid and eventually break if the extension of any segment is too great.

Clipping involves adding a new object, with the approximate appearance of a clip, and associating it with a position on one of the segments of the duct. Any movement of that duct segment is also applied to the clip. A cut of the duct involves dividing the duct segment into two separate segments at the appropriate location. Unlike the other duct segments on either side, these two new segments are only connected at one end to their respective ducts. Because of this, they no longer transfer movement and forces across the cut, and so the duct has now become two separate ducts that can move apart under force. This usually happens immediately the cut is done, as, prior to the cut the duct is typically under tension from one of the users stretching it while the other cuts. The accumulation of forces on the whole duct suddenly is not in equilibrium for each of the two new ducts, creating the resulting movement apart.

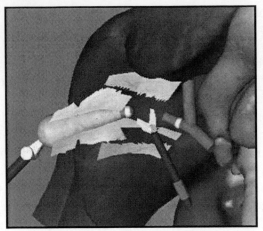

Figure 11. Cutting the cystic duct.

One of the benefits of hand-guiding is the ability to assist a novice in the correct technique of putting the gall bladder/cystic duct system under longitudinal tension. The hand-guiding feature was found to provide a very useful way of indicating the amount of extension that should be applied. The instructor could 'grasp' the student's hand haptically while the student had hold of the fundus of the gall bladder. Then the instructor could pull the student's hand in the right direction with the appropriate amount of force while feeling the resistance of the tension in the duct. This is easily implemented using the system described in section 5.2. Since the force being applied to the student's tool is already being accumulated in an algorithm collecting forces from the duct extension and collisions with other objects, the force from the instructor's guidance, arriving across the network, can be simply added into this calculation as another route from a remote field.

5.5. Data Flow

During a typical cystic duct manipulation there are three sets of data being transmitted between collaborating machines: model state data which is input into algorithms occurring within the *graphics* thread, haptic state data which is used in algorithms occurring during the *haptics* thread and video and/or audio data which is likely to be needed to allow discussion as the two users work.

The model state data is transferred at approximately 30 Hz, as part of the graphics refresh cycle. This rate is limited by the power of the processor and complexity of the logic that needs processing, and runs as fast as possible. Typically the transmission rate needed for this data in the gall bladder simulator is 165,840 bits/sec. Table 1 shows the components of this.

The haptics state data is transmitted at 400 Hz. This figure was determined empirically by winding back the value from a starting point of 1000 Hz to discover the minimum value that could achieve a stable interaction over a network with a latency of 290 ms. The rate is governed explicitly within the code within the 1000 Hz haptic cycle, but is one of the configuration parameters for the program.

Table 1. Components of model state data flow

Data type	Items per cycle	Bytes per item	Bytes	Bits
Position vectors	47	12	564	4512
Orientation vectors	2	16	32	256
Floating point values	2	4	8	64
Boolean values	27	1	27	216
Integer values	15	4	60	480
Total bits/cycle				5528
Typical cycles/second				30
Bits/second				165,840

Table 2. Components of haptic data flow

Data type	Items per cycle	Bytes per item	Bytes	Bits
Position vectors	1	12	12	96
Total bits/cycle				96
Typical cycles/second				400
Bits/second				38,400

The transmission rate for this data is 165,840 bits/sec. Table 2 shows the components which comprise this.

A networked training system such as this needs to be accompanied by an audio channel to allow instructor and student to converse, and perhaps a video channel as well, to enhance the conversation. The video and audio data traffic rate depends on what type of compression is used, but is likely to far exceed that needed for the model and haptics, shown above.

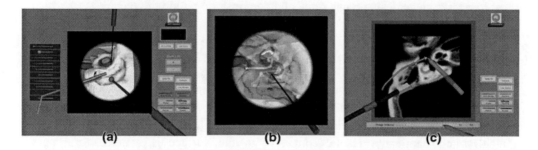

Figure 12. Screen captures of the system in operation. (a) A student drills the bone in the simulated microscope view, with guidance from the instructor. (b) The bone is made transparent to show the anatomical landmarks beneath. (c) The instructor annotates a slice from the CT scan of the bone.

6. Another Simulator: Temporal Bone Surgery

Using components developed for the cholecystectomy (gall bladder) trainer (described above), a simulator aimed at a different type of surgery was developed. The temporal bone simulation system enables an instructor and student to collaboratively explore and drill a volumetric model of the temporal bone located in the skull behind the ear canal. This bone has significant anatomical features embedded within it. The bone must be drilled away to allow access to the middle and inner ear for such operations as mastoidectomy and cochlear implant.

This simulator uses many of the concepts developed for the cholecystectomy simulator described above [14]. It makes use of the virtual marker pen, white board, image viewer, and video player. As with the cholecystectomy system, the main view is an anatomical 3D model of the area of interest, the temporal bone located just behind the ear. It also incorporates the networking feature, allowing an instructor to share the same virtual model and viewpoint as the student. The simulator differs in that interaction involves the drilling away of rigid bone, and the only deformable tissue involved is the ear canal. Components of the middle and inner ear, such as the cochlear and the semi-circular canals are also modeled, as is the facial nerve and sigmoid sinus, embedded within the temporal bone.

The view of the model is through a simulated microscope, to match the microscope used in the real surgery (figure 12). This simulator uses the same type of haptic devices as the gall bladder simulator, but allows each user to have a haptic device in each hand, each controlling a different virtual instrument. It has a powered drill with a number of interchangeable burrs, a suction tool for removing drilled waste and a facial nerve detector, mimicking a device used in real surgery which detects proximity to the facial nerve, as well as the guiding, drawing and erasing tools.

The training procedure involves selecting a drilling burr to carefully drill away the bone to gain access to the middle and inner ear structures. The skill required in this task is in avoiding contact with the facial nerve and sigmoid sinus that are both embedded within the bone. Surgeons must drill until they identify one of these structures and then carefully proceed whilst avoiding any contact with them. The drilling must continue to expose parts of the middle and inner ear to allow various surgical procedures to be carried out on them.

As with the gall bladder simulator, the instructor can use a guiding hand to steer the student in a task, and can also point, draw and demonstrate within the scene.

6.1. Bone Model

A hybrid volume/surface approach to producing a graphical and haptic rendering of an erodable bone model was chosen. A voxel-based system stores the bone volume in a quad-tree structure and a triangulated surface is draped around this. The surface is rendered graphically and haptically. Haptic contact with the surface is mapped to a particular underlying voxel. Contact time, drill speed, burr type and force applied are used to calculate a threshold at which the voxel is deleted. As voxels in the model are removed by drilling, the surface is continuously reconfigured to cover the outermost layer of voxels. The resolution of the voxelization is configurable, the trade-off being the refresh rate. It can be tuned to the best performance for a particular computer power.

6.2. Sharing Instruments

With this simulator, each participant can hold two haptic devices, one in each hand, so, with both instructor and student, there could be four instruments in the scene at one time.

These are tracked separately and can interact with each other. For example the guiding hand can be set to guide the student's left hand tool, right hand tool, or nearest tool whenever the activating button is pressed. Each instrument behaves differently when in contact with the model. The tool itself holds fairly little logic. It is basically a graphic shape and a set of parameters. This behaviour is encoded into the logic of the model components, not the tool. For example, the bone model will erode itself when contacted by a spinning drill. However when contacted by the suction instrument it behaves as a simple hard surface. The drilled dust however, will react to the suction device, and will pass into its nozzle.

During a teaching session an instructor is likely to need to demonstrate various techniques to a student. To allow this, it is necessary to provide a natural way for users at each end of the network to share the various instruments (marker pen, eraser, facial nerve probe, guiding hand, drill handle, sucker). Some of these instruments can be duplicated in both users' hands at the same time. For example, both users could have a marker pen and draw at the same time, without any significant conflict. Others, such as the drill, may cause problems if two exist in the scene and are drilling at the same location.

One way to avoid this is to allow the two to exist, but have them haptically bump into each other if they are too close, preventing them from working on the same part of the model simultaneously. However, since the drill burrs are rigid surfaces, there is no inherent damping in the model, and stability issues are likely to occur in a networked system.

Another method would be to combine the effects of both drills into one resultant action on the model. This is the method used in the *gall bladder* simulator. A similar technique used for this simulator would be more problematical, since the bone surfaces are rigid and therefore would also not have the inherent damping provided by the soft tissue surfaces to aid in sustaining stability under dual manipulation.

Fortunately, for the temporal bone simulator, it was possible to take advantage of the fact that the procedure requires only one drill to be used at any time. By also applying this restriction within the simulator, it is possible to avoid significant complexity. When one user selects the drill, it becomes unavailable to the other user, until it is relinquished.

The method of passing tools between users involves one user placing a tool down and the other picking it up, much as would happen in the real world. The 'putting down' and 'picking up' action is simulated as a touch sensitive tool tray within the scene. Touching a tool label with a tool will disengage and put down the current tool and pick up the touched one. If the drill is in use, its label will be greyed out and not selectable.

6.3. Microscope View

The normal mode of performing this type of surgery is by viewing the region through a stereo microscope. Simulating this is not as straight-forward as scaling the model up or down. This is because a microscope scales the visual representation of the object but does not change the touchable size and shape. The surgeon's hands and the surgical instrument still need to move at the same original scale, regardless of the zoom of the visual representation. To implement this, it was necessary to represent the objects within the microscope twice; firstly for the graphics rendering (with the currently selected scaling to match the zoom of the microscope), and secondly for the haptics rendering, with no scaling applied. Duplication was avoided by including the same geometric model within two branches of the scene-graph; one containing a scaling node in its hierarchy while the other one did not. During the graphics rendering pass, the thread is prevented from rendering the non-scaled branch and during the haptics rendering pass the thread is prevented from rendering the scaled branch. The bone model is attached below each branch.

This mechanism, however, does not accommodate the various instruments that can appear both outside the microscope as well as within the microscope's field of view, depending on their movement. Additionally, it is common for an instrument to extend from the view outside to inside the microscope, so, for example, a drill handle may need to be at normal zoom at one end, and zoomed several times at the other end. Graphical clipping planes are used to achieve this effect. A graphical clipping plane can apply to a scene-graph *group* node and allows the graphical rendering of its enclosed objects only if they are to either side of a 2D plane in 3D space. Placing these planes appropriately around the microscope prevents the non-zoomed versions of the instruments being seen within. A second branch of the scene-graph contains corresponding clipping planes which face in the opposite directions. This branch contains the zoomable, 'within microscope' versions of the same instruments. The effect is that an instrument moving towards the microscope will have any part of itself appear correctly zoomed within the microscope's field of view. As well as this, any *movements* within the microscope are also appropriately zoomed. The method causes the disconnection between the outside shaft of an instrument and the inside view of it – as occurs within a real-world microscope.

6.4. Bone Dust Simulation

The action of the drilling burr on the surface of the bone results in a build-up of bone dust and debris in the vicinity of the drill. This is simulated through a particle system with the capability to emit particles according to various configurable parameters. These include particle size, creation location, creation rate, velocity and 'spray'. The spray parameter controls the variability in the speed and direction of the emitted particles. Without it, they are emitted in a single linear stream. The particles also have the ability to be drawn towards a location in space and to disappear when arriving there. This feature is used in the haptic sucking tool, which draws the particles into its mouth. Because the system is designed for collaboration, it is necessary to replicate any particle generation and sucking on both collaborating machines. However, the accurate replication of each individual particle across the network would constitute an unnecessary use of bandwidth. Since the users would not interact individually with each particle, it proved sufficient to only reproduce the particle emission location, velocity, rate and spray parameters listed above. Such an approximation resulted in the ability to be drilling and creating dust at one end of the network, and sucking the dust from the computer at the other end, with no discernable inconsistencies.

6.5. Assessment

One advantage of using a virtual environment to train surgeons is that the computer can monitor the student's actions and assess the skill and knowledge they display. A prototype of such an assessment technique was implemented in this simulator. The correct technique of drilling bone is to firstly identify (i.e. drill close to but not into) the sigmoid sinus. Once its location and orientation is identified (by a change in the nearby bone texture and color) the surgeon should progress with drill strokes *parallel* to this structure not 'jabbing' towards it. A measure of distance variation as a proportion of total motion is an indication of how parallel the motions were and how much 'jabbing' is occurring.

6.6. Trials

Clinical trials of the temporal bone surgical simulator were conducted by running students through the simulator before assigning them a task of drilling a real, cadarvic temporal bone. These students' performances on the real bone was compared to the performance of students who had spent a similar time undergoing cadarvic training for the skill. It was found that the simulator-trained students had a better understanding of the anatomy and better skill at avoiding mistakes [18]. O'Leary states that

> "Knowledge from the VR transferred well to an actual temporal bone drilling exercise, confirming concurrent validity .... It was encouraging, and perhaps surprisingly so, that the drilling technique was rated as adequate or good for the majority of students, given that this was their first temporal bone drilling experience"

When we developed these simulators, we considered that the networking feature would be something used over a distance, perhaps allowing an instructor to train students in another city or even another country. However, one of the surprising conclusions drawn from the instructors' feedback after the trials was that the networking was one of the most valuable features, *even when both machines were side-by-side*. This was because the instructor can get into the virtual environment with the student and see the model from the student's viewpoint. Without networking, using the haptic workbench in stand-alone mode, an instructor would need to lean over a student to try to indicate or point to something in the scene. They would only be able to point at the mirror and their different viewpoints would likely result in different apparent positions being pointed out. Allowing the instructor to join the student in the virtual world, permits unambiguous indication, demonstration and annotation.

7. Conclusion

We have described some of the issues involved in building a haptic training simulator for teaching surgery in a one-on-one mentoring style. We used two examples taken from the work carried out at the CSIRO ICT Centre [4]; a cholecystectomy simulator and a temporal bone simulator. The former was a prototype used to discover suitable techniques – especially for implementing networking and collaboration between two users. The latter had a larger range of features and a better user interface. This is now in commercially available[16].

The networking feature was discovered to be very valuable to both instructors and students. However, the developer must take care when deciding what parts of the scene to connect to a collaborating machine and how to connect those components in the virtual environment. The CSIRO collaboration toolkit encapsulates much of the complexity involved in the networking and provides a range of components that can be used for these types of connections. This software is now (2010) available as an open source toolkit (available as H3DNetworkingUtils from http://www.ict.csiro.au/downloads.php).

References

[1]   Biggs, S. & Srinivasan, M. (2002). "Haptic Interfaces. *Handbook of Virtual Environments: Design, Implementation, and Applications*". 93-116, Lawrence Erlbaum Associates, Inc., NJ, USA.

[2]   Burns, E., Razzaque, S., Panter, A. T., Whitton, M. C., McCallus, M. R., Brooks, F. P. (2006). Jr. "The Hand is More Easily Fooled than the Eye". Presence: *Teleoperators and Virtual Environments*, **15**(1), 1-15.

[3]   Chong, N., Kawabata, S., Ohba, K., Kotoku, T., Komoriya, K. & Takase, K. (2002). *et al.* "Multioperator teleoperation of Multirobot Systems with Time Delay". *Presence: Teleoperators and Virtual Environments*, **11**(3), 277-303.

[4]   Csiro Ict Centre. CSIRO ICT Centre [Web Page]. URL: www.ict.csiro.au, accessed, **11**, February 2009.

[5]   Kolb, D. A. (1984). *Experiential Learning: experience as the source of learning and development.* New Jersey, USA: Prentice-Hall.

[6]   Gray, H. (2000). "*The Liver*". Gray, H. "*Anatomy of the Human Body*". Bartleby.com; © 2000 Copyright Bartleby.com, Inc. (orig. Philadelphia: Lea & Febiger, 1918), 1188-1202.

[7]   Gunn, C., Hutchins, M. & Adcock, M. (2005). "Combating Latency In Haptic Collaborative Virtual Environments". *Presence: Teleoperators and Virtual Environments*, **14**(3), 313-328.

[8]   Gunn, C., Hutchins, M., Adcock, M. & Hawkins, R. (2003). "Trans-World Haptic Collaboration". In Proceedings of ACM SIGGRAPH 2003, *Conference Abstracts and Applications*, 1, Aug.

[9]   Gunn, C., Hutchins, M., Stevenson, D., Adcock, M. & Youngblood, P. "Using Collaborative Haptics in Remote Surgical Training". In *Proceedings of First Joint Eurohaptics Conference and Symposium on Haptic Interfaces for Virtual Environment and Teleoperator Systems* , 481-482.

[10] H3D.org. H3D [Web Page]. URL: www.H3D.org, accessed 25 October 2009.

[11] Halle, M. (1997). "Autostereoscopic displays and computer graphics". Computer *Graphics,* ACM SIGGRAPH: **31**(2), 58-62.

[12] Hodges, L. F. & Davis, E. T. "Geometric Considerations for Stereoscopic Virtual Environments.". PRESENCE: *Teleoperators and Virtual Environments*, **2**, 1-10.

[13] Holliman, N. (2005*). ",3D Displays, A practical technology ?".* Department of Trade and Industry, UK. Public Service Review: **7**.

[14] Hutchins, M., O'Leary, S., Stevenson, D., Gunn, C. & Krumpholz, A. (2005). "A networked haptic virtual environment for teaching temporal bone surgery". *Studies in Health Technology and Informatics*, **111**, 204-207.

[15] Internet 2. *The Internet 2 Consortium* [Web Page]. URL: http://www.internet2.edu, accessed 23 July 2006.

[16] MedicVision. MedicVision Pty Ltd [Web Page]. URL: www.medicvision.com.au, accessed 31 October 2009.

[17] Miller, G. A. (1956). "The magical number seven, plus or minus two: Some limits on our capacity for processing information". *The Psychology Review*, **63**, 81-97.

[18] O'Leary, S. J., H. M., Stevenson, D., Gunn, C., Krumpholz, A. & Kennedy, G. *et al.* "Validation of a Networked Virtual Reality Simulation of Temporal Bone Surgery". *The Laryngoscope*, **18**(6), 1040-1046,

[19] Reachin Technologies. Reachin API [Web Page]. URL: www.reachin.se, accessed, **27**, April 2006.

[20] *SensAble Technologies.* (2006). SensAble Phantom Haptic Device [Web Page]. URL: www.sensable.com, accessed 30 February.

[21] Seropian, M., Dillman, D., Lasater, K. & Gavilanes, J. (2007). "Mannequin-based simulation to reinforce pharmacology concepts". Simulation in Healthcare : *Journal of the Society for Simulation in Healthcare*, **2**(4), 218-223.

[22] Stevens, W. (1998). "*Unix Network Programming*". 2 edition. Vol. 1. 85-110, Prentice Hall, NJ, USA.

[23] Stevenson, D., Smith, K., Mclaughlin, J., Gunn, C., Veldkamp, J. & Dixon, M. (1999). "Haptic Workbench: A Multi-Sensory Virtual Environment". In Proceedings of The Engineering Reality of Virtual Reality, IS&T/SPIE *Symposium on Electronic Imaging*, **99**, 356-366, Jan.

In: Computer Science Research and the Internet
Editor: Jaclyn E. Morris, pp. 73-107

ISBN: 978-1-61728-730-5
© 2011 Nova Science Publishers, Inc.

Chapter 3

GALOIS FIELD SUM OF PRODUCTS APPROACH TO MULTIPLE-VALUED QUANTUM LOGIC CIRCUIT SYNTHESIS

Mozammel H.A. Khan[*]

Department of Computer Science and Engineering,
East West University, Dhaka, Bangladesh

Abstract

A quantum algorithm is implemented using a quantum logic circuit that uses quantum mechanical phenomena to solve the problem. The quantum logic circuit is constructed with quantum gates using reversible logic synthesis techniques. Most of the quantum algorithms are binary algorithms. However, there are ample possibilities to develop multiple-valued quantum algorithms. The reasons are (i) multiple-valued quantum gates are realizable using existing quantum technologies, (ii) multiple-valued reversible logic synthesis is now possible, and (iii) multiple-valued quantum logic circuit is more compact and manageable than binary quantum logic circuit. The quaternary quantum logic circuit has additional advantage that qubits can be very easily encoded into quaternary qudits by grouping two qubits together. This advantage opens an avenue for using quaternary quantum logic circuit internally in binary quantum algorithms. Though there are other approaches of multiple-valued reversible/quantum logic circuit synthesis, the most promising and practical approach is to synthesize multiple-valued reversible/quantum logic circuit as Galois field sum of products (GFSOP) circuit. The advantage of this approach is that any multiple-valued non-reversible logic function with many input variables can be expressed as minimized GFSOP expression and the GFSOP expression can be realized as cascade of 1-qudit, M-S, Feynman, and Toffoli gates. Moreover, macro-level Feynman and Toffoli gates can be realized on the top of 1-qudit and M-S gates without using any ancilla input constant. In this chapter we have developed effective method for synthesis of ternary and quaternary multiple-output logic functions as GFSOP circuit. For this purpose, we have introduced the concept of Galois filed (GF) with example of GF(3) and GF(4) and discussed the notion of GFSOP expression. We have developed Galois field expansions (GFE) for ternary and quaternary cases and have proposed heuristic algorithm for GFSOP minimization by application of these GFEs. For synthesizing quantum logic circuits with lesser width, we have developed method of realizing macro-level

---

[*] E-mail address: mhakhan@ewubd.edu

ternary and quaternary Feynman and Toffoli gates on the top of 1-qudit and M-S gates without use of any ancilla input. Finally, we have proposed method for multiple-output GFSOP realization as cascade of 1-qudit, M-S, Feynman, and Toffoli gates, which minimizes both the gate count and the width of the synthesized quantum circuit. We have established effectiveness of the GFSOP minimization algorithm with sufficient experimental results. The very important feature of the proposed synthesis method is that the method inherently converts a non-reversible function into a reversible one for GFSOP based realization using quantum gates.

Keywords: Feynman gate realization, Galois field expansion, GFSOP expression, GFSOP minimization, GFSOP synthesis, multiple-valued logic, quantum logic, quaternary logic, reversible logic, ternary logic, Toffoli gate realization

1. Introduction

Landauer [1] proved that binary logic circuits built using classical irreversible gates lead to inevitable heat dissipation, regardless of the technology used to realize the gates. Zhirnov *et al.* [2] showed that heat dissipation in any future CMOS technology will lead to impossible heat removal and thus the speeding-up of CMOS devices will be impossible at some point of time. Bennett [3] proved that for heat not to be dissipated in a binary logic circuit, it is necessary that the circuit be built from reversible gates. *A gate (or circuit) is reversible if there is a one-to-one and onto (bijective) mapping between inputs and outputs.* Thus all output patterns are just permutations of input patterns. Bennett's theorem suggests that every future binary technology will have to use some kind of reversible gates in order to reduce heat dissipation. This is also true for multiple-valued logics, which by themselves demonstrate several potential advantages over binary technology.

Quantum technology is inherently reversible and is one of the most promising technologies for future computing systems [4]. Quantum algorithms allow solving problems much more efficiently than in classical computing. For instance, while classical algorithm needs N steps to search an unstructured database, a quantum Grover algorithm [5] needs only $\sqrt{N}$ steps. Another example is Shor's quantum algorithm [6] for prime factoring, which is exponentially faster than any known classical algorithm. All quantum algorithms are made up of quantum logic circuits that use superposition, entanglement, and interference of the quantum states to solve the problem. A quantum logic circuit is made up of quantum gates, which are inherently reversible in nature. These quantum logic circuits are designed using reversible logic synthesis methods [4]. Thus any development of the reversible logic synthesis method adds values to both classical reversible logic circuit synthesis and quantum logic circuit synthesis.

Multiple-valued quantum gates are realizable using existing quantum technologies [7-14]. The quantum technologies naturally provide *qudits* (quantum digits – the basic unit of multiple-valued quantum information) as quanta. *Qubits* (quantum bits – the basic unit of binary quantum information) are obtained by restricting the dynamics of the technology to just two of these quanta [9]. Thus, qudit realization and qubit realization in the existing quantum technologies are of the similar cost. A major obstacle in the quantum technologies is the limit on the number of coupled qubits (or qudits for multiple-valued case) that can be achieved. For a Hilbert space of N dimension, a binary quantum system, or qubit system, requires $n_2 = \log_2 N$ qubits, whereas a d-valued quantum system, or qudit system, requires $n_d = \log_d N = \dfrac{\log_2 N}{\log_2 d}$ qudits. Therefore, we have

$$\frac{n_d}{n_2} = \frac{\dfrac{\log_2 N}{\log_2 d}}{\log_2 N} = \frac{1}{\log_2 d},$$

which implies that the d-valued quantum system requires $1/\log_2 d$ times fewer qudits than the corresponding number of qubits. For d = 3 and 4, the reduction of the quantum register widths are $1/1.58$ and $1/2$ times, respectively. Thus, the use of d-valued quantum system enables a much more compact and efficient information encoding than for binary quantum system. Specifically, the quaternary quantum system has the advantage that binary qubit system can very easily be encoded into quaternary qudit system by grouping two qubits together into a quaternary qudit value. These advantages of multiple-valued quantum system open avenues for developing multiple-valued quantum algorithms. Moreover, as the realizations of both qubit and qudit are of the similar technological complexity, the d-valued encoded realization of binary quantum logic circuit is more compact and efficient than the binary quantum logic circuit. This advantage also provides possibility to use multiple-valued, specifically quaternary, quantum logic circuit internally in the binary quantum algorithms.

A good number of works have been reported on ternary (d = 3) reversible/quantum logic synthesis [15-35]. There are also several works reported on quaternary (d = 4) reversible/quantum logic synthesis [36-42]. These synthesis methods for both ternary and quaternary reversible/quantum logic circuits can be divided into three broad areas of approaches. In the first approach, technology dependent primitive gates are used for circuit synthesis [17, 19, 21, 23, 25, 27, 30, 34, 38]. This approach produces circuit with low cost but the design methods are generally very difficult to use for functions with many input variables. Within this approach, papers [17, 19, 21, 23, 27, 38] use deterministic methods, whereas papers [25, 30, 34] use Genetic Algorithm based methods. In the second approach, macro-level gates are used [15, 18, 20, 24, 26, 28, 29, 32, 33, 37, 39, 40, 42]. These macro-level gates are realizable on the top of technology dependent primitive gates [35, 36, 43, 44, 45, 46]. This approach is relatively easier, but the produced circuit is of higher cost. This approach is also relatively difficult to use for functions with many input variables. Within this approach, there are also two different kinds of methods. Papers [15, 18, 24, 26, 28, 29, 32, 33, 37, 39, 40, 42] use deterministic methods, whereas paper [20] uses Genetic Algorithm based method. The third approach is to synthesize reversible/quantum logic circuits as Galois field sum of products (GFSOP) circuits [16, 22, 35, 36, 41]. The advantage of this approach is that any multiple-valued function with many input variables can be represented as GFSOP expression [22, 41] and the GFSOP expression can be easily implemented as cascade of multiple-valued 1-qudit, Muthukrishnan-Stroud (M-S) [8], Feynman, and Toffoli gates, where the macro-level Feynman and Toffoli gates are realizable on the top of technology dependent primitive gates like 1-qudit and M-S gates [35, 36, 43, 44, 45, 46]. This approach has additional advantage that GFSOP based circuits are highly testable [47]. This approach extensively uses Feynman and multiple-input Toffoli gates for GFSOP realization. The most remarkable drawback of this approach was that realization of macro-level Feynman and

Toffoli gates on the top of primitive gates required a large number of ancilla input constants [36, 43, 44], which made the synthesized circuit having a very large number of ancilla input constants. Recently, ancilla input free realization of Feynman and Toffoli gates on the top of 1-qudit and M-S gates is reported in [46]. Thus, the GFSOP based synthesis of reversible/quantum multiple-valued logic circuit has become very promising and practical for four reasons: (i) any multiple-valued logic function with many inputs can be easily represented as minimized GFSOP expression, (ii) GFSOP expressions can be easily realized as cascade of 1-qudit, M-S, Feynman, and Toffoli gates, (iii) the realizations of Feynman and Toffoli gates on the top of technology dependent primitive gates now do not require any ancilla input constant, which makes the width of the synthesized circuit minimum, and (iv) the GFSOP based circuits are highly testable.

Methods for GFSOP based reversible/quantum synthesis of ternary [22] and quaternary [36, 41] logic functions are reported. However, the ternary GFSOP minimization method reported in [22] and the quaternary GFSOP minimization method reported in [41] are quite different. Moreover, GFSOP synthesis technique reported in [22] and the quaternary GFSOP synthesis technique reported in [36] are also different. In this chapter, we have discussed generalized methods of GFSOP minimization and GFSOP synthesis, which can be used for ternary, quaternary, and other multiple-valued logic functions with higher bases provided that Galois field can be constructed for that base. The generalized GFSOP based synthesis of reversible/quantum logic circuit has two distinct jobs, one is to represent the function as minimized GFSOP expression and the other is to realize the GFSOP expression as cascade of reversible/quantum 1-qudit, M-S, Feynman, and Toffoli gates. The presented methods of this chapter make possible synthesizing non-reversible multiple-valued multiple-output logic functions as a reversible/quantum circuits.

The rest of the chapter is organized as follows. In Section 2, we have discussed the concept of Galois field (GF) and have shown constructions of GF(3) and GF(4). We have introduced the concept of multiple-valued Galois field sum of products (GFSOP) expressions with examples of ternary and quaternary GFSOP expressions in Section 3. In Section 4, we have developed ternary and quaternary Galois field expansions (GFE) using which ternary and quaternary logic functions can be expressed as GFSOP expressions. We have developed heuristic algorithm for minimization of multiple-valued GFSOP expression and have shown example of minimization of ternary GFSOP expression in Section 5. In Section 6, we have introduced technology dependant ternary and quaternary primitive gates like 1-qudit gates and Muthukrishnan-Stroud (M-S) gates [8]. We have shown realization of multiple-valued 1-reduced Post literals (1-RPL) and reversible literals using 1-qudit and M-S gates in Section 7. In Section 8, we have developed method for realization of multiple-valued Feynman gates on the top of 1-qudit and M-S gates that does not require any ancilla input constant in the realization and have shown examples of realizations of ternary and quaternary Feynman gates. We have developed method for realization of multiple-valued Toffoli gates on the top of 1-qudit and M-S gates that does not need any ancilla input constant in the realization and have shown examples of realizations of ternary and quaternary Toffoli gates in Section 9. In Section 10, we have developed heuristic technique for synthesis of multiple-valued multiple-output GFSOP expressions as cascade of 1-qudit, M-S, Feynman, and Toffoli gates that minimizes the number of 1-qudit gates as well as the width of the realized circuit and have shown example of realization of ternary GFSOP expressions. We have shown experimental results for minimization of ternary and quaternary GFSOP expressions in Section 11. In Section 12, we have concluded the chapter.

2. Galois Field

A field is a set F with two binary operations - addition (denoted by +) and multiplication (denoted by $\cdot$ or juxtaposition), are defined, which satisfies the following axioms:

(A1) $a + (b + c) = (a + b) + c$ (associative law for addition)

(A2) $a + b = b + a$ (commutative law for addition)

(A3)   There is an element 0 (zero) such that $a + 0 = a$ for all a

(A4)   For any a, there is an element $(-a)$ such that $a + (-a) = 0$

(M1) $a \cdot (b \cdot c) = (a \cdot b) \cdot c$ (associative law for multiplication)

(M2) $a \cdot b = b \cdot a$ (commutative law for multiplication)

(M3)   There is an element 1 (not equal to 0) such that $a \cdot 1 = a$ for all a

(M4)   For any $a \neq 0$, there is an element a^{-1} such that $a \cdot a^{-1} = 1$

(D) $a \cdot (b + c) = (a \cdot b) + (a \cdot c)$ (distributive law)

If p is a prime integer, then the *integers mod* p form a Galois field (also known as finite field): its elements are the congruence classes of integers mod p, with addition and multiplication induced from integer mod operations. The Galois field with p elements is abbreviated as GF(p). GF(3) addition and multiplication tables are shown in Tables 1 and 2, respectively. The readers can verify that the operations are integer mod 3 operations.

Table 1. GF(3) addition table

+	0	1	2
0	0	1	2
1	1	2	0
2	2	0	1

Table 2. GF(3) multiplication table

$\cdot$	0	1	2
0	0	0	0
1	0	1	2
2	0	2	1

We can construct GF(p^r), where p is a prime integer and r is any integer. The construction of the field is as follows. First, let F_p be the field of integers mod p. Now choose an irreducible polynomial $f(X)$ of degree r over F_p as below:

$$f(X) = X^r + C_{r-1} X^{r-1} + \cdots + C_1 X + C_0 \qquad (1)$$

Now, the elements of F_p are all the expressions of the form

$$x_0 + x_1 a + x_2 a^2 + \cdots + x_{r-1} a^{r-1} \tag{2}$$

where a is required to satisfy $f(a) = 0$, and $x_0, x_1, x_2, \cdots, x_{r-1} \in F_p$. The number of expressions of the form of (2) is p^r, since there are p choices for each of the r coefficients $x_0, x_1, x_2, \cdots, x_{r-1}$. Adding these expressions is straightforward. To multiply, we have to consider that

$$a^r + C_{r-1} a^{r-1} + \cdots + C_1 a + C_0 = 0 \tag{3}$$

For GF(4), $p = 2$ and $r = 2$. Then (1) reduces to

$$f(X) = X^2 + C_1 X + C_0 \tag{4}$$

Equation (4) remains irreducible if we take $C_1 = C_0 = 1$ and (4) reduces to

$$f(X) = X^2 + X + 1 \tag{5}$$

Also, (2) reduces to

$$x_0 + x_1 a \tag{6}$$

where, $x_0, x_1 \in \{0,1\}$. Now, putting different values of x_0 and x_1 in (6), we can find the four elements of F_4 as follows:

$$0 + 0 \cdot a = 0$$
$$0 + 1 \cdot a = a$$
$$1 + 0 \cdot a = 1$$
$$1 + 1 \cdot a = 1 + a$$

That means, $F_4 = \{0, 1, a, a+1\}$.

The additions of these elements are mod 2 additions as follows:

$$0 + 0 = 0$$
$$0 + 1 = 1$$
$$0 + a = a$$
$$0 + (1+a) = 1 + a$$
$$1 + 0 = 1$$
$$1 + 1 = 0$$
$$1 + a = 1 + a$$
$$1 + (1+a) = a$$
$$a + 0 = a$$
$$a + 1 = 1 + a$$

$$a + a = 0$$
$$a + (1 + a) = 1$$
$$(1 + a) + 0 = 1 + a$$
$$(1 + a) + 1 = a$$
$$(1 + a) + a = 1$$
$$(1 + a) + (1 + a) = 0$$

For GF(4), (3) reduces to

$$a^2 + C_1 a + C_0 = 0 \tag{7}$$

Taking $C_1 = C_0 = 1$, (7) reduces to

$$a^2 + a + 1 = 0 \tag{8}$$

From (8), we have using mod 2 addition

$$a^2 = 1 + a \tag{9}$$

The multiplications of the elements are as follows:

$$0 \cdot 0 = 0$$
$$0 \cdot 1 = 0$$
$$0 \cdot a = 0$$
$$0 \cdot (1 + a) = 0$$
$$1 \cdot 0 = 0$$
$$1 \cdot 1 = 1$$
$$1 \cdot a = a$$
$$1 \cdot (1 + a) = 1 + a$$
$$a \cdot 0 = 0$$
$$a \cdot 1 = a$$
$$a \cdot a = a^2 = 1 + a$$
$$a \cdot (1 + a) = a + a^2 = a + 1 + a = 1$$
$$(1 + a) \cdot 0 = 0$$
$$(1 + a) \cdot 1 = 1 + a$$
$$(1 + a) \cdot a = a + a^2 = 1$$
$$(1 + a) \cdot (1 + a) = 1 + 2a + a^2 = 1 + 2a + 1 + a = a$$

Now, taking $a = 2$, $F_4 = (0,1,2,3\}$ and the addition and multiplication over GF(4) are as shown in Tables 3 and 4, respectively.

In this chapter, unless otherwise explicitly stated, all addition (+) and multiplication (·) operations are GF operations.

Table 3. GF(4) addition table

+	0	1	2	3
0	0	1	2	3
1	1	0	3	2
2	2	3	0	1
3	3	2	1	0

Table 3. GF(4) multiplication table

+	0	1	2	3
0	0	0	0	0
1	0	1	2	3
2	0	2	3	1
3	0	3	1	2

3. Multiple-Valued Galois Field Sum of Products Expression

For expressing a d-valued ($d \geq 3$) logic function as Galois field sum of products (GFSOP) expression, we will use two types of multiple-valued literals – 1-reduced Post literals (1-RPLs) and reversible literals as defined below.

Definition 1. A d-valued ($d \geq 3$) *1-reduced Post literal (1-RPL)* represents a mapping from a variable x to a transformed value x^i, $x^i : \{0,1,\cdots,(d-1)\} \rightarrow \{0,1\}$, such that

$$(\forall i \in \{0,1,\cdots,(d-1)\}) \; x^i = \begin{cases} 1 & \text{if } x = i \\ 0 & \text{otherwise} \end{cases}.$$

The ternary ($d=3$) 1-RPLs are x^0, x^1, and x^2. The ternary 1-RPLs can be expressed using the following GF(3) polynomial expressions:

$$x^0 = 2x^2 + 1 \tag{10}$$

$$x^1 = 2x^2 + 2x \tag{11}$$

$$x^2 = 2x^2 + x \tag{12}$$

The quaternary ($d=4$) 1-RPLs are x^0, x^1, x^2, x^3. The quaternary 1-RPLs can be expressed using the following GF(4) polynomial expressions:

$$x^0 = x^3 + 1 \tag{13}$$

$$x^1 = x^3 + x^2 + x \tag{14}$$

$$x^2 = x^3 + 2x^2 + 3x \tag{15}$$

$$x^3 = x^3 + 3x^2 + 2x \tag{16}$$

This sort of GF polynomial representation of 1-RPLs will be useful in developing Galois field expansions (GFE) in Section 4. In Section 7, we will see that 1-RPLs can be realized on the top of technology dependent primitive 1-qudit and M-S gates.

Definition 2. A d-valued ($d \geq 3$) *reversible literal* represents a bijective mapping from a variable x to a transformed value $x^{<q>}$, $x^{<q>} : \{0,1,\cdots,(d-1)\} \to \{0,1,\cdots,(d-1)\}$, where $<q>$ is a string from the alphabet $\{+,/,0,1,\cdots,(d-1)\}$. There are $d!$ reversible literals.

The $3! = 6$ ternary reversible literals can be grouped into two categories. Let us assume that $a,b \in \{0,1,2\}$ and $a \neq b$. Then, the two groups of ternary reversible literals can be described as follows:

(i) A reversible literal of the form x^{+a} represents a shift of the variable x by a, i.e., $x^{+a} = x + a$. There are three such reversible literals (readers should note that $x^{+0} = x$).

(ii) A reversible literal of the form x^{ab} represents a cyclic change of the value of the variable x, i.e., a becomes b, and b becomes a. There are three such reversible literals.

The six ternary reversible literals can be expressed using the GF(3) polynomial expressions as shown in Table 5.

The $4! = 24$ quaternary reversible literals can be grouped into four categories. Let us assume that $a,b,c,d \in \{0,1,2,3\}$ and $a \neq b \neq c \neq d$. Then, the four groups of quaternary reversible literals can be described as follows:

(i) A reversible literal of the form x^{+a} represents a shift of the variable x by a, i.e., $x^{+a} = x + a$. There are four such reversible literals (readers should note that $x^{+0} = x$).

(ii) A reversible literal of the form x^{ab} represents a cyclic change of the value of the variable x, i.e., a becomes b, and b becomes a; c and d remain unchanged. There are six such reversible literals.

(iii) A reversible literal of the form x^{abc} represents a cyclic change of the value of the variable x, i.e., a becomes b, b becomes c, and c becomes a; d remains unchanged. There are eight such reversible literals.

(iv) A reversible literal of the form x^{abcd} represents a cyclic change of the value of the variable x, i.e., a becomes b, b becomes c, c becomes d, and d becomes a. There are six such reversible literals.

The 24 quaternary reversible literals can be expressed using the GF(4) polynomial expressions as shown in Table 6.

In Section 7, we will see that reversible literals can be realized using technology dependent primitive 1-qudit gates.

The GF polynomial expressions for 1-RPLs and reversible literals will be useful for developing Galois field expansions (GFE) in Section 4.

Table 5. GF(3) polynomial expressions for ternary reversible literals

Reversible literals of category x^{+a}	Reversible literals of category x^{ab}
$x^{+0} = x + 0$	$x^{12} = 2x$
$x^{+1} = x + 1$	$x^{01} = 2x + 1$
$x^{+2} = x + 2$	$x^{02} = 2x + 2$

Table 6. GF(4) polynomial expressions for quaternary reversible literals

Reversible literals of the form x^{+a}	Reversible literals of the form x^{ab}	Reversible literals of the form x^{abc}	Reversible literals of the form x^{abcd}
$x^{+0} = x + 0$	$x^{01} = x^2 + 1$	$x^{012} = 3x + 1$	$x^{0123} = 3x^2 + 1$
$x^{+1} = x + 1$	$x^{02} = 3x^2 + 2$	$x^{013} = 2x + 1$	$x^{0132} = 2x^2 + 1$
$x^{+2} = x + 2$	$x^{03} = 2x^2 + 3$	$x^{021} = 2x + 2$	$x^{0213} = x^2 + 2$
$x^{+3} = x + 3$	$x^{12} = 2x^2$	$x^{023} = 3x + 2$	$x^{0231} = 2x^2 + 2$
	$x^{13} = 3x^2$	$x^{031} = 3x + 3$	$x^{0312} = x^2 + 3$
	$x^{23} = x^2$	$x^{032} = 2x + 3$	$x^{0321} = 3x^2 + 3$
		$x^{123} = 2x$	
		$x^{132} = 3x$	

Readers should note that the length of the superscript for 1-RPLs is one and that of the reversible literals is more than one. Thus, the length of the superscript differentiates which one is a 1-RPL and which one is a reversible literal.

In Section 5, we will see that for writing GFSOP expressions, reversible literals are needed to be multiplied by constants greater than 1. Such multiplication of a reversible literal by a constant is equivalent to another reversible literal and can be determined using the GF polynomial expressions of the reversible literals. Consider the following example:

$$2x^{01} = 2(2x + 1) = x + 2 = x^{+2}.$$

This can also be done using truth table as shown in Table 7. In Table 7, the first column lists all possible values of the variable x, the second column lists the corresponding values produced by the literal x^{01}, and the third column lists the values resulted by multiplying the values of the second column by 2. Inspection of the third column reveals that the values are $x + 2$ making the conclusion that $2x^{01} = x^{+2}$. Equivalent reversible literals for product of constants and reversible literals are given in Table 8.

Table 7. Determination of equivalent reversible literal for $2x^{01}$

x	x^{01}	$2x^{01}$
0	1	2
1	0	0
2	2	1

Table 8. Equivalent reversible literals for product of constant and reversible literal

Ternary literals	Quaternary literals	
$2x = x^{12}$	$2x = x^{123}$	$3x = x^{132}$
$2x^{+1} = x^{02}$	$2x^{+1} = x^{021}$	$3x^{+1} = x^{031}$
$2x^{+2} = x^{01}$	$2x^{+2} = x^{032}$	$3x^{+2} = x^{012}$
$2x^{12} = x$	$2x^{+3} = x^{013}$	$3x^{+3} = x^{023}$
$2x^{01} = x^{+2}$	$2x^{01} = x^{0231}$	$3x^{01} = x^{0321}$
$2x^{02} = x^{+1}$	$2x^{02} = x^{0312}$	$3x^{02} = x^{0132}$
	$2x^{03} = x^{0123}$	$3x^{03} = x^{0213}$
	$2x^{12} = x^{13}$	$3x^{12} = x^{23}$
	$2x^{13} = x^{23}$	$3x^{13} = x^{12}$
	$2x^{23} = x^{12}$	$3x^{23} = x^{13}$
	$2x^{012} = x^{+2}$	$3x^{012} = x^{032}$
	$2x^{013} = x^{023}$	$3x^{013} = x^{+3}$
	$2x^{021} = x^{031}$	$3x^{021} = x^{+1}$
	$2x^{023} = x^{+3}$	$3x^{023} = x^{013}$
	$2x^{031} = x^{+1}$	$3x^{031} = x^{021}$
	$2x^{032} = x^{012}$	$3x^{032} = x^{+2}$
	$2x^{123} = x^{132}$	$3x^{123} = x$
	$2x^{132} = x$	$3x^{132} = x^{123}$
	$2x^{0123} = x^{0213}$	$3x^{0123} = x^{03}$
	$2x^{0132} = x^{02}$	$3x^{0132} = x^{0312}$
	$2x^{0213} = x^{03}$	$3x^{0213} = x^{0123}$
	$2x^{0231} = x^{0321}$	$3x^{0231} = x^{01}$
	$2x^{0312} = x^{0132}$	$3x^{0312} = x^{02}$
	$2x^{0321} = x^{01}$	$3x^{0321} = x^{0231}$

From the definition of reversible literals, it is clear that reversible literals represent 1-qudit permutation operations.

Galois field sum of products (GFSOP) expression is defined using the following definitions.

Definition 3. Product of 1-RPLs and reversible literals are known as *Galois field product (GFP)*. For example, $x^1 y^{02} z^{+2}$ is a ternary GFP and $x^{0231} y^{13} z^0$ is a quaternary GFP.

Definition 4. Sum of GFPs is known as *GFSOP expression*. For example, $x^1 y^{02} z^{+2} + x^{02} y^{+1} z^{12} + xz^1$ is a ternary GFSOP expression and $x^{0231} y^{13} z^0 + x^{012} y^3 z^{23} + yz^{+2}$ is a quaternary GFSOP expression.

Definition 5. If a GFSOP expression contains only 1-RPLs and each GFP contains all variables, then we call that expression a *canonical GFSOP expression*. For example,

$x^1y^2z^0 + x^2y^2z^1 + x^2y^1z^0$ is a ternary canonical GFSOP expression and $x^1y^2z^3 + x^2y^0z^1 + x^0y^2z^3$ is a quaternary canonical GFSOP expression.

Table 9. Truth table of ternary full-adder

ABC	C_oS
000	00
001	01
002	xx
010	01
011	02
012	xx
020	02
021	10
022	xx
100	01
101	02
102	xx
110	02
111	10
112	xx
120	10
121	11
122	xx
200	02
201	10
202	xx
210	10
211	11
212	xx
220	11
221	12
222	xx

The truth table of ternary full-adder is shown in Table 9. Readers should note that, in full-adder, carry inputs are either 0 or 1. Therefore, for carry input $C = 2$, outputs are don't cares as shown in Table 9. Here we have not considered the problem of don't care assignments, and, therefore, we have assumed 0s for all don't care outputs. Canonical GFSOP expression for a function can be written directly from the truth table. In Table 9, the first non-zero output of the sum output S is 1 and the corresponding input combination is $ABC = 001$. When $A = 0$, then $A^0 = 1$; when $B = 0$, then $B^0 = 1$; and when $C = 1$, then $C^1 = 1$. Therefore, when $ABC = 001$, then $A^0B^0C^1 = 1$. Thus, the GFP corresponding to the input combination $ABC = 001$ is $A^0B^0C^1$. If we multiply the GFP $A^0B^0C^1$ by the corresponding output 1, then the resulting GFP is $A^0B^0C^1$, which produces the desired output 1. The third non-zero output of the sum output S is 2 and the corresponding input combination is $ABC = 011$. The GFP for this input combination is $A^0 B^1 C^1$. When $ABC = 011$, then $A^0 B^1 C^1 = 1$. If this GFP is multiplied by the corresponding output 2, then we get the desired output 2. Therefore, the resulting GFP for this output is $2A^0 B^1 C^1$. Similarly, GFPs for all non-zero outputs (don't cares are assumed to be 0s) are determined and summed up to write the canonical GFSOP expression. The canonical GFSOP expressions for the sum output S and the carry output C_o are given in (17) and (18), respectively.

$$S(A,B,C) = A^0 B^0 C^1 + A^0 B^1 C^0 + 2A^0 B^1 C^1 + 2A^0 B^2 C^0 + A^1 B^0 C^0 + 2A^1 B^0 C^1 + \\ 2A^1 B^1 C^0 + A^1 B^2 C^1 + 2A^2 B^0 C^0 + A^2 B^1 C^1 + A^2 B^2 C^0 + 2A^2 B^2 C^1 \tag{17}$$

$$C_o(A,B,C) = A^0 B^2 C^1 + A^1 B^1 C^1 + A^1 B^2 C^0 + A^1 B^2 C^1 + A^2 B^0 C^1 + A^2 B^1 C^0 + A^2 B^1 C^1 + A^2 B^2 C^0 + A^2 B^2 C^1 \tag{18}$$

4. Multiple-Valued Galois Field Expansions

In this section, we will develop ternary and quaternary Galois field expansions (GFE) using which any ternary and quaternary logic function can be expressed as GFSOP expression, respectively.

Definition 6. The *cofactors* of an n-variable d-valued ($d \geq 3$) logic function f with respect to the variable x_i are defined as follows:

$$(\forall j \in \{0,1,\cdots,(d-1)\})\, f_j = f(x_1,\cdots,x_{i-1}, j, x_{i+1},\cdots,x_n)$$

The three ternary cofactors are

$$f_0 = f(x_1,\cdots,x_{i-1},0, x_{i+1},\cdots x_n)$$
$$f_1 = f(x_1,\cdots,x_{i-1},1, x_{i+1},\cdots x_n)$$
$$f_2 = f(x_1,\cdots,x_{i-1},2, x_{i+1},\cdots x_n)$$

The four quaternary cofactors are

$$f_0 = f(x_1,\cdots,x_{i-1},0, x_{i+1},\cdots x_n)$$
$$f_1 = f(x_1,\cdots,x_{i-1},1, x_{i+1},\cdots x_n)$$
$$f_2 = f(x_1,\cdots,x_{i-1},2, x_{i+1},\cdots x_n)$$
$$f_3 = f(x_1,\cdots,x_{i-1},3, x_{i+1},\cdots x_n)$$

Definition 7. A *composite cofactor* is defined as

$$f_{(a_0 \cdot 0)(a_1 \cdot 1)\cdots(a_{(d-1)} \cdot (d-1))} = a_0 f_0 + a_1 f_1 + \cdots + a_{(d-1)} f_{(d-1)}$$

where, $(\forall i \in \{0,1,\cdots,(d-1)\})$ $a_i \in \{0,1,\cdots,(d-1)\}$; $a_i = 1$ is not explicitly written and in that case the braces are omitted.

In this chapter, we have used the following ternary composite cofactors:

$$f_{01} = f_0 + f_1$$
$$f_{02} = f_0 + f_2$$
$$f_{12} = f_1 + f_2$$
$$f_{012} = f_0 + f_1 + f_2$$
$$f_{001} = f_0 + f_0 + f_1$$
$$f_{002} = f_0 + f_0 + f_2$$
$$f_{011} = f_0 + f_1 + f_1$$
$$f_{112} = f_1 + f_1 + f_2$$
$$f_{022} = f_0 + f_2 + f_2$$
$$f_{122} = f_1 + f_2 + f_2$$

We have also used the following quaternary composite cofactors:

$$f_{01} = f_0 + f_1$$
$$f_{02} = f_0 + f_2$$
$$f_{03} = f_0 + f_3$$
$$f_{12} = f_1 + f_2$$
$$f_{13} = f_1 + f_3$$
$$f_{23} = f_2 + f_3$$
$$f_{012} = f_0 + f_1 + f_2$$
$$f_{013} = f_0 + f_1 + f_3$$
$$f_{023} = f_0 + f_2 + f_3$$
$$f_{123} = f_1 + f_2 + f_3$$
$$f_{0123} = f_0 + f_1 + f_2 + f_3$$
$$f_{1(2\cdot2)(3\cdot3)} = f_1 + 2f_2 + 3f_3$$
$$f_{1(3\cdot2)(2\cdot3)} = f_1 + 3f_2 + 2f_3$$

The fundamental d-valued ($d \geq 3$) GFE is given in the following theorem. In the following theorem, we will use the symbol x to represent the variable x_i in an n-variable d-valued ($d \geq 3$) logic function f to make the expressions more readable.

Theorem 1. Any n-variable d-valued ($d \geq 3$) logic function f can be expanded with respect to the variable x using the following fundamental Galois field expansion (GFE):

$$f = x^0 f_0 + x^1 f_1 + \cdots + x^{(d-1)} f_{(d-1)}$$

Proof. We will prove the theorem using perfect induction.

If $x = 0$, then $f = x^0 f_0 + x^1 f_1 + \cdots + x^{(d-1)} f_{(d-1)} = 1 \cdot f_0 + 0 \cdot f_1 + \cdots + 0 \cdot f_{(d-1)} = f_0$.

If $x = 1$, then $f = x^0 f_0 + x^1 f_1 + \cdots + x^{(d-1)} f_{(d-1)} = 0 \cdot f_0 + 1 \cdot f_1 + \cdots + 0 \cdot f_{(d-1)} = f_1$.

Similarly, if $x = (d-1)$, then

$$f = x^0 f_0 + x^1 f_1 + \cdots + x^{(d-1)} f_{(d-1)} = 0 \cdot f_0 + 0 \cdot f_1 + \cdots + 1 \cdot f_{(d-1)} = f_{(d-1)}.$$

Thus, we have the theorem.

[End of Proof]

The fundamental ternary GFE (TGFE) and quaternary GFE (QGFE) are given in (19) and (20), respectively.

$$\text{TGFE 1: } f = x^0 f_0 + x^1 f_1 + x^2 f_2 \tag{19}$$

$$\text{QGFE 1: } f = x^0 f_0 + x^1 f_1 + x^2 f_2 + x^3 f_3 \tag{20}$$

Fundamental GFEs are GFEs using only 1-RPLs. Application of fundamental GFE on all variables of a d-valued ($d \geq 3$) logic function produces canonical GFSOP expression.

Based on TGFE 1 of (19), we have developed 15 TGFEs using 1-RPLs and reversible literals as given in the following theorem.

Theorem 2. Any n-variable ternary logic function f can be expanded with respect to the variable x using any of the following 15 TGFEs:

TGFE 2: $f = x^0 f_{01} + x^{02} f_1 + x^2 f_2$

TGFE 3: $f = x^{+1} f_0 + x^1 f_{01} + x^2 f_2$

TGFE 4: $f = x^0 f_{02} + x^1 f_1 + x^{+2} f_2$

TGFE 5: $f = x^{01} f_0 + x^1 f_1 + x^2 f_{02}$

TGFE 6: $f = x^0 f_0 + x^1 f_{12} + x^{12} f_2$

TGFE 7: $f = x^0 f_0 + x f_1 + x^2 f_{12}$

TGFE 8: $f = x^1 f_{012} + x^{02} f_1 + x^{+2} f_2$

TGFE 9: $f = x^{+1} f_0 + x^1 f_{012} + x^{12} f_2$

TGFE 10: $f = x^{01} f_0 + x f_1 + x^2 f_{012}$

TGFE 11: $f = f_0 + x f_{112} + x x^{12} f_{012}$

TGFE 12: $f = f_0 + x^{12} f_{122} + x x^{12} f_{012}$

TGFE 13: $f = f_1 + x^{+2} f_{022} + x^{+2} x^{01} f_{012}$

TGFE 14: $f = f_1 + x^{01} f_{002} + x^{+2} x^{01} f_{012}$

TGFE 15: $f = f_2 + x^{+1} f_{001} + x^{+1} x^{02} f_{012}$

TGFE 16: $f = f_2 + x^{02} f_{011} + x^{+1} x^{02} f_{012}$

Proof. Substituting (10), (11), and (12) in (19), we have

$$
\begin{aligned}
f &= (2x^2 + 1) f_0 + (2x^2 + 2x) f_1 + (2x^2 + x) f_2 \\
&= (2x^2 + 1) f_0 + (2x^2 + 1 + 2x + 2) f_1 + (2x^2 + x) f_2 \\
&= (2x^2 + 1)(f_0 + f_1) + (2x + 2) f_1 + (2x^2 + x) f_2 \\
&= x^0 f_{01} + x^{02} f_1 + x^2 f_2
\end{aligned}
$$

Thus, we have TGFE 2. Similarly, we can prove TGFE 3 through TGFE 16.

[End of Proof]

Based on QGFE 1 of (20), we have developed nine QGFEs using 1-RPLs and reversible literals as given in the following theorem.

Theorem 3. Any n-variable quaternary logic function f can be expanded with respect to the variable x using any of the following nine QGFEs:

QGFE 2: $f = f_0 + x^1 f_{01} + x^2 f_{02} + x^3 f_{03}$

QGFE 3: $f = f_1 + x^0 f_{01} + x^2 f_{12} + x^3 f_{13}$

QGFE 4: $f = f_2 + x^0 f_{02} + x^1 f_{12} + x^3 f_{23}$

QGFE 5: $f = f_3 + x^0 f_{03} + x^1 f_{13} + x^2 f_{23}$

QGFE 6: $f = f_{012} + xx^{23} f_{03} + x^{+1} x^{01} f_{13} + x^{+2} x^{0312} f_{23}$

QGFE 7: $f = f_{013} + xx^{23} f_{02} + x^{+1} x^{01} f_{12} + x^{+3} x^{0213} f_{23}$

QGFE 8: $f = f_{023} + xx^{23} f_{01} + x^{+2} x^{0321} f_{12} + x^{+3} x^{0213} f_{13}$

QGFE 9: $f = f_{123} + x^{+1} x^{01} f_{01} + x^{+2} x^{0312} f_{02} + x^{+3} x^{0213} f_{03}$

QGFE 10: $f = f_0 + xx^{23} f_{0123} + x^{23} f_{1(2\cdot 2)(3\cdot 3)} + x f_{1(3\cdot 2)(2\cdot 3)}$

Proof: Substituting (13), (14), (15), and (16) in (20), we have

$$
\begin{aligned}
f &= (x^3 + 1) f_0 + (x^3 + x^2 + x) f_1 + (x^3 + 2x^2 + 3x) f_2 + (x^3 + 3x^2 + 2x) f_3 \\
&= f_0 + x^3 f_0 + (x^3 + x^2 + x) f_1 + (x^3 + 2x^2 + 3x) f_2 + (x^3 + 3x^2 + 2x) f_3 \\
&= f_0 + [(x^3 + x^2 + x) + (x^3 + 2x^2 + 3x) + (x^3 + 3x^2 + 2x)] f_0 + (x^3 + x^2 + x) f_1 + (x^3 + 2x^2 + 3x) f_2 + (x^3 + 3x^2 + 2x) f_3 \\
&= f_0 + (x^3 + x^2 + x)(f_0 + f_1) + (x^3 + 2x^2 + 3x)(f_0 + f_2) + (x^3 + 3x^2 + 2x)(f_0 + f_3) \\
&= f_0 + x^1 f_{01} + x^2 f_{02} + x^3 f_{03}
\end{aligned}
$$

Thus, we have QGFE 2. Similarly, we can prove QGFEs 3 through 10.

[End of Proof]

5. Minimization of Multiple-Valued Galois Field Sum of Products Expression

Application of GFE 1 on variables of a d-valued ($d \geq 3$) logic function produces a canonical GFSOP expression. However, application of other GFEs on variables of a d-valued ($d \geq 3$) logic function produces a non-canonical GFSOP expression that leads to minimization of GFSOP expression. In this section, we have developed heuristic algorithm for GFSOP minimization for d-valued ($d \geq 3$) non-reversible logic functions expressed as output vector. For incompletely specified function, the don't care outputs are replaced by 0s.

The size of the minimized GFSOP expression depends on both variable ordering and GFE selection for the variables for application of GFEs. Here we have proposed a heuristic algorithm for simultaneous variable ordering and GFE selection with the view to maximize the number of zeros in the transformed vector. The n-variable d-valued ($d \geq 3$) logic function f is represented by its output vector as an array with indices 0 to $d^n - 1$, where the indices correspond to the input values. The don't care outputs of incompletely specified functions are replaced by 0s. For the proposed heuristic algorithm, we consider groups of d^{n-i} length for $i = 1, 2, \cdots, n$ starting from the group boundary index jd^{n-i} for $j = 0, 1, \cdots, d^i - 1$. For example, if $d = 3$, $n = 3$ and $i = 1$, then the group length is 9 and the groups start from group boundary indices 0, 9, and 18, respectively. If such a group contains all 0s, then the cofactors resulting from that group will all be 0. We have designated such a group of d^{n-i} 0s by Z_i.

The following heuristic algorithm simultaneously determines variable ordering and GFEs for variables:

1. For all n variables, find expansions for all the GFEs. For each variable-GFE pair, compute Z_1 through Z_n.
2. Select the variable-GFE pair with the highest Z_1 value. In case of a tie, break it using Z_2 through Z_n. This selection will produce maximum number of 0s in different group lengths in the transformed vector. If the tie can not be resolved using Z_2 through Z_n, break it arbitrarily.
3. For the next transformation, repeat steps 1 and 2 for the remaining variables. Repeat this process until $n-1$ variables are transformed.
4. For the last variable, find expansions for all the GFEs and select the variable-GFE pair with the highest Z_n value. This selection will produce maximum number of 0s in the final transformed vector. In case of tie, break it arbitrarily.
5. For multi-output function, repeat steps 1 to 4 for all output functions separately. Then, identify the common GFPs.

We illustrate the heuristic algorithm using ternary full-adder function as shown in Table 9. The sum output is

$$S(A, B, C) = [010\ 120\ 200\ 120\ 200\ 010\ 200\ 010\ 120]^T \qquad (21)$$

where the vector entry is the output value and the index of the vector entry is the input combination. The algorithm identifies variable A as the first variable and the corresponding expansion is TGFE 8. After application of TGFE 8 on the variable A of the vector of (21), the transformed vector is

$$[000\ 000\ 000\ 120\ 200\ 010\ 200\ 010\ 120]^{T} \tag{22}$$

The algorithm identifies variable B as the second variable and the corresponding expansion is TGFE 8. After application of TGFE 8 on the variable B of the vector of (22), the transformed vector is

$$[000\ 000\ 000\ 000\ 200\ 010\ 000\ 010\ 120]^{T} \tag{23}$$

The only remaining variable is C and the algorithm identifies TGFE 1 as the best GFE for this variable. After application of TGFE 1 on the variable C of the vector of (23), the final transformed vector is

$$[000\ 020\ 001\ 000\ 001\ 012\ 000\ 000\ 000]^{T} \tag{24}$$

The final transformed vector has five non-zero elements, whereas the original output vector has 12 non-zero elements resulting into a significant minimization. Minimized ternary GFSOP expression is written from the final transformed vector of (24) as discussed later in this section.

Now, we see the minimization of carry output, which is

$$C_{o}(A,B,C) = [000\ 000\ 010\ 000\ 010\ 110\ 010\ 110\ 110]^{T} \tag{25}$$

The algorithm identifies variable C as the first variable and the corresponding expansion is TGFE 1. After application of TGFE 1 on the variable C of the vector of (25), the transformed vector is

$$[000\ 001\ 011\ 001\ 011\ 111\ 000\ 000\ 000]^{T} \tag{26}$$

The algorithm identifies variable A as the second variable and the corresponding expansion is TGFE 1. After application of TGFE 1 on the variable A of the vector of (26), the transformed vector is

$$[000\ 001\ 011\ 001\ 011\ 111\ 000\ 000\ 000]^{T} \tag{27}$$

The only remaining variable is B and the algorithm identifies TGFE 11 as the best expansion for this variable. After application of TGFE 11 on the variable B of the vector of (27), the final transformed vector is

$$[000\ 001\ 000\ 010\ 100\ 000\ 012\ 120\ 000]^{T} \tag{28}$$

The final transformed vector has seven non-zero elements, whereas the original output vector has nine non-zero elements resulting into some minimization.

Now, we will see writing ternary GFSOP expression for sum output form (24). The first non-zero element of the final vector of (24) is 2, whose index is 4 and the input combination is $ABC = 011$. As the value of the variable A is 0, we take the product corresponding to the 0th location of TGFE 8 (corresponding to the cofactor f_{012}), which is A^1. As the value of the variable B is 1, we take the product corresponding to the 1st location of TGFE 8 (corresponding to the cofactor f_1), which is B^{02}. As the value of the variable C is 1, we take the product corresponding to the 1st location of TGFE 1, which is C^1. Then these three products are multiplied with the output constant 2 resulting into the product $2A^1B^{02}C^1$. The constant 2 can be eliminated by multiplying it with any reversible literal of the product term using the results from Table 8. For example $2B^{02} = B^{+1}$. Therefore, the product term $2A^1B^{02}C^1$ can be rewritten as $A^1B^{+1}C^1$. Similarly, determining product terms for all non-zero elements and then summing them up, we find the minimized GFSOP expression from (24) as follows:

$$S(A,B,C) = A^1B^{+1}C^1 + A^1B^{+2}C^2 + A^{02}B^{02}C^2 + A^{02}B^{+2}C^1 + A^{+1}B^{+2}C^2 \qquad (29)$$

The GFSOP expression of (29) is a minimized GFSOP expression having only five product terms. The corresponding canonical GFSOP expression of (17) has 12 product terms.
Similarly, the minimized GFSOP expression for carry output from (28) is

$$C_o(A,B,C) = A^0BC^2 + A^1C^1 + A^1BC^0 + A^2C^1 + 2A^2C^2 + A^2BC^0 + A^2B^{12}C^1 \qquad (30)$$

In Section 10, we will see realization of minimized ternary GFSOP expressions of (29) and (30).
Using the same heuristic algorithm, quaternary non-reversible functions can be minimized as quaternary GFSOP expressions.

6. Some Multiple-Valued Primitive Quantum Gates

Any unitary operation can theoretically be realized using quantum technologies [4]. Specifically, any d-valued ($d \geq 3$) unitary operation represented by a $d \times d$ unitary matrix, such as ternary unitary operation represented by a 3×3 unitary matrix and quaternary unitary operation represented by a 4×4 unitary matrix, can be realized using liquid ion-trap quantum technology [8] as 1-qudit gate. We will represent a 1-qudit gate using the symbol of Figure 1, where A is the input variable, z is any unitary operation, and A^z is the output of the gate after unitary operation z is applied on the input A. The unitary operation z includes any possible unitary operation represented by a $d \times d$ unitary matrix including the permutation operations corresponding to six ternary and 24 quaternary reversible literals discussed in Section 3.
Muthukrishnan and Stroud [8] proposed a liquid ion-trap realizable 2-qudit d-valued ($d \geq 3$) controlled quantum gate family, where a unitary operation is applied on the controlled input when the value of the controlling input is $d - 1$. We will refer to this family of gates as Muthukrishnan-Stroud (M-S) gate family. The symbol of M-S gate is shown in Figure 2. The input A is the controlling input and the input B is the controlled input. The output P is

exactly equal to the input A (pass through output). The output Q is equal to B^z when $A = d - 1$ and equal to B when $A \neq d - 1$, where z is any possible unitary operation including permutation operations corresponding to six ternary and 24 quaternary reversible literals.

7. Realization of Multiple-Valued Literals Using Primitive Quantum Gates

The multiple-valued reversible literals, such as six ternary and 24 quaternary reversible literals discussed in Section 3, are permutation transforms of input values to output values, which are unitary in nature. These reversible literals can be realized using 1-qudit gates.

We have proposed here a method for realization of d-valued ($d \geq 3$) 1-RPLs using 1-qudit and M-S gates as shown in Figure 3. The value of a is chosen in such a way that when the value of $A = i$, then the controlling value of the M-S gate is $x = i + a = d - 1$ to produce $A^i = 1$. The value of b is chosen in such a way that $a + b = 0$ to restore the value of A at the output. The values of a and b for realization of ternary and quaternary 1-RPLs are given in Table 10. The realizations of d-valued ($d \geq 3$)1-RPLs require three primitive gates and one ancilla input constant (*any additional input other than the primary input used in the design is called ancilla input*). However, the reader can readily verify that the 1-RPL A^{d-1}, such as ternary A^2 and quaternary A^3, can be realized using only one M-S gate.

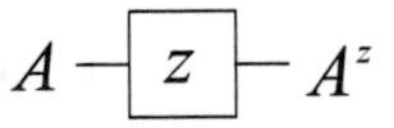

$$A - \boxed{z} - A^z$$

Figure 1. Symbol of d-valued ($d \geq 3$) 1-qudit gate.

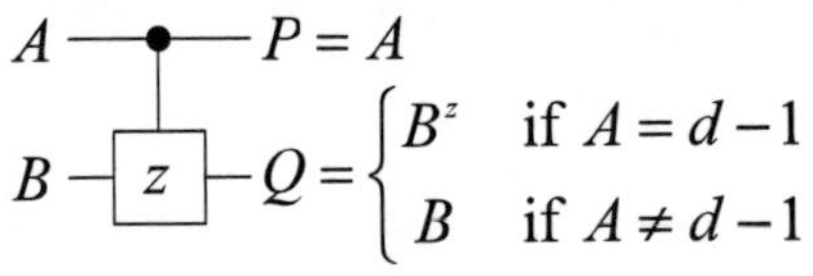

$$A \longrightarrow\!\!\bullet\longrightarrow P = A$$
$$B - \boxed{z} - Q = \begin{cases} B^z & \text{if } A = d - 1 \\ B & \text{if } A \neq d - 1 \end{cases}$$

Figure 2. Symbol of d-valued ($d \geq 3$) Muthukrishnan-Stroud (M-S) gate family.

Table 10. Values of a and b for realization of ternary and quaternary 1-RPLs

	Ternary		Quaternary	
$A = i$	a	b	a	b
0	2	1	3	3
1	1	2	2	2
2	0	0	1	1
3			0	0

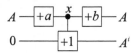

Figure 3. Realization of d-valued ($d \geq 3$) 1-RPLs using quantum gates.

8. Multiple-Valued Feynman Gate

The symbol of d-valued ($d \geq 3$) Feynman gate is shown in Figure 4, where A, B are inputs and $P = A$, $Q = A + B$ are outputs. Feynman gate is a macro-level gate and needs to be realized on the top of 1-qudit and M-S gates.

For realization of Feynman gate on the top of 1-qudit and M-S gates, we propose the architecture of Figure 5. The architecture does not require any ancilla input constant. When $A = 0$, the output $Q = 0 + B = B$ and we need not to apply any operation on the input B. When $A = i \in \{1, 2, \cdots, d-1\}$, we need to apply $+i$ operation on B using M-S gate to make the output $Q = i + B = A + B$. For doing this, we need to make the corresponding controlling value of the M-S gate equal to $d - 1$ by providing an effective shift of $+x_i$ to the input $A = i$ at the controlling point. This implies that

$$(\forall i \in \{1, 2, \cdots, d-1\}) \ i + x_i = d - 1. \tag{31}$$

Figure 4. Symbol of d-valued ($d \geq 3$) Feynman gate.

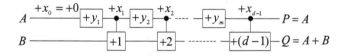

Figure 5. Architecture for realization of d-valued ($d \geq 3$) Feynman gate.

Table 11. Values of y_i and x_i for realization of ternary and quaternary Feynman gate using architecture of Figure 5

	Ternary		Quaternary	
$A = i$	y_i	x_i	y_i	x_i
0		0		0
1	1	1	2	2
2	2	0	3	1
3			1	0

This effective shift to the input $A = i$ is made by cascaded 1-qudit gates, which requires that

$$(\forall i \in \{1,2,\cdots,d-1\})\, x_i = x_{i-1} + y_i. \tag{32}$$

Solving (31) and (32) for ternary and quaternary cases, we have the values of y_i and x_i as given in Table 11. Using these values of y_i and x_i, the realizations of ternary and quaternary Feynman gates are shown in Figures 6 and 7, respectively. Realization of ternary Feynman gate requires four primitive gates and realization of quaternary Feynman gate needs six primitive gates. The architecture of Figure 5 can be used for realization of any d-valued Feynman gate if GF(d) can be constructed, that is, if d is a prime or a prime power. *In general, realization of d-valued Feynman gate using the architecture of Figure 5 requires $2(d-1)$ primitive gates and no ancilla input constant.*

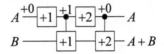

Figure 6. Realization of ternary Feynman gate.

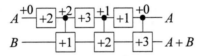

Figure 7. Realization of quaternary Feynman gate.

9. Multiple-Valued Toffoli Gate

The symbol of d-valued ($d \geq 3$) 3-qudit Toffoli gate is shown in Figure 8, where A, B, C are inputs and $P = A$, $Q = B$, $R = C + AB$ are outputs. Toffoli gate is a macro-level gate and needs to be realized on the top of 1-qudit and M-S gates.

For realization of d-valued ($d \geq 3$) 3-qudit Toffoli gate on the top of 1-qudit and M-S gates, we propose the architecture of Figure 9. The proposed architecture does not require any ancilla input constant. In the architecture of Figure 9, the inputs A and B are used as the controlling line and the controlled line, respectively, for circuits 1, 2, and 3. The first circuit produces $(\forall A)\, X = xB$, where $x \in \{1,2,\cdots,d-1\}$. The second circuit produces $(\forall A)\, Y = yX = xyB$, where $y \in \{1,2,\cdots,d-1\}$. The third circuit produces $(\forall A)\, Q = zY = xyzB$, where $z \in \{1,2,\cdots,d-1\}$. The condition $(\forall A)\, Q = xyzB = B$ requires that

$$(\forall A \in \{0,1,\cdots,d-1\})\, xyz = 1. \tag{33}$$

The two Feynman gates in the architecture of Figure 9 produce $R = C + X + Y = C + (x + xy)B = C + AB$, which requires that

$$(\forall A \in \{0,1,\cdots,d-1\})\, x + xy = A. \tag{34}$$

Solving (33) and (34) for ternary and quaternary cases, we get the values of x, y, and z as given in Table 12. Based on these values, the realizations of ternary and quaternary 3-qudit Toffoli gates are shown in Figures 10 and 11, respectively. There are some 1s in Table 12. Multiplications by these 1s are not required, since they do not change the values. The other multiplications are done using M-S gates. For this purpose, we need to provide controlling value of $(d-1)$ at the controlling points for all values of A by using cascaded 1-qudit gates similar to that done for Feynman gate realizations. Ternary $2\times$ operation can be realized using 12 permutation operation. Quaternary $2\times$ and $3\times$ operations can be realized using 123 and 132 permutation operations, respectively. Realization of ternary 3-qudit Toffoli gate requires $8 + 2\times4 = 16$ primitive gates and no ancilla input constant. Realization of quaternary 3-qudit Toffoli gate needs $14 + 2\times6 = 26$ primitive gates and no ancilla input constants.

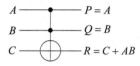

Figure 8. Symbol of d-valued ($d \geq 3$) 3-qudit Toffoli gate.

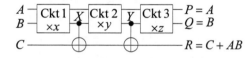

Figure 9. Architecture for realization of d-valued ($d \geq 3$) 3-qudit Toffoli gate.

Table 12. Values of x, y, and z for realization of ternary and quaternary Toffoli gates using the architecture of Figure 9

	Ternary			Quaternary		
A	x	y	z	x	y	z
0	1	2	2	1	1	1
1	2	1	2	2	2	2
2	1	1	1	3	2	1
3				1	2	3

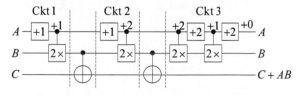

Figure 10. Realization of ternary 3-qudit Toffoli gate.

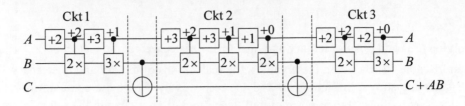

Figure 11. Realization of quaternary 3-qudit Toffoli gate.

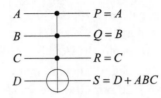

Figure 12. Symbol of d-valued ($d \geq 3$) 4-qudit Toffoli gate.

d-valued ($d \geq 3$) Toffoli gates with more than three qudits are often used in the GFSOP synthesis. The symbol of d-valued ($d \geq 3$) 4-qudit Toffoli gate is shown in Figure 12. For realization of d-valued ($d \geq 3$) 4-qudit Toffoli gate on the top of 1-qudit and M-S gates, we propose the architecture of Figure 13. In the architecture of Figure 13, the input A is used as the controlling line and the input C is used as the controlled line for circuits 1, 2, and 3. The input B remains unchanged in all three circuits. The first circuit produces $(\forall A)\, X = xC$, where $x \in \{1, 2, \cdots, d-1\}$. The second circuit produces $(\forall A)\, Y = xyC$, where $y \in \{1, 2, \cdots, d-1\}$. The third circuit produces $(\forall A)\, R = xyzC$, where $z \in \{1, 2, \cdots, d-1\}$. The condition $(\forall A)\, R = xyzC = C$ requires that

$$(\forall A \in \{0, 1, \cdots, d-1\})\, xyz = 1. \tag{35}$$

The two 3-qudit Toffoli gates in Figure 13 produce $S = D + BxC + BxyC = D + (x + xy)BC = D + ABC$, which requires that

$$(\forall A \in \{0, 1, \cdots, d-1\})\, x + xy = A. \tag{36}$$

Equations (35) and (36) are exactly the same as (33) and (34) and their solutions are as shown in Table 12. Based on these values, the realizations of ternary and quaternary 4-qudit Toffoli gates are shown in Figures 14 and 15, respectively. Realization of ternary 4-qudit Toffoli gate requires $8 + 2 \times 16 = 40$ primitive gates. Realization of quaternary 4-qudit Toffoli gate needs $14 + 2 \times 26 = 66$ primitive gates.

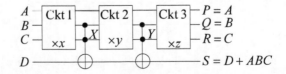

Figure 13. Architecture for realization of d-valued ($d \geq 3$) 4-qudit Toffoli gate.

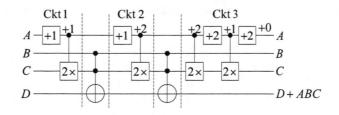

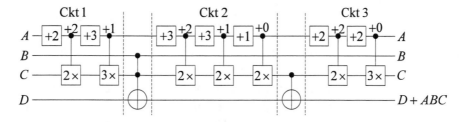

Figure 14. Realization of ternary 4-qudit Toffoli gate.

Figure 15. Realization of quaternary 4-qudit Toffoli gate.

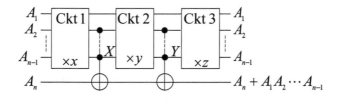

Figure 16. Architecture for realization of d-valued ($d \geq 3$) n-qudit ($n \geq 3$) Toffoli gate.

The architecture of Figure 13 can be generalized for realization of d-valued ($d \geq 3$) n-qudit ($n \geq 3$) Toffoli gate using $(n-1)$-qudit Toffoli gates as shown in Figure 16. Readers should note that the Feynman gate can be considered as a 2-qudit Toffoli gate. The input A_1 is the controlling input and the input A_{n-1} is the controlled input in all three circuits. The inputs A_2 through A_{n-2} are unchanged. The two Toffoli gates are $(n-1)$-qudit Toffoli gates. The values of x, y, and z are as shown in Table 12. The architecture of Figure 16 can be used for realization of any d-valued ($d \geq 3$) Toffoli gate if GF(d) can be constructed, that is, if d is a prime or a prime power. *Realization of ternary n-qudit ($n \geq 3$) Toffoli gate requires 8 + 2×[number of primitive gates for ternary $(n-1)$-qudit Toffoli gate] primitive gates. Realization of quaternary n-qudit ($n \geq 3$) Toffoli gate needs 14 + 2×[number of primitive gates for quaternary $(n-1)$-qudit Toffoli gate] primitive gates.*

10. Realization of Multiple-Valued Multiple-Output GFSOP Expressions

Multiple-output d-valued ($d \geq 3$) GFSOP expressions can be realized as a cascade of 1-qudit, M-S, Feynman, and Toffoli gates. In the GFSOP realizations, the 1-RPLs are realized using 1-qudit and M-S gates and the reversible literals are realized using 1-qudit gates as discussed in Section 7. The product terms are generated and summed with other product terms using Toffoli gates. For realization of literals, necessary copies of the concerned input is made using Feynman gate. To reduce the number of additional copies of the input, we will generate the literals along the same copy of the input. To reduce the number of 1-qudit gate, we will use a literal as many times as possible before changing it to another literal. For this purpose, we have developed heuristic technique for literal and product ordering as discussed below using the example of ternary full-adder function as given in (29) and (30):

Step 1: Determine the literal counts for each variable in the given GFSOP expressions. Order the literals for each variable in the decreasing order of count. Break the tie arbitrarily. If any product term has more than one literals of the same variable, then rearrange the literals in the given GFSOP expressions in the increasing order. This rearrangement of the literals will make the most frequent literal appears first in the product term. The literal counts and their orders for GFSOP expressions of (29) and (3) are given in Table 13. As no product term of these GFSOP expressions has more than one literals of the same variable, literal rearrangement is not required for these GFSOP expressions.

Table 13. Literal ordering for each variable of the GFSOP expressions of (29) and (30)

Variable A			Variable B			Variable C		
Literal	Count	Order	Literal	Count	Order	Literal	Count	Order
A^1	4	1	B^{+1}	1	3	C^1	5	1
A^{02}	2	3	B^{+2}	3	1	C^2	5	2
A^{+1}	1	4	B^{02}	1	4	C^0	2	3
A^0	1	5	B	3	2			
A^2	4	2	B^{12}	1	5			

Step 2: Determine the score for each product term of the given GFSOP expressions as sum of its literal counts. Order the product terms in the decreasing order of scores. Break the tie using decreasing number of matches with the preceding product term. The scores and the orders of the product terms of the GFSOP expressions of (29) and (30) are given in Table 14. The product term $A^1B^{+2}C^2$ has the highest score 12 and assigned the order 1. The product terms $A^1B^{+1}C^1$, $A^{02}B^{+2}C^1$, and $A^2B^{12}C^1$ have scores 10. The numbers of matches of the product terms $A^1B^{+1}C^1$, $A^{02}B^{+2}C^1$, and $A^2B^{12}C^1$ with the preceding product term $A^1B^{+2}C^2$ (order 1) are 1, 1, and 0, respectively. The tie between the product terms $A^1B^{+1}C^1$ and $A^{02}B^{+2}C^1$ is broken arbitrarily. Thus, the order of the product terms $A^1B^{+1}C^1$, $A^{02}B^{+2}C^1$, and $A^2B^{12}C^1$ are assigned to be 2, 3, and 4, respectively. The orders of the other product terms are determined similarly. In the GFSOP realization, the product terms are implemented in the increasing order as discussed below.

Table 14. Product term ordering of the GFSOP expressions of (29) and (30)

Product Term	Function	Score	Order
$A^1 B^{+1} C^1$	S	10	2
$A^1 B^{+2} C^2$	S	12	1
$A^{02} B^{02} C^2$	S	8	11
$A^{02} B^{+2} C^1$	S	10	3
$A^{+1} B^{+1} C^2$	S	7	12
$A^0 BC^2$	C_o	9	9
$A^1 C^1$	C_o	9	6
$A^1 BC^0$	C_o	9	10
$A^2 C^1$	C_o	9	5
$2A^2 C^2$	C_o	9	7
$A^2 BC^0$	C_o	9	8
$A^2 B^{12} C^1$	C_o	10	4

This sort of literal rearrangement and product term ordering will ensure that most frequent literals appear in consecutive product terms and the literals can be realized once and used for generating the concerned product terms. This will help reduce number of 1-qudit gates needed to generate the literals as discussed in GFSOP synthesis method given below.

We have developed a method for synthesis of multiple-output GFSOP expressions using cascade of 1-qudit, M-S, Feynman, and Toffoli gate as discussed below:

Step 1: Count the maximum number of literals of each variable appearing in any product term of the GFSOP expressions. If these numbers are more than one, then create additional copies of the variables using Feynman gate. In the GFSOP expressions of (29) and (30), the maximum number of literals of all variables appearing in any product term is one and, for this specific example, no additional copy of any variable is needed. If any variable has 1-RPLs in the GFSOP expression, then add an input constant 0 line with that variable as shown in Figure 17 for variables A and C. If some constants cannot be eliminated from the GFSOP expressions, then add those constant input lines as shown in Figure 17 by adding input constant 2. For realizing the outputs, add constant 0 lines for each output as shown in Figure 17 for sum output S and carry output C_o.

Step 2: Realize the product terms according to their increasing order as determined in Table 14. For the first product term $A^1 B^{+2} C^2$, generate 1-RPL A^1 using the method discussed in Section 7, that is, generate the effective shift $+1$ of the variable A by using a $+1$ 1-qudit gate along the variable A line and then add an M-S gate between the controlling line A and the constant 0 input line dedicated for generating 1-RPLs as shown in Figure 17. Generate the reversible literal B^{+2} by using a $+2$ 1-qudit gate along the line B as shown in Figure 17. Generate the 1-RPL C^2 similarly. The three literals are then multiplied by a 4-qudit Toffoli gate and added to the constant 0 line dedicated for the sum output S as shown in Figure 17.

For the second product term $A^1B^{+1}C^1$, the 1-RPL A^1 is already generated. Generate reversible literal B^{+1} along the line B using a +2 1-qudit gate in cascade with the previous 1-qudit gate +2. The new 1-qudit gate can be determined as shown in Table 15. In Table 15, the first column lists all possible values of input B, the second column lists the values produced by the previous reversible literal B^{+2}, and the third column lists the values to be produced by the needed reversible literal B^{+1}. Now, we need a 1-qudit gate that will generate the output of the third column taking input of the second column. A closer inspection of the second and third columns shows that the required 1-qudit gate is +2. Generate 1-RPL C^1 similarly. The already generated 1-RPL A^1 and the newly generated two literals B^{+1} and C^1 are then multiplied to produce the product term $A^1B^{+1}C^1$ and added this to the previous product term $A^1B^{+2}C^2$ using another 4-qudit Toffoli gate as shown in Figure 17. The other product terms of the GFSOP expressions are generated and summed in the similar ways as shown in Figure 17. In Figure 17, 1-RPLs of a variable are generated along the same constant 0 line dedicated for generating 1-RPLs of that variable. For example, 1-RPLs A^0, A^1, and A^2 are generated along the same line. Depending on the value of the variable A only one 1-RPL will be generated along the line, since all the controlling values will never be 3 simultaneously. However, 1-RPLs A^1 and A^2 are generated thrice and twice, respectively. This will create no problem, since they are part of different product terms, where the other literals are different.

Table 15. Generation of the reversible literal B^{+1} from the reversible literal B^{+2}

Input B	Output of the previous reversible literal B^{+2}	Output of the reversible literal B^{+1} to be generated
0	2	1
1	0	2
2	1	0

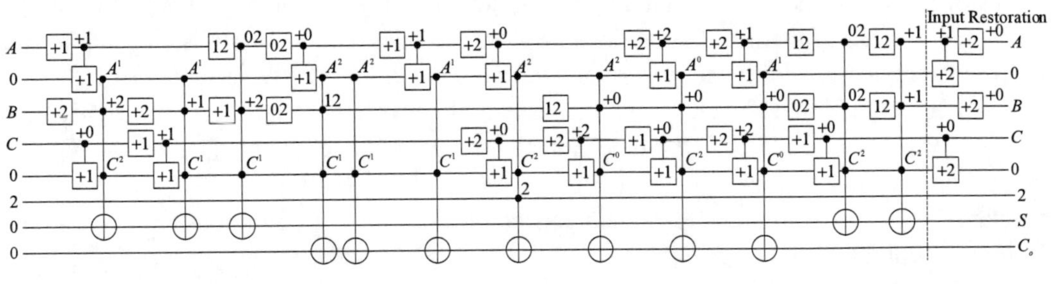

Figure 17. Realization of ternary GFSOP expressions of (29) and (30) using cascade of 1-qudit , M-S, Feynman , and Toffoli gates.

Step 3. Restore the inputs at the output to make the quantum circuit coherent. The last 1-RPL generated for the variable A is A^1. Generation of 1-RPL A^1 is done using an M-S gate with +1 effective shift of the variable A as controlling value and a +1 operation in the M-S gate. If we add another M-S gate with same controlling value and +2 operation, that is, +1 effective shift of the variable A and a +2 operation of the M-S gate, then the constant 0 input dedicated for generating 1-RPLs will be restored, since +1 + 2 = 0. The last effective shift of variable A is +1. If we add a +2 1-qudit gate along the line A, then the variable A will be restored, since $+1 + 2 = 0$. Restorations of all inputs are done similarly as shown in Figure 17. Input restoration is important for making the quantum circuit coherent and to reuse the same inputs in other parts of a larger quantum circuit. For example, this sort of input reuse is done in the oracles of Grover's quantum search algorithm [4, 5]

The GFSOP synthesis technique proposed here ensures that the literal that is used more than once is tried to be generated once and used in concerned product terms generations. This will eventually reduce the number of 1-qudit gates needed. Generating the literals along the same line, rather than using many copies of the variable, will reduce the width of the synthesized circuit.

11. Experimental Results

We have implemented the ternary and quaternary GFSOP minimization algorithms using C language on a PC. We have experimented with the following functions:

prod$n$: input $x_0, x_1, \cdots, x_{n-1}$; output $y = (x_0 x_1 \cdots x_{n-1})\,\mathrm{GF}(d)$. [Output is the $\mathrm{GF}(d)$ product of n input variables.]

sum$n$: input $x_0, x_1, \cdots, x_{n-1}$; output $y = (x_0 + x_1 + \cdots + x_{n-1})\,\mathrm{GF}(d)$. [Output is the $\mathrm{GF}(d)$ sum of n input variables.]

sqsum$n$: input $x_0, x_1, \cdots, x_{n-1}$; output $y = \left(x_0^2 + x_1^2 + \cdots + x_{n-1}^2\right)\mathrm{GF}(d)$. [Output is the $\mathrm{GF}(d)$ sum of squares of n input variables.]

avg$n$: input $x_0, x_1, \cdots, x_{n-1}$; output $y = \mathrm{int}[(x_0 + x_1 + \cdots + x_{n-1})/n]\,\mathrm{GF}(d)$. [Output is the integer part of the average of n input variables expressed $\mathrm{GF}(d)$ value.]

$n$cy$r$: input $x_0, x_1, \cdots, x_{n-1}$; output $y = x_0 x_1 \cdots x_{r-1} + x_1 x_2 \cdots x_r + \cdots + x_{n-1} x_0 \cdots x_{r-2}\ \mathrm{GF}(d)$. [A d-valued ($d \geq 3$) GFSOP function of n input variables, where the product terms consist of r input variables in cyclic order. For example, 3cy2 is $y(a,b,c) = (ab + bc + ca)\,\mathrm{GF}(d)$.]

hadd: d-valued ($d \geq 3$) half-adder.

hsub: d-valued ($d \geq 3$) half-subtractor

fadd: d-valued ($d \geq 3$) full-adder. For carry input $C_i > 1$, outputs are assumed to be 0.

fsub: d-valued ($d \geq 3$) full-subtractor. For borrow input $C_i > 1$, outputs are assumed to be 0.

Experimental results of 20 ternary functions are shown in Table 16. The experimental results show that a significant minimization over canonical GFSOP expression is achieved for prod$n$, sum$n$, sqsum$n$, and $n$cy$r$ functions and the minimizations of other functions are also quite satisfactory. Moreover, minimizations of prod$n$, sqsum$n$, sum2, and 4cy3 functions are exact minimization. Experimental results of 20 quaternary functions are shown in Table 17. The experimental results show that a significant minimization over canonical GFSOP expression is achieved for prod$n$, sum$n$, sqsum$n$, avg2, avg10, 4cy$n$, 10cy$n$, hsub functions and the minimizations of other functions are also quite satisfactory. Moreover, the minimizations of prod$n$ and sum$n$ functions are exact minimization.

Mozammel H.A. Khan

Table 16. Experimental results of ternary functions

Function name	Number of input	Number of output	Number of canonical products	Number of minimized product	% of minimization over canonical GFSOP
prod2	2	1	4	1	75.00
prod4	4	1	16	1	93.75
prod10	10	1	1024	1	99.90
sum2	2	1	6	2	66.67
sum4	4	1	54	10	81.48
sum10	10	1	39366	682	98.27
sqsum2	2	1	8	2	75.00
sqsum4	4	1	48	4	91.67
sqsum10	10	1	39528	10	99.97
avg2	2	1	6	5	16.67
avg4	4	1	50	31	38.00
avg10	10	1	34001	17589	48.27
4cy2	4	1	36	8	77.78
4cy3	4	1	42	4	90.48
10cy2	10	1	39204	79	99.80
10cy3	10	1	35802	74	99.79
hadd	2	2	9	5	44.44
hsub	2	2	9	5	44.44
fadd	3	2	21	12	42.86
fsub	3	2	21	12	42.86

Table 17. Experimental results of quaternary functions

Function name	Number of input	Number of output	Number of canonical products	Number of minimized product	% of minimization over canonical GFSOP
prod2	2	1	9	1	88.889
prod4	4	1	81	1	98.765
prod10	10	1	59049	1	99.998
sum2	2	1	12	2	83.333
sum4	4	1	192	4	97.917
sum10	10	1	786432	10	99.999
sqsum2	2	1	10	4	60.000
sqsum4	4	1	160	8	95.000
sqsum10	10	1	655360	20	99.997
avg2	2	1	8	4	50.000
avg4	4	1	221	134	39.367
avg10	10	1	985733	272945	72.310
4cy2	4	1	120	20	83.333
4cy3	4	1	122	8	93.443
10cy2	10	1	588288	272	99.954
10cy3	10	1	558560	260	99.535
hadd	2	2	18	11	38.889
hsub	2	2	19	9	52.632
fadd	3	2	40	25	37.500
fsub	3	2	40	25	37.500

12. Conclusion

Multiple-valued logic has many advantages over binary logic. The major advantage is that multiple-valued encoded realization of binary logic function is more compact than original binary realization. Multiple-valued quantum gates are realizable in current quantum technologies [7-14] and their costs are almost similar to the cost of binary quantum gates [9]. As the multiple-valued encoded realization of binary function is more compact, its quantum realization cost will be lesser than that of binary realization. This advantage makes multiple-valued reversible/quantum logic synthesis very promising. Successful methods for synthesis of multiple-valued quantum logic circuit also creates possibility of developing multiple-valued quantum algorithms as well as using multiple-valued quantum circuits internally in the binary quantum algorithms.

Multiple-valued logic functions can be very easily represented as GFSOP expression and the GFSOP expression can be realized as cascade of reversible gates. This approach uses Feynman and multiple-input Toffoli gates for the cascade. Previously, multiple-valued Toffoli gate realization required many ancilla constants [36, 43, 44] making the realized GFSOP based reversible/quantum logic circuit very wide. Ancilla input constant free realizations of d-valued ($d \geq 3$) Feynman and n-qudit ($n \geq 3$) Toffoli gates on the top of 1-qudit and M-S gates as presented in this chapter makes this GFSOP based synthesis more promising and practical than the earlier.

In this chapter, we have developed 16 ternary Galois field expansions (TGFE) and 10 quaternary GFEs (QGFE). Then, we have developed heuristic algorithm for minimization of non-reversible d-valued ($d \geq 3$) logic function as GFSOP expression using application of GFEs. After that, we have shown method for realization of multi-output GFSOP expressions as cascade of 1-qudit, M-S, Feynman, and Toffoli gates. To reduce the number of 1-qudit gates in the realization, we have developed literal ordering and product ordering techniques. The developed technique for GFSOP synthesis is such that the width of the synthesized reversible/quantum circuit and the total number of reversible/quantum gates required are as minimum as possible. The proposed GFSOP synthesis method also restores the inputs at the outputs making the quantum circuit coherent and providing possibility of reusing the inputs in other parts of a larger quantum circuit.

Experimental results of ternary and quaternary functions show a significant minimization over canonical GFSOP expressions. Some of the functions produce exact minimum results.

The proposed GFSOP synthesis method implicitly converts a non-reversible function into a reversible function for synthesis using reversible/quantum gates. The proposed method can be extended for any d-valued ($d \geq 3$) non-reversible logic function if GF(d) can be constructed, that is, if d is a prime or a prime power

The proposed GFSOP minimization method works with completely specified functions. In our experiments, we have replaced the don't care outputs by 0s. Further study can be done on value assignment for don't care outputs such that the method can take advantage of don't cares to further minimization of the incompletely specified functions.

As the realizations of Feynman and Toffoli gates do not require any ancilla input constant and the GFSOP synthesis method presented here uses as minimum copies of a variable as possible, the proposed synthesis method is suitable for quantum circuit synthesis with less ancilla input constants, which is a favorable and desirable attempt, since quantum register width is a major constraint in quantum technology.

References

[1]   Landauer, R. (1961). "Irreversibility and heat generation in the computational process," *IBM Journal of Research and Development*, vol. 5, 183-191.

[2]   Zhirnov, V. V., Kavin, R. K., Hutchby, J. A. & Bourianoff, G. I. (2003). "Limits to binary logic switching – a Gedanken model," *Proceeding of the IEEE*, vol. 91, no. 11, 1934-1939.

[3]   Bennett, C. H. (1973). "Logical reversibility of computation," *IBM Journal of Research and Development*, vol. 17, 525-532.

[4]   Nielsen, M. & Chuang, I. (2000). *Quantum Computation and Quantum Information*, Cambridge University Press.

[5]   Grover, L. K. (1996). "A fast quantum mechanical algorithm for database search," *Proceedings of 28th ACM Symposium on Theory of Computing*, 212-219.

[6]   Shor, P. W. (1994). "Algorithm for quantum computation: discrete logarithms and factoring," *Proceedings of 35th Annual Symposium on Foundations of Computer Science*.

[7]   Burlakov, A. V., Chekhova, M. V., Karabutova, O. V., Klyshko, D. N. & Kulik, S. P. (1999). "Polarization state of a biphoton: quantum ternary," *Physical Review A* **60**, R4209.

[8]   Muthukrishnan, A. & Stroud, C. R. (2000). Jr., "Multivalued logic gates for quantum computation," *Physical Review A*. vol. 62, 052309/1-8.

[9]   Bartlett, S., deGuise, D. & Sanders, B. (2002). "Quantum encodings in spin systems and harmonic oscillators," *Physical Review A*, **65**, 052316.

[10] Das, R., Mitra, A., Kumar, V. & Kumar, A. (2003). "Quantum information processing by NMR: Preparation of pseudo pure states and implementation of unitary operations in a single-qutrit system," *arXiv:quant-ph/0307240v1*, 31 July.

[11] Klimov, A. B., Guzman, R., Retamal, J. C. & Saavedra, C. (2003). "Qutrit quantum computer with trapped ions," *Physical Review A*, vol. 67, 062313.

[12] Daboul, J., Wang, X. & Sanders, B. C. (2003). "Quantum gates hybrid qudits," *Journal of Physics A: Mathematical and General*, vol. 36, no. 14, 7063-7078.

[13] Kunio, F. (2003). *"The controlled-U and unitary transformations in two-qudit,"* arXiv:quant-ph/0304078.

[14] McHugh, D. & Twamley, J. "Trapped-*ion qutrit spin molecule quantum computer*," http://arXiv.org/abs/quant-ph/0506031.

[15] Perkowski, M., Al-Rabadi, A. & Kerntopf, P. (2002). "Multiple-valued quantum logic synthesis," *Proceedings of 2002 International Symposium on New Paradigm VLSI Computing*, Sendai, Japan, December, 12-14, 41-47.

[16] Khan, M. H. A., Perkowski, M. A. & Kerntopf, P. (2003). "Multi-output Galois field sum of products synthesis with new quantum cascades," *Proceedings of 33rd IEEE International Symposium on Multiple-Valued Logic (ISMVL 2003)*, Tokyo, Japan, 16-19 May, 146-153.

[17] Al-Rabadi, A. N. (2004). "Quantum circuit synthesis using classes of GF(3) reversible fast spectral transforms," *Proceedings of 34th IEEE International Symposium on Multiple-Valued Logic (ISMVL 2004)*, Toronto, Canada, 19-22 May, 87-93.

[18] Curtis, E. & Perkowski, M. (2004). "A transformation based algorithm for ternary reversible logic synthesis using universally controlled ternary gates," *Proceeding of International Workshop on Logic and Synthesis (IWLS 2004)*, Tamecula, California, USA, 2-4 June.

[19] Denler, N., Yen, B., Perkowski, M. & Kerntopf, P. (2004). "Synthesis of reversible circuits from a subset of Muthukrishnan-Stroud quantum multi-valued gates," *Proceeding of International Workshop on Logic and Synthesis (IWLS 2004)*, Tamecula, California, USA, 2-4 June.

[20] Khan, M. H. A. & Perkowski, M. A. (2004). "Genetic algorithm based synthesis of multi-output ternary functions using quantum cascade of generalized ternary gates," *Proceedings of 2004 IEEE Congress on Evolutionary Computation (CEC 2004)*, Portland, Oregon, USA, 19-23 June, 2194-2201.

[21] Bullock, S. S., O'Leary, D. P. & Brennen, G. K. (2005). "Asymptotically optimal quantum circuits for d-level systems," *Physical Review Letters*, vol. 94, 230502.

[22] Khan, M. H. A., Perkowski, M. A., Khan, M. R. & Kerntopf, P. (2005). "Ternary GFSOP minimization using Kronecker decision diagrams and their synthesis with quantum cascades," *Journal of Multiple-Valued Logic and Soft Computing*, vol. 11, 567-602.

[23] Yen, B., Tomson, P. & Perkowski, M. (2005). "Sum of non-disjoint cubes covering generation for multi-valued systems of base 2, for use in Muthukrishnan-Stroud quantum realizable gates: an extension of the EXOR covering problem," *Proceedings of International Workshop on Logic and Synthesis (IWLS)*.

[24] Khan, M. H. A. & Perkowski, M. A. (2005). "Quantum realization of ternary encoder and decoder," *Proceedings of 7th International Symposium on Representations and Methodology of Future Computing Technologies (RM 2005)*, Tokyo, Japan, 5-6 September.

[25] Khan, M. M. R., Khan, M. H. A. & Akbar, M. M. (2005). "Evolutionary algorithm based synthesis of multi-output ternary reversible circuits using quantum cascades," *Proceedings of 7th International Symposium on Representations and Methodology of Future Computing Technologies (RM2005)*, Tokyo, Japan, 5-6 September.

[26] Yang, G., Song, X., Perkowski, M. & Wu, J. (2005). "Realizing ternary quantum switching networks without ancilla bits," *arXiv:quant-ph/0509192v1*, 27 Sep.

[27] Khan, F. S. & Perkowski, M. (2005). "Synthesis of ternary quantum logic circuits by decomposition," *arXiv:quant-ph/0511041v1*, 4 Nov.

[28] Miller, D. M., Maslove, D. & Dueck, G. W. (2006). "Synthesis of quantum multiple-valued circuits," *Journal of Multiple-Valued Logic and Soft Computing*, vol. 12, no. 5-6.

[29] Khan, M. H. A. (2006). "Design of reversible/quantum ternary multiplexer and demultiplexer," *Engineering Letters*, vol. 13, no. 2, 65-69.

[30] Khan, M. M. R., Sujan, M. G. A. & Khan, M. H. A. (2006). "Post-EA simplification of ternary reversible circuit," *Proceedings of 9th International Conference on Computer and Information Technology (ICCIT 2006)*, Dhaka, Bangladesh, 21-23 December.

[31] Kerntopf, P., Perkowski, M. A. & Khan, M. H. A. (2006). "On universality of general reversible multiple-valued logic gates", *Journal of Multiple-Valued Logic and Soft Computing*, vol. 12, no. 5-6, 417-429.

[32] Khan, M. H. A. & Perkowski, M. A. (2007). "Quantum ternary parallel adder/subtractor with partially-look-ahead carry," *Journal of System Architecture*, vol. 53, no. 7, 453-464.

[33] Khan, M. H. A. (2008). "Design of reversible/quantum ternary comparator circuits," *Engineering Letters*, vol. 16, no. 2, 178-184.

[34] Khanum, R., Kamal, T. & Khan, M. H. A. (2008). "Genetic algorithm based synthesis of ternary reversible/quantum circuit," *Proceedings of 11th International Conference on Computer and Information Technology (ICCIT 2008)*, 25-27 December, Khulna, Bangladesh, 270-275.

[35] Khan, M. M. M., Biswas, A. K., Chowdhury, S., Hasan, M. & Khan, A. I. (2009). "Synthesis of GF(3) based reversible/quantum logic circuits without garbage output," *Proceedings of 39th IEEE International Symposium on Multiple-Valued Logic (ISMVL 2009)*, Naha, Okinawa, Japan, 21-23 May, 98-102.

[36] Khan, M. H. A. & Perkowski, M. A. (2007). "GF(4) based synthesis of quaternary reversible/quantum logic circuits," *Journal of Multiple-Valued Logic and Soft Computing, vol. 13*, 583-603.

[37] Khan, M. H. A. (2007. "Reversible realization of quaternary decoder, multiplexer, and demultiplexer circuits," *Engineering Letters*, vol. 15, no. 2, 203-207).

[38] Khan, M. H. A. (2007). "Synthesis of incompletely specified multi-output quaternary function using quaternary quantum gates", *Proceedings of 10th International Conference on Computer and Information Technology (ICCIT 2007)*, Dhaka, Bangladesh, 27-29 December.

[39] Khan, M. H. A. (2008). "A recursive method for synthesizing quantum/reversible quaternary parallel adder/subtractor with look-ahead carry," *Journal of Systems Architecture*, vol. 54, no. 12, 1113-1121.

[40] Khan, M. H. A. (2008). "Synthesis of quaternary reversible/quantum comparators," *Journal of Systems Architecture*, vol. 54, no. 10, 977-982.

[41] Khan, M. H. A., Siddika, N. K. & Perkowski, M. A. (2008). "Minimization of quaternary Galois field sum of products expression for multi-output quaternary logic function using quaternary Galois field decision diagram," *Proceedings of 38th IEEE International Symposium on Multiple-Valued Logic (ISMVL 2008)*, 22-24 May, Dallas, TX, USA, 125-130.

[42] Khan, M. H. A. (2009). "Scalable architecture for synthesis of reversible quaternary multiplexer and demultiplexer circuits," *Proceedings of 39th IEEE International Symposium on Multiple-Valued Logic (ISMVL2009)*, 21-23 May, Naha, Okinawa, Japan, 343-348.

[43] Khan, M. H. A. (2004). "Quantum realization of ternary Toffoli gate using ion-trap realizable Muthukrishnan-Stroud primitive gates," *Proceedings of 7th International Conference on Computer and Information Technology (ICCIT 2004)*, Dhaka, Bangladesh, 26-28 Dec, 369-371.

[44] Khan, M. H. A. (2006). "Quantum realization of quaternary Feynman and Toffoli gates," *Proceedings of International Conference on Electrical and Computer Engineering (ICECE 2006)*, Dhaka, Bangladesh, 19-21 December, 157-160.

[45] Khan, A. I., Nusrat, N., Khan, S. M., Hasan, M. & Khan, M. H. (2007). "Quantum realization of some ternary circuits using Muthukrishnan-Stroud gates", *Proceedings of 37th IEEE International Symposium on Multiple-Valued Logic (ISMVL 2007)*, 14-16 May, Oslo, Norway.

[46] Khan, M. H. A. (2009). "Quantum realization of multiple-valued Feynman and Toffoli gates without ancilla input," *Proceedings of 39th IEEE International Symposium on Multiple-Valued Logic (ISMVL2009)*, 21-23 May, Naha, Okinawa, Japan, 103-108.

[47] Kalay, U., Hall, D. & Perkowski, M. (1998). *"A minimal and universal test set for multiple-valued Galois field sum-of-products circuits,"* Proceedings of 7th International Workshop on Post-Binary ULSI Systems (ULSIWS 19980, Fukuoka, Japan, May, pp. 50-51.

In: Computer Science Research and the Internet
Editor: Jaclyn E. Morris, pp. 109-132

ISBN: 978-1-61728-730-5
© 2011 Nova Science Publishers, Inc.

Chapter 4

QUANTUM SOLUTIONS FOR FUTURE SPACE COMMUNICATION

Laszlo Bacsardi[a], Laszlo Gyongyosi[b], Marton Berces[c] and Sandor Imre[d]

Department of Telecommunications, Budapest University of Technology
and Economics, Budapest, Hungary

Abstract

In the last decades quantum theory – a theory based on quantum mechanical principles – has appeared in space research. Quantum theory based communication offers answers for some of nowadays' technical questions in satellite communication. In our point of view, the quantum computing algorithms can be used to affirm our free-space communication in the following four ways: open-air communication, earth-satellite communications, satellite broadcast and inter-satellite communication. Quantum cryptography – cryptography based on quantum theory principles – gives better solutions for communication problems e.g. key distribution than the classical cryptographic methods, which have been found to have vulnerabilities in wired and wireless systems as well. The long distance quantum communication technologies in the future will far exceed the processing capabilities of current silicon-based devices. In current network technology, in order to spread quantum cryptography, interfaces able to manage together the quantum and classical channel must be implemented. Currently, the quantum cryptographic key generation systems (QKD) have been realized in metro-area networks over couple of ten kilometers The QKD can be used in wired or wireless (free-space) environment as well. The free-space based QKD solutions can achieve megabit-per-sec data rate communication. Long-distance open-air and satellite quantum communication experiments have been demonstrated the feasibility of extending quantum channel from ground to satellite, and in between satellites in free-space. The satellite based single photon links already allow QKD on global scale. In this chapter we introduce how the quantum principles will affect the world of space communication. We summarize the ideas from the past until present and show solutions to set up an efficient quantum channel for the quantum based satellite communication.

---

[a] E-mail address: bacsardi@hit.bme.hu
[b] E-mail address: gyongyosi@hit.bme.hu
[c] E-mail address: berces@hit.bme.hu
[d] E-mail address: imre@hit.bme.hu

1. Introduction

The history of space communication started more than 50 years ago. The humankind entered into the space age in the International Geophysical Year, with the successful launch of the first men-made satellite, the Sputnik-1 on October 4, 1957. [1] The little equipment with weight of 83.6 kg changed our view about the space forever. After less than 12 years the first man landed on the Moon. In the 70's we launched spacecrafts to explore the far universe (the Voyagers, the Pioneer 10, 11), and currently the Voyager-1 is the farthest man-made object from the Earth. [2]

In the 80's the Russian space station, the Mir was constructed. Now we have an International Space Station orbiting around the Earth, and the Americans, the Chinese, the Indians and the Europeans as well would like to go to the Moon, to the Mars and beyond that. But the exact date for that kind of long manned journey is still uncertain.

The first communication satellite was the Sputnik-1, which was equipped with an on-board radio-transmitter. The first American communication satellite was the SCORE (Signal Communications Orbit Relay Equipment), which broadcasted a Christmas greeting from U.S. President Eisenhower in 1958. However, it was just a relay satellite equipped with an onboard tape recorder. The first phone communication & TV broadcast via satellite was possible with launch of Echo-1 on February 4, 1962. The first commercial communication satellite, the Telstar-1 was launched July 10, 1962. The first geostationary satellite was the Syncom 3, launched on August 19, 1964, and it was used to relay experimental television coverage on the 1964 Summer Olympics in Tokyo, Japan to the United States. The first Indian communication satellite, the Aryabhata was launched on 19 April 1975. [3]

Until now hundreds of satellites have been launched, and we have many applications which are based on satellite communication. The global navigation, the weather forecast, the remote sensing, the telecommunication, the emergency alert system are just a few examples.

We use the satellite communication for many years, and nowadays we know its limits. This is why it is worth to examine the possible connection between the satellite communication and the quantum based communication.

For a well functioning communication, we need a channel coding to handle the errors appearing in a communication channel. In quantum computing the classical error coding methods cannot be used. This led to the development of quantum based error correction methods and algorithms. However, they are mostly based on quantum and not classical theorems [4]. Quantum communication in free-space can be implemented successfully, even if the measurement apparatus and quantum gates can cause error in the communication. Including the quantum gates, which being used to correct the errors of the quantum communication channel. To reach this goal, many fault-tolerant algorithms have been developed, and these methods make possible to use free-space quantum channel, and free-space QKD systems [5].

At present, the optical QKD is limited to a distance of approximately 100 km, however free-space quantum cryptography makes possible to transmit the photons in long distances. The free-space quantum communication can be extended to *ground-to-satellite* or *satellite-satellite* quantum communication, which could be an ideal application for global quantum cryptography. One of the main advantages of the usage of space for future quantum communication is the loss-free and distortion-free optical communication. In the space, the communication between satellites can exploit the advantages of vacuum, where the noise of the channel can be negligible. Entanglement can be used in satellite communication, to enhance the security level of key agreement process, and to realize a more secure communication compared to faint pulse QKD technology [4].

This chapter is organized as follows. In Section 2 we give some basics about the space communication. In Section 3 the details of the free-space quantum channel are discussed. In Section 4 we introduce the quantum key distribution which provides new ways to transmit information securely. Section 5 is about the present and future approaches in quantum space communication.

2. Space Communication

Since the first telephone call was made in the 19th century, telecommunications has gone through a lot of changes and became part of our everyday lives. Nowadays numerous alternative solutions exist for every aspect of electronic communications, such as telephone calls, text messages, email, etc. Beside these one way channels are also in use, such as television or radio. Many of these use satellites to operate. As they become more popular and available to more and more people it is vital to find more effective solutions for information transmission. Not to mention that for instance the geostationary orbit is almost full. Quantum information based systems can be a really effective way to exploit the hidden possibilities of the channels and satellites.

From our point of view the communication between two parties can be divided into the following four categories: open-air communication, earth-satellite communications, satellite broadcast and inter-satellite communication.

2.1. Communication Schemes

Open-air communication stands for the communication between two entities on ground, for instance two antenna towers. So in this case no satellite is involved but this scenario needs to be mentioned as we can gain useful channel models by experimenting in this environment. Apart from this there are different communication scenarios, as the usage of the satellites are various. When talking about satellite broadcast a central station sends the signal to the satellite directly from earth. After that, the satellites broadcast it back to the earth. The typical utility for this scheme is the television broadcast. That is done by geostationary satellites as they seem to be a single point in the sky that does not move at all.

Inter-satellite communication is when two satellites transmit data to each other. It can be implemented between any two satellites that are in line of sight.

Earth-satellite communication is when one party is the satellite the other one is an earth station.

2.2. Frequencies and Orbits

In the early days (1960-1970) the typical communication frequency was around a couple of tens and a couple of hundreds MHz. Later on it became a couple of GHz. Today's satellites usually transmit at 4 or 12GHz [6].

Satellites revolve around the Earth following circular or elliptical trajectories. These trajectories are called orbits. The most commonly used orbits are as follows [6]:

- Elliptical orbits with a 64 degree angel to the equatorial plane. This type of orbit was adopted by the USSR for the MOLYNA system with a period of 12 hours. Advantages of this orbit are: insensitivity of the irregularities of the terrestrial gravitational potential and the satellites can cover large areas of the high latitude when they pass to the apogee for a large faction of their orbital period. With a 12 hour orbital period this coverage is provided for 8 hours. Studies showed that with 8 satellites that have 8 hour orbital period the most important markets (East Asia, Europe, North America) can be entirely covered.
- Circular Low Earth Orbits (LEO). These orbits have a distance from the surface of several hundred kilometers and since it is circular, the attitude of the satellites is constant. It provides lower coverage and the orbit has nearly 90 degree inclination. Several tens of satellites can cover the entire globe providing real time communication.
- Circular Medium Earth Orbits (MEO). The radius is about 10 000 and the inclination about 50 degrees. With 10 or 15 satellites and 6 hour period a continuous coverage of the Earth can be provided.
- Circular orbits with zero inclination. The most popular is the geostationary orbit. That has 35 786 km elevation and the orbit period is exactly one day. This means that the satellite from the Earth look like a single point in the sky, allowing large number of users to receive the signal from it with cheap equipment. [7]

These orbits are shown in Figure 1.

2.3. Some Interesting Applications

The international long distance telephony was the first application of the satellite communication. Although we use submarine communication cables currently, there are several islands and regions where the satellite based transmission is the only way for the communication (like some regions of Africa, Antarctica, Australia, China, Russia, Australia). The satellite phones use either LEO or GEO orbit satellites.

The television companies use GEO orbit satellites for broadcasting different TV-channels to the customers. Two satellite types are used: the Fixed Service Satellites (FSS) and the Direct Broadcast Satellite. The FSS are used for broadcast feeds from a local station to the television network (e.g. live shots). The DBS transmit to small DBS satellite dishes (usually 45 to 60 cm in diameter).

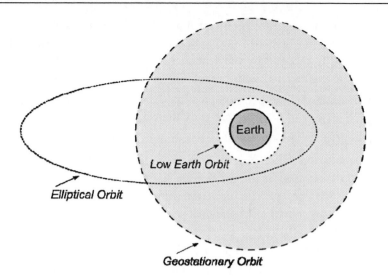

Figure 1. Illustrating different orbits around Earth.

One of the most well-known applications is the global navigation satellite system (GNSS). This is a space based navigation system which is providing reliable positioning services to worldwide users in all weather anywhere on the Earth or near the Earth, where four or more GPS satellites could be seen. The satellites broadcast signals which can be used by GPS receivers to provide three-dimensional location and a precise time. There are several GPS based applications in the field of location-based services, navigation, wildlife management, road pricing, geophysical sciences, rescue etc. Currently the NAVSTAR Global Positioning System is the only full operational GNSS which is operated by United Sates. The Russian GLONASS is in the process to being restored, the European Union's Galileo scheduled to be operational in 2014. China would like to expend its Beidou navigation system to a global system called Compass.

For the communication we can use satellite radio, which covers a much wider geographical range than the terrestrial radio. The amateur radio operators use special satellites (Orbiting Satellite Carrying Amateur Radio - OSCAR) which have been designed to transmit amateur radio traffic. But we can use the satellites to carry internet traffic, and many users who are located in remote areas can connect to the internet.

3. Free-Space Quantum Channel

In the physical realizations of quantum states, the space of the qubits is a continuous space, and the unitary transformations applied on the qubits, are also continuous transformations. The unitary quantum transformations have finite precision, and to realize an idealistic quantum channel, the qubits have to be perfectly isolated from its environment. In practical implementations, it is possible to correct the errors caused by decoherence, quantum noise and interaction with the environment [8].

In free-space quantum channel, the most important problems are the noise of free-space channel, and the long distance communication. However, the problem of preserving the state of qubits, and avoid the error of quantum gates and measurements can be corrected by quantum error correction algorithms. In quantum communications - similarly to classical systems -, the information is encoded into a message M, which represents a longer string of symbols s. The string is encoded by the sender, Alice. Alice uses a code alphabet of size n, and every symbols are associated with probability p_s. The sent symbols are decoded on the receiver side, by Bob. In quantum communication, Alice uses a quantum states to encode the information, which states can be represented by their density matrices ρ_s. The probability of a given density matrix ρ_s, represents the probability distribution p_s of the given message. Bob's decoding process on the other side, is made by measurements on each of the received quantum states. The outcomes of the measurements are real positive numbers, belonging to the same alphabet of size n. The communication over the quantum channel can be summarized as the communication of classical sources with random events, using a quantum channel for communication [9, 10].

If Alice sends classical information through the quantum channel, the alphabet of the quantum symbols used to code the classical information must be made of pure quantum states. The transmission of classical information over *satellite quantum channel* with no prior entanglement between the sender (Alice) and the recipient (Bob) is illustrated in Figure 2. The sender's classical information denoted by A_i encoded into a quantum state $|\psi_A\rangle$. The encoded quantum states are sent over the satellite quantum channel, In the decoding phase, Bob measures state $|\psi_A\rangle$, the outcome of the measurement is the classical information B_i.

A qubit can be described by the two-dimensional Hilbert space $\mathbb{C}^2$, and the operators acting on the quantum system is generated by the Pauli matrices,

$$\sigma_x = \begin{pmatrix} 0 & 1 \\ 1 & 0 \end{pmatrix}, \ \sigma_y = \begin{pmatrix} 0 & -i \\ i & 0 \end{pmatrix}, \ \sigma_z = \begin{pmatrix} 1 & 0 \\ 0 & -1 \end{pmatrix}. \tag{1}$$

In generally, for a Pauli matrix σ_k, $Tr(\sigma_k) = 0$ and $\sigma_k^2 = I$, where $k = x, y, z$. The set of states for a qubit in the computational basis $\{|0\rangle, |1\rangle\}$, is the *eigenbasis* of σ_z, thus $\sigma_z |0\rangle = |0\rangle$ and $\sigma_z |1\rangle = -|1\rangle$. A generic *pure* state can be given by

$$|\psi\rangle = \alpha|0\rangle + \beta|1\rangle, \tag{2}$$

and the *projector* of the state is $|\psi\rangle\langle\psi| = \frac{1}{2}(1 + \hat{n} \cdot \vec{\sigma})$, where $\hat{n}$ is the *Bloch vector*, and it can be given by $\hat{n} = (2\operatorname{Re}(\alpha\beta^*), 2\operatorname{Im}(\alpha\beta^*), |\alpha|^2 - |\beta|^2)$. For *pure* state the *norm* of Bloch vector is 1, and these vectors cover the Bloch sphere [9].

The *pure* quantum states of a *two-level* system can be given by unit vectors in spherical coordinates,

$$|\psi\rangle = \cos\frac{\theta}{2}|0\rangle + e^{i\varphi}\sin\frac{\theta}{2}|1\rangle \tag{3}$$

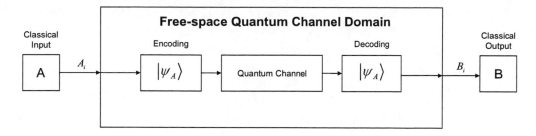

Figure 2. Transmission classical information through the free-space quantum channel.

The state $|\psi\rangle$ can be given by state $|+\hat{n}\rangle$, and it is the eigenstate for the eigenvalue $+1$ of $\hat{n}\cdot\vec{\sigma}$, with $\hat{n}=\hat{n}(\theta,\varphi)=(\sin\theta\cos\varphi,\sin\theta\sin\varphi,\cos\theta)$ where $\theta\in[0,\pi]$ and $\varphi\in[0,2\pi]$. A ρ *mixed* state can be expressed by a $|\psi\rangle\langle\psi|=\dfrac{1}{2}(\mathbf{1}+\hat{n}\cdot\vec{\sigma})$ projector on a *pure* quantum state.

The quantum states sent to quantum channel can be represented by their density matrix. We denote by $\mathbf{S}(\mathbb{C}^d)$ the space of all density matrices of size $d\times d$, and we call it a *d-level* system [8, 11]. A one-qubit system is a *two-level* system [12], and its density matrix can be expressed as

$$\rho=\begin{pmatrix}\dfrac{1+z}{2} & \dfrac{x-iy}{2}\\[2mm]\dfrac{x+iy}{2} & \dfrac{1-z}{2}\end{pmatrix},\ x^2+y^2+z^2\leq1,\ x,y,z\in\mathbb{R}. \qquad (4)$$

Alice's pure quantum state can be expressed by a density matrix ρ_A, whose rank is one, while a state with rank two is called *mixed*. According to the noise $\mathcal{N}$ of quantum channel, Alice's sent pure quantum state becomes a mixed state, thus Bob will receive a mixed state denoted by σ_B. A pure state has special meaning in quantum information theory and it is on the *boundary of the convex object*. A density matrix which is *not pure* is called *mixed state*.

For one-qubit states, the condition for ρ to be pure is simply expressed as $x^2+y^2+z^2=1$, and it is on the surface of the Bloch ball [12].

In Figure 3. we illustrated the general model of noisy quantum channel.

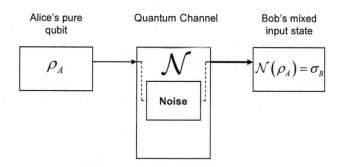

Figure 3. General model of a noisy quantum channel.

The map of the quantum channel is a trace-preserving and completely positive map, and it can be given by a linear transform $\mathcal{N}$ which maps quantum states to quantum states. The noise of the channel can be modeled by a linear transform

$$\mathcal{N}: M(\mathbb{C};d) \to M(\mathbb{C};d) \tag{5}$$

where $\mathcal{N}\left(\rho\left(\mathbb{C}^d\right)\right) \subset \rho\left(\mathbb{C}^d\right)$. Thus, if Alice sends quantum state $\rho(x,y,z)$ on the quantum channel, the channel maps it as follows:

$$\left\{ (x',y',z') \middle| \rho'(x',y',z') = \mathcal{N}\left(\rho(x,y,z)\right), (x,y,z) \right\}. \tag{6}$$

The image of quantum channel's linear transform $\mathcal{N}$ is an ellipsoid. To preserve the condition for density matrix ρ, the eavesdropper's cloning transformation $\mathcal{N}$ must be trace-preserving, i.e. $Tr\mathcal{N}(\rho) = Tr(\rho)$, and it must be completely positive, i.e. for any identity map I, the map $\mathcal{N} \otimes I$ maps a semi-positive Hermitian matrix into a semi-positive Hermitian matrix. Thus, in our satellite communication based, the channel is modeled by a *TPCP* map [13].

The capacity of the satellite channel $C(\mathcal{N})$ for given noise $\mathcal{N}$, can be defined as follows [9, 10]:

$$C(\mathcal{N}) = \max_{p_1,\ldots,p_n,\rho_1,\ldots,\rho_n} S\left(\mathcal{N}\left(\sum_{i=1}^{n} p_i(\rho_i) \right) \right) + \sum_{i=1}^{n} p_i S(\mathcal{N}(\rho_i)), \tag{7}$$

where $S(\rho) = -\rho \log \rho$ is the von-Neumann entropy.

4. Free-Space Quantum Key Distribution

In present classical cryptographic methods, the key exchange is generally based on public key methods. The security of modern cryptographic methods like asymmetric cryptography, relies heavily on the problem of factoring integers. In the future, if *quantum computers* become reality, any information exchange using current classical cryptographic schemes will be immediately insecure. Current classical cryptographic methods are not able to guarantee long-term security. Other cryptographic methods, with absolute security must be applied in the future.

Quantum cryptography provides new ways to transmit information securely, using the fundamental principles of quantum-mechanics. As classical cryptography uses and manipulates classical bits, quantum cryptography does the same with qubits, to realize provably, *absolute secure* communication [14, 15]. In quantum cryptographic schemes, the secret information is not encoded directly into the quantum states, the qubits are used only to generate a secret cryptographic key, shared between two legal parties, called Alice and Bob. The main idea behind the quantum cryptographic protocols was the absolute secure key distribution, hence we rather call these cryptographic methods as *Quantum Key Distribution (QKD)* systems.

The QKD schemes will have a deep relevance in future's secure space quantum communication, because these cryptographic systems can provide unbreakable quantum communication. As we can conclude, there exist several fields, where private information must be send through a *free-space* quantum communication channel. The QKD schemes solve the problem of key exchange, however to provide provably safeness, some security steps are integrated after the process of quantum-based key exchange [d13]. Using quantum cryptography, the safety of future's space communication against various forms of possible attacks can be guaranteed.

Using free-space quantum channel, an absolutely invulnerable quantum communication can be implemented for long distances, and for global spreading of QKD systems. In this section, we discuss the three basic QKD protocols, namely the *BB84* protocol, *B92* protocol and the *EPR-based QKD* protocol. The QKD protocols are symmetric cryptographic systems, where the action of encryption, transforms the original message into an encoded message. The reverse operation of encryption is called decryption, which decodes the encoded message into the original message. The decryption operation is based on a secret key, which key is symmetric, hence the sender and the receiver have the same one to encode and decode the given message. In classical cryptography, the provably secure *OTP* (*One-Time Pad*) cryptography can not be realized in practice without the problem of sharing long keys. However, classical cryptography without key exchange was solved by using asymmetric keys. These asymmetric public-key cryptosystems are not provably secure systems, and using quantum computers, these schemes *will be broken* easily in the future.

Contrary to classical cryptography, quantum cryptography means distributing secret keys over a public communication channel, and not encrypting and decrypting of qubits. The QKD protocols' main task is to realize an absolute secure *key exchange* process on the quantum channel. In future space communication, the free-space channel is a communication channel involving long distances. The free-space QKD implementations use photons, the elementary particles of light to realize quantum bits. The polarization states of photons are related to the logical values of quantum states, and the particles of special photon-pairs can form entanglement [9].

In this section, we overview the working mechanism of three basic QKD protocols, and they applications in future space communication, finally we discuss the relevant physical free-space QKD implementations.

4.1. Behind the Security of QKD Schemes

The security of QKD schemes relies on the *no-cloning* theorem [16]. Contrary to classical information, in a quantum communication system the quantum information cannot be copied perfectly. If Alice sends a number of photons $|\psi_1\rangle, |\psi_2\rangle, ..., |\psi_N\rangle$ through the free-space quantum channel, an eavesdropper is not interested in copying an arbitrary state, only the possible polarization states of the attacked QKD scheme. To copy the sent quantum state, an eavesdropper has to use a quantum cloner machine, and a known "*blank*" state $|0\rangle$, onto which the eavesdropper would like to copy Alice's quantum state. If Eve wants to copy the *i*-th sent photon $|\psi_i\rangle$, she has to apply a unitary transformation U, which gives the following result:

$$U\left(|\psi_i\rangle\otimes|0\rangle\right)=|\psi_i\rangle\otimes|\psi_i\rangle,\tag{8}$$

for each polarization states of qubit $|\psi_i\rangle$. As it has been proven by the no-cloning theorem, a photon chosen from a given set of polarization states can be cloned perfectly only, if the polarization angles in the set that are distinct, are all mutually orthogonal [16]. As we can conclude, the quantum states in the QKD schemes can be copied perfectly only, if the quantum states are related to each other as the classical bits related to each other.

The unknown non-orthogonal states cannot be cloned perfectly, the cloning process of the quantum states is possible only if the information being cloned is classical, hence the quantum states are all orthogonal. The polarization states in the QKD protocols are not all orthogonal states, which makes no possible to an eavesdropper to copy the sent quantum states [16].

In Figure 4. we illustrated Eve's quantum cloner on the quantum channel. Alice's pure state is denoted by ρ_A, the eavesdropper's quantum cloner transformation is denoted by $\mathcal{L}$. The mixed state received by Bob, is represented by σ_B.

An eavesdropper has no a priori information about the bases of the polarization states, hence Eve has to measure each photon in a random basis. Eve might try partial cloning, and better copying strategies, but she has no chance to clone the whole key perfectly, only a small set of the final can be copied by Eve.

The fundamental property behind the security of QKD schemes is, that it is not possible to an eavesdropper to eavesdrop the quantum channel without the fact, that the legal parties Alice and Bob becoming aware of it. An eavesdropper cannot intercept the sent qubits successfully, however Eve may have luck, and she can re-generate some intercepted qubits in the same bases. An other possible attack could be the man-in-the-middle attack, however the attack works only for a small subset of the whole key. Statistically, the success probability of an eavesdropper's attack against QKD schemes decreases *exponentially*, as the legal parties increment *linearly* the length of the qubit string. To increase the security of key exchange process, an extra phase integrated into the QKD schemes, which contains two extra phases, called *information reconciliation* and *privacy amplification* [14, 15].

4.2. The BB84 Protocol

The first QKD protocol was the *BB84* protocol, the inventors of the protocol were C. H. Bennett and G. Brassard, and they published their solution in 1984 [5].

In the general model of free-space BB84 protocol, Alice, the sender sends light signals to Bob, using free-space optics devices. Alice and Bob have single-photon sources, and they can produce photons in any polarization states $|\leftrightarrow\rangle,|\updownarrow\rangle,|\nearrow\rangle,|\nwarrow\rangle$ using rectilinear $\{|\leftrightarrow\rangle,|\updownarrow\rangle\}$ and diagonal $\{|\nearrow\rangle,|\nwarrow\rangle\}$ bases. Alice and Bob make their photon-measurements independently in the two bases, chosen randomly. The measurements in the rectilinear or diagonal bases can be described in the terms of basic Pauli-transformations Z, and X [5].

In the first step, Alice puts the random-generated polarized photon sequence through the free-space quantum channel. In this phase, Alice encodes logical 0 by polarization state $|\leftrightarrow\rangle$

or $\left|\nearrow\right\rangle$ at random, and similarly she encodes logical 1 using polarization states $\left|\updownarrow\right\rangle$ or $\left|\searrow\right\rangle$, chosen randomly [5].

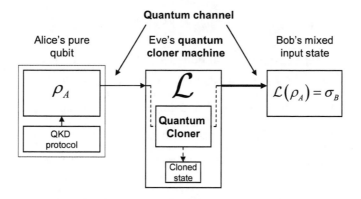

Figure 4. The eavesdropper's quantum cloner on the quantum channel.

The random bases and the random logical bits can be described by two random sequences $B=(b_1,b_2,...b_N)$ and $L=(l_1,l_2,...l_N)$, where b_i is the *basis* of the i-th qubit, and l_i is the *logical value* of the i-th random qubit. Each of the two sequences are $N=(4+\Delta)n$ bits length, where Δ is a small integer number. Using these initial $N=(4+\Delta)n$ length sequences, after the key agreement phase, the desired key length is *2n* [5]. Using sequences $B=(b_1,b_2,...b_N)$ and $L=(l_1,l_2,...l_N)$, Alice generates an N-length qubit sequence as follows [5, 17]:

$$\left|\psi\right\rangle = \left|\psi_{b_1l_1}\right\rangle \otimes \left|\psi_{b_2l_2}\right\rangle \otimes...\otimes \left|\psi_{b_Nl_N}\right\rangle$$
$$= \bigotimes_{i=1}^{N}\left|\psi_{b_il_i}\right\rangle, \tag{9}$$

where $\left|\psi_{b_il_i}\right\rangle$ denotes the i-th qubit, encoded in basis b_i, with logical value l_i. Alice generates the i-th single qubit $\left|\psi_{b_il_i}\right\rangle$ according to the BB84 qubit-photon encoding convention:

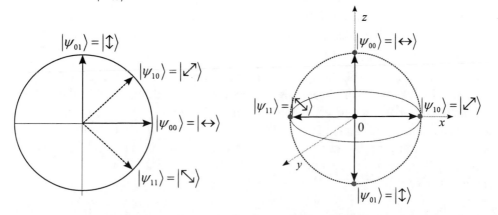

Figure 5. The four possible polarization states of BB84 protocol.

$$|\psi_{00}\rangle = |\leftrightarrow\rangle,$$
$$|\psi_{01}\rangle = |\updownarrow\rangle,$$
$$|\psi_{10}\rangle = |\nearrow\rangle,$$
$$|\psi_{11}\rangle = |\searrow\rangle.$$

(10)

We note, that other possible conventions can be used in the protocol. The basis state $b_i = 0$ encodes the logical bit l_i in the quantum basis $\{|\leftrightarrow\rangle, |\updownarrow\rangle\}$, and $b_i = 1$ encodes bit l_i in the basis $\{|\nearrow\rangle, |\searrow\rangle\}$. The logical bit $l_i = 0$ determines the choice of state to $|\leftrightarrow\rangle$ or $|\nearrow\rangle$, and similarly, $l_i = 1$ restrict the state space into polarization states $|\updownarrow\rangle$ or $|\searrow\rangle$. After the encoding process, Alice puts the N-qubit length string $|\psi\rangle$ on the free-space quantum channel [5].

In Figure 5. we illustrated the four possible polarization states of BB84 protocol.

In the next phase, Bob, at the end of the free-space quantum channel, receives the photons and makes a measurement on every photon, according to his random choice of *rectilinear* $\{|\leftrightarrow\rangle, |\updownarrow\rangle\}$ or *diagonal* $\{|\nearrow\rangle, |\searrow\rangle\}$ bases. The measurements in these bases can be viewed as a random choice between Pauli transformations Z and X, and the correct measurement with *+1* eigenvalue represents the correct choice, and a *-1* measurement will be called a wrong measurement. In the right measurements, Bob has chosen the same basis as Alice, in the wrong measurements the bases are differ, and these wrong measurements result 0 bit information. The right basis choices corresponds to measuring $|\updownarrow\rangle$ and $|\leftrightarrow\rangle$ with Z basis, and $|\nearrow\rangle, |\searrow\rangle$ with X basis [5]. The right basis choices of Bob give correct logical state, however in the case of wrong basis choice, Bob's bits will be random. The results of wrong measurements are not correlated to Alice's original sequence.

If Alice sent $|\psi\rangle$ to the free-space channel, then Bob will receive the state $\rho = \mathcal{N}(|\psi\rangle\langle\psi|)$, where $\mathcal{N}$ characterizes the noise of the channel. Bob produces a random sequence $B' = (b_1', b_2', \ldots b_N')$ of length $N = (4+\Delta)n$, which represents the chosen bases of his measurements. In this sequence, $b_i' = 0$ represents the Z-measurement basis, and $b_i' = 1$ represents the X-measurement basis. In this phase, Bob has only 50% chance to choose the right basis, and the results of his measurements will generate a random sequence $L' = (l_1', l_2', \ldots l_N')$ of length $N = (4+\Delta)n$ [5, 17].

In the next phase, Bob tells Alice his measurement-basis sequence, using a public communication channel. Bob keeps his bits he has measured, in secret. After Bob has sent the measurement-basis sequence, Alice will know the right choices of Bob. Alice uses the public channel to send back to Bob a logical sequence, which tells to Bob, where his measurements were right, and which logical bits are to be discarded. After this step, Bob and Alice will have a bit sequence, which contains those bits, where they have used the *same* measurement bases.

Using the public channel, the wrong logical bits could be discarded from sequences $L = (l_1, l_2, \ldots l_N)$ and $L' = (l'_1, l'_2, \ldots l'_N)$. It has been proven, that with a sufficiently large sequence $N = (4 + \Delta)n$, the valid bits in sequences L and L' are at least $2n$, with high probability [5].

As we can conclude, the probability of Bob choosing the right measurement basis is only fifty percent, and if Alice sends a longer sequence through the free-space quantum channel, the valid and the discarded bit sequence will be longer. The final key represents a shared secret key, which key can be used to encrypt and decrypt messages over a classical channel, thus the shared secret quantum key can be used in classical crypto algorithms. The key can be applied for one-time-pad (OTP) encoding and decoding, or it can be used in other classical cryptosystems, like Data Encryption Standard (DES) and Advanced Encryption Standard (AES)[9].

4.2.1. Improving Security Level of Quantum Key Distribution

The logical sequences $L = (l_1, l_2, \ldots l_N)$ and $L' = (l'_1, l'_2, \ldots l'_N)$ with length $2n$, represents the logical states of quantum bits, where Alice and Bob have chosen the same bases. For a noiseless and idealistic free-space quantum channel, the sequences L and L' are perfectly match, but in practice, according the noise of quantum channel or an eavesdropper Eve, these bits of two sequences might have been modified. To discard the corrupted bits, Alice selects a random subset of n bits from her sequence $L = (l_1, l_2, \ldots l_N)$, and sends it to Bob over the public channel, which channel is assumed to be error-free. This step is called *information reconciliation* phase. In this phase, Bob receives the sequence, and compares the corresponding n-bit subset of his sequence $L' = (l'_1, l'_2, \ldots l'_N)$. In the next phase, Bob tells Alice the number of errors in the n-bit length subset of previously detected key, over the public channel. If the number of errors is over a certain threshold, the parties abort the protocol, otherwise they use the agreed key with error-correction techniques.

However, in this phase, an eavesdropper could be able to derive some partial information about the key, thus Alice and Bob will sacrifice a smaller secret key from the remaining n-bit length string. This final step is called as *privacy amplification*, and in this phase Alice and Bob can be sure, that an eavesdropper's information about their secret key is approximately zero [5].

The techniques of *information reconciliation* and *privacy amplification* give a higher level to the quantum secret key agreement process, the effectiveness and importance of these techniques in the security of QKD systems have been proven mathematically [17].

4.3. The B92 Protocol

C. H. Bennett, one of the invertors of the first QKD protocol, in 1992 published the simplified version of the four state BB84 protocol [18]. The B92 protocol based on the fundamental principles of quantum mechanics like BB84, however it uses *only two* polarization states.

Similarly to BB84, in the first step Alice generates a random sequence $B = (b_1, b_2, \ldots b_N)$ of $N = (4 + \Delta) n$ bit length, and an N-length qubit string:

$$
\begin{aligned}
|\psi\rangle &= |\psi_{b_1}\rangle \otimes |\psi_{b_2}\rangle \otimes \ldots \otimes |\psi_{b_N}\rangle \\
&= \bigotimes_{i=1}^{N} |\psi_{b_i}\rangle,
\end{aligned}
\tag{11}
$$

where b_i is the basis of the i-th qubit [4]. The i-th qubit $|\psi_{b_i}\rangle$ in the string is generated according to B92 coding convention, as

$$
\begin{aligned}
|\psi_0\rangle &= |\leftrightarrow\rangle, \\
|\psi_1\rangle &= |\nearrow\rangle.
\end{aligned}
\tag{12}
$$

In Figure 6. we illustrated the two possible polarization states of B92 protocol.

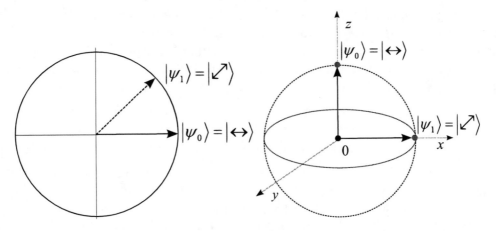

Figure 6. The two possible polarization states of B92 protocol.

After Alice has sent the photon-string through the quantum channel, Bob receives the block $|\psi\rangle$, and produces his random string $B' = (b_1', b_2', \ldots b_N')$ of length $N = (4 + \Delta) n$. In the measurement process, Bob chooses rectilinear basis $\{|\leftrightarrow\rangle, |\updownarrow\rangle\}$ if $b_i' = 0$, and diagonal basis $\{|\nearrow\rangle, |\searrow\rangle\}$ if $b_i' = 1$. The outcome of Bob's measurement is a random bit sequence of $L' = (l_1', l_2', \ldots l_N')$ of length $N = (4 + \Delta) n$ [18].

If Bob chooses the right bases Z and X to measure states $|\psi_0\rangle = |\leftrightarrow\rangle$ and $|\psi_1\rangle = |\nearrow\rangle$, the outcome of the measurement will be deterministic, since in either cases Bob will obtain logical value $l_i' = 0$. On the other hand, if Bob uses wrong basis, thus $b_i \neq b_i'$, then his outcome will *randomly* $l_i' = 0$ or $l_i' = 1$, with equal probability 50%.

In the B92 protocol - contrary to BB84 -, the information about the right bases should not to be exchanged publicly, because if Bob measures $l_i' = 1$, he will be sure that he made a *wrong* measurement. Bob tells to Alice only his logical bit sequence $L' = (l'_1, l'_2, ... l'_N)$ over the public channel, while keeping the measurement-basis sequence $B' = (b'_1, b'_2, ... b'_N)$ in *secret*.

Only the basis pairs b_i, b'_i yielding Bob's logical value $l'_i = 1$, will be retained by Alice and Bob. The operation generates two logical subsets of measurement sequences with at least *2n* valid bits, and the public knowledge of the logical bits $l'_i = 1$, does not tell an eavesdropper anything about the values of bases b_i, b'_i, which have equal probabilities of being 0 or 1 [18]. The security steps, like information reconciliation and privacy amplification is the same as that of BB84 [5, 17].

4.4. Entanglement-based Quantum Key Distribution

Entanglement has deep relevance in quantum communications, and especially in free-space quantum communication. The phenomena of entanglement can be integrated into QKD systems, the entangled EPR or Bell states can be physically generated by entangled photons. The idea of entanglement-based quantum cryptography was first published by Arthur K. Ekert, in 1991 [19].

In the entanglement based QKD scheme, Alice and Bob share an ensemble of $N = (4 + \Delta)n$ entangled-states, based on one of the four Bell-states, for example:

$$|\beta_{00}\rangle = \frac{|00\rangle + |00\rangle}{\sqrt{2}} \qquad (13)$$

The shared *N*-length state $|\psi\rangle$ can be expressed as the tensor product of the EPR-states as:

$$|\psi\rangle = |\beta_{00}\rangle_1 \otimes |\beta_{00}\rangle_2 \otimes ... \otimes |\beta_{00}\rangle_N$$
$$= \bigotimes_{i=1}^{N} |\beta_{00}\rangle_i = \frac{1}{\sqrt{2^N}} (|00\rangle + |11\rangle)^{\otimes N}. \qquad (14)$$

In Figure 7. we illustrated the schematic model of entanglement based QKD.

In the EPR-based QKD scheme, the legal parties measure the photons in rectilinear base $\{|\leftrightarrow\rangle, |\updownarrow\rangle\}$, or in diagonal base $\{|\nearrow\rangle, |\nwarrow\rangle\}$, using optical devices. After the measurements, they will keep only those qubits, where the bases were the same.

Similarly to BB84 and B92 protocols, Alice and Bob generate a random measurement-basis sequences $B = (b_1, b_2, ... b_N)$ and $B' = (b'_1, b'_2, ... b'_N)$, of length $N = (4 + \Delta)n$. The outcomes of the measurements generate the random logical-bit sequences $L = (l_1, l_2, ... l_N)$ and $L' = (l'_1, l'_2, ... l'_N)$.

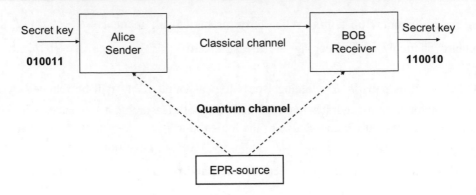

Figure 7. Entanglement based QKD protocol.

In the measurement process of the i-th entangled state $\left|\beta_{00}\right\rangle_i$, if Alice uses basis $\{\left|\leftrightarrow\right\rangle,\left|\updownarrow\right\rangle\}$ to measure her first qubit, she will collapse Bob's qubit into $\left|\psi\right\rangle_B = \left|\leftrightarrow\right\rangle$ or $\left|\psi\right\rangle_B = \left|\updownarrow\right\rangle$, and the logical value of her measurement will be $l_i = 0$ or $l_i = 1$, with equal probability.

On the other hand, if Alice uses diagonal basis $\{\left|\nearrow\right\rangle,\left|\searrow\right\rangle\}$ to measure her first quantum bit, she will collapse Bob's state into $\left|\psi\right\rangle_B = \left|\nearrow\right\rangle$ or $\left|\psi\right\rangle_B = \left|\searrow\right\rangle$, and the logical value of her measurement will be randomly $l_i = 0$ or $l_i = 1$.

The collapse of Bob's qubit is based on the *nonlocality property* of entangled quantum states. In the next phase, if Bob make a measurement on his collapsed state $\left|\psi\right\rangle_B$ with the same basis as Alice's, then the logical value of his measurement l_i' will exactly match with Alice's logical bit l_i [11, 19].

After Bob's measurements, Alice and Bob compare the measurement bases b_i, b_i' and they will keep only the logical bits l_i, l_i' where $b_i = b_i'$. As we can conclude, the steps of EPR-based QKD scheme are very similar to BB84, however the parties have to share a set of entangled states before the communication [11, 19].

We note, that in practical free-space quantum communication, implementation of entanglement-based QKD could be a more complex issue, than single qubit communication, however the error-sensitivity of single qubit communication could be decreased [20, 21].

4.5. Physical QKD Implementations

In the physical QKD implementations, the errors caused by quantum channel noise are unavoidable, even if there is no eavesdropping activity on the quantum channel. The free-space quantum channels are not idealistic quantum channels, thus the advanced quantum error-correction methods plays a fundamental role in the achievability of implemented QKD protocols. To increase the security level of these protocols, the legal parties assume, that all of the errors were caused by the eavesdropper's quantum cloner machine, and they make some security steps after the first round of key agreement.

The quantum key distribution schemes can be used in two ways, because these QKD protocols can be implemented as a One-Time-Pad encoder and decoder, and they can be integrated into classical cryptographic methods, like DES, AES. In a larger free-space communication network, QKD schemes can be situated somewhere within the lower layer of the global network security architecture. The QKD-based key agreement in the lower network layers, provide a *provably secure* key agreement, and the agreed key can be used by the classical crypto algorithms in the higher level of the architecture [15].

As we have showed, the secret key agreement phase of the QKD schemes is not always identical, thus the legal parties have to do some further security processing and error-correction. These steps are called as information reconciliation and privacy amplification, which phases have deep, and mathematically proven relevance in the security of QKD schemes.

The physical free-space implementations of the discussed BB84, B92 and EPR-based QKD protocols are all have to face with the problem of long distance quantum communication. In the physical implementations, the main issue is to protect the coherence of the polarization states, however the perturbation of physical devices and the communication over the free-space channel causes decoherence. The decoherence of quantum systems is an elementary nature of physical implementations, and it is an unavoidable property of quantum communication systems. We note, that the negative effects of decoherence can be eased by using quantum error correction algorithms. The quantum error correction schemes have a deep relevance in free-space quantum communication to avoid quantum channel noise, and these approaches are applicable to QKD protocols.

The laboratory implementations of free-space QKD systems are based on photons, which photons are sent through the air. The free-space QKD communication was implemented successfully, for example by Gisin et al. in 2002, Dusek et al. in 2006, Lo, Popescu and Spiller in 2001 or Bouwmeester, Ekert and Zeilinger in 2000 [4, 13]. In Germany, free-space QKD was implemented over 23.4 km. In future QKD experiments, this distance can be extended to range more than 100 kilometers. The ground free-space QKD approaches can be combined with satellite communication, and a secure key exchange can be realized between any two arbitrary locations on the globe in the future [8, 22].

5. Present and Future Quantum Approaches in Space Communication

The present quantum approaches in space communication mostly used for secure key exchanging. The current free-space and satellite QKD schemes use *weak laser pulses*, instead of single photon communication. The logical values of the quantum bits are encoded by photon polarizations, using multilaser sources and optical receiver units.[22].The proposed satellite based quantum key distribution scheme used optical devices, improved spatial filtering and narrowband passfilter to control the transmitter lasers. In this free-space QKD implementation, the error rate was below 6%, and the polarization preparation devices and analysis modules were stable [22, 23].

5.1. Satellite Quantum Key Distribution

Using low, medium and geostationary satellite systems, the future's free-space quantum communication should be able to realize secret key agreement over long distances, and QKD can be extended to achieve global quantum data protection. The future free-space satellite QKD schemes can be applied basically in two schemes [24, 25]:

1. Global quantum key distribution based on *satellite-to-ground* faint pulse quantum communication,
2. Simultaneous key generation between ground stations using *EPR-based* QKD scheme.

In Figure 8. we illustrated the schematic of a *global key exchange* QKD system in free-space. The global key free-space QKD scheme uses symmetric key encoding at the space satellite modules, and the decoding process is implemented at ground level. According to the security requirements of free-space communication, the global key free-space method requires the generation of new keys regularly. In this scheme, QKD is applied during the key upload to satellites, which key will be used by the satellite module to data scrambling. The satellites scramble the transmitted data to the licensed users only, and in this process, a QKD based key can be applied efficiently to ensure the advantages of quantum mechanics.

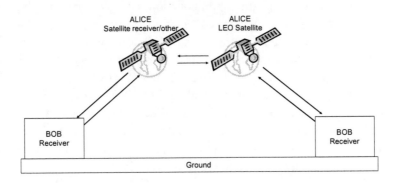

Figure 8. Global key exchange based free-space QKD.

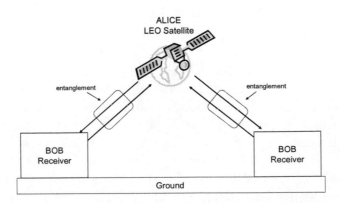

Figure 9. Satellite-to-ground free-space QKD.

The global key exchange based QKD scheme uses faint pulse quantum cryptography, the bitrate of the key agreement process is about 1000 bit/sec. The tested implementations have worked between 600 km and 2000 km distances. The global key exchanging satellite QKD systems can be implemented with more than one ground receiving stations for a single satellite module. The exchanged keys can be used by ground stations on long distances [4].

In Figure 9. we illustrated a *satellite-to-ground* free-space QKD scheme, the proposed model uses entangled photons. The bitrate of the key agreement process in the current implementations is greater than 100 bit/s. The secret key agreement process requires two optical paths from the space module to the ground communication module, which increments the error rate in the current solutions. Another drawback of polarization based satellite-to-ground QKDs, that according to the movement of the Earth, Alice and Bob rotate to each other, thus it is necessary to continuously compensate this movement in polarization detection [22, 23].

The communication in the satellite-to-ground QKD schemes can be based on entangled photon pairs. The EPR-based free-space quantum cryptography uses the EPR-based QKD scheme, discussed in the previous section. In practical implementations, there are still many challenges to use entanglement however the free-space EPR technology can be implemented easily in current free-space QKD realizations [11, 19, 20, 21].

According to the physical problems of generating and controlling entangled photons, in the near future, the free-space QKD communication will be able to realize the global key exchange model, where EPR-states are not required. We note that the cost of this approach is lower, but still high compared to other classical free-space communication systems.

5.2. Devices and Tools in Free-space Quantum Communication

The physical realization of a free-space quantum channel is not an idealistic channel. The single-photon communication is not appropriate in noisy, practical implementations. In the faint pulse QKD schemes, the transmitter uses weak pulses of light, with orthogonally polarized pulses. The number of the photons per pulse is limited, it is usually chosen as *0.1* photons per pulse [4, 22, 23]. On the other side, the receiver uses a single-photon counting detector to measure the pulses. In the measurement phase, the receiver converts the light into electronic pulses, the measurement bases are switched randomly. Along the transmission of the pulses, only a few fractions of the pulses will be used in the secret key. The lost and detected pulses measured with different bases are dropped out from the key.

In the practical implementations, the transmitter contains a laser diode, a mirror, relay lens, and spatial filter. The single photon communication is approximated by the polarization coded faint pulses. The transmitter module launches the faint light pulse in one of the possible polarization states into the quantum channel. Alice's faint pulse contains an average photon number of approximately 0.1. The light of the laser diode is combined with a mirror the spatial filter is used to achieve spatial indistinguishability [4].

In Figure 10. we illustrated the general configuration of Alice's free-space transmitter module. The system uses weak coherent pulses, with polarization modulation. The field programmable gate array performs the signal processing [20].

Bob's receiver system consists of a telescope with computer controlled pointing. In many outdoor applications, the resolution of the telescope system is the limiting factor. The receiver module consists of beamsplitters, polarization beamsplitters (PBS) and photon counting avalanche diodes [22]. The polarization is changed by polarization rotator half-wave plates. Bob splits the incoming photons to the analyzers by the beam splitter truly random, hence no random generators required in the receiver module. The detection time of each photon is recorded in Bob's module, and a delay time is used between the detections, to discriminate the measurement bases. In the tested physical approaches, the overall optical detection efficiency of Bob's module was about 17%, with timing jitter smaller than one nano-second [22].

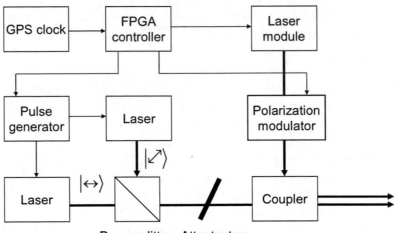

Figure 10. Configure of Alice's transmitter.

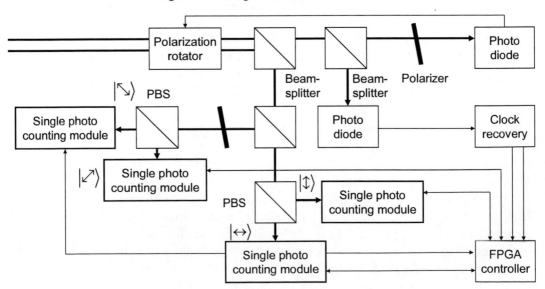

Figure 11. Configuration of Bob's receiver.

In Figure 11. we illustrated the configuration of Bob's receiver module, the module synchronizes data clock recovery, and controls the photon detection. The results of the measurements are recorded on a storage device, integrated into the receiver device [4].

5.3. Quantum Communication in the Near Future

One of the biggest challenges in free-space QKD implementations are the extremely high precision of optical devices, the nano-second time interval synchronization of key exchange process, and the generation of entangled photons in long distances [20, 21]. The free-space EPR-based QKD methods was first tested and demonstrated successfully in Wien, at about 600 m range. The raw key rate of the testbed implementation was about 20 bit/sec [24, 25]. Later, free-space quantum key distribution system has been implemented over several kilometers [23]. Future free-space QKD applications can include direct communication between satellites, where the secret quantum key agreement process will be achieved between satellites in the space. The current low, medium and geostationary earth orbit satellites between the range of 1000 km and 35,000 km, can be used for this purpose, to achieve secure future space quantum communication [22]. However, the fiber based results are promising as well. Japanese Researches at National Institute of Information and Communications Technology (NICT) reported a QKD field test through a 97 km installed fiber. They established the clock transmission technique for long distance QKD without degrading the quantum signal, using an optical amplifier for the clock signal, narrowband filters on both quantum and clock signals. [26]

One promising project is the Space-QUEST (Quantum Entanglement in Space Experiments), which is led by a European research consortium. This project is supported by the European Life and Physical Sciences in Space Programme of ESA, aiming at a quantum communications space-to-ground experiment from the International Space Station. According to their mission scope, to bring quantum entanglement for the first time in the space environment will open a new range of fundamental physics experiments. [27]

Other interesting application for free-space optical links is the interconnection of airships placed in the stratosphere, so called High Altitude Platforms (HAPs). The HAPS can offer a cost-effective solution for broadband data access in regions where only little terrestrial infrastructure exists. In the satellite communication it can be a good solution for the downlink of earth observation data gathered by LEO satellites. [28].

Italian researches reported the first experimental implementation of a scheme for single-photon exchange between a satellite and an Earth-based station. They have built an experiment that mimics a single photon source on a satellite, exploiting the telescope at the Matera Laser Ranging Observatory of the Italian Space Agency to detect the transmitted photons. They were able to detect returns from satellite Ajisai, a low-earth orbit geodetic satellite, whose orbit has a perigee height of 1485 km. [29]

5.4. Redundancy-Free Quantum Communication

To further increase the effectiveness of a quantum communication system some other tricks can be applied. For example there is the possibility to decrease the overhead on the channel caused by bits used for error correction. In classical systems, error correction can be performed only with the help of some redundancy. The error correction capabilities are required for any form of a large scale computation and communication. In classical systems the simplest form to give redundancy to the communication is to encode each bit more than once, however in quantum communication the error correction can be done by much more complex strategies. Currently, many quantum error correction techniques have been introduced to overcome the limitations of quantum theory principles. In these proposals, redundancy is required for successful error correction, because the quantum states are cannot be cloned perfectly, or cannot be measured nondestructively. If we could use redundancy-free solutions, they could be very useful in the long-distance aerial communication, because there would be no need to use redundant error correction codes as nowadays. With the redundancy-free techniques the effective capacity of the satellite link would also be increased.

At our department we developed different redundancy-free solutions for free-space quantum communication [8]. We would like to provide error correction by sending certain amount of qubits over a noisy quantum channel. The qubits are independent and each contains information that needs to be processed. Our initial assumption is that the channel rotates the qubit with a ω degree that is considered to be constant so far. We wish to create a system where error correction is possible. By this, not a complete restoration of the initial qubits is meant. The transmission is considered successful when at the end of the channel the qubit remains in its original state's ε environment.

To achieve this we mix the qubits and send them over the channel, as shown in Figure 12. What we expect to happen at the measurement is that the error for one qubit is distributed among the others' environment (its neighbors). By being so, the error remains in an ε environment for each qubit. For the communication we use n long qubits so that $2^n = N$, where n is the length of the qubits and N is the size of the space. We can construct a description which leads to a redundancy-free solution because the classical states are coded into the eigenvectors of the U matrix. With the appropriate selection of the matrix A we can restore one quantum bit sent over the channel without any other (redundant) information. The whole algorithm is described in [8].

We can consider the redundancy-free implementation of an unitary error correcting operator $\mathcal{R}_\theta$. The protocol achieves the redundancy-free quantum communication using *local unitary operations* and *unitary matrices*. The whole algorithm can be found in [8].

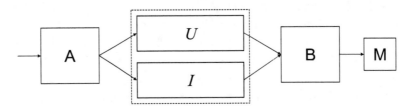

Figure 12. Our channel model for redundancy free-error correction. *A* and *B* are appropriated selected matrixes, M denotes the measurement. The quantum channel transforms a unitary transformation with *p* probability and an identity transformation with *1-p* probability.

Conclusion

As everyday life is getting faster and more communication intensive it requires researchers and engineers to respond to the growing needs. Cost efficiency is also an important issue. In telecommunication applications where the air is used as the channel the most crucial issue to solve is how to transmit as many bytes at a given frequency in a second as possible. This is true for cellular phone system as well as for satellites. In both case one way to determine the system's efficiency is to measure the number of bytes sent per second. The more we are able to squeeze through the channel the more efficient the system is.

In this chapter we have summarized the bases of quantum information based communication system. We gave a short introduction to satellites and open air communication. An overview of the quantum based key distribution schemes was also presented. The modern approaches to quantum theory based satellite communication were also described. Beside these we gave a solution to how to create more effective free space communication via quantum channels.

Although the development of the implementations of quantum based computing system is not as rapid as many hoped decade(s) ago, the existing result are promising. In the other hand the need for satellites are unquestionable. We think that mixing the useful and well working devices with new and promising techniques (such as quantum communication) can lead to systems that may be the foundations of tomorrow's communication.

References

[1]   Tim Furniss. *A History of Space Exploration*. Mercury Books, 2006.

[2]   Parkinson, BW; Stansell, T; Beard, R; Gromov, K. *A history of satellite navigation. Navigation*, 1995, 109-164.

[3]   Evans, BG. *Satellite communication systems*. IET, 1999.

[4]   Dusek, M; Lutkenhaus, N; Hendrych, M. Quantum Cryptography. http://arxiv.org/abs/quant-ph/0601207, 2006.

[5]   Bennett, CH; Brassard, G. Quantum cryptography: Public key distribution and coin tossing. In Proceedings of the IEEE International Conference on Computers, *Systems and Signal Processing*, 1984, 175-179.

[6]   Dennis Roddy. *Satellite Communications*, Prantice-Hall 1989.

[7]   Gérard Maral, Michael Bousquet. Satellite Communications Systems, System, *Techniques and Technology*. Wiley, 2002.

[8]   Bacsardi, L; Gyongyosi, L; Imre, S. Solutions for Redundancy-free Error Correction in Quantum Channel. *In Proceedings of Quantum Comm*, 2009.

[9]   Imre, S; Ferenc, B. *Quantum Computing and Communications: An Engineering Approach. Wiley*, 2005.

[10] Michael, A; Nielsen, Isaac, L. Chuang. *Quantum Computation and Quantum Information*, Cambridge University Press, 2000.

[11] Bennett, CH; Brassard, G; Ekert, AK. Quantum cryptography. *Sci. Am.*, 1992, Vol 267(4), 50.

[12] Gyongyosi, L; Imre, S. Fidelity Analysis of Quantum Cloning Based Attacks in Quantum Cryptography. In: *Proceedings of the 10th International Conference on Telecommunications - ConTEL 2009*. Zagreb, Croatia, 221-228.

[13] Scarani, V; Kurtsiefer, C. The black paper of quantum cryptography: real implementation problems. arXiv:0906.4547, 2009.

[14] Koashi, M; Adachi, Y; Yamamoto, T; Imoto, N. Security of Entanglement-Based *Quantum Key Distribution with Practical Detectors*. http://arxiv.org/abs/0804.0891, 2008.

[15] Lo, HK; Chau. HF. Unconditional security of quantum key distribution over arbitrarily long distances. *Science*, 283, 2050, 1999.

[16] Wootters,WK; Zurek, WH. A single quantum cannot be cloned. *Nature*, 1982, 299, 802-803.

[17] Tsurumaru, T; Tamaki, K. Security Proof for QKD Systems with Threshold Detectors. http://arxiv.org/abs/0803.4226, 2008.

[18] Bennett, CH; Bessette, F; Brassard, G; Salvail, L; Smolin, J. Experimental quantum cryptography. *J. Cryptol.* 1992, Vol 5, 3=28.

[19] Ekert, AK. Quantum cryptography based on Bell's theorem *Phys. Rev. Lett.,* 1991, 67, 661-663.

[20] Ho, C; Lamas-Linares, A; Kurtsiefer, C. Clock synchronization by remote detection of correlated photon pairs. *New Journal of Physics*, 2009 11, 045011.

[21] Ling, A; Peloso, MP; Marcikic, I; Scarani, V; Lamas-Linares, A; Kurtsiefer, C. Experimental quantum key distribution based on a Bell test. *Physical Review A* 78, 020301, 2008.

[22] Schmitt-Manderbach, T; Weier, H; Fürst, M; Ursin, R; Tiefenbacher, F; Scheidl, T; Perdigues, J; Sodnik, Z; Kurtsiefer, C; Rarity, JG; Zeilinger, A; Weinfurter, H. Experimental Demonstration of Free-Space Decoy-State Quantum Key Distribution over 144 km. *Physical Review Letters* 2007, PRL 98, 010504.

[23] Beaudry, NJ; Moroder, T; Lutkenhaus, N. (2008). Squashing Models for Optical Measurements in Quantum Communication. http://arxiv.org/abs/0804.3082.

[24] Bacsardi, L. Using Quantum Computing Algorithms in Future Satellite Communication. *Acta Astronautica*, 2005, Vol 57, 224-229.

[25] Bacsardi, L. Satellite communication over quantum channel. *Acta Astronautica*, 2007, Vol 61, 151-159.

[26] Tanaka, A; Fujiwara, M; Nam, SW; Nambu, Y; Takahashi, S; Maeda, W; Yoshino, K; Miki, S; Baek, B; Wang, Z; Tajima, A; Sasaki, M. & Tomita, A. Ultra fast quantum key distribution over a 97 km installed telecom fiber with wavelength division multiplexing clock synchronization. *Opt. Express*, 2008, 16(15), 11354-11360.

[27] Ursin, R. et all, Space-QUEST. Experiments with quantum entanglement in space, Proceedings of the 2008 *Microgravity Sciences and Process Symposium*, 2008.

[28] Fuchs, C; Giggenbach, D. Optical Free-Space Communication on Earth and in Space Regarding Quantum Cryptography Aspects, *LICST* 1867-8211, 82-95.

[29] Villoresi, P. et al. Experimental verification of the feasibility of a quantum channel between space and Earth. *New Journal of Physics*, 2008, 10, 033038.

In: Computer Science Research and the Internet ISBN: 978-1-61728-730-5
Editor: Jaclyn E. Morris, pp. 133-151 © 2011 Nova Science Publishers, Inc.

Chapter 5

VIRTUAL REALITY AS A TOOL FOR MACHINING-PROCESSES SIMULATION AND EVALUATION

A. Markos Petousis[1], Nickolas Bilalis[2,*]
and S. Nickolas Sapidis[3]

[1]Technological Education Institute of Crete, Estavromenos,
71004 Heraklion, Crete, GREECE
[2]Department of Production Engineering & Management, Technical University of Crete,
Kounoupidiana, 73100, Chania, Crete, GREECE
[3]Department of Product and Systems Design Engineering, University of the Aegean,
Ermoupolis, 84100, Syros, GREECE

Abstract

Recently, virtual reality systems have been presented for simulation of machining processes, aiming at the determination of specific machining parameters, such as the required fixtures and the machining environment, the cutting tool dynamics, the chip shape and volume, and the shape of the cutting tool.

A methodology is presented in this chapter for the development of a virtual environment for 3 axis milling process simulation. The technological and research challenges involved in this methodology are described.

The operation of a new system developed by the authors for machining-process simulation in a virtual environment is presented. This system integrates a virtual reality environment with computational and graphical models for the simulation of three axis milling processes. A computational model has been developed for the visualization of the milling process in the virtual environment and graphical model has been developed for the calculation of quantitative data related to surface roughness of machined surfaces.

Keywords: Virtual Manufacturing, virtual machining, virtual milling, machining simulation, surface roughness

---

[*] E-mail address: nbilalis@isc.tuc.gr, Fax: +302821037253

1. Introduction

The production process simulation is a critical part in the design of the production process, since it allows the study of process parameters in close to real conditions. The development of computer graphics considerably extended simulation applications capabilities. Virtual Reality initially was only exploited for visualization and interaction between the product and the designers. The development of the computational systems along with the increase of the Virtual Reality functionalities and the integration of production simulation models, significantly extended Virtual Reality capabilities for production processes study.

Virtual Reality based systems focus on the study of specific production processes, such as machining processes and are mainly used as supplementary tools of the simulation system. With the development of techniques for the study of production processes parameters, the available tools for the study of the product have been considerably improved, allowing the development of more accurate, complete and detailed virtual models.

In current study the required technologies for the development of a machining processes simulation virtual environment are presented and the most significant research systems are reviewed. This study also proposes a methodology for the development of a virtual environment for machining-process simulation. The technological and research challenges involved in this methodology are described. These challenges involve cutter path determination, three-dimensional visualization, material removal simulation, and quantitative-data estimation using graphical models related to the actually performed process. A graphical model for surface roughness has been developed and is presented in the current study. This model has been exploited in the development of a virtual environment for machining processes simulation. Finally, the operation of the whole system developed by the authors for machining-process simulation in a virtual environment is presented.

2. Virtual Environment Systems for Machining Processes Simulation

Virtual reality has been used for the simulation of several different industrial processes, such as the development of virtual prototypes and the real time simulation of manufacturing processes 0. In particular for the machining processes, virtual environments have been used for the study of different parameters. Studies aiming at the verification of the process are related mainly with the determination of the process feasibility, with the predefined set of process parameters. In the system of Dae Kyun Baek et al. 0 a prediction model of chip volume per tooth in milling operations using a numerical control (NC) verification model was developed. The chip volume is important machining process parameter for the determination of the cutting forces and the prediction of the chip load on a cutter tooth. For the determination of the chip volume, the cutter swept volumes along the path were calculated from the information obtained from NC codes as well as the feed-rate.

The system of X. Tian et al. 0 for a predefined NC program, where feedrate, spindle speed and cutter path are determined, determines the possibility of collisions during the execution of the machining process. Studies of specific process parameters, such as cutting force, power, tool-life and surface roughness, aim to optimize their values, by modifying the NC program 0, 0, in order to improve machining process results, such as the machining accuracy. Li et al. 0 developed a framework of a NC program optimization system based on virtual machining. The framework is developed based on an actual machining system, including a machine tool, a cutting tool, a set of fixture and a workpiece. With this framework, the machining process driven by a NC program in the actual environment can be simulated, to acquire adequate information for error compensation and cutting parameter optimization. The NC program is interpreted according to the programming regulations of NC instructions and a syntax check report is given; as the virtual machining process is going on. Collision detection is also carried out according to the relative position of the moving geometrical models of virtual machining environment. Finally, virtual workpiece is produced for accuracy prediction and evaluation.

Systems aiming at the design, modelling and implementation of production plans are focused on errors detection in the executed operations 0-0. Chryssolouris et al. 0 developed a virtual machine shop environment in order to support process verification in terms of geometrical, technical and economic characteristics. The features of this environment enable the user to set up a process, to operate a machine tool, to edit and execute an NC part program in an immersive and interactive way. Jitender et al. 0 presented an overview of a comprehensive finite element method (FEM) based milling process plan verification model and associated tools. The method is considering the effects of fixturing, operation sequence, tool path and cutting parameters. The milling process is simulated in a transient 3D virtual environment and the part thin wall deflections and elastic–plastic deformations during machining are predicted.

Because of the nature of the virtual reality technology, several studies are aiming at the visualization of the machining process results 0-0. In order to achieve that, the intersection between the cutter and the workpiece must be determined, exploiting process kinematics 0, the cutter swept volume must be calculated 0 and the chip removal can also be simulated, with the exploitation of appropriate illumination models 0. Peng et al. 0 developed a novel Virtual Reality-based system for interactive modular fixture configuration design. A multi-view based modular fixture assembly model was exploited to assist information representation and management. Based on geometric constraints, a precise 3D manipulation approach was proposed to improve intuitive interaction and accurate 3D positioning of fixture components in virtual space. Thus, the modular fixture configuration design task can precisely be performed in virtual space. Jang et al. 0 developed a voxel-based simulator for multi-axis CNC machining. The simulator displays the machining process in which the initial workpiece is incrementally converted into the finished part. The voxel representation is used to model efficiently the state of the in-process workpiece, which is generated by successively subtracting tool swept volumes from the workpiece. The voxel representation also simplifies the computation of regularised Boolean set operations and of material removal volumes. By using the material removal rate measured by the number of removed voxels, the feedrate can be adjusted adaptively to increase the machining productivity.

Virtual reality has also been exploited for training in machining processes 0, 0, 0, 0. Mousavi et al. 0 studied the application of haptic feedback in Virtual Reality to enhance user performance in manufacturing. The aim of the study was to improve the results from the usage of Virtual Reality as a tool for training applications in manufacturing, since haptic interfaces have the potential to enhance communication and interaction via the computer enabling affective expressive interpersonal communication and enriching interaction by haptic feedback. Duffy et al. 0 developed an intelligent virtual reality-based training system to take advantage of the way people appear to respond to auditory and visual cues. Training scenarios were developed based on the idea that many times human errors in industry are shown to coincide with conditions that are infrequently encountered. Knowledge and auditory cues for different machining conditions for a computer-numerical-control (CNC) milling machine were built into the existing knowledge base. A simulated tool breakage that consisted of an animation, text and sound of glass breaking was integrated into a virtual training sequence and was triggered by the failure to stop operation in the poor cutting condition represented by sub-optimum spindle speed and cutting sound. An analysis was conducted to determine the impact of the simulated accident on decision-making performance in a real machining task.

For the implementation of a virtual reality system for machining processes simulation, technologies, such as cutter path determination, material removal simulation and quantitative data related to the executed process calculation must be exploited and integrated in the virtual environment.

For the determination of the cutter path from the CAD/CAM system data several methods have been presented 0 - 0. Methods are diversified according to the cutter geometry and the number of axis of the CNC machine. Methods aim at the determination of the parallel to the geometry trajectory, in which the cutter has to move in order to produce the required shape. In most of the methods the geometry of the part is approximated with parametric surface boundaries in the 3d space from which the offset trajectory is being determined, according to the type and the geometry of the selected cutter.

Workpiece material removal simulation in solid models is determined by defining the sweep volume of the cutter as a three dimensional geometrical model. This geometrical model is being subtracted from the workpiece with the use of Boolean operations to produce the new shape of the workpiece. For sweep volumes calculation the three dimensional model geometry and the cutter trajectory are being mathematically defined 0.

In solid modelling systems 0, surfaces and edges are expressed with mathematical equations and the intersections between the surfaces and the edges of each model are determined. In systems where the three dimensional geometry is defined with polygons, algorithms have been presented for the determination of the section between polygons (polygon clipping algorithms) 0. These algorithms are used in solid modelling systems for the visualization of the subtracted geometry.

Another approach for the implementation of Boolean operations between three dimensional geometries is based in the differentiation and approximation of the model geometry. For the determination of the intersection between geometrical models, the intersection between each elementary geometrical model is determined. The intersecting elementary geometrical models are removed from the geometry. Octree 0 is a geometry differentiation method being used in Boolean operations 0. Octree is based in the approximation of the three dimensional geometry with elementary cubic volumes and the further subdivision of each volume until the geometry is approximated with adequate accuracy. Marching cubes is a similar to octree method, which was used along with finite elements for material removal simulation in machining 0.

Finally, the most important exploitation of the virtual reality technology in machining simulation systems is the determination of quantitative data, such as the machined surface roughness 0 and the cutting forces 0 - 0. Machined surface quality, cutting forces, required power and cutter wear, are all production quantitative parameters that contribute in the improvement of the machining result appraisal during the product design phase. Prior to the introduction of quantitative data determination tools in the production design processes, empirical or experimental methods were used.

CAM systems are the most common machining simulation tools, but they are unable to provide quantitative data for the machining process. Quantitative data are determined in different systems that employ mainly analytic or numerical methods. Antoniadis et al. 0 presented a numerical method for quantitative data determination (cutting forces and surface roughness) in milling processes with ball end cutting tools. The method is based in workpiece modelling by linear segments that decrease their height at the interaction point with the cutter cutting edge. From the cut out part of the needle, in every step of the differentiated cutting tool movement, the size of the cutting chip is determined and from that the cutting forces are calculated. From the remaining needles shape the machined surface is determined which is used for surface roughness determination. Engin et al. 0 proposed a generalized mathematical model for predicting cutting forces, vibrations, dimensional surface finish and stability lobes in milling. The model is based in the mathematical modelling of the cutter with helical flutes defined in a parametric volume. Liu et al. 0 developed a model for the determination of peripheral milling dynamic parameters. The model is based in the determination of the vibrations between the workpiece and the cutter that influence cutting forces. The geometry and kinematics of the cutter are considered for the determination of the machined surface, from which surface roughness is being calculated.

Several analytical methods have been presented for surface roughness parameters determination in milling processes. These methods are considering the cutting speed, the feed, the depth of cut and vibrations as parameters and employ mathematical equations, such as the multiple regression equation 0 for the determination of the surface roughness parameters. Tseng et al. 0 state that in conventional metal removal processes an exact prediction of surface roughness is difficult to achieve, due to the stochastic nature of the machining processes and they propose the use of a data mining technique to solve the quality assurance problem in predicting the acceptance of computer numerical control (CNC) machined parts, rather than focusing on the prediction of precise surface roughness values. Rough set theory data mining technique was applied to derive rules for the process variables that contribute to the surface roughness. The proposed rule-composing algorithm and rule-validation procedure was tested with the historical data the company has collected over the years. The results indicate a higher accuracy over the statistical approaches in terms of predicting acceptance level of surface roughness.

For the calculation of the cutting forces in milling, research is focused on different processes parameters, such as the determination of the cutting forces equation coefficients 0 and the chip thickness 0. Generic mathematical approaches have also been presented 0 - 0. These models focus on processes in different machining surfaces types, such as inclined surfaces 0 or freeform surfaces 0. Additionally, models employing visualization technologies, such as solid modelling tools 0, for the determination of the intersection between the cutter and the workpiece have been presented. Moreover, models have been presented for the study of specific cutting conditions, such as the vibrations between the cutter and the workpiece 0.

In the systems described in the current section, virtual reality graphics environments have been integrated with mathematical models, in order to extend their functionalities, by adding the capability to determine critical quantitative parameters of the simulated machining process. The current study proposes an integrated methodology for the development of a virtual reality based milling processes visualization and simulation system, capable of determining the roughness of the machined surfaces in the virtual environment.

3. Ethodology for the Development of a Virtual Environment for 3 Axis Milling Process Simulation

In this section a methodology is proposed for the development of a virtual reality based milling processes visualization and simulation system, capable of determining the roughness of the machined surfaces in the virtual environment.

In the proposed methodology (Figure 1) different technologies required in order to achieve such a simulation and visualization system are developed and integrated. Each of these technologies contains different algorithms, which are diverted to equivalent software libraries during the development process of such systems.

In Figure 1 these algorithms and software libraries are listed. The system contains main and auxiliary subsystems, each of which is developed with an equivalent technology and serves a specific functionality in the virtual environment. For each of the subsystems' technologies a simulation model was developed.

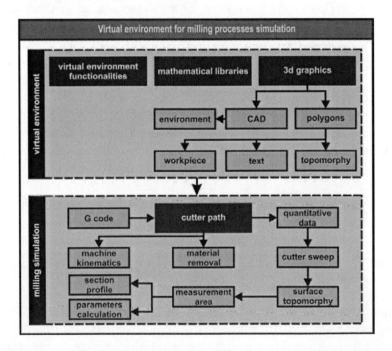

Figure 1. Methodology for the development of a virtual reality based milling processes visualization and simulation system.

With respect to machining process quantitative data estimation the proposed model integrates a graphical model for surface roughness estimation and a virtual tool for measurement and display of the results. Surface roughness in machining is a parameter related with the geometrical characteristics of the abnormalities produced by the cutter in the machined surface. Surface roughness is an important parameter in machining, since it affects surface quality and product functional characteristics. Good surface roughness reduces friction on the machined surface, increases product wear resistance, improves product appearance and mechanisms functionality.

In the next sections the technology for the development of each of the virtual environment subsystems simulation models is described.

3.1. Cutter Path Determination

In the proposed methodology the CNC milling machine part production program file produced in the CAM software (G-code commands program file) is being read from its file.

A parsing algorithm has been developed. This algorithm parses and recognizes the G-code commands and the corresponding numerical values in each command. The information is converted into linear, curvilinear and rotational mathematical equations of the cutter trajectory in space 0. The developed algorithm supports compensation. Compensation is the cutter trajectory offset to the defined geometry at a distance equal to the cutter radii, in which the cutter has to move, in order to produce the defined geometry. So, if a compensation G-code command has been defined, the algorithm determines the equivalent offset cutter trajectory. In this case the coordinates of the geometry vertices and the cutter radii are given in the G-code command and the CNC machine controller has to determine the offset trajectory from these data.

The linear, curvilinear and rotational mathematical equations of the cutter trajectory in space are exploited for the visualization of the cutter movement relative to the workpiece in the virtual environment, in order to preserve the cutting conditions defined in the G-code program file. This integration of the virtual environment with the CAM software, through the G-code program file was necessary, in order to ensure that the process studied in the proposed system is the same with the one produced in the CAM system and to be able to verify the quantitative data calculated with this methodology with experiments executed in real production environments. The verification process is mainly based on the execution of a G-code program file in the real and the virtual environment, calculation of the surface roughness quantitative data (surface topomorphy and surface roughness parameters values) with the developed model in the virtual environment, measurement of the corresponding surface roughness data in the real experiment and comparison of the two results 0.

3.2. Three Dimensional Geometrical Models

For the development of the system, the geometrical models of the environment were produced with the use of CAD and polygons tools.

Solid and surface models are used in contemporary systems for three dimensional geometry definitions. Several methods have been presented for geometrical models visualization. In most graphics systems three dimensional geometry is visualized with the use of shaded polygons (usually triangles), which approximate the shape of the geometry

In the proposed system, the machine shop building, the machines, the cutters and the environment parts where drafted with the use of Pro Engineer. Workpiece geometrical model is defined with the use of virtual environment dynamic geometry tools that provide the ability to modify the geometrical model shape in real time. The use of dynamic geometry is necessary, in order to visualize the material removal from the workpiece during machining processes simulation.

3.3. Workpiece Material Removal Simulation

In the proposed methodology the material removal is visualized by modifying workpiece polygon vertices coordinates, according to cutter position in real time. For the modification of the workpiece polygon vertices, the coordinates of the vertices are compared with the coordinates of the lowest cutter section, in each position of the cutter trajectory. The cutter trajectory is expressed as sequence of linear and curvilinear mathematical equations in the 3d space. To visualize the machine axis kinematics and the material removal, the cutter is placed in discrete positions on the trajectory. In each position the cutter lowest section coordinates are compared with the workpiece vertices coordinates. This comparison checks if a workpiece vertex is inside the cutter volume at the current cutter position. For every vertex inside the cutter volume, its Z coordinate is decreased to the lowest cutter section Z coordinate at this position. This process is repeated for all the workpiece vertices in the cutter position area. In this way the workpiece shape is changing in real time, during the machining process simulation, according to the cutter movements in space.

The algorithm for the determination of the intersection between the workpiece and the cutter and the visualization of the workpiece material removal when simulating a milling process in the virtual environment is shown in Figure 2.

3.4. Quantitative Data Parameters Determination in Machining Processes

In the proposed methodology a model has been developed 0 for the determination of surface roughness parameters in the machined surface. The model is able to determine the machined surface topomorphy and calculate surface roughness parameters values (R_a, R_y, R_{ti}, R_z). The machined surface topomorphy and all the data calculated with this model are visualized in the virtual environment (Figure 3).

In the presented model, cutter motion relative to the workpiece is simulated, monitored and studied, according to the predefined cutting conditions, for the determination of the machined surface topomorphy. In the model the parameters that are considered in surface roughness formation are the cutting speed, feed, cutting depth, cutter diameter, height, cutter end, number of teeth and cutting edges geometry. Parameters that contribute to the surface roughness formation, such as the cutter material, quality and type of cutter, quality of jigs and fixtures, the use of lubricant and vibrations in the machining process are not considered.

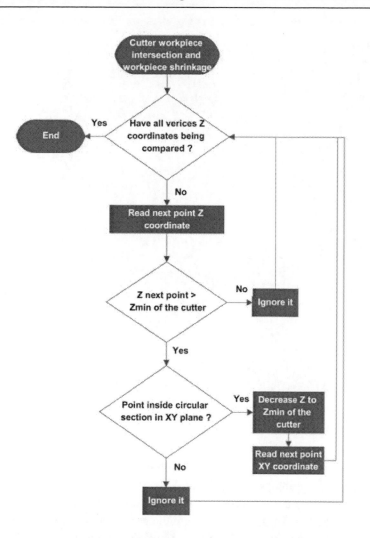

Figure 2. Workpiece material removal algorithm.

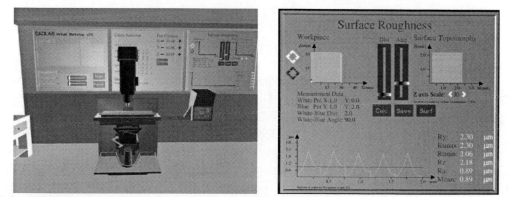

(a) the quantitative data table (on the right) in the virtual environment
(b) Up Milling, sz=0.2mm/rev,edge, txy=0.4mm, tz=0.3mm, ball-end cutter D20, z=1, P02 (TiN), Ck60

Figure 3. Surface Roughness results calculated with the developed model as they are presented in the virtual environment.

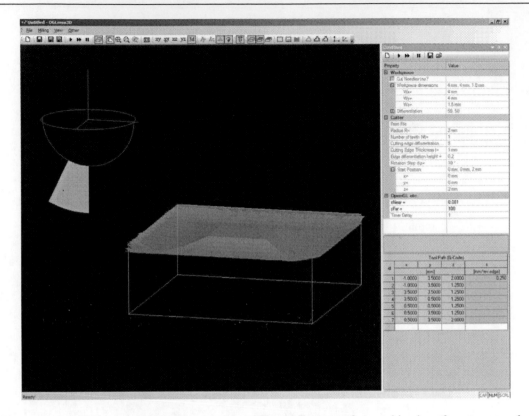

Figure 4. OpenGL machining processes simulation environment for machined surface topomorphy determination.

The model for the determination of the machined surface topomorphy was implemented in a three dimensional graphics environment developed in OpenGL (Figure 4). In the model the cutter motion relative to the workpiece is being simulated according to cutting conditions defined in the G code file. These conditions are the tool path, the spindle speed in rpm and the feed in mm/min. During simulation the cutter sweep surface is calculated, by determining cutting edges sweep surface. From the cutting edges sweep surface the machined surface of the process is determined.

For the determination of cutting edges sweep surface during machining simulation, the cutter is being modelled, according to the shape and number of its cutting edges. Cutting edges shape is defined from the outer edge profile of each cutting edge, which defines the overall cutter profile. Each cutting edge is being differentiated in equal elementary segments that could be considered as straight lines. The number of segments for the differentiation of the cutting edge is being chosen in the software interface.

The cutter path relative to the workpiece is also being differentiated. The cutter is being successively placed in the differentiated path positions, according to the cutting conditions (spindle speed, feed). When the cutter is placed in the next discrete position of the tool path, it changes its position in space but it also revolves around the axis of revolution at an angle calculated from the spindle speed. The sweep surface of each cutting edge is determined and stored for each two adjacent discrete positions. For the determination of the cutting edge sweep surface, between two discrete positions, every differentiated cutting edge segment is stored. For every cutting edge segment, between two adjacent positions (Figure 5a) a linear surface is defined (Figure 5b), which is subsequently divided into four triangular surfaces, by adding a node in the "middle" of the surface (Figure 5c). This is necessary in order to avoid crossed cutting edge segment ends (Figure 6) and to convert the linear surface into four flat surfaces.

The sweep surface of each differentiated cutting edge segment between two adjacent positions is defined by the four triangle surfaces (Figure 7). The sweep surfaces produced by all differentiated cutting edge segments form the cutting edge sweep surface between two adjacent positions of the cutter path. This process is repeated for all the cutting edges of the selected cutter in this specific machining process.

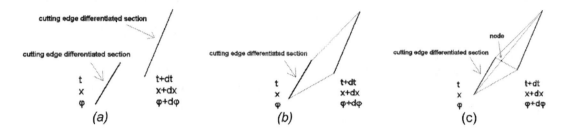

Figure 5. Sweep surface of a differentiated cutting edge segment.

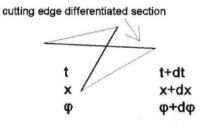

Figure 6. For specific ball end cutter positions, two adjacent positions of the differentiated cutting edge segments could produce the shape shown.

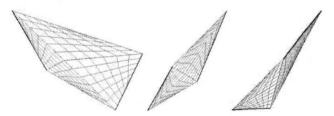

Figure 7. Sweep surface of a differentiated cutting edge segment for two adjacent cutter path positions.

The process for the determination of the cutting edge sweep surface between two discrete cutter path positions is repeated for the entire cutter path, to determine the sweep surface of the cutter during the machining process (Figure 8). The part of the sweep surface inside the workpiece limits is the machined surface that is the geometry produced by the cutter during this machining process. A clipping algorithm is used to determine the part of the sweep surface inside the workpiece limits (Figure 9).

Sweep surface has overlapping triangles, since part of each cutting edge sweep is being overlapped by the next cutting edge sweep or the next cutter pass sweep. The final workpiece surface must be determined from the clipped cutter sweep surface. The final machined surface is the one defined by the lower part of the clipped cutter sweep surface. If the cutter sweep surface is projected from its down side, the final machined surface topomorphy is derived, since the overlapped triangles are not visible in this projection, because the hidden line algorithm projects on the user interface only the geometry visible in each point of view. This final machined surface topomorphy is derived from this projection in the form of cloud of points. The coordinates for the cloud of points are determined. The pixels used to visualize the machined surface are converted into X and Y coordinates in the graphics environment coordinate system. For these pixels the Z coordinate is derived from the visualization system Z buffer, which provides the distance between the camera and the object visualized in each pixel. In surface roughness parameters determination, the difference between the lowest and the highest edge on a surface profile is considered, so this value for the Z coordinate is suitable. Calculations for surface roughness parameters are being performed in a transformed coordinate system, which is locally defined in the surface profile. The cloud of points coordinates describing the machined surface topomorphy are exported in a text file and they are used to calculate quantitative parameters for the machined surface roughness.

Figure 8. Cutting edges sweep surface along the cutter path.

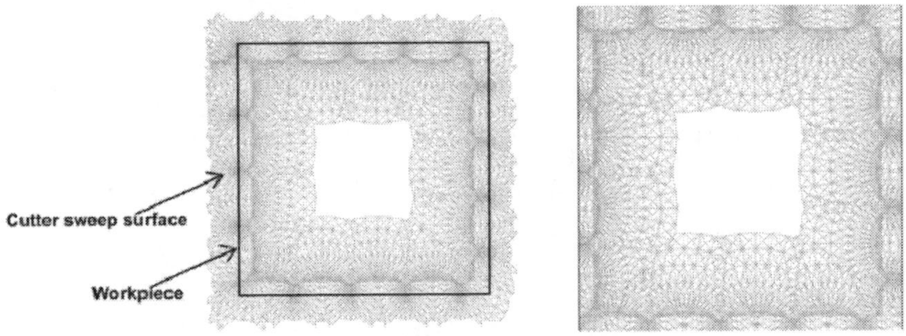

Figure 9. Clipping algorithm for the cutter sweep surface. The constructed geometry is the part of the cutter sweep surface inside workpiece limits.

In order to determine the surface roughness parameters, the user has to define the measurement plane on the machined surface. This process is followed in real surface roughness measurements. For the determination of the measurement plane, a handler was developed on the equivalent quantitative data table on the virtual environment. The handler defines a plane vertical to the machined surface in which topomorphy will be determined and surface roughness parameters will be calculated from this topomorphy. System user defines the position of each handler end. Handler ends define surface roughness measurement plane limits.

For surface roughness parameters determination, cloud points on the vertical measurement plane defined by the system user or in a small width distance from the plane are retrieved from the exported in the previous step cloud of points file. This is necessary because the direction for measurement is randomly selected by the system user, so the number of topomorphy cloud points exactly on the measurement plane may be small and as a result surface roughness parameters calculation accuracy could be decreased. From the points on the selected measurement plane, the topomorphy of the machined surface within the plane limits is determined and surface roughness parameters such as R_a, R_y, R_{ti}, R_z and surface topomorphy mean line are calculated. In the quantitative data table, surface topomorphy and mean line are visualized in a specially developed graph and also surface parameter values are shown.

The results calculated with the developed model for machined surface roughness parameters determination, were verified with data determined in cutting experiments and by another numerical model that was integrated to the system. The results were found to be in agreement with both the numerical model and the experiments 0.

4. The Proposed Virtual Machining Process Simulation System

CAD lab from the Technical University of Crete developed a virtual machine shop environment based on the methodology presented in this study. The virtual environment was developed with the commercial Virtual Reality platform PTC Developer Toolkit and ANSI C programming language for the realistic visualization of the machining processes. A complete machine shop is being visualized and the functional characteristics of a three axes CNC milling machine are being simulated. The structure of the machining processes simulation system is shown in Figure 10.

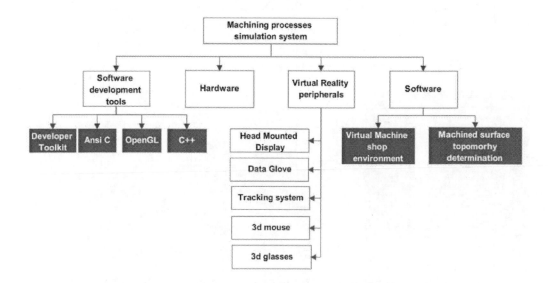

Figure 10. Structure of the machining processes simulation system.

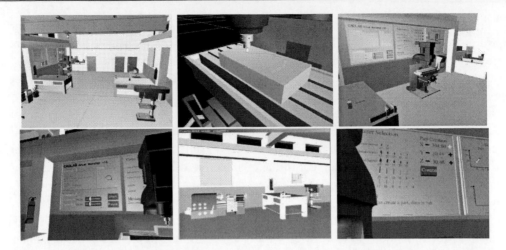

Figure 11. Machining processes simulation virtual environment.

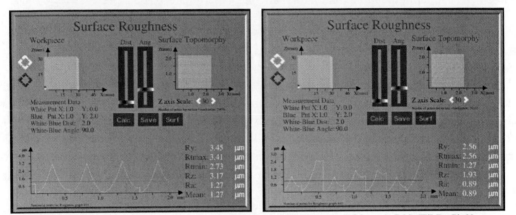

Up Milling, sz=0.2mm/rev,edge, txy=0.5mm, tz=0.3mm, ball-end cutter D20, z=1, P02 (TiN), Ck60
Up Milling, sz=0.3mm/rev,edge, txy=0.3mm, tz=0.3mm, ball-end cutter D20, z=1, P02 (TiN), Ck60

Figure 12. Quantitative data for surface roughness parameters and the measurement area topomorphy in the virtual environment for different machining conditions.

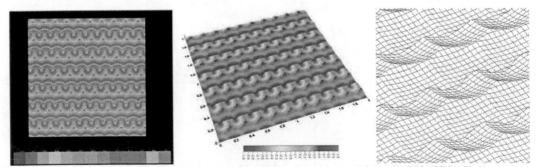

Up Milling, sz=0.2mm/rev,edge, txy=0.3mm, tz=0.3mm, ball-end cutter D20, z=1, P02 (TiN), Ck60

Figure 13. 3d representations of the machined surface topomorphy.

In Figure 11 the virtual environment for machining processes simulation is presented. The user can fly trough the virtual environment, interact with all the objects and manually manipulate the CNC machine. For the execution of a machining process, the user has to select workpiece dimensions and cutter from the corresponding data table. The CNC machine executes the defined machining process. CNC machine axes move realistically according to the path and the feed defined in the program and spindle revolves with the predefined speed. During machining process simulation, workpiece material removal is being visualized when the cutter intersects the workpiece and data related to the process are being visualized. Moreover, information like the G-code command simulated in the CNC machine, feed, spindle speed and cutter trajectory are being visualized in a data table. When the simulation is completed, user is able to select the surface roughness measurement area in the equivalent virtual environment data table and hence acquire quantitative data for surface roughness parameters and the measurement area topomorphy (Figure 12). Finally, the entire machined surface topomorphy (Figure 13) can be visualized as a three dimensional model, that can be inspected from different perspectives.

Aim of the developed a virtual machine shop environment is the integration of virtual environments with production design processes. The system extends CAM system capabilities, since it provides higher level visualization functionalities and quantitative data for the production process defined in the CAM system. So, the developed virtual machine shop environment could be employed as a verification tool, providing qualitative and critical quantitative data for the machining process defined in the CAM system. It can also be exploited as a training tool, because of the realistic visualization of the executed processes in the virtual environment.

5. Verification of the Developed Model for Machining Processes Quantitative Data Calculation

The results acquired by the model were verified with the experimentally verified machining simulation numerical model MSN (Milling Simulation by Needles) 0 and data from experiments. A verification model has been developed that follows a two steps process for the verification of the system results 0. First the machined surface topomorphy accuracy is validated and then the calculated parameter values are being directly compared. Moreover, a wide variety of cutting experiments was implemented with different cutting conditions (up/down milling, change of feed, step over and depth of cut) to directly quantitatively and qualitatively verify the model results. Figure 14 shows a typical correlation performed between the computational and the experimental results for two different cutting conditions. The left image of this figure shows the experimental topomorphy. The middle and the right image of the same figure shows the computationally produced surface topomorphy, in two different ways, in iso-surface form and in 3D form. The correlation between the experimental and the computational results exhibits that the topomorphies are in good agreement, considering that there are parameters that could not be taken into account in the developed computational model. Overall the verification of the developed model showed that the results acquired by the system are in agreement with both the employed numerical model and the experimental results.

6. Conclusions

Currently there is a tendency for Virtual Reality characteristics and production processes models integration. This tendency is leading to the creation of the next generation simulation systems that will provide quantitative data for the process, increased visualization, fly through and interaction capabilities in a virtual environment. Functionality for achieving an exact representation of reality is still missing from the virtual environments for machining processes simulation presented so far, but the comprehension of what is actually being carried out in the real world is improved. The research in this area is showing adequate maturity but the final form of these simulation systems for use in real industrial environments has not yet been delimited, although significant systems have been presented.

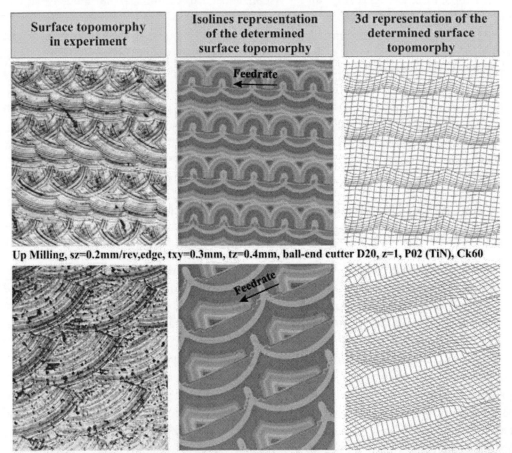

Figure 14. Comparison between the experimental and the determined surface topomorphy.

This study proposes a methodology for the development of a machining processes simulation system with Virtual reality functional characteristics. In this methodology the required technologies for the development of a virtual environment for machining processes simulation are presented and integrated. Each of these technologies is a different research area. A virtual environment for milling processes simulation has been developed with this methodology. The virtual environment provides realistic visualization of the executed milling process, it is integrated with CAM systems, but the most significant capability of the environment is that it is able to calculate and visualize in 3d quantitative data related with the machined surface roughness. All the required algorithms for the development of the virtual environment have been developed by the authors. The model for the calculation of quantitative data related to the machined surface roughness is based on the Z buffer of the graphics subsystem. The model was verified with data from real experiments and a numerical model. The verification process showed that, although the verification method followed does not completely confront the stochastic behaviour of machining processes, the results acquired by the system are in agreement with both the employed numerical model and the experimental results, making the model suitable for integration in production design processes. This result can easily lead to the conclusion that 3d graphics and Virtual Reality environments are nowadays capable of not only visualizing real world processes, but also provide data related with these processes which is either not feasible or very difficult to be determined with conventional methods.

Acknowledgment

The project is co-funded by the European Social Fund and National Resources – EPEAEK II –IRAKLITOS

References

Antoniadis, A., Savakis, K., Bilalis, N. & Balouksis, A. (2003). "Prediction of surface topomorphy and roughness in ball end milling", *Advanced Manufacturing Technology*, Vol. 21, 965-971.

Antonio Jimeno, Alberto Puerta, (2007). "State of the art of the virtual reality applied to design and manufacturing processes", *International Journal of Advanced Manufacturing Technology*, Vol. 33, 866-874.

Bilalis, N. & Petousis, M. (2008). "Development of a virtual environment for surface topomorphy and roughness determination in milling operations", Transactions of the ASME, Journal of Computing and Information Science in Engineering, Special Issue Advances in Computer *Aided Manufacturing*, Vol. 8, No 2.

Bilalis, N., Petousis, M., Antoniadis, A. (2009). "Model for surface roughness parameters determination in a virtual machine shop environment", *International Journal of Advanced Manufacturing and Technology*, Vol. 40, Issue 11.

Blackmore, D., Leu, M. C. & Wang, L. (1997). "The sweep envelope differential equation algorithm and its application to NC machining verification", *CAD*, Vol. 29, No 9, 629-637.

Brunet, P. & Navazo, I. (1990). "Solid representation and operation using extended Octrees", *ACM Transactions on Graphics*, Vol. 9, No 2, 170-197.

Chérif, M., Thomas, H., Furet, B. & Hascoët, J. Y. (2004). "Generic modeling of milling forces for CAD/CAM applications", *Machine Tools and Manufacture*, Vol. 44, No 1, 29-37.

Chryssolouris, G., Mavrikios, D., Fragos, D., Karabatsou, V. & Pistiolis, K. (2002). "A novel virtual experimentation approach to planning and training for manufacturing processes-the virtual machine shop", *International Journal of Computer Integrated Manufacturing*, Vol. 15, No 3, 214-221.

Csaba Antonya and Doru Talaba, (2007). "Design evaluation and modification of mechanical systems in virtual environments", *Virtual Reality*, Vol. 11, 275-285.

Dae Kyun Baeka, Tae Jo Kob, Hee Sool Kim, (2006). "Chip volume prediction using a numerical control verification model", *International Journal of Machine Tools & Manufacture*, Vol. 46, 1326-1335.

Ding, S., Mannan, M. A. & Poo, A. N. (2004). "Oriented bounded box and octree based global interference detection in 5–axis machining of free-form surfaces", *CAD*, Vol. 36, 1281-1294.

Duffy, V. G., Ng, P. W. & Ramakrishnan, A. (2004). "Impact of a simulated accident in virtual training on decision making performance", *Industrial Ergonomics*, Vol. 34, 335-348.

Engin, S. & Altintas, Y. (2001). "Mechanics and dynamics of general milling cutters. Part II: Inserted cutters", *Machine Tools and Manufacture*, Vol. 41, 2213-2231.

Fleisig, R. V. & Spence, A. D. (2005). "Techniques for accelerating B-Rep based parallel machining simulation", *CAD*, Vol. 37, 1229-1240.

Jang, D., Kim, K. & Jung, J. (2000). "Voxel-Based Virtual Multi-Axis Machining", *Advanced Manufacturing Technology*, Vol. 16, 709-713.

Jeong Hoon Ko, Won Soo Yun, Dong Woo Cho, (2003). "Off-line feed rate scheduling using virtual CNC based on an evaluation of cutting performance", *CAD*, Vol. 35, 383-393.

Jitender, K. (2008). Rai, Paul Xirouchakis, "Finite element method based machining simulation environment for analyzing part errors induced during milling of thin-walled components", *International Journal of Machine Tools & Manufacture*, Vol. 48, 629-643.

Lamikiz, A., Lacalle, L. N., Sanchez, J. A. & Salgado, M. A. (2004). "Cutting force estimation in sculptured surface milling", *Machine Tools and Manufacture*, Vol. 44, 1511-1526.

Larue, A. & Altintas, Y. (2005). "Simulation of flank milling processes", *Machine Tools and Manufacture*, Vol. 45, 549-559.

Lee, T. S. & Lin, Y. J. (2000). "A 3D predictive cutting force model for end milling of parts having sculptured surfaces", *Advanced Manufacturing Technology*, Vol. 16, 773-783.

Li, H. Z., Liu, K. & Li, X. P. (2001). "A new method for determining the undeformed chip thickness in milling", *Materials Processing Technology*, Vol. 113, No 1, 378-384.

Li, J. G., Yao, Y. X., Xia, P. J., Liu, C. Q. & Wu, C. G. (2008). "Extended octree for cutting force prediction", International *Journal of Advanced Manufacturing Technology*, Vol. 39, 866-873.

Li, J. G., Zhao, H., Yao, Y. X. & Liu, C. Q. (2008). "Off-line optimization on NC machining based on virtual machining", *International Journal of Advanced Manufacturing Technology*, Vol. 36, 908-917.

Lin, Y. & Shen, Y. L. (2004). "Enhanced virtual machining for sculptured surfaces by integrating machine tool error models into NC machining simulation", *Machine Tools and Manufacture*, Vol. 44, 79-86.

Liu, X. & Cheng, K. (2005). "Modeling the machining dynamics in peripheral milling", *Machine Tools and Manufacture*, Vol. 45, 1301-1320.

Lo, C. C. (1999). "Real Time generation and control of cutter path for 5 axis CNC machining", *Machine Tools and Manufacture*, Vol. 39, 471-478.

Lou, M. S. J. C., Chen, C. & Li, C. M. (1999). "Surface Roughness prediction technique for CNC End Milling", *Industrial Technology*, Vol. 15, No 1, 1-6.

Milenkovic, V. (1993). "Robust Polygon Modeling", *CAD*, Vol. 25, No 9, 546-566.

Mousavi, M. & Aziz, F. A. (2008). State of the art of haptic feedback in virtual reality in manufacturing, Proceedings - *International Symposium on Information Technology*, Vol. 3.

Ong, S. K., Jiang, L. & Nee, A. Y. C. (2002). "An Internet Based Virtual CNC Milling System", *Advanced Manufacturing Technology, Vol 20*, 20-30.

Peng Gaoliang, Wang Gongdongb, Liu Wenjiana, Yu Haiquan, "A desktop virtual reality-based interactive modular fixture configuration design system", Computer-Aided Design, Article in Press

Peng, Q., Hall, F. R. & Lister, P. M. (2000). "Application and evaluation of VR-based CAPP system", *Materials processing Technology*, Vol. 107, 153-159.

Ratchev, S., Nikov, S. & Moualek, I. (2004). "Material removal simulation of peripheral milling of thin wall low rigidity structures using FEA", *Advances in Engineering Software*, Vol. 35, 481-491.

Sun, S., Luo, L., Li, G., Zou, X. & Yang, J. (2008). "The virtual simulation system of numerical control machining", 2008 International Workshop on Modelling, *Simulation and Optimization*, 289-293.

Tian, X., Deng, H., Fujishima, M. & Yamazaki, K. (2007). "Quick 3D Modeling of Machining Environment by Means of On-machine Stereo Vision with Digital Decomposition", *Annals of the CIRP*, Vol. 56.

Tseng, T. L., Kwon, Y. & Ertekin, Y. M. (2005). "Feature based rule induction in machining operation using rough set theory for quality assurance", *Robotics and Computer Integrated Manufacturing*, Vol. 21, 559-567.

Wang, S. M., Chiou, C. H. & Cheng, Y. M. (2004). "An improved dynamic cutting force model for end milling process", *Materials Processing Technology*, Vol. 148, 317-327.

Wang, T. Y., Wang, G. F., Li, H. W., Lin, J. B. & Wu, Z. Y. (2002). "Construction of a realistic scene in virtual turning based on a global illumination model and chip simulation", *Materials Processing Technology*, Vol. 129, 524-528.

Wang, W. J., Wang, T. Y., Fan, S. B. & Wang, W. Y. (2008). Research on material removal algorithm model in virtual milling process based on adaptive dynamic quadtrees algorithm", *Applied Mechanics and Materials, Volume 10-12*, 822-827.

Woo Soo Yun, Dong Woo Cho, "Accurate 3-D cutting force prediction using cutting condition independent coefficients in end milling", *Machine Tools and Manufacture*, Vol. 41, No 4, 463-478, 2000.

Yao, Y., Li, J., Lee, W. B., Cheung, C. F. & Yuan, Z. (2002). "VMMC: A test bed for machining", *Computers in industry*, Vol. 47, 255-268.

Zhang, I., Deng, J. & Chan, S. C. F. (2000). "A next generation NC machining system based on an NC Feature Unit and Real Time tool path generation", *Advanced Manufacturing Technology*, Vol. 16, 889-901.

In: Computer Science Research and the Internet
Editor: Jaclyn E. Morris, pp. 153-168

ISBN: 978-1-61728-730-5
© 2011 Nova Science Publishers, Inc.

Chapter 6

VIRTUAL ENVIRONMENTS TO THE NEURAL SIMULATION

Regina Célia Coelho[*,1] *and Nivaldi Calonego Jr.*[2,**]

[1] Universidade Federal de São Paulo (UNIFESP), Rua Talim,
330 – Vila Nair, São José dos Campos - SP – Brazil
[2]State University of Mato Grosso (UNEMAT), Faculdade de
Ciências Exatas – Departamento de Computação,
Av. São João s/n – Cavalhada, Cáceres- MT - Brazil

1. Introduction

Nervous systems and the mechanisms underlying their operation are very complex. Computational simulators to model these systems may also become very complex and, consequently, be difficult to define, comprehend and manage. Thus, it is crucial there are software tools that support discussion, development and exchange of computational models.

To try to simulate and understand neural systems, researchers in computational neuroscience have used mathematical or algorithmic models, being some of them are too complex to be treated analytically and must be evaluated numerically on a computer. The main motivation for the development of neural simulators is the fact that scientific questions can be answered with a single modeling system.

In a neural simulation, it is desirable to follow interact with the scene and, sometimes, to modify the results by altering some parameters or introducing some new information. It is also desirable to be able to examine the formation of the neural structure, by observing each new element being added, in a nondeterministic way, forming a whole new structure, as well as to interact, navigate or even immerse in the structure being formed, as in a virtual reality environment. It is necessary to give special attention to the neural modeling in these simulations, since studies have shown that morphology of neural cells is an important factor in the behavior of the neural cell (Kossel, Löwel and Bolz, 1995; Linden, 1993; Purves, 1988;

---

[*] E-mail address: rccoelho@unifesp.br. Phone: +55 12 3942 5568.
[**] E-mail address: nivaldi.calonegojr@gmail.com. Phone: +55 65 3221 0508.

Wässle, 1986). These studies have proved that the more complex the function of the cells, the more complex will be its morphology. Unfortunately, the morphology of the neural cell is usually either taken straight from experimental data (compartmental models), or simplified with coarse approximations, or, still, neglected altogether, but it is hardly ever modeled. Thus, the study of correlation between morphology and physiology requires more than analytical approaches. It requires numerical simulations whose understanding could be greatly improved if simulations results were visualized and interacted by scientists or students.

Those numerical simulations can happen in several scales. For instance, modeling molecular interactions with individual neuron cells, such as neurochemical factors influencing the neuron growth; modeling the neuron signal processing, such as the potential actions in a compartmented approach; modeling a lot of cells in the tissue level, where the neurons interact one with another to answer for input stimuli. An innovative approach could insert dynamical features to better understand the neuron growth conditions when its environmental circumstances change.

This paper presents a review of some of the most common virtual environments to the neural simulation and a technological approach to make feasible the visualization of the simulation of neuron birth, growth and death, at the neural tissue level. This is called Distributed Environment to Neural Simulation (DENS).

2. Overview of Simulation Environments

Over time, different simulation systems have been developed, some of them being dedicated to construct the morphologically detailed neurons models. The neural simulators NEURON [Hines, 1984, 1989, 1997, 2000] and GENESIS [Bower, 1998, 2003] are the most used to model whole cells or a small network, while MCell [Stiles, 1998, 2001a, 2001b] is chosen to model individual particles in complex geometries. In the same line, there is NEST [Gewaltig, 2007] used to simulate large neural networks. Except for MCell, all these softwares are used to simulate electrophysiological experiments. NEST simulator is specifically designed for distributed simulations of very large networks, while NEURON and GENESIS simulators are designed for complete simulation environment with graphical interface and tools for representation of model structure and analysis of the results. MCell was designed to simulate the chemical properties of cells and consider three-dimensional properties of extracellular domains.

There are some simulators that use L-systems [Fijters, 1974] in their methodologies. One of them is L-Neuron [Ascoli, 2000], which generates the cells using stochastic L-System and has an interaction and visualization environment. It generates morphologically realistic neural networks, but it relies on the a priori limitation strategy in which the specification of artificial neuron is limited to combinations of statistically determined values of morphological properties. Another simulator is EvOL-Neuron [Nielsen, 2006a, 2006b, 2008], a tool that also uses L-system to generate artificial neurons, but without putting a priori limitations on the candidate artificial neurons [Nielsen, 2006b].

Other software that implements reaction of electrical signals of cells is A-Cell-3D [Ichikawa, 2005]. It considers 3D morphology of neurons (but not features of natural cells) and it is used to simulate biochemical reactions and electrical circuits in 3D cells generated by a simulation program.

While L-Neuron is based on recursive rules using a Lindenmayer-system formalism, i.e., looping rules given by a Lindenmayer-string, NeuGen [Edehard, 2006; Aluri, 2005] implements a straightforward algorithm which utilizes forward-stepping rules.

The following is a brief description of each of these neural simulators.

Neuron

NEURON[1] is a simulation environment free and open source used to simulate empirically neurons and small neural networks based on biological neurons and neural circuits [Hines,1984; Hines,1989; Hines,1997]. This simulator allows the inclusion of membrane properties of the cells, as for instance, extracellular potential near the membrane, multiple channel types, in homogeneous channel distribution, ionic accumulation and diffusion [Brette, 2007]. It is efficient to model problems that range from parts of single cells to a few cells in which the membrane properties (for instance, calculation of ionic concentration, extracellular potential, etc.) have a crucial role. NEURON supports implementation of distributed models of networks that will run in a parallel computation environment, where each processor integrates the equations for its subnet [Migliore,2006]. The models defined by NEURON may include electronic circuits, including resistors, capacitors, voltage, current sources, and operational amplifiers. Its main characteristic is to allow the user to handle the cable properties of neurons without having to deal directly with compartments. It allows users to simulate the biophysical properties of membrane and cytoplasm, the branches of neurons, and the effects of synaptic communication between cells.

Instead of the NEURON users having to deal directly with compartments of the cells, the cells are represented by sections, where each one has its own anatomical and biophysical properties, which can be assembled into branched architectures. The sections are a continuous unbranched cable (analogous to an unbranched neurite) and they can be connected together to form branched trees, endowed with properties that can vary continuously with position along their lengths. The properties of each section do not need to be constant. Instead, they can vary along its length [Hines, 1997]. It supports two different specification languages: HOC and MODL [Hines, 2000]. Thus, models can be created, for instance, by writing programs in an interpreted language based on HOC, which has been enhanced to simplify the task of representing the properties of biological neurons and networks. It is possible to increase the ability to exchange model specifications with other simulators through the Extensible Markup Language (XML) [Brette, 2007].

NEURON's computational engine uses algorithms that are tailored to the model system equations [Hines,1984; Hines,1989; Hines,1997].

NEURON fully supports hybrid simulations and analytically computable artificial spiking cells.

---

[1] http://www.neuron.yale.edu

Genesis

GENESIS[2] (the GEneral NEural SImulation System) was designed to be an extensible general simulation system for the realistic modeling of neural and biological systems [Bower, 1998]. It is widely used for single cell or cells network modeling. Just as NEURON, GENESIS system consists of a precise sequence of instructions to specify how to create and combine parts of the model, or be, the user specify how the models should be created using the internal data structures of a simulator [Canon, 2007]. Its specification language is SLI, a high-level scripting language. It uses an interpreter with pre-compiled object types, which allows that user interacts and modifies a simulation in run time [Brete, 2007]. It is possible to simulate since subcellular components, including their biochemical reactions [Bhalla, 2004], until large networks [Nenadic, 2003]. Here, the cell models are defined including dendritic morphology and ionic conductances and the neural networks are defined duplicating known axonal projection patterns.

GENESIS environments graphical allow running simulations with or without scripting. It includes a customizable user interface that can be used by users who are not specialized. Its simulator and interface are based on a building "block approach" (object-oriented approach), where simulations are constructed from modules and generate outputs, and the neurons are constructed from compartments and variable conductance ion channels and these compartments are linked to form multi-compartmental neurons. If these neurons are linked, it is possible to form neural networks. This modularity allows quickly construct a new simulation or to modify an existing simulation by changing modules that are chosen from a library or database of standard simulation components [Bower, 2003].

There is a version of parallel GENESIS, known as PGENESIS. It is used on simulations involving tens of thousands of cells.

Nest

NEST (Neural Simulation Tool) is a simulation environment for large heterogeneous networks of neurons with a small number of compartments [Gewaltig, 2007]. It has been developed by the NEST Initiative[3] that was founded in 2001 with the goal to collaborate in the development of simulation methods for biologically realistic neural networks. There is a lot of use for models that focus on the dynamics, size, and structure of neural systems rather than on the detailed morphological and biophysical properties of individual neurons, as for instance, models of sensory processing (visual or auditory cortex of mammals), models of network activity dynamics (laminar cortical networks), models of spike-synchronization in fccd-forward networks, learning and plasticity in models of sensory processing. It allows combining different types of neurons and different synapse models, and structuring networks into layers, areas and subnetworks. The layers and subnetworks are implemented storing the nodes of a network as a tree where the subnetworks are the branches and the neurons and devices are the leaves [Gewaltig, 2007]. The goal of NEST is to try to maintain a close correpondence to an electrophysiological experiment [Diesmann, 2002].

---

[2] http://www.genesis-sim.org/GENESIS/
[3] http://www.nest-initiative.org

Just as, GENESIS, NEST uses the specification language SLI, a stack-oriented programming language with postfix notation. Thus, its user interface is a simulation language interpreter which processes a rather high level expressive language with a simple syntax. Beside this, the interpreter provides a set of basic data structures which are used to exchange data between modules. The simulation language is used for data pre and post-processing, specification of parameters and for the compact description of the network structure and the protocol of the virtual experiment [Brete, 2007; Diesmann, 2002].

The simulation kernel of NEST is divided into two parts [Diesmann, 2002]:

i) a set of abstract base classes used to define neural elements at different abstraction levels;

ii) a simulation driver, used to control the simulation kernel.

NEST can take advantage of multiple processors, cores, or computers in a local network. Communication overhead is minimized by communicating in intervals of the minimum propagation delay between neurons [Morrison, 2005]. On computer cluster, each computer creates its own part of the network and on single computers, the networks are distribuited over the available processors, where each processor runs one part [Gewaltig, 2007].

One extension module that allows simulations to be coded using the Python programming language is PyNEST[4]. Thus, instead of NEST's SLI language, it uses Python language, which has a more convenient syntax and gives us access to many supplementary packages [Eppler, 2008].

MCell

MCell[5] (Monte Carlo cell) is an environment for cellular microphysiological simulations. It uses highly optimized Monte Carlo algorithms and 3D cellular models to simulate the movements and reactions of molecules within and between cells. Monte Carlo algorithms are used to track the stochastic behavior of discrete molecules in space and time for interacting with other discrete molecules, called ligands and effectors, heterogeneously distributed within the 3D geometry of the cellular microphysiology. Ligands encounter cell membrane boundaries and effectors molecules as they diffuse. Encounters may result in chemical reactions governed by user specified reaction mechanisms, but the final outcome of each encounter is decided by comparing the value of a random number to the probability of each possible outcome [Balls, 2004]. Thus, molecular diffusion and reactions are modeled using a stochastic treatment of phenomenological rates, and the simulation time step can often be on the microsecond scale for signals lasting from milliseconds to seconds [Casanova, 2007].

MCell simulation environment tolerates hundreds of thousands of surface mesh objects, where each mesh may be composed of millions of polygons, and this requires about the same amount of time as simulation of a highly simplified structure. It is possible to generate highly realistic reconstructions of cellular or subcellular boundaries to define the 3D diffusion space, which can be populated with molecules of different kinds [Stiles, 2001b]. These molecules

---

[4] http://www.nest-initiative.org/index.php/PyNEST
[5] http://www.mcell.psc.edu/; http://www.mcell.cnl.salk.edu

may react with others that are released periodically from different locations within the structure, to simulate the production of biological signals.

Besides including the development and use of highly realistic 3D biological structures, MCell simulations allow realistic movements and interactions of individual molecules within the structures.

MCell simulation uses a high-level model description language (MDL) designed for readability by scientists. Thus, in a simulation, one or more MDL input files are parsed to create the objects, and execution begins for a specified number of time-step iterations.

An extension of MCell simulator, called MCell-K, has been developed to increase its capacity of processing. It uses the KeLP (Kernel Lattice Parallelism) infrastrutucture[6], a framework for implementing portable scientific applications on distributed memory parallel computers that, in MCell-K, manages distributed pointer-based data structures, including molecule migration among processors, and facilitates load balancing. With MCell-K is possible to simulate extra-cellular dynamics in a specialized neural structure in the cerebellum (cerebellar glomerulus) [Balls, 2004].

A-Cell-3D

A-Cell-3D [Ichikawa, 2005] is software to model and simulate reaction-diffusion and electrical processes within the 3D morphology of a neuron. It generates and compartmentalizes 3D morphologies of cell (or part of it) on a small whole number of parameters. It has functions for embedding biochemical reactions and electrical equivalent circuits in the generated 3D morphology, automatically generating a simulation program for spatiotemporal numerical integration.

A-Cell-3D is an evolution of A-Cell [Ichikawa, 2001]. Unlikely A-Cell, A-Cell-3D considers the geometric properties of a neuron and, if it is necessary, it models just a single compartment, but does not consider the features of natural cells.

It is possible to specify the membrane surface density in A-Cell-3D, what is converted to the number of molecules on each membrane. It also constructs biochemical reaction and Hodgkin-Huxley models, which should be embedded in the desired compartments. A-Cell3D allows viewing compartments embedded with specified reactions, what is important to view the location of embedded reaction in the 3D morphology.

One important characteristic of A-Cell-3D is the simulation program, written in C language, generated automatically by it, base on the constructed 3D model, to simulate the Ca^{2+} dynamics in the spine/dendrite shape [Ishikawa, 2005]. Once executed this simulation program, the calculation results are stored as a binary file, which can be read by A-Cell-3D.

L-Neuron

L-Neuron[7] implements a stochastic L-System and a mathematical description of the topology extracted from natural cells to generate the artificial cells anatomically indistinguishable form their real counterparts. It implements sets of recursive

---

[6] http://cseweb.ucsd.edu/groups/hpcl/scg/kelp/
[7] http://krasnow.gmu.edu/cn3/L-Neuron/index.htm

neuroanatomical rules that parsimoniously describe dendritic geometry and topology by locally inter-correlation morphological parameters, instead of using standard L-systems, and read in experimental data (statistical distribution) to generate virtual cells. The L-neuron stochastically samples parameter values from experimental statistical distributions to generate virtual neurons within several morphological classes. Statistical distributions can be measured from computer files of reconstructed neurons in several commonly used formats. These features are extracted from several traced format, such as EUTECTIC, SWC and NEUROLUCIDA notation. Generated neurons can be converted in several 3D-graphic formats and saved as compartmental files compatible with electrophysiological simulators, such as the GENESIS and NEURON simulators [Ascoli, 2000].

L-Neuron uses Hillman's algorithm [Hillman, 1979] to generate the neurons. This algoritm defines some parameters, called "fundamentals", as enough features to describe completely and precisely the dendritic growth. Another algorimth used by L-Neuron is the Tamori [Tamori, 1993], that introduces the concept of efective volume as fundamental parameter to calculate the bifurcation angles and diameters. Finally, it also uses algorithm's Burke [Burke, 1992], that deals of statistical features of angles and diameters.

It is also possible to simulate tropism in L-Neuron, imitating the efects of neurotrophic factors and growth cones.

L-Neuron can be run on a standard desktop workstation to visualize the large data sets, but it is used to generate individual cells, not a neural network.

EvOL-Neuron

EvOL-Neuron (Evolucionaty Optimization of L-systems) [Nielsen, 2006a, 2006b, 2008] is a method for artificial neurons generation that explores the immense parameter space for morphologies. It is based on L-systems [Lindenamyer, 1968] and evoluctionary computation [Kosa, 1992]. The candidate neurons (2D or 3D) are generated by L-system and validated by evolutionary computation (genetic algorithm), which optimizes the accuracy of those candidate neurons by exploring the parameter space [Nilesen, 2008]. In generation phase just virtual neurons are created, and, in the validation phase, good virtual neurons are selected. EvOL-Neuron supposes all neural morphologies can be approximated with a standard L-system and can be found efficiently by applying evolutionary computation, and it does not impose any a priori limitation on candidate neural morphologies. Just on the validation phase limitations are imposed on candidate virtual neurons [Nielsen, 2006a, Nielsen, 2006b].

During the generation of each artificial neuron, this neuron can suffer fitness, by the evolutionary computation, to approximate it to the real neurons and the survival neurons in this fitness are used in a new iteration, generating a new population of neurons. The fitness value reflects the biological accuracy of the generated artificial neuron with respect to the prototype neuron. Thus, the artificial neurons resultants of the iterations are morphologically and statistically similar to the real neurons [Nielsen, 2006a].

The fact of this method to implement a *posteriori* constraining strategy, allows the search the complete parameter space for virtual neurons that conform to current biological knowledge, what it means to specify which properties the neuron should obey [Nielsen, 2008].

There are two limitations in this method: realistic variability and the lack of guarantee to find good structures [Nielsen, 2008].

In EvOL-Neuron, it is possible to model trophic fields, but just in two dimensions.

NeuGen

NeurGen[8] is a tool for generation and description of dendritic and axonal morphology of realistic neurons and neuronal networks in 3D. It is possible to generate real neural network geometries and to simulate networks of synaptically connected neurons in a cortical column [Eberhard, 2006]. It directly supports geometry formats for using the NEURON simulation software via HOC files.

NeuGen generates neural cells of morphological classe of the cortex, and synaptically connected neural networks and it is based on sets of descriptive and iterative rules which represent the axonal and dendritic geometry of neurons by iter-correlating morphological parameters. The synapses in NeuGen are created by distributions and/or distance between cells and the interconnections are made due to realistic connectivity patterns in a cortical column by experiments. Its input configuration contains parameter for the different neuron cell type morphologies. The configuration parameters for a base neuron class are inherited to all its subclasses (sppecialized neurons) [Aluri, 2005].

NeuGen tool is useful for geometric modeling and the construction of the morphology of cells.

3. Distributed Environment to Neural Simulation

Distributed Environment to Neural Simulation (DENS) is a virtual environment to model and simulate morphologically realistic neural cells. This environment was developed considering five issues [Coelho, 2009]:

(i) possibility to observe the dynamics of growth of the cells and formation of the neural netoworks;

(ii) possibility to observe the interactions with models leading to an understanding of the interplay between aspects of development, such as environmental influence and the development of the whole structure;

(iii) simulation of interactions between cells;

(iv) navigation and following the structure growth, observing each new element being added in a non-deterministic way, forming a whole new structure;

(v) exploration of the cellular plasticity.

DENS is divided into modules shown in Figure 1. There are two major parts (Simulator and Viewer), where each is divided into other sub-models and the arrowed lines represents exchange between the modules. To visualize some characteristics of plasticity of neural cells (or structure neural) it is possible to include some trophic field in the simulation environment. Simulator module is responsible for generating the realistic morphologically neurons (or

---

[8] http://atlas.gcsc.uni-frankfurt.de/~neugen/

neural structures) and sends the results to Viewer module, responsible for showing graphically the results and allowing the interactions with the users.

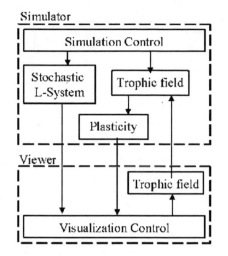

Figure 1. Modules of DENS [Coelho, 2009].

DENS allows one to see an animation, for instance, the neural growth process of the structure, and interact with the neural structure generated.

One of the major advantages of DENS is the possibility of having different users interacting into the same neural structure, even if they are located in different places. In that case, the interaction occurs by exchange of messages between them and the virtual environment. For instance, a user can insert a new neural cell and/or a trophic field and it will be possible all the users see this (or these) alteration (s) in the neural structure.

3.1. Simulator Module

Before detailing the Simulator module, it is necessary to define the parts a neuron constituent parts which are involved in the simulation. At high level, we can divide a neuron into two parts: *soma* (cell body) and *neurites* (any *branch* (dendrite or axon) that comes out of the soma). Neurites are divided into *branch element* and *natural end*. Just if a neurite is a dendrite, it may have bifurcations. Branch element is either the piece between two succeeding bifurcations, or the piece between a bifurcation and a natural end, or the piece between a tree origin and a bifurcation, and the neuron shape depends on branch element shape properties (color, texture, tortuosity, etc.). Natural end is each branch termination. Each branch element is formed by successive parts, called *compartments* (branch element atomic part), responsible for tortuosity of a branch element. Figure 2 illustrates all this parts of neuron [Coelho, 2009].

The simulator generates neural cells based in functions of density of probability (fdp), one for each morphological feature: compartment length, branch length, θ and ϕ angles of compartment, θ and ϕ angles of branch, thickness. These fdps were not equally evaluated along the growth process. Ten hierarchical branching levels was identified for the muddy puppy eyes neuron cells. So, each feature has ten fdps, one for each branching level. Others two distributions were applied to evaluate the probability for branching at each level, and the probability of a number of soma efferent neuritis [Coelho, 2002].

The neuron drawing process is better seen as a turtle drawer algorithm for 3D spaces, where a cursor mimics a pencil tip drawing in the air. Firstly, a spherical soma is drawn (representing the soma), and the number of efferent neurites (η) is randomly found based on the fdp_η. Next, the compartment length (σ_i), i.e. the distance that the cursor must move drawing a line in the next step, is also randomly evaluated according to fdp_σ. At same moment, the branch length (β_j) is defined by the fdp_β to locate a 3D position for the branching occurrence, for each level j. Two angles must be defined for the compartment: the angle between the new segment and the normal plane formed by the two last step segments (ϕi), and the angle between the new compartment and the perpendicular vector with the last compartment (θi). As illustrates the Figure 3, the branches (β_l) are resultant from the concatenation of some compartments (σ_1, σ_2, and σ_3). Similarly, the angles for branches are defined, since two compartments must derive from a unique location. One of the compartment will take the fdp_ϕ and other, fdp_θ. However, the other compartment requires two other fdps for each one of two angles ϕ_j and θ_j [Coelho, 2002].

The neuron growth was simulated by rotating the turtle cursor to the segments that are to be drawn or branched. Therefore, the simulation can be followed up by displaying step-by-step each step segment (in Viewer module).

During the generating of each part of each neuron, some data are sent to Viewer module to allow the visualization of the scene being formed. These data are generated obeying a context-free, regular, parametric, and stochastic L-system. This grammar is used to all the data sent have a homogeneous namespace, where each neural cell piece is specifically named (more detail about this grammar can be obtained in [Coelho, 2009]).

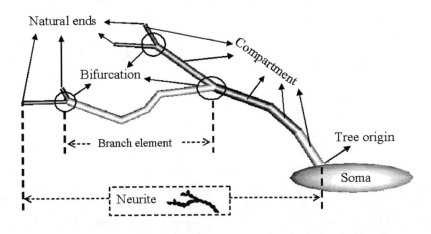

Figure 2. Parts of neuron [Coelho, 2009].

3.2. Viewer Module

The *Viewer* module is responsible for rendering, tracking and navigation systems. There is a protocol between the rendering and the tracking systems that identify the objects received and the respective action to be taken. The grammar is the key concept for interaction, and linking the rendering and the tracking systems, once that it is responsible for defining names for each branch created. This branch element identification creates a unique identifier for each branch element in the whole neural system. More than that, it creates a hierarchical namespace partition, analogous to a tree data structure, as shown in Figure 4.

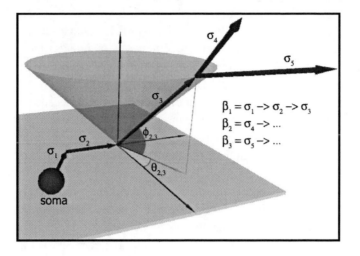

Figure 3. Parts of one neural cell and some angles used.

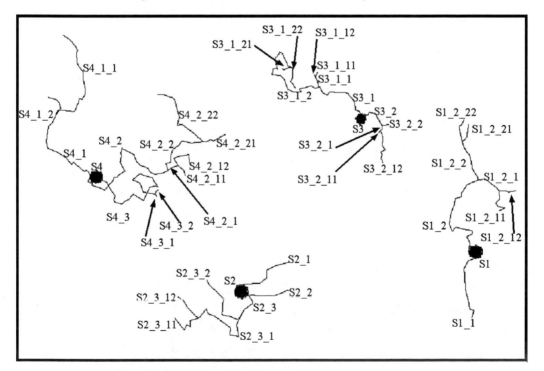

Figure 4. Example of namespaces generated by each branch element [Coelho,2009].

Viewer allows interaction with the neurons in growth, as well as the insertion of influence fields (simulating trophic fields). A distributed architecture was built to accomplish the visualization of neural structure, coming from a simulator and processed by a proxy node.

The user can interact with the scene by sending commands to change scene elements, or changing simulator parameters.

3.3. Distributed Environment

DENS is interesting to allowing geographically distributed users work together in its virtual environment shared through a computer network to interact and analyze the neural structure generated. It is used to generate a few neurons.

Figure 5 illustrates the logical connections between modules of this simulation environment. The main module is user's interactions module, because it allows that users send interaction commands directly to Server module over the network by the Proxy module.

The Simulator generates data that are transferred bye Proxy module, which transforms the data into object parts (in general, compartments) and send them to the Server. The Server runs the Interaction module, which parses the commands to handle the objects in the scene rendered by *OpenVRML* procedures. In this case, the *Proxy* transforms the data input to output the VRML code, by meeting the code templates in the *Proxy*.

Proxy module is responsible to manage exchanges of messages between the Simulator and the Viewer. Each instance of the *Proxy* module, labeled as Pi in Figure 5, has its own configuration file, and controls the *Viewer* module Vij instance. This approach leaves the user to check the qualitative visualization properties enabling users to see simultaneous different points of view.

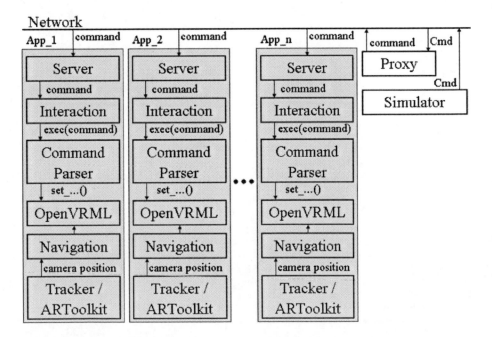

Figure 5. Instances of the visualization application, proxy and simulator [Coelho, 2009].

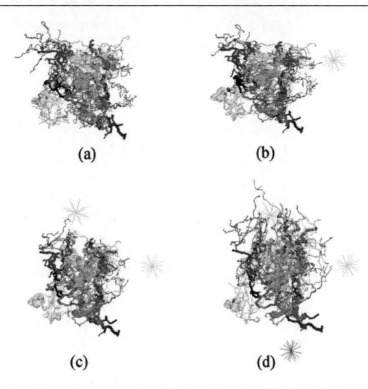

(a)   (b)

(c)   (d)

Figure 6. Examples of neural reorganization with insertion of trophic field. (a) Initial neural structure with 15 cells; (b) first reorganization of structures when an attraction field is inserted; (c) new reorganization after the insertion of a new attraction field; (d) new reorganization after the insertion of a repulsion field (the darkest field) [Coelho, 2009].

The *Proxy* also manages the requisitions of users in collaborative activities such as save some neural structure state, or multicast user messages, supporting not only internal commands, but commands which may be distributed to the viewers.

DENS allows that the user edits, interacts or executes the neural structure after the simulator had produced it.

A relevant interaction feature is the insertion of trophic field. According to Perry and Maffei [Perry, 1988], the sprouting of some chemotrophic factors can lead to neural reorganization. This visualization approach leaves to introduce several fields, either attraction or repulsion fields, with different strengths in the same structure. Supposing that each field emulates a new chemotrophic factor sprouting into the structure, analysis about what will happen to the cells could be done, even if the present fields had their strengths changed, or different fields were introduced into the neural structures.

The reorganization caused by inserting a trophic field into the structure implies a new position computation for each node, which depends on its field distance (the closer the distance, the larger the field influence) and its soma distance (the stronger the distance, the larger the field influence), as seen in equation (I).

Figure 5 illustrates the steps of the neural structure steering after the trophic fields were inserted. By observing Figure 5 (b) and (c), the dendritic arborization was reorganized in the direction of the attraction field. The Figure 5 (d) shows a major dendritic arborization reorganization going to the attraction field in the top of the structure. That occurred after a repulsion field had been inserted at the bottom of the neural structure, which resulted in the repulsion of dendritic arborization to the new trophic field.

4. Conclusion

Virtual environment to the neural growing simulation has became a powerful tool for neuroscientists to examine and better understand the development of some cells, mainly because several parameters of biological neural structures are not known by the researchers. The neural cells simulation is an essential tool to support studies about the neural structure development, neural plasticity, neurogenesis, and signal interaction among different neural cells. Neural modeling and simulation has become important because, unlike a mathematic computational simulation and modeling, several parameters of biological structures are unknown by the researcher.

This chapter presented some the most known neural simulators existing and a distributed environment to neural simulation (DENS) that simulates the growth neural and several other aspects related to the neurogenesis, such as, the results of the neural reorganization after the inclusion of trophic fields or neural death. Some of these simulators are projected mainly to simulate compartmental model (NEURON, GENESIS, NEST, MCell, A-Cell-3D), and others are more interested in modelling the neural morphology of natural cells (L-Neuron, EvOL-Neuron, NeurGen, and DENS). It is possible to get the results of one simulator (considering the cellular shape) and use as entrance of the other simulator (considering the compartmental model). Thus, it is possible to have a very interesting study about the neural structures, since virtual environments to neural simulation where are considered realistic neuromorphic models are considered, are essential for allowing the user to have full control over the parameters involved.

References

Aluri, A. (2005). Stochastic generation of biologically accurtate brain networks, *Master thesis*, BNL, Texas A&M University.

Ascoli, G. A. & Krichmar, J. L. (2000). L-neuron: A modeling tool for the efficient generation and parsimonious description of dendritic morphology. *Neurocomputing*, 32-33, 1003- 1011.

Balls, G., Baden, S. B., Kispersky, T., Bartol, T. M. & Sejnowski, T. J. (2004). A large scale Monte Carlo simulator for cellular microphysiology. *Proceedings of the 18th International Parallel and Distributed Processing Symposium*, (IPDPS).

Bhalla, U. S. (2004). Signaling in small subcellular volumes: II. Stochastic and diffusion effects on synaptic network properties. *Biophysical Journal*, **87**, 745-753.

Bower, J. M. & Beeman, D. (1998). *The Book of Genesis: Exploring realistic neural models with the GEneral NEural SImulation System* (2nd edition), Teleos Publishing, SpringerVerlag New York.

Bower, J. M., Beeman, D. & Hucka, M. (2003). The GENESIS Simulation System, in: *The Handbook of Brain Theory and Neural Networks*, Second edition (M.A. Arbib, Ed.), Cambridge, MA, MIT Press, 475-478.

Brete, R., Rudolph, M., Carnevale, T., Hines, M., Beeman, D., Bower, J. M., Diesmann, M., Morrison, A., Goodman, P. H., Harris Jr., F. C., Zirpe M., Natschläger, T., Pecevski, D., Ermentrout, B., Djurfeldt, M., Lansner, A., Rochel, O., Vievile, T., Muller, E., Davison, A. P., el Boustani, S. & Destexhe, A. (2007). Simulation of networks of spiking neurons: a review of tools and strategies. *Journal of Computational Neuroscience,* **23**(3), 349-398,.

Burke, R. E., Marks, W. B. & Ulfhake, B. (1992). A parsimonious description of motoneurons dendritic morphology using computer simulation, *Journal of Neuroscience,* **12**, 2403-2416.

Cannon, R. C., Gewaltig, M. O., Gleeson, P., Bhalla, U. S., Hines, M. L., Howell, F. H., Muller, E., Stiles. J. R., Wils, S. & De Shutter, E. (2007). Interoperability of neuroscience modeling software: current status and future directions. *Neuroinformatics,* **5**(2), 127-38.

Casanova, H., Bartol Jr., T. M., Stiles, J. & Berman, F. (2001). Distributing Mcell simulations on the grid. The *International Journal of High Performance Computing Applications,* **15**(3), 243-257.

Coelho, R. C. & Costa, L. F. (2002). Realistic neuromorphic models and their application to neural reorganization simulations. *Neurocomputing,* **48**, 555-571.

Coelho, R. C., Calonego Jr., N. & Consularo, L. A. (2009). A technique to visualize neural structures generated by contex-free, parametric and stochastic L-system, *Virutal Reality,* (in press).

Diesmann, M. & Gewaltig; M. O. (2002). NEST: An Environment for Neural Systems Simulations. In Plesser, T; Macho, V. (eds). Forschung und wissenschaftliches Rechnen, Beitrage zum Heinz-Billing-Preis, Volume 58 GWDG-Bericht of Göttingen (D): Ges. *Fuer Wissenschaftliche Datenverarbeitung,* 43-70.

Fijters, D. & Lindenmayer, A. (1974). A model for the growth and flowering of aster novae-angiae on the basis of table <1,0> L-systems. *In:* Rozenberg, G., Salomaa, A. L-Systems, *Lecture Notes in Computer Science,* Springer, v. 15, 24-52.

Eberhard, J., Wanner, A. & Wittum, G. (2006). NeuGen: a tool for the generation of realistic morphology of cortical neurons and neural networks in 3D, *Neurocomputing,* **70**(1-3), 327-342.

Eppler, J. M., Helias, M., Muller E., Diesmann, M. & Gewaltig, M. O. (2008). PyNEST: A convenient interface to the NEST simulator. *Frontiers in Neuroinformatics,* **2**, 12.

Gewaltig, M. O. & Diesmann, M. (2007). NEST (Neural Simulation Tool). *Scholarpedia* **2**(4), 1430.

Hillman, D. E. (1979). Neuronal shape parameters and substructures as a basis of neuronal form, In: Schmitt, F., editor, *The Neurosciences,* 4th Study Program, MIT Press, *Cambridge,* 477-498.

Hines, M. (1984). Efficient computation of branched nerve equations. *International Journal of Bio-Medical Computing,* **15**, 69-76.

Hines, M. (1989). A program for simulation of nerve equations with branching geometries. *International Journal of Bio-Medical Computing,* **24**, 55-68.

Hines, M. L. & Carnevale, N. T. (1997). The NEURON simulation environment. *Neural Computation,* **9**, 1179-1209.

Hines, M. L. & Carnevale, N. T. (2000). Expanding NEURON's Repertoire of Mechanisms with NMODL. *Neural Computation,* **12**, 9951007.

Ichikawa, K. (2001). A-Cell: graphical user interface for the construction of biochemical reaction models. *Bioinformatics,* **17**, 483-484.

Ichikawa, K. (2005). A Modeling Environment With Three-Dimensional Morphology,A-Cell-3D, and Ca2+ Dynamics in a Spine, *Neuroinformatics*, **3**(1), 49-64.

Koza, J. (1992). *Genetic programming: On the programming of computers by means of Natural Selection.* MIT Press, Cambridge.

Kossel A., Löwel S. & Bolz J. (1995). Relationships between dendritic fields and functional architecture in striate cortex of normal and visually deprived cats. *The Journal of Neuroscience*, **15**, 3913-3926.

Lindenmayer, A. (1968). Mathematical models for cellular interaction in development, *Journal of Theoretical Biology*, **18**, 300-315.

Linden, R. (1993). Dendritic competition in the developing retina: ganglion cell density gradients and laterally displace dendrites. *Visual Neuroscience*, **10**, 313-324.

Migliore, M., Cannia, C., Lytton, W. W., Markram, H. & Hines, M. L. (2006). Parallel network simulations with NEURON. *Journal of Computational Neuroscience,* **21**, 119-129.

Morrison, A., Mehring, C., Geisel, T., Aertsen, A. & Diesmann, M. (2005). Advancing the boundaries of high connectivity network simulation with distributed computing. *Neural Computation*, **17**, 1776-1801.

Nenadic, Z., Ghosh, B. K. & Ulinski, P. (2003). Propagating waves in visual cortex: A large scale model of turtle visual cortex. *Journal of Computational Neuroscience,* **14**, 161-184.

Nielsen, B. T., Tuyls, K. & Postma, E. (2006a). EvOL – Neuron: methods and prospects. In Extended Abstract, **15**[th] *Annual Computational Neuroscience Meeting* (CNS)., Edingurgh, UK.

Nielsen, B. T., Tuyls, K. & Postma, E. (2006b). *Shaping realistic neuronal morphologies: an evolutionary computation method*, International Joint Conference on Neural Networks, Vancouver, BC, Canada, 16-21.

Nielsen, B. T., Tuyls, K. & Postma, E. (2008). EvOL – Neuron: neuronal morphology generation, *Neurocomputting*, **71**(4-6), 963-972.

Perry, V. H. & Maffei, L. (1988). Dendritic competition: competition for what? *Developmental Brain Research*, **41**, 195-208.

Purves, D. (1988). *Body and Brain- A Trophic Theory of Neural Connections.* Harvard University Press, United States of America.

Stiles, J. R. & Bartol, T. M. (2001a). Monte Carlo methods for simulating realistic synaptic microphysiology using MCell. In DeSchutter, E., editor, Computational Neuroscience: *Realistic Modeling for Experimentalists*. CRC Press.

Stiles, J. R., Bartol, T. M., Salpeter, E. E. & Salpeter, M. M. (1998). Monte Carlo simulation of neurotransmitter release using MCell, a general simulator of cellular physiological processes. In Bower, J. M., editor, *Computational Neuroscience*, pages 279–284, New York, NY, Plenum Press.

Stiles, J. R., Bartol, T. M., Salpeter, M. M., Salpeter, E. E. & Sejnowski, T. J. (2001b). Synaptic variability: new insights from reconstructions and Monte Carlo simulations with MCell. In Cowan, W., Sudhof, T., Stevens, C., editors, *Synapses*. Johns Hopkins University Press.

Tamori, Y. (1986). Theory of dendritic morphology, *Physical Review E* **48**, 3124-3129, 1993.

Wässle, H. Sampling of visual space by retinal ganglion cells. In: J. D., *Visual Neuroscience*. Pettigrew, K. J. Sanderson, & W. R. Levick, eds. Cambridge University Press, 19-32.

In: Computer Science Research and the Internet ISBN: 978-1-61728-730-5
Editor: Jaclyn E. Morris, pp. 169-183 © 2011 Nova Science Publishers, Inc.

Chapter 7

A BIOINFORMATIC WEB SERVER TO CUT PROTEIN STRUCTURES IN TERMS OF PROTEIN UNITS

Jean-Christophe Gelly[*] *and Alexandre G. de Brevern*[**]

INSERM UMR-S 665, Dynamique des Structures et Interactions des
Macromolécules Biologiques (DSIMB), Université Paris Diderot –
Paris 7, Institut National de Transfusion Sanguine (INTS), 6,
rue Alexandre Cabanel, 75739 Paris cedex 15, France

Abstract

Analysis of the architecture and organization of protein structures is a major challenge to better understand protein flexibility, folding, functions and interactions with their partners and to design new drugs.

Protein structures are often described as series of α-helices and β-sheets, or at a higher level as an arrangement of protein domains. Due to the lack of an intermediate vision which could give a good understanding and description of protein structure architecture, we have proposed a novel intermediate view, the Protein Units (PUs). They are novel level of protein structure description between secondary structures and domains. A PU is defined as a compact sub-region of the 3D structure corresponding to one sequence fragment, defined by a high number of intra-PU contacts and a low number of inter-PU contacts. The methodology to obtain PUs from the protein structures is named Protein Peeling (PP). For the algorithm, the protein structures are described as a succession of Cα. The distances between Cα are translated into contact probabilities using a logistic function. Protein Peeling only uses this contact probability matrix. An optimization procedure, based on the Matthews' coefficient correlation (MCC) between contacts probability sub matrices, defines optimal cutting points that separate the region examined into two or three PUs. The process is iterated until the compactness of the resulting PUs reaches a given limit. An index assesses the compactness quality and relative independence of each PU.

---

[*] E-mail addresses: jean-christophe.gelly@univ-paris-diderot.fr, alexandre.debrevern@univ-paris-diderot.fr. Mailing address: Dr. de Alexandre G. de Brevern, INSERM UMR-S 665, DSIMB, Université Paris Diderot – Paris 7, Institut National de Transfusion Sanguine (INTS), 6, rue Alexandre Cabanel, 75739 Paris cedex 15, France
[**] The authors wish it to be known that, in their opinion, the first and the last authors should be regarded as joint First Authors.

Protein Peeling is a tool to better understand and analyze the organization of protein structures. We have developed a dedicated bioinformatic web server: Protein Peeling 2 (PP2). Given the 3D coordinates of a protein, it proposes an automatic identification of protein units (PUs). The interface component consists of a web page (HTML) and common gateway interface (CGI). The user can set many parameters and upload a given structure in PDB file format to a perl core instance. This last component is a module that embeds all the information necessary for two others softwares (mainly coded in C to perform most of the computation tasks and R for the analysis). Results are given both textually and graphically using JMol applet and PyMol software. The server can be accessed from http://www.dsimb.inserm.fr/dsimb_tools/peeling/. Only one equivalent on line methodology is available.

Introduction

The proteins are a succession of amino acids joined together by peptide bonds. They are crucial macromolecules implicated in major physiological processes and also most of the diseases. Since the elucidation of the first protein structure by Max Perutz and John Kendrew in the late 50's (Kendrew et al. 1958; Perutz et al. 1960), it was experimentally demonstrated that functional proteins adopt a three dimensional structure (3D) defined by the spatial arrangement of the atoms of its amino acids. Protein 3D structures are still resolved using X-ray crystallography since the last 50 years (Kendrew et al. 1958). The process by which a protein adopts this three-dimensional structure under natural condition from an initial disordered state is called folding. Native protein structures are maintained by inter-residue interactions. Anfinsen demonstrated that the amino acid sequence alone contain all the information needed to obtain a functional protein structure (Anfinsen et al. 1961). Otherwise molecular mechanism responsible for this self-assembly is poorly understood and remains one of the most fundamental problems in biological sciences.

From the beginning of biochemical sciences, interesting characteristics have been determined or theoretically predicted. Thus, some amino acids favor to adopt local structures called repetitive secondary structures: α-helix and β-sheet due to their physicochemical properties. The combination of theses secondary structures elements and other non-regular form the final structure of the protein and characterize a particular and functional protein topology (Richardson 1981).

Various studies had also shown that protein structure fold can be represented into units called protein structural domains. Proteins can be constituted by one unique domain while others are combinations of many ones. Domains represent not only structural meaningful elements but also facilitate the understanding of protein architecture. Quasi structural independence is the major characteristic of domains. Sometimes theses domains had also a well defined function and were evolutionary conserved (Ponting and Russell 2002). One aim is to simplify analysis into more significant component based on geometric and physicochemical properties. Indeed great part of protein domains are organized around a hydrophobic core and some are able to fold independently and exhibit a well defined topology. More than one thousand different domains have been identified in structural databases, e.g., SCOP (Murzin et al. 1995), CATH (Orengo et al. 1997) or FSSP (Holm and Sander 1997). Defining automatic procedures for reliable domain assignment is an essential task for the generation of pertinent domain databases used for relevant scientific studies

(Heger et al. 2005). The main idea behind these approaches is that the inter-domain interaction is weaker than the intra-domain interaction.

Despite availability of these various tools, it remains hard to describe and understand protein structures diversity with theses methodologies. A clear gap exists between an elementary view of protein structure as a succession of secondary structure elements, and a more complex view of protein structural domains. It lacks a level of description complementary between secondary structures and domains, a kind of intermediate view of structural organization and complexity. Some authors have proposed such a supplementary level, consistent with folding models. Wetlaufer was the first to examine the organization of known structures and suggested that the early stages of 3D structure formation, *i.e.*, nucleation, occur independently in separate parts of these molecules (Wetlaufer 1973; 1981). These folding units have been proposed to fold independently during the folding process, creating structural modules which give birth to the native structure.

Protein domains identification methods. Protein structures can be seen as composed of single or multiple functional domains that can fold and function independently. Dividing a protein into domains is useful for more accurate structure and function determination and explanation of folding process. Automatic domain parsing is based on a common simple principle: inter-domain interaction is weaker than the intra-domain interaction and intra-domain are strong enough to maintain stability (Wetlaufer 1973; Rossman and Liljas 1974; Richardson 1981; Wetlaufer 1981). Domain definition is simply the result of this cutting process. Many different procedures to assign protein structural domains have been developed. DETECTIVE method is based on the idea that domains have a hydrophobic interior (Swindells 1995), while Wodak and Janin used an iterative approach based on surface areas with an iterative cleavage of the native structure (Wodak and Janin 1981). Gaussian network model could also be used (Kundu et al. 2004). Different algorithms to hierarchically split proteins into compact units have been proposed (Lesk and Rose 1981; Wodak and Janin 1981; Sowdhamini and Blundell 1995; Swindells 1995; Tsai and Nussinov 1997; Kundu et al. 2004). Their goal was to describe protein structure at different organization levels (Taylor 2007). Nonetheless, the problem of dividing a protein structure into domains is not yet solved.

PUU (Holm and Sander 1994) is a recursive top-down approach which uses a hypothetical model of autonomously folding units corresponding to protein domains. A hierarchical 5-level filtering process is applied during partitioning of the structure, it tries to conserve long length protein fragment, cut flexible regions and not secondary structure. DomainParser uses a top-down approach to domain decomposition implemented using a graph theoretical approach (Xu et al. 2000; Guo et al. 2003). Its main problem is the failure to continue successful partitioning. Protein Domain Parser (Alexandrov and Shindyalov 2003) is based on the assumption that the expected number of contacts between two domains depends on their surface areas. DOMAK (Siddiqui and Barton 1995), 3Dee (Dengler et al. 2001; Siddiqui et al. 2001), DETECTIVE (Swindells 1995), DALI (Holm and Sander 1998), STRUDL (Wernisch et al. 1999), and DDOMAIN (Zhou et al. 2007)) are build on similar approaches. Interestingly, they are often benchmarked on a manual definition of structural domains (Joshi 2007) as SCOP (Murzin et al. 1995). The difficulty of defining automatically structural domains has been often been shown, *e.g.*, (Holland et al. 2006) and no consensus could be easily found. An important point is the size of protein domains which always remains important (often more than a hundred residues) and so does not reflect protein folding early steps.

Small compact unit identification methods. Thus, many researchers have tried to determined smaller protein units which could represent earlier event of the protein folding and the smallest basic element of structure organization. The most common view was to define a hierarchically splitting of proteins into compact units (Go 1981; Lesk and Rose 1981; Wodak and Janin 1981; Janin and Wodak 1983; Sowdhamini and Blundell 1995; Tsai and Nussinov 1997; Guo et al. 2003; Pugalenthi et al. 2005). During the 70's Wetlaufer proposed that the early stages of 3D structure formation, *i.e.*, nucleation, occur independently in separate parts of these molecules (Wetlaufer 1973; 1981). These folding units have been proposed to fold independently during the folding process, creating structural modules which can be assembled to give the native structure.

Go identifies basic structural unit by $C\alpha$-$C\alpha$ distance map and visual inspection of protein structures (Go 1981) while Janin and Wodak algorithm search along polypeptide the partitioning point generating units with the smallest surface interaction (Janin and Wodak 1983). Folding unit as defined by Lesk & Rose (Lesk and Rose 1981) are selected by a bottom-up hierarchical approach using inertial ellipsoids minimal area of small fragments. Later many methods based on different principles have been proposed. One of the most recent methodology is DIAL (Sowdhamini and Blundell 1995; Pugalenthi et al. 2005) and his database (Sowdhamini et al. 1996). DIAL algorithm determined small compact unit by hierarchical approach based on distances between secondary structure elements.

Protein Unit and Protein Peeling. We have likewise developed a method called Protein Peeling (Gelly et al. 2006a). This algorithm dissects a protein into Protein Units (PUs). A PU is a compact sub-region of the 3D structure corresponding to one sequence fragment. The basic principle is that each PU must have a high number of intra-PU contacts, and, a low number of inter-PU contacts. Thus, organization of protein structures can be considered in a hierarchical manner: secondary structures are the smallest elements, and, Protein Units are intermediate elements leading to structural domains.

Bioinformatics methodology needs to be widely available and distributed to be useful for the scientific community. A web server (http://www.dsimb.inserm.fr/dsimb_tools/peeling/) dedicated to Protein Peeling, has been developed for this purpose. It is now the second improved version of our approach (Gelly et al. 2006b).

Methodology of Protein Peeling

Protein Peeling algorithm works from the $C\alpha$-contact matrix translated into contact probabilities. A PU (or the protein at the beginning) is associated to a protein sequence s comprised between positions $[i, j]$, ($i < j$, $i=1$ and $j=N$ at the beginning). The sequence is cut into two parts s_1 and s_2 associated with the positions $[i, m]$ and $[m + 1, j]$ respectively. The symmetric contact probability sub-matrix associated to the sequence s is shared into 3 sub-matrices corresponding to the sum of the contact probabilities between the residues of s_1 with itself (noted A), s_2 with itself (B), and, s_1 with s_2 (C). To assess the presence of numerous contacts within the sub-units s_1 and s_2 and a limited number of contacts between them,

Matthews' coefficient correlation (*MCC*) is used (Matthews 1975). The *MCC* measure is translated into a *partition index*, $PI_{ij}(m)$:

$$PI_{i,j}(m) = \frac{AB - C^2}{(A+C)(B+C)}$$

Thus, the quality of the splitting of the PU into two sub-units is quantified via a correlation. The complete absence of contacts between these two sub-units (*i.e.*, $C = 0$) leads to a maximal value of the partition index (*i.e.*, 1). A large presence of contacts between sub-units ($C > 0$) induces a low *PI* value. The cutting process cuts in 2 or 3PUs. To characterize the compactness of PUs defined, a compaction index (*CI*) based on mutual information is calculated (Etchebest et al. 2005; Hazout 2007)., it uses the sum of the probabilities associated with each PUs and indicates when to stop cutting, when it reaches a given threshold *R* (see (Gelly et al. 2006a) for more details and especially the Figure 1).

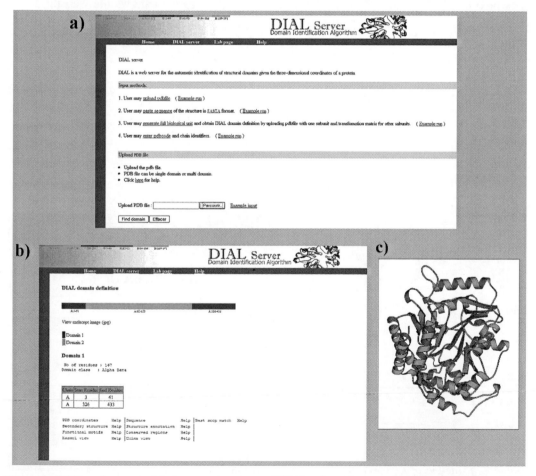

Figure 1. *DIAL web server*. (a) the entrance page of DIAL where the use upload the PDB file, (b) the result of DIAL cutting process of dialkylglycine decarboxylase (PDB code 1ZOB), (c) visualization of the cutting with Molscript software (Kraulis 1991).

The process is recursively done. It is iterated until the compactness of the resulting PUs reaches a given limit, fixed by the user. A refinement of cutting is carried out thanks to the method of *pruning* which checks that PUs lately generated are compact (Gelly et al. 2006b).

Comparable Approaches

The only comparable method is so DIAL. The approach is available at http://caps.ncbs.res.in/DIAL/. It considers small units as clusters of secondary structure elements. In a first step, α-helices and β-strands are first clustered using inter-secondary structural distances between Cα positions. In a second step, dendograms based on this distance measure are used to identify sub-domains. Their goal was to describe the different levels of protein structure organization.

Figure 1 shows the use of DIAL Web server to cut the structure of dialkylglycine decarboxylase (PDB code 1ZOB (Berman et al. 2000)). Figure 1a shows the website, Figure 1b is the result of cutting by DIAL of dialkylglycine decarboxylase. For this particular protein, two regions are found. They are represented on the structure on Figure 1c. It is a nice static view of the protein using molscript software (Kraulis 1991).

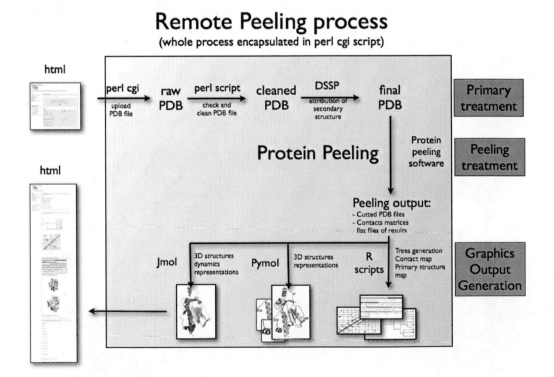

Figure 2. *Principle of PP2 web server.* All the different steps of the process are presented with the actions done and the language / software.

Protein Peeling Web Server

The flowchart representation of Protein Peeling web server is shown on Figure 2. Different languages and softwares are used. The web page in HTML shows on the upper left is the entrance point of PP2 webserver (see Figure 3, http://www.dsimb. inserm.fr/ dsimb_tools/peeling/). After the submission of PDB file by the user, the common gateway interface (CGI) gets the values from the web form and transmitting it to the perl core instance. Then PDB file undergoes appropriate treatment. It start by the cleaning of the PDB files to ensure a correct format and afterward by the launching of secondary structure assignment done by DSSP software (Kabsch and Sander 1983). Then, the perl module launches the protein peeling main software (done in C language for computational efficiency), that reads the clean PDB file, the secondary structure assignment and the different options. The protein peeling process is done and compactness indices are computed.

Protein Peeling v2

an approach for splitting a 3D protein structure into proteins units

Home
tools to use our peeling
method
About method
how "peeling" a protein
Contacts
to send an email to
authors

announcement

19/01/2005
-Peeling launched
10/02/2006
-Peeling2 launched
25/02/2009
-After a transfer
Peeling2 is back

Peeling a protein

This method take an input pdb file and peel it.

Browse for your 3D structure file (pdb file format):

[   ] [Parcourir...]

[PEEL IT]

Options

Prune tree :	○Yes ◉No CI cut-off:	0.2
Choose a specific R-value :	95	
Minimal size of protein unit :	16	
Minimal size of secondary structures :	8	
Take into account only regular secondary structure for Peeling :	○Yes ◉No	
Cut-off distance between atom :	8.0	
Delta parameter in logistic function :	1.5	
Maximal size of protein unit :	0	

Figure 3. *Web page of Protein Peeling 2*. On the left part is given the different information needed (methods and contacts). On the right part, the pdb file is the only obligation; all the options are given by default and could be changed.

In a second step, render programs perform visualization of results. R software scripts (Ihaka and Gentleman 1996) are dedicated to visualize (i) the hierarchical peeling of the protein structures, (ii) the probabilities contact matrix and (iii) schematic representation of PUs in sequence with their contents in secondary structures. Two visualization softwares are used:

(i) Ray tracing proteins structures relies on PyMol (DeLano 2002) which gives excellent rendering. The perl core creates a dedicated PyMol script which is used and is also given to the user which can adapt to its own needs. The format conversion and the post-rendering of the pictures was managed by ImageMagick suite (ImageMagick).

(ii) An interactive visualization is also possible through the JMol applet (JMol) which is based on a Java Virtual Machine.

The perl core generates finally a complete web page (see Figure 2, left) that summarizes all the output information.

Example of Protein Cutting

Figures 4 and 5 show the cutting of dialkylglycine decarboxylase through Protein Peeling approach (PDB code 1ZOB). Figure 4b shows the dendogram obtained with default parameters; the cutting is so quite impressive. For R^2 equals to 20, a first event appears, it cuts the protein into two much misbalanced PUs (1-26 and 27-431). In a recent study (Faure et al. 2009), we have shown that Protein Peeling can detect mobile extremities. These last have fewer constraints than the hydrophobic core of the protein and so are often considered as "mobile" (Jacob and Unger 2007). Our "mobile" extremities have been detected as PU, representing less than 20% of the size of protein which are cut early in the process of peeling and is not cut again. Half of the proteins have been detected associated to mobile extremities. Here, our mobile N-terminus (residue 1-26) is mainly helical which the case is for 2/3 of N-termini. As α-helices are not conditioned by long range contacts within the sequence like β-sheets; this tendency seems logical. Its CI value is low (0.26).

The second cutting event is for R^2 equals to 70, the splitting event is not a simple dual one, but three PUs are generated, with one short (27-59) and two longer PUs (60-326 and 327-431). The first one mainly composed of β-strands will not be cut again as the last one which is a bundle of 3 α-helices and 3 β-strands. They are associated to very high CI values (2.49 and 3.75 respectively). Next cutting events cut so the central PUs into 3 PUs and at the end finally into 8 PUs.

Depending on the purpose of the research, the final number PUs and / or their lengths and contents can be different. Here some PUs are only 20 residues long and associated to low CI, e.g., PU 60-80 has null CI. It is so interesting to come back at previous cutting events. Our web server allows coming back to each cutting events. It is also always possible to change the options concerning length, R^2 values, etc.

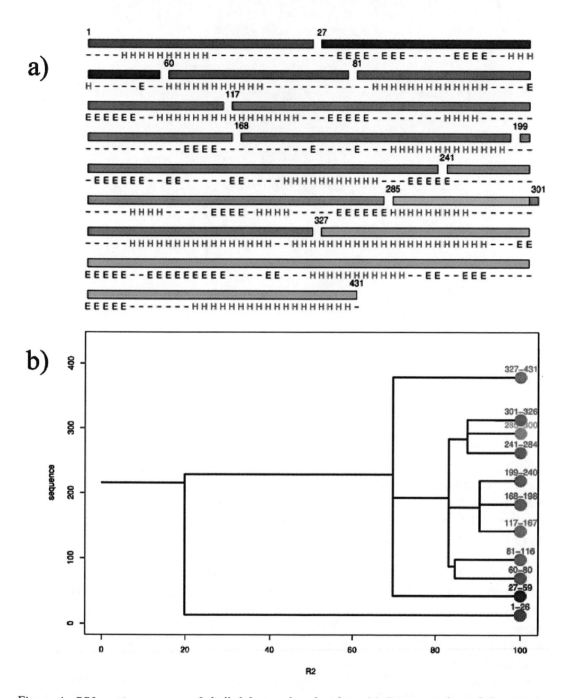

Figure 4. *PP2 cutting process of dialkylglycine decarboxylase.* (a) Representation of the protein sequence with delineation of the different PUs in different colors. Are also given the secondary structure assignment done by DSSP (Kabsch and Sander 1983). (b) Dendograms of the PP2 cutting. Is shown for each R^2 value the number of generated PUs (Ihaka and Gentleman 1996).

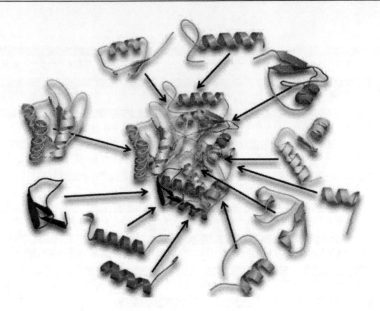

Figure 5. *PP2 cutting process of dialkylglycine decarboxylase.* Are shown all the different PUs generated for a very high R^2 value.

Conclusion

The three-dimensional structure is the core of protein functions and is mainly determined by its amino acid sequence. Nonetheless, the protein folding is not completely understood (Clark 2008). Several models have been proposed for protein folding, *e.g.*, the framework model (Ptitsyn and Rashin 1975; Udgaonkar and Baldwin 1988), the diffusion-collision model (Karplus and Weaver 1994), the hydrophobic collapse model (Rackovsky and Scheraga 1977) or the nucleation and growth mechanism (Fersht 1997). George Rose proposed a simple hierarchical model (Rose 1979), which assemblies small units in a hierarchical manner (Lesk and Rose 1981; Baldwin and Rose 1999a; b; Haspel et al. 2003a; b) coupled with the hydrophobic effect as the driving force (Dill 1985; Dill and Chan 1997). It leads to the construction of protein domains and complete folds.

Analyzing protein structures in terms of protein domains has been a long and fruitful research area for a long time. Many different approaches have been proposed (Holm and Sander 1994; Siddiqui and Barton 1995; Swindells 1995; Holm and Sander 1998; Wernisch et al. 1999; Xu et al. 2000; Anselmi et al. 2001; Dengler et al. 2001; Siddiqui et al. 2001; Alexandrov and Shindyalov 2003; Guo et al. 2003; Emmert-Streib and Mushegian 2007; Joshi 2007; Zhou et al. 2007). They are based on numerous processes and algorithms. Most of them had initially an available website, but surprisingly at the time of this review none is functional.

Protein domains are also evolutionary units of proteins. The prediction of protein domains from sequence information can improve tertiary structure prediction (Chivian et al. 2003) and enhance protein function annotation (Holland et al. 2006), but domains also been used to help structure determination (Campbell and Downing 1994), guide protein engineering (Guerois and Serrano 2001) and mutagenesis (Nielsen and Yamada 2001). Hence, some approaches have been proposed to predict protein structural domains from the sole knowledge of the sequence. For instance, DOMAC (http://www.bioinfotool.org/domac.html) is a hybrid domain prediction web service integrating template-based and *ab initio* methods (Cheng 2007). Its template-based method is accurate enough for guiding protein structure prediction, structure determination, function annotation, mutagenesis analysis and protein engineering. Other are more specialized as OPUS-Dom (Wu et al. 2009), a *de novo* method for predicting protein domain boundaries. Its methodology is based on a coarse-grained folding method, which constructs low-resolution structural models from a target sequence by folding a chain of vectors representing the predicted secondary-structure elements.

Analyzing protein structures in terms of small compact protein units is a less common research. As we shown only two methods are available at this time, DIAL and Protein Peeling. Interest of DIAL is the proposition of potential alternative splitting events. Interest of Protein Peeling is the availability of numerous options allowing a real expertise of the protein structure. Moreover, visualization tools allow a direct analysis of the cutting through JMol applet while PyMol script and accompanying Figures are of great quality. In the same way, the different Figures generated through R software, (i) dendogram showing the entire process of splitting, (ii) the presentation of PUs with secondary structures and (iii) contact map with delineation of PUs, are an efficient representation. All these points make the Protein Peeling web server a unique tool to analyze protein structures.

In the same way, our database of pre-cutting proteins provides useful materials for further analysis on structure, size, composition in amino acid and secondary structures of protein units. Such experiments open the way to other ambitious development like construction of three dimensional structures of proteins with protein units as it has been shown with similar approaches (Haspel et al. 2003a; Inbar et al. 2003). As shown, Protein Units a valuable tools to understand protein folding, predict protein structure, identify structural domains. Futures developments will concern mainly the use of PUs for classification and for prediction purposes.

Acknowledgments

This work was supported by grants from the Ministère de la Recherche, Université Paris Diderot – Paris 7, National Institute for Blood Transfusion (INTS) and the National Institute for Health and Medical Research (INSERM).

References

Alexandrov, N. & Shindyalov, I. (2003). PDP: protein domain parser. *Bioinformatics,* **19**, 429-430.

Anfinsen, C. B., Haber, E., Sela, M. & White, F. H. Jr. (1961). The kinetics of formation of native ribonuclease during oxidation of the reduced polypeptide chain. *Proc Natl Acad Sci, U S A,* **47**, 1309-1314.

Anselmi, C., Bocchinfuso, G., Scipioni, A. & De Santis, P. (2001). Identification of protein domains on topological basis. *Biopolymers,* **58**, 218-229.

Baldwin, R. L. & Rose, G. D. (1999a). Is protein folding hierarchic? I. Local structure and peptide folding. *Trends Biochem Sci,* **24**, 26-33.

Baldwin, R. L. & Rose, G. D. (1999b). Is protein folding hierarchic? II. Folding intermediates and transition states. *Trends Biochem Sci,* **24**, 77-83.

Berman, H. M., Westbrook, J., Feng, Z., Gilliland, G., Bhat, T. N., Weissig, H., Shindyalov, I. N. & Bourne, P. E. (2000). The Protein Data Bank. *Nucleic Acids Res,* **28**, 235-242.

Campbell, I. D. & Downing, A. K. (1994). Building protein structure and function from modular units. *Trends Biotechnol,* **12**, 168-172.

Cheng, J. (2007). DOMAC: an accurate, hybrid protein domain prediction server. *Nucleic Acids Res,* **35**, W354-356.

Chivian, D., Kim, D. E., Malmstrom, L., Bradley, P., Robertson, T., Murphy, P., Strauss, C. E., Bonneau, R., Rohl, C. A. & Baker, D. (2003). Automated prediction of CASP-5 structures using the Robetta server. *Proteins,* 53 Suppl **6**, 524-533.

Clark, A. C. (2008). Protein folding: Are we there yet? *Archives of Biochemistry and Biophysics,* **469**, 1-3.

DeLano, W. L. T. (2002). The PyMOL Molecular Graphics System *DeLano Scientific, San Carlos, CA, USA.* http://www.pymol.org.

Dengler, U., Siddiqui, A. S. & Barton, G. J. (2001). Protein structural domains: analysis of the 3Dee domains database. *Proteins,* **42**, 332-344.

Dill, K. A. (1985). Theory for the folding and stability of globular proteins. *Biochemistry,* **24**, 1501-1509.

Dill, K. A. & Chan, H. S. (1997). From Levinthal to pathways to funnels. *Nat Struct Biol,* **4**, 10-19.

Emmert-Streib, F. & Mushegian, A. (2007). A topological algorithm for identification of structural domains of proteins. *BMC Bioinformatics,* **8**, 237.

Etchebest, C., Benros, C., Hazout, S. & de Brevern, A. G. (2005). A structural alphabet for local protein structures: improved prediction methods. *Proteins,* **59**, 810-827.

Faure, G., Bornot, A. & de Brevern, A. G. (2009). Analysis of protein contacts into Protein Units. *Biochimie,* **91**, 876-887.

Fersht, A. (1997). Nucleation mechanism in protein folding. *Curr. Opin. Struct. Biol,* **7**, 3-9.

Gelly, J. C., de Brevern, A. G. & Hazout, S. (2006a). 'Protein Peeling': an approach for splitting a 3D protein structure into compact fragments. *Bioinformatics,* **22**, 129-133.

Gelly, J. C., Etchebest, C., Hazout, S. & de Brevern, A. G. (2006b). Protein Peeling 2: a web server to convert protein structures into series of protein units. *Nucleic Acids Res,* **34**, W75-78.

Go, M. (1981). Correlation of DNA exonic regions with protein structural units in haemoglobin. *Nature,* **291**, 90-92.

Guerois, R. & Serrano, L. (2001). Protein design based on folding models. *Curr Opin Struct Biol,* **11**, 101-106.

Guo, J. T., Xu, D., Kim, D. & Xu, Y. (2003). Improving the performance of DomainParser for structural domain partition using neural network. *Nucleic Acids Res,* **31**, 944-952.

Haspel, N., Tsai, C. J., Wolfson, H. & Nussinov, R. (2003a). Hierarchical protein folding pathways: a computational study of protein fragments. *Proteins,* **51**, 203-215.

Haspel, N., Tsai, C. J., Wolfson, H. & Nussinov, R. (2003b). Reducing the computational complexity of protein folding via fragment folding and assembly. *Protein Sci,* **12**, 1177-1187.

Hazout, S. (2007). Entropy-derived measures for assessing the accuracy of N-state prediction algorithms. In *Recent Advances in Structural Bioinformatics*. (ed. A.G. de Brevern), pp. 395-417. Research signpost, Trivandrum, India.

Heger, A., Wilton, C. A., Sivakumar, A. & Holm, L. (2005). ADDA: a domain database with global coverage of the protein universe. *Nucleic Acids Res, 33*, D188-191.

Holland, T. A., Veretnik, S., Shindyalov, I. N. & Bourne, P. E. (2006). Partitioning protein structures into domains: why is it so difficult? *J Mol Biol, 361*, 562-590.

Holm, L. & Sander, C. (1994). Parser for protein folding units. *Proteins, 19*, 256-268.

Holm, L. & Sander, C. (1997). Dali/FSSP classification of three-dimensional protein folds. *Nucleic Acids Res, 25*, 231-234.

Holm, L. & Sander, C. (1998). Dictionary of recurrent domains in protein structures. *Proteins, 33*, 88-96.

Ihaka, R. & Gentleman, R. (1996). R: a language for data analysis and graphics. *J Comput Graph Stat, 5*, 299-314.

ImageMagick. http://www.imagemagick.org.

Inbar, Y., Benyamini, H., Nussinov, R. & Wolfson, H. J. (2003). Protein structure prediction via combinatorial assembly of sub-structural units. *Bioinformatics* 19 Suppl, 1, i158-168.

Jacob, E. & Unger, R. (2007). A tale of two tails: why are terminal residues of proteins exposed? *Bioinformatics, 23*, e225-230.

Janin, J. & Wodak, S. J. (1983). Structural domains in proteins and their role in the dynamics of protein function. *Prog Biophys Mol Biol, 42*, 21-78.

JMol. http://jmol.sourceforge.net/.

Joshi, R. R. (2007). A Decade of Computing to Traverse the Labyrinth of Protein Domains. *Current Bioinformatics, 2*, 113-131.

Kabsch, W. & Sander, C. (1983). Dictionary of protein secondary structure: pattern recognition of hydrogen-bonded and geometrical features. *Biopolymers, 22*, 2577-2637.

Karplus, M. & Weaver, D.L. 1994. Protein folding dynamics: the diffusion-collision model and experimental data. *Protein Sci, 3*, 650-668.

Kendrew, J. C., Bodo, G., Dintzis, H. M., Parrish, R. G., Wyckoff, H. & Phillips, D. C. (1958). A three-dimensional model of the myoglobin molecule obtained by x-ray analysis. *Nature, 181*, 662-666.

Kraulis, P. (1991). MOLSCRIPT: a program to produce both detailed and schematic plots of protein structures. *J. Appl. Cryst., 24*, 946-950.

Kundu, S., Sorensen, D. C. & Phillips, G. N., Jr. (2004). Automatic domain decomposition of proteins by a Gaussian Network Model. *Proteins, 57*, 725-733.

Lesk, A. M. & Rose, G. D. (1981). Folding units in globular proteins. *Proc Natl Acad Sci U S A, 78*, 4304-4308.

Matthews, B. (1975). Comparison of the predicted and observed secondary structure of T4 phage lysozyme. *Biochim. Biophys. Acta, 405*, 442-451.

Murzin, A. G., Brenner, S. E., Hubbard, T. & Chothia, C. (1995). SCOP: a structural classification of proteins database for the investigation of sequences and structures. *J Mol Biol, 247*, 536-540.

Nielsen, P. K. & Yamada, Y. (2001). Identification of cell-binding sites on the Laminin alpha 5 N-terminal domain by site-directed mutagenesis. *J Biol Chem, 276*, 10906-10912.

Orengo, C. A., Michie, A. D., Jones, S., Jones, D. T., Swindells, M. B. & Thornton, J. M. (1997). CATH--a hierarchic classification of protein domain structures. *Structure*, **5**, 1093-1108.

Perutz, M. F., Rossmann, M. G., Cullis, A. F., Muirhead, H., Will, G. & North, A. C. (1960). Structure of haemoglobin: a three-dimensional Fourier synthesis at 5.5-A. resolution, obtained by X-ray analysis. *Nature*, **185**, 416-422.

Ponting, C. P. & Russell, R. R. (2002). The natural history of protein domains. *Annu Rev Biophys Biomol Struct*, **31**, 45-71.

Ptitsyn, O. B. & Rashin, A. A. (1975). A model of myoglobin self-organization. *Biophys Chem*, **3**, 1-20.

Pugalenthi, G., Archunan, G. & Sowdhamini, R. (2005). DIAL: a web-based server for the automatic identification of structural domains in proteins. *Nucleic Acids Res*, **33**, W130-132.

Rackovsky, S. & Scheraga, H. A. (1977). Hydrophobicity, hydrophilicity, and the radial and orientational distributions of residues in native proteins. *Proc Natl Acad Sci U S A*, **74**, 5248-5251.

Richardson, J. S. (1981). The anatomy and taxonomy of protein structure. *Adv Protein Chem*, **34**, 167-339.

Rose, G. D. (1979). Hierarchic organization of domains in globular proteins. *J Mol Biol*, **134**, 447-470.

Rossman, M. G. & Liljas, A. (1974). Letter: Recognition of structural domains in globular proteins. *J Mol Biol*, **85**, 177-181.

Siddiqui, A. S. & Barton, G. J. (1995). Continuous and discontinuous domains: an algorithm for the automatic generation of reliable protein domain definitions. *Protein Sci*, **4**, 872-884.

Siddiqui, A. S., Dengler, U. & Barton, G. J. (2001). 3Dee: a database of protein structural domains. *Bioinformatics*, **17**, 200-201.

Sowdhamini, R. & Blundell, T. L. (1995). An automatic method involving cluster analysis of secondary structures for the identification of domains in proteins. *Protein Sci*, **4**, 506-520.

Sowdhamini, R., Rufino, S. D. & Blundell, T. L. (1996). A database of globular protein structural domains: clustering of representative family members into similar folds. *Fold Des*, **1**, 209-220.

Swindells, M. B. (1995). A procedure for detecting structural domains in proteins. *Protein Sci*, **4**, 103-112.

Taylor, W. R. (2007). Evolutionary transitions in protein fold space. *Curr Opin Struct Biol*, **17**, 354-361.

Tsai, C. J. & Nussinov, R. (1997). Hydrophobic folding units derived from dissimilar monomer structures and their interactions. *Protein Sci*, **6**, 24-42.

Udgaonkar, J. B. & Baldwin, R. L. (1988). NMR evidence for an early framework intermediate on the folding pathway of ribonuclease A. *Nature*, **335**, 694-699.

Wernisch, L., Hunting, M. & Wodak, S. J. (1999). Identification of structural domains in proteins by a graph heuristic. *Proteins*, **35**, 338-352.

Wetlaufer, D. B. (1973). Nucleation, rapid folding, and globular intrachain regions in proteins. *Proc Natl Acad Sci U S A*, **70**, 697-701.

Wetlaufer, D. B. (1981). Folding of protein fragments. *Adv Protein Chem*, **34**, 61-92.

Wodak, S. J. & Janin, J. (1981). Location of structural domains in protein. *Biochemistry,* **20**, 6544-6552.

Wu, Y., Dousis, A. D., Chen, M., Li, J. & Ma, J. (2009). OPUS-Dom: applying the folding-based method VECFOLD to determine protein domain boundaries. *J Mol Biol,* **385**, 1314-1329.

Xu, Y., Xu, D. & Gabow, H. N. (2000). Protein domain decomposition using a graph-theoretic approach. *Bioinformatics,* **16**, 1091-1104.

Zhou, H., Xue, B. & Zhou, Y. (2007). Ddomain: Dividing structures into domains using a normalized domain-domain interaction profile. *Protein Sci,* **16**, 947-955.

In: Computer Science Research and the Internet
Editor: Jaclyn E. Morris, pp. 185-195

ISBN: 978-1-61728-730-5
© 2011 Nova Science Publishers, Inc.

Chapter 8

SERVER BASED STRATEGIES FOR ADVANCED VISUALIZATION IN RADIOLOGY

P.M.A. Van Ooijen

University Medical Center Groningen, the Netherlands

Abstract

With the increasing amount of data being produced by radiological imaging modalities such as Magnetic Resonance Imaging (MRI) and especially Multi Detector Computed Tomography (MDCT) with datasets ranging up to over 1000 individual slices of half a millimeter thickness the demand for other visualization methods than just paging through all these slices in a stack is also growing rapidly. Traditionally, the evaluation of such datasets would be performed on dedicated workstation, powerful enough to handle the large amounts of data at acceptable speed using more advanced visualization techniques such as maximum intensity projection (MIP), Multi Planar Reformation (MPR) and three-dimensional volume rendering (VR). Although the need certainly existed, the more widespread use of these advanced visualization techniques was hampered by the fact that these tools were expensive and only available at a limited number of locations in the hospital. However, higher availability of advanced visualization has nowadays grown into a requirement to keep up with the growing data production. To meet this requirement, server based strategies for advanced visualization have found their way in to the clinical practice in radiology. In this chapter the different levels of "thickness" of the server-client combinations will be covered as well as the current state-of-the-art both for the intranet of the hospital and for tele-medicine on the internet. Next implementation requirements will be covered that are obligatory to provide the conditions under which a server based advanced visualization system can strive within radiological practice. Besides this description of past and present we will also try to provide a view into the future and discuss where the server based advanced visualization could lead us.

Introduction

With the increasing amount of data being produced by radiological imaging modalities such as Magnetic Resonance Imaging and especially Multi Detector Computed Tomography with datasets ranging up to over 1000 individual slices of half a millimeter thickness the demand for other visualization methods than just paging through all these slices is also growing rapidly. Even larger volumes of data from 4D CT and MR including multi-phase and functional studies are pushing towards the limits of the existing environments even further. Trying to send all this data to several dedicated workstations throughout the hospital not only causes a data-overload of the physicians that have to deal with all these data but also has repercussions on the technical infrastructure. The increasing data stream with, for example, 1GB of data for a single CT examination or up to 4GB for a multi-phase cardiac CT examination strains the operation of older servers, consume large portions of the network bandwidth, and surpasses the capacity of workstation memory and graphics boards causing slow-down of the software by repeated harddrive access while swapping data back and forth between internal memory and harddrive. With the projected development of an increase of the inplane resolution of CT from 512x512 to 1024x1024 per axial slice, the total amount of data from CT (which is responsible for a large portion of the data production in most modern hospitals) will again increase by a factor of four. Therefore, solutions need to be developed and implemented now to keep up with this ever growing data production.

One solution is to minimize the data to be evaluated by using advanced visualization techniques to obtain a clinically meaningful composite image. This requires advanced three-dimensional (3D) and 4-dimensional (4D) visualization, segmentation and analysis of those large datasets in a fast and simple manner that can be performed by a radiologist with or without some pre-work being done by a specialized radiological technician.

Some decades ago, the only way to perform advanced visualization in radiology was by using very expensive high-end graphic super computers running on UNIX such as the ones produced by SGI/Silicon Graphics. Gradually these capabilities were shifted to the desktop with the advances in graphics capabilities of regular MS Windows/INTEL based personal computers that were driven forward rapidly by the graphically very demanding and financially very lucrative market of computer gaming. This led to solutions based either on the central processing unit (CPU) in those computer systems or, more dedicated, on the graphics processing unit (GPU). Recently, the next transition has taken place where the computationally expensive calculations required for high end 3D and 4D image visualization and processing are not performed at the local machine but on a server with the local machine only acting as a client. This client-server based advanced visualization has now come of age and can be deployed throughout radiology departments and even the entire healthcare enterprise with the high-end tools and pre-configured workflows that, until recently, were only known from the fat-client full workstations. Besides this, the client server design also provides a suitable platform to be used for tele-radiology and tele-medicine.

Thin-Client to Web-Client

One of the main advantages of the use of client-server technology using thin-clients or web-clients is the elimination of the data transport between the server and the client. Previously, a thick-client workstation had to transfer all the DICOM data to the workstation itself consuming a large network bandwidth and resulting in multiple databases throughout the hospital all with their own local version of the patient data. In the case of a client-server setup all data remains at the server side where all the computational expensive work is performed and only the results of these computations in the form of one or multiple viewports on the client side will be transferred over the network. Full control over the datasets and the available tools is provided by the client.

This setup improves data integrity because only one copy of the data is available residing on the server in one central database system instead of multiple copies on every workstation. Furthermore, it also frees up network bandwidth and it avoids peak bandwidth problems. As a result, advanced visualization with full features including 3D and 4D imaging becomes available to any physician anywhere in- and outside the hospital regardless of the speed of the network connection or the speed or memory of the computer hardware at the client side.

One issue currently in the spotlight, which is also used by the different vendors to differentiate their implementations from each other on the commercial market, is the type of client applications to use. The different types all have their own advantages, disadvantages and required level of maintenance. In a recent paper, Toland et al defined a classification of the different types of clients into five degrees of thickness [TOLAND06]. In their paper Toland et al state that "The thinner the client, the less effect it has on the hosting work station. In contrast, a thick client consumes the work station's resources and often prevents a work station from being used to effectively run anything other than the client application."

The thickness of a certain application based on the subdivision into the five degrees of thickness proposed by Toland et al. can be determined by two to four simple questions. The first question is whether the system uses an installer (such as a setup.exe) to install itself on the local machine. If not, that it will probably run within a webbrowser which leads to the next question whether it requires the use of a non-standard browser plug-in. If not, then Toland classifies the application as a true thin client. If the application does require a webbrowser plugin then Toland classifies the application as an enhanced browser (also referred to as a web client).

When an installation is required, then the next question is whether the application requires the installation of JAVA or .NET. If so, Toland classifies the application as a virtual machine. If not, then the final possible question would be whether the setup can be downloaded or not. If the answer on this final question is yes, then Toland classifies it as a web-deployable thick client, if not then Toland classifies it as a thick client.

A true thin client as specified by Toland is the most flexible solution. The only requirement is a standard webbrowser which makes it platform independent and the same client can run just as well on Microsoft Windows as on Linux or Mac (providing that support for multiple different webbrowsers is guaranteed). Besides the standard browser based files (e.g. cookies) these clients leave no files or changes on the local machine and most of the processing is performed at the site of the server.

The enhanced browser application also runs within a webbrowser environment, but it requires some additional software such as ActiveX or Java. Because of this, platform dependency is introduced again and extra installation effort is required for the local machine. Furthermore, the maintenance is also more difficult because the (often set to automatic) updates of ActiveX and Java might disturb the performance of the application software because it was not optimized nor tested for the newer versions.

Examples of virtual machines are Java (Sun Microsystems) and .Net (Microsoft), they function at a layer above the operating system to provide a consistent application environment. Applications can be developed in Java or .Net without concerns about the operating system.

Web-deployable thick clients are thick-clients that are downloadable from a server. They come in the form of an installation file containing both executables and dynamic link libraries. Web-deployable thick clients are aware of their current version and will prompt the user to download and install a new version when it comes available through the server.

The use of a client software package has advantages in that the client software is more easily programmed and can contain more functionality than a webclient. Furthermore, a client software package is not dependent on a webbrowser environment where a webclient is. Another technical aspect which is more flexible in a client software package is the method of communication with the server and the security protocols used. The programmer can make his/her own choices and is not limited to the capabilities of a webbrowser. Login structures are setup in such a way that the client can be adapted to the user's needs and workflow with capabilities to support a single logon by automatic login or by inheriting login information from the windows logon.

However, the use of a client software package limits the platforms to use as client machines, since a windows client will not run on a Linux workstation and vise versa. Therefore, most of the systems available on the commercial market are targeted at the Windows environment which is the most common environment in current PACS installations. Some vendors, however, are also developing client software for more 'exotic' operating system environments such as clients for use on the iPhone or iPod Touch.

Thick clients are the traditional workstations. Software is installed on the local machine by use of a CD or DVD and in most cases by entering a license key connected to that particular machine. The software application extensively uses the hardware components of the local machine such as the CPU, internal memory and video card (GPU – Graphics Processing Unit). Therefore, high requirements are usually defined for the configuration of the local machine including, in some cases, dedicated special purpose hardware components specifically designed for the software application.

One component which Toland failed to include in his subdivision into the different thicknesses of applications is the question, in case of advanced visualization, where the rendering and post-processing takes place and thus where the original DICOM data reside. In advanced imaging, generally, when the DICOM data is transferred to the local machine we are talking about client-side rendering which, in most cases, implies a thick client or a web-deployable thick client. However, when the DICOM data remains at the server (server-side rendering), all processing and visualization is done at the server side and only results are transferred to the clients. This is generally referred to as a thin- or web-client solution. Therefore, an extensive subdivision in advanced imaging could be somewhat different than the one proposed by Toland and would require inclusion of more different properties.

Another issue which is not covered by Toland in his classification is the use of dedicated hardware components compared to the use of standard of-the-shelve components. This usage of special purpose, dedicated, hardware components can be found both in thick clients on the local machine and in client-server solutions on the server side. However, this might highly effect aspects such as cost and speed.

Although dedicated hardware will provide higher rendering speeds and more capabilities at the moment of introduction, this will most probably decrease over time. Reason for this is that the lifetime of this type of hardware is mostly much longer than that of more general hardware because of the relatively smaller market which requires longer life-time to break-even on the development investments. For the same reason dedicated hardware will be relatively expensive.

It has to be noted that although currently with increasing thickness, the available functionality in the application will also increase, the current trend is towards more advanced functionality into thinner clients because of increasing server capacity at decreasing cost. Furthermore, maintenance cost of web-deployable thick clients and thick clients are much higher because the software resides on the client system and thus problems can arise at the client side. Also, the web-deployable thick client and thick clients are operating system dependent and put higher demands on the clients concerning OS version, drivers and hardware.

From a maintenance point of view, the advantages of server-based clients (varying from the true thin client to the virtual machine) are widespread availability of web browsers, platform independence and simple and straightforward installation of new users, by providing access to the server and downloading the required plug-ins or applets on first visit [KOTTER06] [Zhang03] provided the user has a login that allows this installation. Furthermore, updates and upgrades of the server-client based system is only required on the server side, after which the clients will automatically update through installation of new plug-ins or applets upon activation. Maintenance and support do not require physical presence at the end-user machine, but everything can be done on the server or remotely [TOLAND06].

With a true thin-client, the maintenance effort is even lower because no files or changes are present on the host computer and thus all maintenance will be performed solely at the server.

Currently the server-client approach is mainly used for institutional wide systems (eg, PACS web viewers) where more department specific solutions still require more functionality and therefore are still often based on thick clients.

Current Practice

In current practice the server-client model for advanced visualization is used both within hospitals and outside hospitals as tele-medicine (or tele-radiology) solution.

In-Hospital Use

A transition to server-side rendering support by some form of server-client model has been in progress over the past years. This transition has changed the way in which hospitals use and distribute advanced imaging to the users [OOIJEN04]. In many cases, the server of the client-server advanced imaging system is used as a temporary storage of thin-slices [MEENAN06]. In other cases, all thin-slices are stored at the central PACS and the client-server advanced imaging system is used to fetch the data from this PACS [OOIJEN08].

In both cases the main advantage is that advanced visualization becomes available at any place throughout the hospital at relatively low additional efforts and cost. The requirements on local networks probably will not be an issue. Most radiology departments are used to high volume data transfer from modalities to PACS and to workstations and will have high speed networks. Therefore, the network speed required to send all the data from the PACS or modalities to the rendering server will not be much of a problem. Because of the use of a client-server setup requirements for the clients are much lower and therefore the hospital wide LAN (Local Area Network) will most probably be quite sufficient for adequate use of advanced visualization throughout the enterprise. Note that with thick clients waiting time to get data into a workstation at departments outside radiology could be quite long and thus very inefficient consequently requiring an upgrade of (large parts of) the hospital network to allow adequate use of advanced visualization throughout the enterprise.

In general, it is agreed that advanced visualization is a requirement and that this will gradually extend from radiology only to also being deployed at other departments. This in itself is not possible using thick clients because of the sheer costs of installation and maintenance. Therefore, the use of client-server based models using thin client viewers that can be installed anywhere in the hospital are the only way this transition of advanced visualization to outside radiology can be achieved [VERSEL09] [FRATT09]

Tele-Medicine

In the hospital intranet, in most cases, the network itself will not be the bottleneck. However, in case of tele-medicine, more specifically tele-radiology, the bottleneck can in most cases be found at the side of the physician working at home. Private internet connections are available in different setups ranging from ADSL to Cable and at many different speeds depending on the subscription. In a typical university hospital in the Netherlands, the speeds of the connections used by the staff radiologists ranged from 256 kbps to 768 kbps for upload and from 1200 kbps to 4000 kbps for download [OOIJEN07]. This difference in upload and download is not problematic since in case of server-side advanced imaging, the highest requirements are on the download speed and not on the upload speed which is only used to transfer the interaction information. However, the rendering speed that can be achieved is depending on the network speed and compression may have to be used at lower bandwidths. When using compression, one has to be careful since higher levels of compression may lead not only to acceptable speed, but also to severe image degradation leading to inadequate, non-diagnostic, image quality.

Besides the speed issue, the issue of security and patient data safety and privacy becomes a very important point when sharing data outside the healthcare institution's firewalls.

A common setup is the use of Virtual Private Network (VPN) connections using user name and password authentication in combination with some sort of unique, one time usable, code. This unique code can be generated by a code generator which requires a pincode for the user and subsequently provides a login code to enable the VPN connection or alternatively, the VPN login code is sent to a predefined mobile phone as a text message.

Besides the security already provided by the VPN, the client-server setup can also, additionally, employ data encryption in the communication to guarantee private and secure communication between the client and the server.

The local hardware requirements at the site of the user heavily depend on what tasks a radiologist wants to perform from home. If the system at home is only used for tele-consultation, requirements are low. The radiologist (supervisor) has to evaluate the image data but diagnosis is not required. In this case a simple PC or laptop would be sufficient. However, when full reporting capabilities are required at home, medical grade computer screens have to be installed (and regularly calibrated). Furthermore, if voice dictation would also be added from home, the requirements for the network connection and the local machine will become higher and additional hardware has to be included (speechmike, headset, etc.).

Implementation Requirements

To be able to be used in the very demanding field of healthcare, there are several additional implementation requirements that are crucial for acceptance. These requirements are on the integration of the server-client system into the normal workflow and, as mentioned earlier, on the image quality of the system in relation to the speed of the system.

Integration into the Normal Workflow

To really introduce advanced visualization to the radiologist or other physicians, it needs to be fully integrated into the normal workflow. This was always a main disadvantage of the dedicated, fat client, workstations. The availability of these workstations was limited to a few workstations per department and radiologists had to move from their regular workspace to this workstation to perform advanced visualization. Furthermore, the access to the workstation was further diminished because multiple users (radiologists, radiological technicians) had to use the same workstation. However, with the introduction of server based advanced visualization it became possible to overcome these problems of the workstations, under the condition that the server-client setup could offer similar to the same functionality and speed to the user.

The integration of a server-client system has to be defined at different levels and the system has to be able to 'talk' to several other computer systems running in the hospital.

First, integration into the Picture Archiving and Communication System (PACS) is the main requirement. This integration is in the first place needed to obtain data from the PACS and to have the ability to export results such as reports or secondary captures to the PACS in DICOM format. In the second place, it should also be able to integrate seamlessly with the PACS client application at the workstation of the radiologist such that the advanced visualization viewer application an be launched directly from within the PACS worklist or from the PACS viewing window loading only the data present at the PACS workstation at the time of activation.

Another possible system running at merely every digital radiology department that the advanced visualization system has to be able to interface with is the Radiological Information System (RIS). This RIS can provide the worklist of the radiologist. In such a situation it should also be possible to start the advanced visualization client directly from the RIS.

Trade-off Image Quality and Delivery Speed

A main point against client-server, or more specifically webbased, advanced visualization of the skeptics is the argument that to obtain adequate speed in the delivery of the results of the visualization the vendors have to apply a too high level of compression which leads to low quality images that cannot be used for primary diagnosis and are only suited for referral purposes. In some cases, such as in teleradiology, where only very low network bandwidth is available, this is partly true because compression has to be used. In many cases, however, this compression is only applied during interaction and full resolution is presented when the user interaction is stopped.

Economic and Technical Benefits

The introduction of thin-client viewing in the clinical setting has a number of economic and technical benefits. The most relevant of these are listed here (adapted from [VISAGE09] [BUCK09]).

- Cost savings
  - Use of available hardware
  - Only server upgrade
  - Maintenance
- Increased efficiency
  - Clinical Efficiency
  - Workflow Efficiency
- Network resource savings
- One centralized database system
- System scalability

Cost savings can be both direct and indirect. The direct cost savings are made achieved all thin client solutions for advanced visualization are available virtually and will run with sufficient performance on any clinical quality personal computer. Therefore, hospitals do not have to invest in advanced hardware for 3D image viewing throughout the hospital or at remote sites.

Furthermore, because of the use of a central server that services multiple thin-client computers cost savings can be made in the three or five year hardware upgrade cycle. The requirements and costs for upgrading thick client workstations during each cycle is much higher than the costs involved with a regular upgrade cycle of the server hardware and a, less regular, upgrade cycle of the less-demanding thin-client hardware.

Maintenance costs will be lower because of automatic installation of client software without having dedicated personnel being at the actual workstation and decrease in man-hours required for software and hardware maintenance.

Efficiency gains from the availability of advanced visualization using server-client solutions are to be found in many different areas. Clinical and workflow efficiency gain can be found from the ability of thin client technology to deliver 2D datasets and advanced imaging technologies to the desktop of the physician not only at the radiology department, but anywhere throughout the healthcare enterprise and thereby speeding up the diagnostic and therapeutic process in a time preserving and user-friendly fashion. Another efficiency gain can be perceived where, before the introduction of client-server rendering, 3D rendering would be performed at a dedicated workstation located at the CT or MR scanner. This could, in such a setup, cause diminished use of the scanner because post-processing had to be performed. By allowing the post-processing to be performed using client-server systems, the time formerly spent doing the post-processing can be spent to scan more patients and thus increase workflow efficiency. More practically, by providing advanced imaging capabilities at the workstation of the clinicians and radiologists, the image analysis is shifted from radiological technicians that would merely perform pre-processing of the data for the physician to the physicians themselves who actually have to make the diagnosis.

The cost of updating physical network infrastructure to enhance the network speeds is costly. Not only because of the high costs of cabling and network hardware components, but also because of the high cost in fte (full time equivalent) for the labor intensive installation of al the required miles of cabling. Although network attached storage systems will be able keep up with the enormous data growth, the network speeds will probably not resulting in a situation where data can be stored but not retrieved in a proper way. The introduction of server-client systems for advanced visualization could tackle this problem. Because of the use of thin-client solutions, the demand on network resources is low because the transfer of enormous amounts of DICOM data only takes place between the rendering server and the PACS or imaging modalities. After the DICOM data is loaded into the rendering server, only screen-updates are shared with the thin-clients which dramatically reduces the requirements on the network.

When using multiple thick clients distributed over the hospital, just as many different databases with patient DICOM data will exist. When using a client-server system, only one database with patient information will be present using a single, centralized, database management system, because all DICOM data remains at the server and is not physically distributed to the clients. This has advantages technically, because of the reduced overhead and maintenance costs, but also legally because of the reduced risk of unauthorized access or loss of vital information.

The use of a client-server model in most cases also adds to the scalability of the solution. One server allows multiple users to use advanced visualization, while deploying a cluster can service even more users and introduces redundancy into the equation thus reducing downtime due to computer failures and facilitating easy maintenance without downtime. By using such a cluster setup with multiple servers and advanced software or hardware load balancing, optimal speed and availability can be guaranteed by having the cluster act as if it were one single server with one single database.

Future Directions

In 2007, Nagy predicted that "The next generation of PACS will rely heavily upon server-side video rendering for large datasets. The first three generations of architecture simply cannot handle the large volumetric datasets being generated by today's CT and magnetic resonance imaging scanners"[NAGY07]. It seems that this prediction has already become reality in some healthcare institutions and will rapidly spread to others.

A clear trend is now visible to move from thick to thin in the medical applications. All vendors are presenting their own 'thin client' solutions for advanced visualization purposes with varying degrees of thickness. This trend will continue to progress in the coming years and where currently the most advanced tools still require the use of a thick client in most cases, these will also be migrated into the thin client solutions in the near future.

In general the enormous increase in data production with modern medical acquisition devices, such as Computed Tomography and Magnetic Resonance Imaging, has introduced the problem of not being able to transfer all this data around throughout the healthcare enterprise.. This problem could be solved by the widespread introduction of client-server advanced visualization using server-side rendering and processing [Meenan06] which very likely will take place in many healthcare institutions in the near future.

After this first transition to client server systems within hospitals the PACS and advanced visualization capabilities will most probably move towards cloud computing and end up in being regional, national or even international cloud computing systems providing advanced capabilities to all users at high speed and low costs.

Conclusion

The use of client-server applications for advanced visualization is coming of age. The implementation in the clinical setting is growing as an increasing number of vendors move over from thick client solutions to some sort of client-server setup. With the current versions of the various thin client applications, the capability of advanced imaging with high levels of automation has arrived to the desktop of any radiologist or physician throughout the healthcare enterprise. This capability blurs the lines between advanced 3D fat-client workstations and general thin-client 3D so it is no longer necessary to choose between the two and accept compromises. By this, the use of advanced visualization will increase dramatically over the coming years, driven by the ever increasing amount of data produced by contemporary medical acquisition devices.

References

[FRATT09] Fratt L. IT Enables Excellence in Cardiovascular Medicine at the Cleveland Clinic. *CMIO;Sept/Oct*, 2009, 18-21.

[KOTTER06] Kotter E, Baumann T, Jäger D, Langer M. Technologies for image distribution in hospitals. *Eur Radiol*, 2006, 16, 1270-1279.

[MEENAN06] Meenan C, Daly B, Toland C, Nagy P. Use of a Thin-Section Archive and Enterprise 3D Software for Long-Term Storage of Thin-Slice CT Data Sets. *J. Digit Imaging*, 2006, 19(Suppl.1), 84-88.

[NAGY07] Nagy, PG. The Future of PACS. *Med. Physics*, 2007, 34(7), 2676-2682.

[OOIJEN04] Ooijen PMA van, Bongaerts AHH, Witkamp R, Wijker A, Tukker W, Oudkerk M. Multi-Detector Computed Tomography and 3-Dimensional Imaging in a Multi-vendor Picture Archiving and Communications System (PACS) Environment. *Acad Radiol*, 2004, 11, 649-660.

[OOIJEN07] Ooijen PMA van. Enabling off-hour teleconsultation from home, including fast 3D Visualization using AquariusNET. *In: Clinical Case Studies in the Third Dimension, TeraRecon, San Mateo*, 2007.

[OOIJEN08] Ooijen PMA van, Broekema, A; Oudkerk, M. Use of a Thin-Section Archive and Enterprise 3D Software for Long-Term Storage of Thin-Slice CT Data Sets – A Reviewers' Response. *J Digit. Imaging*, 2008, 21(2), 188-192.

[TOLAND06] Toland C, Meenan C, Toland M, Safdar N, Vandermeer P, Nagy P. A suggested classification guide for PACS client applications: the five degrees of thickness. *J. Digit Imaging*, 2006, 19(Suppl.1), S78-83.

[VERSEL09] Versel N. Health Information Exchange – Patient Data on the Move. *CMIO;Sept/Oct*, 2009, 4-8.

[VISAGE09] The Economic Benefits of Thin Client Technology. *White Paper, Visage Imaging*, 2009.

[ZHANG03] Zhang, J; Sun, J; Stahl, JN. PACS and Web-based image distribution and display. *Comput Med Imaging Graph*, 2003, 27, 196-206.

In: Computer Science Research and the Internet
Editor: Jaclyn E. Morris, pp. 197-209

ISBN: 978-1-61728-730-5
© 2011 Nova Science Publishers, Inc.

Chapter 9

WEBGBROWSE 2.0 – A WEB SERVER SUPPORTING MULTIPLE VERSIONS OF THE GENERIC GENOME BROWSER FOR CUSTOMIZABLE GENOME ANNOTATION DISPLAY

Ram Podicheti[1], V. Kashi Revanna[2] and Qunfeng Dong[2,3]

[1]Center for Genomics and Bioinformatics, Indiana University,
1001 E. 3rd Street, Bloomington, Indiana 47405-7005, USA
[2]Department of Biological Sciences, University of North Texas,
1155 Union Circle #305220, Denton, Texas 76203-5017, USA
[3]Department of Computer Science and Engineering, University of North Texas,
1155 Union Circle #305220, Denton, Texas 76203-5017, USA

Abstract

Genome browsers are critical bioinformatics tools for biologists to visualize genome annotations and the other sequence features along a reference sequence. GBrowse is one of the most popular genome browsers used by the research community. However, its installation and configuration prove to be difficult for many biologists. We have developed a web server, WebGBrowse, which takes a user-supplied annotation file in GFF3 format, guides users through the configuration of the display of each genomic feature, and allows them to visualize the genome annotation information via the GBrowse software. This chapter describes an upgraded WebGBrowse server, WebGBrowse 2.0, which provides users with a choice to display their genome annotation with different versions of the GBrowse software. The modular design of WebGBrowse 2.0 allows easy integration of future GBrowse upgrades. We have also developed a web-based GFF3 template generator to facilitate the preparation of the required annotation file in the correct format. The entire WebGBrowse 2.0 package is portable and can be freely downloaded and installed locally.

Introduction

Each sequenced genome must go through a series of bioinformatics computations to produce biologically meaningful annotation information. Genome annotation data typically include the coordinates of genes, regulatory elements, and repetitive regions with reference to the genome sequence. Genome browsers present an integrated graphical view of all these genomic annotations, which are organized as tracks of information layered along by the reference sequence. Users can navigate through different sections of the genomic sequence by zooming and keyword searching. For many scientists, "Seeing is believing." That is why genome browsers are among the most popular bioinformatics software that are actively used by biologists.

Currently, there exist two types of genome browsers: (i) standalone applications and (ii) web servers. Examples of standalone genome browser systems include GenoViz (http://genoviz.sourceforge.net/) and IGV (http://www.broad.mit.edu/igv). Besides having to install and maintain the software on the user's local computer, the biggest limitation of the standalone genome browsers is their weakness in data sharing. That is, the visualization through the standalone genome browsers is restricted to local users sitting in front of their computers where the software is installed. If different computers must be used (*e.g.*, users are away in the conference or there are collaborators located in different institutions), the software and data file must be copied to other computers for off-site use.

In contrast, a web-based genome browser easily allows distributed usages for analyzing the same data. The three most popular web-based genome browser systems used by biological research community are the Generic Genome Browser (GBrowse) (Stein *et al.*, 2002), Ensembl's genome browser (Stalker *et al.*, 2004), and the UCSC genome browser (Karolchik *et al.*, 2003). Other web-based genome browsers are also available, *e.g.*, xGDB (Schlueter *et al.*, 2006) and CoGe (Lyons *et al.*, 2008). A web-based genome browser easily allows distributed usages for analyzing the same data. Users do not need to install any software to use them. In principle, most web-based genome browsers can also be installed on the user's local computer. If properly configured, biologists can use such locally installed genome browsers as a web server for data sharing. However, these web-based genome browsers are sophisticated software packages whose installation and configuration instructions are usually intended for professional bioinformaticians. A typical biologist would find it overwhelming to install, configure, and maintain the software. For example, a GBrowse installation has to be preceded by a proper set up of Perl (http://www.perl.org), GD (http://search.cpan.org/dist/GD/), BioPerl (http://www.bioperl.org/), and other dependencies – a non-trivial challenge for biologists who are not computer savvy. In addition, biologists are not always equipped with the adequate computer resources (*e.g.*, the required UNIX-based operating system).

Therefore, in order to allow users to enjoy the functionalities of web-based genome browsers while avoiding the hassle of installation and configuration, we have developed a web server, WebGBrowse (Podicheti *et al.*, 2009), which allows biologists to upload their own genomic annotation data for display. Users can configure the display of each genomic feature visualize their data with an instance of GBrowse pre-installed on a web server. We chose the GBrowse system as the backend workhorse because GBrowse has a large user base due to its installation in many biological research community databases, *i.e.*, existing GBrowse users will find the same navigation and display style of GBrowse in the WebGBrowse server. Users do not need to install any software on their computers to use WebGBrowse, which can be easily accessed by using any standard web browsers (*e.g.*, Firefox, Internet Explorer, etc.).

Since our original WebGBrowse publication (Podicheti *et al.*, 2009), the GBrowse software has gone through significant upgrade from version 1.x to version 2.0. GBrowse 1.x has been widely used in the research community since 2002; GBrowse 2.0 was released in 2009, and represents a significant rewrite of the version 1.x with enhanced user experience by using Ajax programming technology (http:// en. wikipedia. org/ wiki/ Ajax_% 28programming%29) as well as more flexible configuration options for system administrators. Both of these major GBrowse versions will be available simultaneously because version 1.x likely will remain widely used by many major biological databases. In addition, different users may favor different versions of GBrowse due to a desire to continue using GBrowse 1.x for familiarity. In addition, new GBrowse releases may become available, further diversifying the GBrowser instances available for use. Therefore, it is important to provide different versions of GBrowse for users to easily choose and compare. In addition, some users will want to migrate from version 1.x to 2.0 with minimal effort. A naïve solution would be to provide separate servers hosting different GBrowse versions, which not only results in redundant work (*e.g.*, duplication of the web interface) but also causes significant inconvenience for users (*e.g.*, having to upload the same dataset to different servers). Instead, we have developed WebGBrowse 2.0, where multiple versions of GBrowse can be seamlessly integrated. Users only need to upload their dataset once and go through the same configuration process as in the original WebGBrowse sever, then choose to display their genome annotation with either the traditional GBrowse 1.x or GBrowse 2.0. In the following sections, we describe the detailed implementation and usage of WebGBrowse 2.0.

Materials and Methods

Figure 1 illustrates the architecture of WebGBrowse 2.0. Individual components are described below.

GBrowse

The GBrowse software was downloaded from the GMOD web site (http://gmod.org/wiki/Gbrowse). Both version 1.70 (*i.e.*, the latest stable version of 1.x) and version 2.0 of GBrowse are currently installed at the WebGBrowse 2.0 server. To prevent any potential interference of different versions on the same server, they are installed on separate machines with shared physical disk for accessing common data files and the supporting database.

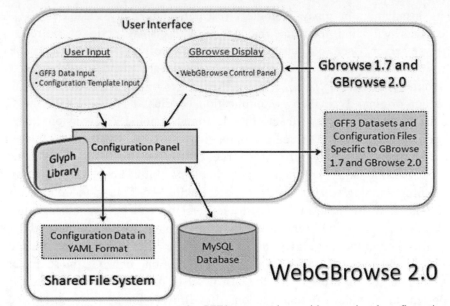

WebGBrowse interface allows users to input the GFF3 content along with an optional configuration template. A Configuration Panel follows the content validation which provides the interface for individual track configuration. The Configuration Panel is powered by a Glyph Library which provides a configurable set of parameters for each glyph. The configuration panel, as a result of its interaction with the user, outputs the configuration data which is saved into a network file system. This data is finally converted into individual configuration files specific to GBrowse 1.7 or GBrowse 2.0 depending on the user's requirements. The corresponding GBrowse libraries preinstalled on the WebGBrowse server render the GBrowse display. A WebGBrowse Control Panel allows the users to download the resultant configuration information and to navigate back to the configuration panel to continue with further changes to the configuration settings. A MySQL database helps maintain the history of datasets submitted to WebGBrowse associated with each specific email address.

Figure 1. Schematic overview of WebGBrowse 2.0 architecture.

Annotation Data File

Users must supply their genome annotation file in Generic Feature Format version 3 (GFF3) format. GFF3 is a standard format for representing genomic features in a tab-delimited plain text file, which consists of 9 tab-delimited columns that specify each sequence feature (*e.g.*, gene, mRNA, CDS, UTR, or any other sequence characteristic that can be physically mapped to reference genome; specified in column 3) and their corresponding genomic coordinates (start and end positions in column 4 and column 5, respectively). The genomic DNA sequence can also be provided in GFF3 file. The complete format specification for GFF3 is available at http://www.sequenceontology.org/gff3.shtml. Through a provided web form, users can upload their GFF3 files to the WebGBrowser server. Once the GFF3 data file is uploaded, WebGBrowse automatically validates the data file and stores it as a file-based database for the pre-installed GBrowse system.

Gbrowse Configuration File

The GBrowse software requires a configuration file for specifying the location of the GFF3 data file as well as other display settings including, for example, feature tracks, shape, font, and color. For every user-uploaded GFF3 data file, WebGBrowse creates a corresponding GBrowse configuration file. Specifically, WebGBrowse identifies a list of genomic features that can be displayed as "tracks" in GBrowse where a track is defined as horizontal display of instances of a particular feature type displayed beneath the reference genomic sequence. For example, predicted genes and proteins can be displayed as two separate tracks in genome browser. The feature list is derived based on the values from the feature type column (*i.e.*, the third column) and the feature source column (*i.e.*, the second column) of the GFF3 data file. Each feature (*e.g.*, gene or quantitative data such as tiling array hybridization intensity values) will be displayed as a different track in GBrowse. Each created configuration file is assigned a unique name based on a time stamp and session ID encrypted by MD5 hash (http://en.wikipedia.org/wiki/MD5). All of the configuration files are stored in the default GBrowse installation directory named *gbrowse.conf*. For GBrowse 2.0, a master configuration file is updated to point to each set of individual GBrowse configuration files.

Glyph Library

In order to properly display each feature, the GBrowse system requires that the appearance of each feature (*e.g.*, color, height, shape, font; also see http://gmod.org/wiki/index.php/CONFIGURE_HOWTO) must be a properly defined "glyph" in the configuration file where glyph refers to the shape of the feature, *e.g.*, using box to represent genes or exons of genes. For inexperienced users, it can be a tedious process to prepare the feature configuration. A key function of WebGBrowse is to provide a user-friendly editor in which a configuration panel lets users choose from more than 40 different glyph styles (*e.g.*, line, box, arrow; also see http://webgbrowse.cgb.indiana.edu/webgbrowse/glyphdoc.html) to properly display the features of interest. Users can also specify the color, font, label and many other characteristics specific to the glyph for the selected genomic feature. Each selected feature can be reviewed for further editing. The above configuration panel is driven by a glyph library that stores various configurable parameters specific to each of the Bio::Graphics::Glyph types in a YAML format file (http://www.yaml.org/), which is used by the HTML::FormEngine Perl library to generate the web forms users interact with.

Modification of the GBrowse Interface

WebGBrowse preserves any intrinsic functions provided by GBrowse such as the ability to download the sequence or annotation of a displayed genomic region as well as any custom annotation tracks. However, while GBrowse makes all the annotated genomes available in the "Data Source" pull-down menu for visualization, WebGBrowse is designed to limit access to an individual user's data by disabling the pull-down menu to encapsulate different users. In addition, we have also added a WebGBrowse control panel in the GBrowse display that allows users to return to the track configuration panel if additional editing is desired. It also allows users to download the generated GBrowse configuration file.

A Supporting Database

A MySQL database was implemented to store users' email addresses and the names of their configuration files. The database is used for associating users with their submitted data. Specifically, when users submit their GFF3 data files, they also have the option of providing their email addresses. If provided, a URL link to the GBrowse display page will be emailed to the user. The email also contains a link to access all the previously submitted datasets from the same user. Providing the email address also allows the user to perform the configuration process in multiple sessions. The progress can be saved at any stage by clicking a "Save Progress" button in the configuration panel and WebGBrowse will send a link to the email address provided. The configuration process can be resumed by clicking on that link at a later time.

GFF3 Template Generator

One of the most common feedbacks we have received from WebGBrowse users is a need for help in preparing the required GFF3 annotation file. Typically, biologists must deal with a large variety of output formats produced by many different bioinformatics programs. For example, there exist more than a dozen of *ab initio* gene prediction programs, each having its own output format. Although some format-conversion tools exist (*e.g.*, the BioPerl script *bp_genBank2gff3.pl* that can convert annotation file in GenBank format to the GFF3 format), specific parsers must be written for many of the existing bioinformatics programs to convert their outputs into GFF3 format. Therefore, for typical biologists who do not have programming skills, they need to seek help from bioinformaticians. Compared with setting up GBrowse, preparing GFF3 data file is a much smaller problem. The involved programming task is not difficult. For example, any bioinformatics students with basic programming skill can usually transform any raw data file into tab-delimited GFF3 files. But most bioinformaticians may be intimidated with GBrowse set-up and maintenance. However, most biologists and many bioinformaticians are not familiar with the GFF3 format specification. Based on the feedback of our users, we have developed a web-based GFF3 template generator, which guides the users step by step through simple web forms on producing a valid sample GFF3 file based on the subset of their genome annotations (*e.g.*, the length of the genome of their interest, the start and end position of some genomic features). The obtained sample GFF3 data file can be used as a template for the programmer to convert the entire dataset.

Notes

The following section briefly describes the usage of WebGBrowse 2.0 server. An illustrated tutorial was developed on the WebGBrowse 2.0 website at http://webgbrowse. cgb.indiana.edu/webgbrowse/tutorial.html. Additional description on the usage of the original

WebGBrowse server is also available (Podicheti and Dong, 2010). WebGBrowse 2.0 shares many key user interfaces with the original WebGBrowse.

1. Use any web browser (*e.g.*, Firefox) to open the URL http://webgbrowse. cgb.indiana.edu to access the WebGBrowse 2.0 web server (Figure 2A). Click the button "Browse..." in the *GFF3 File* section and upload the genome annotation file. We suggest that users try the sample dataset first, which can be downloaded by clicking the link "[Sample GFF3 File]", which was modified from the GFF3 example provided in the GBrowse installation package. This dataset presents typical feature types that can be configured to illustrate the default generic display, protein-coding genes, quantitative data display, and so on. For large data files, users can choose to upload the compressed *.gz* or *.zip* formats, and WebGBrowse can uncompress such files automatically. Provide an email address in the text input field under "Email address". Although this step is optional, it will allow for configuration in multiple sessions, results to be sent via email, and documentation of previous submissions.

2. Click the button "Submit" to send the uploaded GFF3 data to WebGBrowse and open a "Configuration Panel", where feature tracks may be added, edited or deleted from the GBrowse display. At the configuration panel, provide a short description for their dataset in the "Description" field. From the section labeled "Add New Track" (Figure 2B), select a feature from the "Feature" menu, which lists all the unique features derived from the dataset that can be configured into individual GBrowse tracks. For each selected feature, select its shape from the pull-down menu marked "Glyph". A glyph library with a sample image and short description for each selected glyph will be displayed.

3. After clicking the button "Add Track", a floating "Glyph Parameters Form", where the parameters for the selected glyph are displayed, will appear (Figure 2C). The presented configurable parameter set is specific to the type of glyph chosen. Each parameter field has a brief description explaining the purpose of the parameter. If an email address was provided in step 1, a "Save Progress" button will appear at the top right corner of the configuration panel. Clicking the "Save Progress" feature will cause WebGBrowse to email a link to the address provided where configuration can be resumed at any time. Users can change any default parameter values (*e.g.*, the color of the displayed track). More parameters can be viewed by clicking the link "Advanced Section". Once finished setting the parameter values, click the button "Save and Continue" to go back to the configuration panel and add all the desired tracks.

4. The configured tracks and their corresponding configuration settings will be listed under the section "Tracks Added" in the configuration panel (Figure 2D). To edit existing track configuration settings, select the track in the section "Tracks Added" and click the button "Edit Track". Tracks can also be deleted by clicking the button "Delete Track".

5. After adding and configuring all tracks, select the button "Display in GBrowse 1.70" or "Display in GBrowse 2.0" to visualize the features in via either version of the GBrowse software. A familiar display style of GBrowse will appear (Figure 2E, 2F).

Novice GBrowse users can follow the GBrowse tutorial available at OpenHelix (http://www.openhelix.com/gbrowse).

6. In addition to the conventional GBrowse display, there is a "WebGBrowse Control Panel" displayed at the top of the window. Clicking that button that allows further changes to the configuration file as well as a mechanism to download the generated configuration file. Click the button "Edit Configuration" in the WebGBrowse control panel to return to the configuration panel. To save the configuration to a file, click the button "Download Configuration" in the WebGBrowse control panel. To use the downloaded configuration file as a template while configuring another similar dataset, after performing step 1 with the new dataset, click the "Browse..." button in the "Configuration File to be used as a template" section of the "WebGBrowse Input Form" and upload the configuration file.

7. At the GFF template generator (Figure 3A), first provide a basic description of the reference genome (*i.e.*, name and length) then upload or paste a FASTA-format sequence into the form. Fill out the "feature" table (where each row corresponds to the columns of GFF3 format; Figure 3B) to view or download the generated GFF3 data file (Figure 3C).

Discussion

Typically, community databases set up web-based genome browsers for their user community. For example, users can browse annotations for fly genomes at FlyBase (Drysdale, 2008), *C. elegans* genomes at WormBase (Harris *et al.*, 2009), vertebrate genomes at Ensembl (Hubbard *et al.*, 2009), and plant genomes at PlantGDB (Dong *et al.*, 2005). In the past, this strategy had worked well for the research community because the numbers of available genome sequences was relatively small. In fact, it used to take a considerable amount of time to get a genome sequenced and the community databases usually partnered with each sequencing consortium to coordinate the display of the sequenced genomes.

Increasingly, however, such a display strategy in centralized community databases is not sufficient to satisfy the diverse needs of researchers. Specifically, with the rapid advent of DNA sequencing technologies, it has become easier for individual biology laboratories to engage in genome sequencing directly. Sequencing targets can be a particular species, strain, or regions of the genome for some individual in a population. This is especially true for member of the microbial research community because the sequencing microbial genomes has become nearly trivial. Due to limited bioinformatics resources, centralized community database will be unlikely to accommodate such diverse genomic data display needs in a timely fashion that meets researchers' demands.

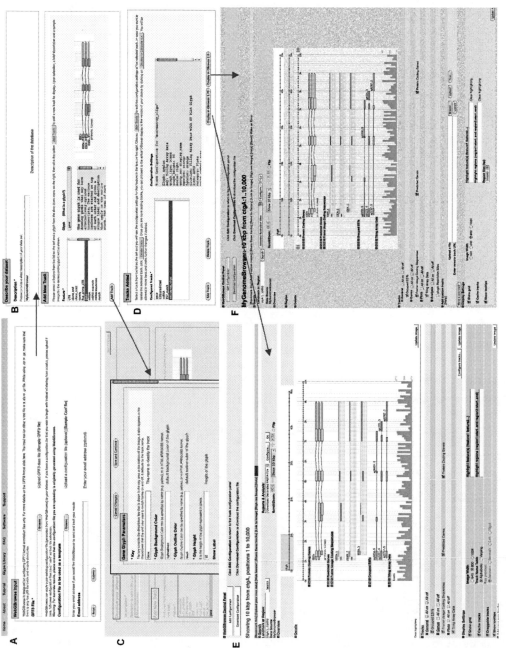

Figure 2. Screenshots of WebGBrowse. See text for details.

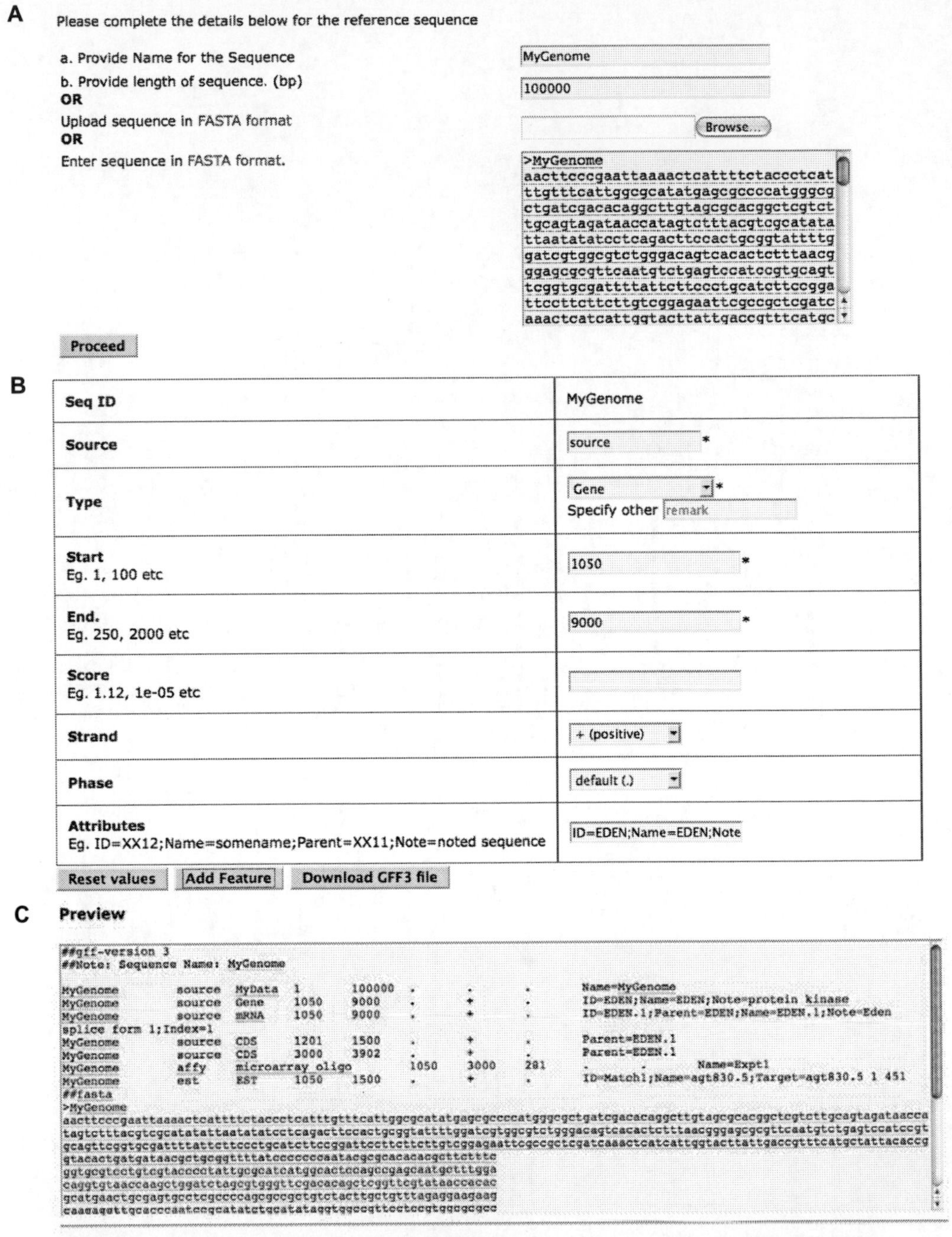

A   Please complete the details below for the reference sequence

     a. Provide Name for the Sequence   `MyGenome`

     b. Provide length of sequence. (bp)   `100000`
     OR

     Upload sequence in FASTA format   (Browse...)
     OR

     Enter sequence in FASTA format.

```
>MyGenome
aacttcccgaattaaaactcattttctaccctcat
ttgtttcattggcgcatatgagcgccccatgggcg
ctgatcgacacaggcttgtagcgcacggctcgtct
tgcagtagataaccatagtctttacgtcgcatata
ttaatatatcctcagacttccactgcggtattttg
gatcgtggcgtctgggacagtcacactctttaacg
ggagcgcgttcaatgtctgagtccatccgtgcagt
tcggtgcgatttattcttccctgcatcttccgga
ttccttcttcttgtcggagaattcgccgctcgatc
aaactcatcattggtacttattgaccgtttcatgc
```

[Proceed]

B

Seq ID	MyGenome
Source	`source` *
Type	Gene ▾ * Specify other `remark`
Start Eg. 1, 100 etc	`1050` *
End. Eg. 250, 2000 etc	`9000` *
Score Eg. 1.12, 1e-05 etc	
Strand	+ (positive) ▾
Phase	default (.) ▾
Attributes Eg. ID=XX12;Name=somename;Parent=XX11;Note=noted sequence	`ID=EDEN;Name=EDEN;Note`

[Reset values]   [Add Feature]   [Download GFF3 file]

C   **Preview**

```
##gff-version 3
##Note: Sequence Name: MyGenome

MyGenome     source  MyData            1      100000  .     .     .    Name=MyGenome
MyGenome     source  Gene           1050     9000    .     +     .    ID=EDEN;Name=EDEN;Note=protein kinase
MyGenome     source  mRNA           1050     9000    .     +     .    ID=EDEN.1;Parent=EDEN.1;Name=EDEN.1;Note=Eden
splice form 1;Index=1
MyGenome     source  CDS            1201     1500    .     +     .    Parent=EDEN.1
MyGenome     source  CDS            3000     3902    .     +     .    Parent=EDEN.1
MyGenome     affy    microarray oligo  1050   3000  281    .     .    Name=Expt1
MyGenome     est     EST            1050     1500    .     +     .    ID=Match1;Name=agt830.5;Target=agt830.5 1 451
##fasta
>MyGenome
aacttcccgaattaaaactcattttctaccctcatttgtttcattggcgcatatgagcgccccatgggcgctgatcgacacaggcttgtagcgcacggctcgtcttgcagtagataacca
tagtctttacgtcgcatatattaatatatcctcagacttccactgcggtattttggatcgtggcgtctgggacagtcacactctttaacgggagcgcgttcaatgtctgagtccatccgt
gcagttcggtgcgatttattcttccctgcatcttccggattccttcttcttgtcggagaattcgccgctcgatcaaactcatcattggtacttattgaccgtttcatgctattacaccg
gtacactgatgataacgctgcggtttatcccccaatacgcgcacacacgctcttc
ggtgcgtcctgtcgtaccctattgcgcatcatggcactccagccgagcaatgctttgga
caggtgtaaccaagctggatctagcgtgggtcgacacagctcggttcgtataaccacac
gcatgaacctgcgagtgcctcgccccagcgccgctgctcacttgctgtttagaggaagaag
caaaagattgcacccaatccgcatatctgcatataagtggccgttcctccgtggcgcgcc
```

Figure 3. Screenshots of GFF3 template. See text for details.

      Although GBrowse and the UCSC genome browser allow users to add their own tracks, such custom tracks can only be displayed along the reference genomes provided by the centralized community databases. In other words, users still cannot display their own whole genomes of interest. For example, FlyBase currently deploys genome browsers for 12 sequenced species. But if a researcher has just sequenced another *Drosophila* species that is not included in FlyBase, he/she cannot add this newly sequenced genome to FlyBase. This is the biggest motivation for developing WebGBrowse: to enable researchers to easily display their own genome sequences and annotation.

Future Work

The GFF3 data file can be stored in the GBrowse system either as a file-based or MySQL-based database. We have applied the file-based database mechanism for the simplicity of implementation. In the future, we plan to migrate to a MySQL-based database to provide faster performance for large datasets.

In addition, WebGBrowse is currently developed as a standard web server for manual interaction with biologists. We plan to extend WebGBrowse to utilize Web Services, thus integrating the WebGBrowser system into the emerging network of online bioinformatics resources that facilitate interoperable machine-to-machine interaction among biological databases and other bioinformatics resources. For example, the results of other online gene prediction and alignment tools could be directly sent to WebGBrowse for display.

Availability

The WebGBrowse web server is freely accessible, using a web browser at http://webgbrowse.cgb.indiana.edu. Although typical biologists will not try to install WebGBrowse (they will just use the web server that we have already provided instead), the software, written in Perl, is also available for local installation. WebGBrowse is released the Apache 2.0 open source license so that other developers can further improve the code and contribute to the project and some institutions could limit the need to access to outside web servers.

Conclusion

Instead of relying on centralized community databases to set up user-specific genome browser, biologists need a visualization tool that can be easily used for displaying their own genomes of interest. We have developed WebGBrowse for biologists to simply upload their genome data and display the annotations on integrated GBrowse software at our web server. This allows biologists to enjoy the functionalities of web-based genome browsers while avoiding the installation hassle while also retaining the freedom to configure the display of each genomic feature. Because multiple version of GBrowse system have become available and each has a unique user interface, we have extended the original WebGBrowse to allow researchers to select their favorite version for visualization.

Acknowledgements

RP designed and implemented WebGBrowse 2.0. KR implemented the GFF template generator. QD conceived the project and guided the development process, and drafted this chapter. We thank Dr. Carolyn Lawrence for her critical reading of the manuscript. Future correspondences should be sent to Qunfeng.Dong@unt.edu. This work was supported in part by the Indiana METACyt Initiative of Indiana University, funded in part through a major grant from the Lilly Endowment, Inc.

References

Dong, Q., Lawrence, C. J., Schlueter, S. D., Wilkerson, M. D., Kurtz, S., Lushbough, C. & Brendel, V. (2005). Comparative plant genomics resources at PlantGDB, *Plant Physiol*, **139**, 610-618.

Drysdale, R. (2008). FlyBase : a database for the Drosophila research community, *Methods Mol Biol*, **420**, 45-59.

Harris, T. W., Antoshechkin, I., Bieri, T., Blasiar, D., Chan, J., Chen, W. J., De La Cruz, N., Davis, P., Duesbury, M., Fang, R., Fernandes, J., Han, M., Kishore, R., Lee, R., Muller, H. M., Nakamura, C., Ozersky, P., Petcherski, A., Rangarajan, A., Rogers, A., Schindelman, G., Schwarz, E. M., Tuli, M. A., Van Auken, K., Wang, D., Wang, X., Williams, G., Yook, K., Durbin, R., Stein, L. D., Spieth, J. & Sternberg, P. W. (2009). WormBase: a comprehensive resource for nematode research, *Nucleic Acids Res*.

Hubbard, T. J., Aken, B. L., Ayling, S., Ballester, B., Beal, K., Bragin, E., Brent, S., Chen, Y., Clapham, P., Clarke, L., Coates, G., Fairley, S., Fitzgerald, S., Fernandez-Banet, J., Gordon, L., Graf, S., Haider, S., Hammond, M., Holland, R., Howe, K., Jenkinson, A., Johnson, N., Kahari, A., Keefe, D., Keenan, S., Kinsella, R., Kokocinski, F., Kulesha, E., Lawson, D., Longden, I., Megy, K., Meidl, P., Overduin, B., Parker, A., Pritchard, B., Rios, D., Schuster, M., Slater, G., Smedley, D., Spooner, W., Spudich, G., Trevanion, S., Vilella, A., Vogel, J., White, S., Wilder, S., Zadissa, A., Birney, E., Cunningham, F., Curwen, V., Durbin, R., Fernandez-Suarez, X.M., Herrero, J., Kasprzyk, A., Proctor, G., Smith, J., Searle, S. & Flicek, P. (2009). Ensembl 2009, *Nucleic Acids Res*, **37**, D690-697.

Lyons, E., Pedersen, B., Kane, J., Alam, M., Ming, R., Tang, H., Wang, X., Bowers, J., Paterson, A., Lisch, D. & Freeling, M. (2008). Finding and comparing syntenic regions among Arabidopsis and the outgroups papaya, poplar, and grape: CoGe with rosids, *Plant Physiol*, **148**, 1772-1781.

Karolchik, D., Baertsch, R., Diekhans, M., Furey, T. S., Hinrichs, A., Lu, Y. T., Roskin, K. M., Schwartz, M., Sugnet, C. W., Thomas, D. J., Weber, R. J., Haussler, D. & Kent, W. J. (2003). The UCSC Genome Browser Database, *Nucleic Acids Res*, **31**, 51-54.

Podicheti, R. & Dong, Q. (2010). Using WebGBrowse to Visualize Genome Annotation on GBrowse, *Cold Spring Harbor Protoclos*, in press.

Podicheti, R., Gollapudi, R. & Dong, Q. (2009). WebGBrowse--a web server for GBrowse, *Bioinformatics*, **25**, 1550-1551.

Schlueter, S. D., Wilkerson, M. D., Dong, Q. & Brendel, V. (2006). xGDB: open-source computational infrastructure for the integrated evaluation and analysis of genome features, *Genome Biol*, **7**, R111.

Stalker, J., Gibbins, B., Meidl, P., Smith, J., Spooner, W., Hotz, H. R. & Cox, A. V. (2004). The Ensembl Web site: mechanics of a genome browser, *Genome Res*, **14**, 951-955.

Stein, L. D., Mungall, C., Shu, S., Caudy, M., Mangone, M., Day, A., Nickerson, E., Stajich, J. E., Harris, T. W., Arva, A. & Lewis, S. (2002). The generic genome browser: a building block for a model organism system database, *Genome Res*, **12**, 1599-1610.

In: Computer Science Research and the Internet
Editor: Jaclyn E. Morris, pp. 211-220

ISBN: 978-1-61728-730-5
© 2011 Nova Science Publishers, Inc.

Chapter 10

VIRTUAL APPLICATIONS IN ENT MEDICINE

T. Mallepree[1], D. Bergers[1] and J. Lamprecht[2]

[1] University of Duisburg-Essen, Production Technology and Product Development,
Duisburg, Germany
[2] Alfried Krupp Krankenhaus, Essen, Germany

Abstract

Virtual three-dimensional (3D) models of the individual human anatomy support the understanding in ENT (ear, nose, throat) medicine significantly. The interdisciplinary coactions of medicine and engineering enabled encompassing developments in reconstructing complex anatomies. Different fields of application can benefit from virtual models such as pre-surgery planning, medical education, and postoperative planning and patient information. To date, various visualization systems are available but according processes are not compatible and lead to time consuming efforts by veering away from medical needs. To overcome that limitations standardization is necessary to realize. Therefore, this chapter intends to state the substantial needs of ENT medicine on virtual environments.

1. Introduction

Biomodeling allows patient specific models to be derived for medical evaluation. Such virtual models are generated by means of computed tomography (CT) or magnetic resonance imaging (MRI) to obtain anatomical geometries. Both scanning methods are commonly conducted in clinical practice and offer image slices of the human body. Since Alberti (Alberti, 1980) published the first idea to generate 3D-models by computed-tomography (CT) images, research was done to set up processes producing 3D-models. A stack of image slices are used to connect the acquired anatomical contours in the third dimension in order to build a volume model. For using three-dimensional (3D) anatomical models in medicine effectively, it is firstly essential to state the intended use of 3D models in medicine and secondly the according technical realization. Most studies investigating analysis and use of medical image data are, thus far, restricted to either visualization and required model reconstruction algorithms (Shi et al., 2006; Kalender, 1995; Lee & Lin, 2001;) or post applications

(Silverstein et al., 2005; Hu, 2005; Parikh et al., 2004; Cai et al., 2004). In addition, the basic medical needs remain unknown in various contributions (e.g., Tsuzuki et al., 2009; Paloc et al., 2001). To overcome these drawbacks current limitations are determined to formulate appropriate demands of how technical developments can contribute to virtual applications in ENT medicine effectively. The technical realization includes discussing the necessary data processes and subsequent applications like Virtual Reality (VR). A VR system enhances the comprehension by adding stereovision and interactivity (Parikh et al., 2004). Future trends of integrated computational aids are discussed as well.

2. Virtual Aids in Medicine

Current applications in medicine comprise various technical developments in which virtual environments play a major role. Mann (1965) from the Massachusetts Institute of Technology formulated as first the vision of an instrument that gives the surgeon the possibility to choose from different treatment approaches. According to Mann´s perspective a surgeon would get encompassing treatment approaches if he would be able to pick from several choices of treatment to achieve the best result for the patient. In reality the medical expert cannot evaluate different plans; he has to decide for one specific action. The basis for providing the surgeon an evaluation instrument is the generation of a virtual environment. For setting up a patient specific treatment plan, a patient specific virtual model is essential. In order to predict a surgical outcome, all real attributes from the biological system may have to be embedded in the virtual patient model. Steps have been done to implement motion and tissue characteristics in a virtual model (Tsuzuki et al., 2009; Biederer et al., 2009). That approaches herald a new era of technical contributions to medicine. But still little steps have been done in comparison to developments that can be found in the aviation industry for example. The virtual prototyping of the Boeing 777 airplane included a simulation of 3 million parts (Liou, 2007). Nevertheless, it is obvious that virtual applications can play a major role in medicine.

The process of medical prototyping starts with the tomographic scan of a patient's relevant anatomical part. This process of capturing image data to reconstruct an identical part of an existing one is Reverse Engineering (RE) (Hieu et al., 2005). During a tomographic-scan, a set of 2D-image slices is scanned. This image set consists of arranged images scanned in a successive sequence.

Each image layer represents a two-dimensional gray-scaled value image (Handels, 2000). Every gray-scaled value is a pixel that is converted into a voxel, a volumetric pixel, by combining several 2D-image layers in the third dimension. The principle is to connect the contours of each 2D-image layer in z-direction (third dimension) by interpolation (Gibson et al., 2006). That procedure is the process of three-dimensional (3D) tomographic reconstruction. For example, the main challenge in reconstructing the human nose is that the fine structures of the nose are visible only by conducting specific tomographic scans with specific scan parameters. Additionally, scanned medical images need a conversion step into a 3D model being ready for VR processing if that should be the succeeding course of action. This is the key demand for the proposed use of medical images for medical evaluation using post applications.

In the following a state of the art review is presented in order to demonstrate the multifarious fields of application of virtual models in medicine. Thereby, it is the objective to convey to a conclusion about the coupling between medicine and engineering.

2.1. Virtual Reality in Medicine

Virtual reality is a human-machine interface, which enables to experience a computer generated environment as reality including an addressing of various senses (Hennig, 2001). An additional formulation is defined by Szekely and Satava (1999) as follows: "the principal aim of VR technology is to present virtual objects or complete scenes in a way identical to their natural counterpart". In summary, VR based-systems include 3D visualization via head mounted displays or specific display screens, devices for interaction and position tracking such as data gloves and force-feedback instruments, and recently emotional (Han et al., 2009) and olfactory (Richard et al., 2006) feedback.

Virtual reality is finding a wide acceptance in the medical community and its potential benefits come into focus (Greenleaf & Piantanida, 2003). The interaction with the data of medical visualizations accelerates the display of 3D tomographic image data of individual patients. Medical visualization in VR environments enables medical experts to understand 3D image information in less time with less elaboration. Several medical fields like surgery planning, medical education, and patient information get encompassing possibilities from VR visualizations with medical image data.

According to Koročsec et al. (2005), it is obvious that VR in medicine has not met the primarily prospects. One reason might be that VR-based systems are not widely accepted in the clinical world. To date, VR-based systems are still exceedingly expensive and data processes are not efficiently working in coaction with existing computer based model building processes. Currently, there exists the Virtual Reality Modelling Language (VRML) only (ISO, 2004) for establishing open standard applications. The most VR-based systems are operated with VRML based data models that allow static visualization only (Koročsec et al., 2005; Neugebauer et al., 2007; Mallepree & Bergers, 2008).

Pre-surgery Planning

It is part of the daily clinical practice to use 3D models for planning and optimization of surgical interventions preoperatively (Székely & Satava, 1999). There are areas, such as ENT surgery, in which a surgery is not possible without preoperative planning by means of virtualized anatomical structures by means of CT or MRI. One of the most apparent utilizations of 3D visualizations in virtual environments is the display and exploration of complex anatomical structures (Warrick, 1998; Haluck, 2000, Friedl, 2002). Therefore, various approaches have brought the benefit of 3D medical models into focus. Most of the published contributions present applications in neurosurgery (Shahidi et al., 1995; Adler et al., 1997; Hernes et al., 2003; Stadie et al., 2008), orthopaedic, maxillofacial, and general sugery (Rosen et al., 1996; Bargar et al., 1998; Verma et al., 2002; Leu et al., 2008).

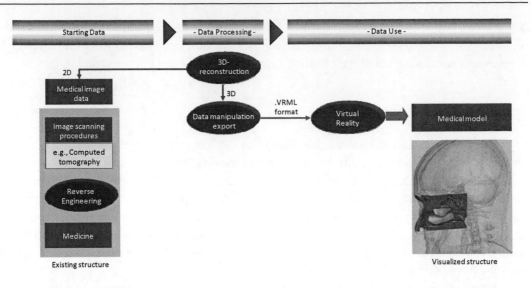

Figure 1. Data process.

Pre-surgery planning by means of virtual medical models also refers to a virtual based simulation of surgical procedures. Surgical simulation systems allow surgeons to train and improve their skills in a virtual environment. VR-based simulation systems support the medical expert in performing a surgery on a virtual medical model by only using reconstructed image data from patients. The task of a virtual surgery system is to accurately simulate the behavior of tissues (skin, muscles, internal organs, bones) under cutting operations (Gutiérrez et al., 2008). For example Lee et al. (2001) introduced a pre-surgical computer aided planning system that allows testing rhinoplasty interventions prior to surgery. Mallepree and Bergers (2009) demonstrated the generation of an animated .VRML model of the human nose with all its facets as basis to explain a pathological anatomy for surgical intervention.

There are several studies that demonstrate that VR-based surgery simulation can remarkably enhance the surgical procedure (e.g., Seymour et al., 2002).

However, there are limitations to discuss. According to Gutiérrez et al. (2008), the VR-based simulation of a surgery necessitates real-time computer graphics and haptic interfaces. Additionally, the 3D graphical display of an anatomy is a precondition for accurate intervention planning. The generation of individual model geometries requires still manual input and deep knowledge about the related process parameters in the process of image segmentation and volume meshing. Various contributions demonstrate the use of virtual models for medical evaluation (Valvoda et al., 2005) but the process parameters for individual model reconstruction remain unknown. Both, fast and accurate model reconstruction and visualization is still under development. The 3D reconstruction of soft tissue is often inaccurate because of inappropriate tomographic data sets of complex anatomies and connected tissues. A user-friendly software program that enables the medical expert to determine anatomical regions of interest independent from the CT or MRI system is still missing.

Medical Education

To date, 2D images and corpses are used in medical education to impart knowledge about the human anatomy. However, there are situations in which anatomies of living persons have to be evaluated. For example, the nasal cavity collapses back upon itself if tissue necrosis appears. In such a case it is helpful to have an analogous virtual model including a VR-based system.

Medical education belongs to one of the most developable fields of application for VR based systems. According to Székely and Satava (1999) computerized 3D teaching atlases that represent different aspects of anatomy, physiology, and pathology can revolutionize the teaching of anatomy to medical students.

With the increase of complexity of better medical techniques, the procedures are also getting more and more complex. Pletcher et al (2000) presented a VR-based system for medical education that included an according training tool treatment simulation in an immersive virtual reality CAVE system. An additional development of Hamilton et al. (1999) was an integrated computer assisted learning (CAL) applications into the undergraduate medical curriculum. The objective was to accomplish an increase in student numbers whilst perpetuating the quality standards of medical education.

Various causes exist for a non prevalent implementation of VR in medical education. According to Haluck et al. (2001), these include a lack of familiarity, high costs, need for numerous upgrades, and inadequate effectiveness in use. To identify factors for the underuse, a survey (139 respondents) across the United States has been conducted by Haluck et al. (2001). They found out that virtual environments in medical education have not been incorporated into surgical education on a widespread basis. They detected that there is a need for learning opportunities outside of the operating room and a role for VR in surgical training. The main concern was being seen in a lack of validation and potential requirements for frequent system upgrades.

According to Friedl et al. (2002) VR-based systems, allowing total immersion, are not available so far. However, one can see the current VR visualizations as being a step towards this direction. But the ultimate goal of VR based systems in advanced surgical education is the real time simulation of treatments procedures with photo-realistic appearance (Stoyanov et al., 2003) and precise force feedback responses while running on a desktop computer system.

Postoperative Planning and Patient Information

VR-based systems have demonstrated in some extent beneficial contribution to postoperative planning. A contribution by Rubin et al. (1996) showed "fly through" visualizations of large vessels, which allowed to determine the positioning of inserted stents in a follow-up step after intraaortic stent placement. The field of rehabilitation also profits from VR applications. VR shows the ability to individualize treatment needs (Schultheis & Rizzo, 2001) by giving the opportunity for experiential, active learning (Weiss et al., 2004). Greenleaf and Tovar (2004) demonstrated the opportunity of VR for disabled or injured patients that can retrieve parts of functionality by practicing tasks in virtual environments.

In sum, there is to state that VR-based systems are used in postoperative treatments but not for patient information. A better understanding of the clinical situation by means of an applied VR display would contribute to patient satisfaction enormously. That implicates a need for a fast processing of individual model data that contain the needed complexity of anatomical structures. Future developments are necessary in order to simplify the process of data acquisition, 3D reconstruction, and model visualization in a virtual environment.

3. Conclusion

The major finding of this report is that virtual models are very advantageous in medical applications. Interaction with a virtual medical model allows one to evaluate a wide range of approaches and medical situations.

Two dimensional (2D) images require that the surgeon mentally determines 3D images from 2D slices. That demand can be difficult and error prone, particularly for more complex structures such as the human nose. This process is not standardized yet, and should be optimized by means of virtual applications.

The current limitations related to virtual applications in ENT medicine are the following:

- **Usability**
  - VR display systems (expensive, error prone in operation, difficulties in handling for non technical users)
  - Data generation (Process parameters for scanning, 3D reconstruction, model visualization)
  - Process complexity (non existence of standards in processing medical image data)
  - Process repeatability
  - Inflexibility of VR display systems (stationary system installation)

- **Model accuracy**
  - Display of complex anatomical structures
  - Process accuracy (scanning, 3D reconstruction)
  - Display of inner and outer anatomical structures (pre- surgery planning in ENT medicine)

- **Generation of individual medical models**

- **Processing time**
  - Time from scanning to model delivery

- **User interaction in virtual scenery**
  - Model manipulation
  - Display of alternatives (patient information)

- **Field of application**
  - Actual medical needs
  - Allocation of case and application

The major deficiency in generating medical models is accuracy (Mallepree & Bergers, 2009). Caused by non-optimal chosen scan parameters a final model deviation is the consequence. Inaccurate medical models are a problem when it comes to model evaluation processes which use the model as basis for simulation runs. Current developments deal with finding better approaches in model acquisition that enable to obtain a model of appropriate accuracy.

Another major deficiency in generating medical models is the need of CT scanning and therefore exposing the patient to radiation. MRI scanners are better when it comes to radiation levels, but they have the disadvantage that the patient has to be stay motionless for up to a longer time span. Edge detection in the image segmentation process is in most cases also better when using CT.

To solve the current constrictions in order to use virtual applications effectively it is essential to install a process that supports surgery planning, patient information, and medical education. Those fields of use implicate various demands on engineering to develop processes that generate individual 3D models of the nose, which show accurately the specific details of the nasal cavity, paranasal sinuses, and the outer shape of the nose and the surrounding details from the forehead to the mouth. Detailed 3D models should support the ENT surgeon in balancing different options of how to execute final surgery and should enhance patient information as well as anatomical understanding exceedingly. VR and according virtual post processes should be further developed by placing more emphasis on the patient. Virtual applications can cover education, rehabilitation, and information of the patients; preventive healthcare could even benefit in the future. Internet based communication between medical experts may contribute to patient care by means of enhanced treatment plans and quick access to specific knowledge. However, security restrictions necessitate a careful data handling. Security standards for electronic based individual and patient-related data transfer are still under development.

In case of demonstrating alternative surgical procedures the surgeon should have the possibility of getting interaction into the virtual scenery and the possibility to manipulate the model. The possibility to add animated sequences should be in focus additionally in order to guide medical experts, patients, and students in cases in which complex spatial relations are existent. In addition, different VR applications for improving the virtual impression have to be introduced such as stereoscopic visualization by means of 3D transportable monitors and high resolution power walls. Current computer–user interfaces are cumbersome and unhandy to transport, making them less serviceable. Handy and transportable display devices and appendent computers may come into the market such as multiview autostereoscopic displays and portable stereoscopic 3D projectors. These devices enable the surgeons to make patient-related information forthcoming at the patient's bedside. According to Krapichler et al. (1999) the acceptance of virtual environment depends largely on the intuitiveness and convenience of the human-machine interface. A VR-based system should match with the needs and requirements of the user, not vice versa.

The detected medical demands should be realized with a process that enables to derive 3D models of highest accuracy and resolution and even a virtual environment that is transportable and easy to use. Especially, in ENT medicine there remain considerable tasks to cope with to establish virtual applications successfully for mainstream healthcare.

References

Adler, JR Jr., Chang, S. D., Murphy, M. J., Doty, J., Geis, P. & Hancock, S. L. (1997). The Cyberknife: a frameless robotic system for radiosurgery. *Stereotact Funct Neurosurg*, **69**, 124-128.

Alberti, C. (1980). Three-dimensional CT and structure models; *British Journal of Radiology*, **53**, 261-262.

Bargar, W. L., Bauer, A. & Boerner, M. (1998) Primary and revision total hip replacement using the Robodoc system. *ClinOrthop*, **12**, 82-91.

Biederer, J., Dinel, J., Remmert, G., Jetter, S. & Nill, S., et al. (2009) 4D-Imaging of the Lung: Reproducibility of Lesion Size and Displacement on Helical CT, MRI, and Cone Beam CT in a Ventilated Ex Vivo System. *International Journal of Radiation Oncology*Biology*Physics*, **73**(3), 919-926.

Cai, Y. Y., Chui, C. K. & Ye, X. Z., et al. (2004). Simulation-based virtual prototyping of customized catheterization devices. *ASME Trans J Comput Inform Sci Eng.*, **4**(2),132-139.

Friedl, R., Preisack, M., Klas, W., Rose, T., Stracke, S., Quast, K., Hannekum, A. & Gödje, O. (2002). Virtual Reality and 3D Visualizations in Heart Surgery Education. *The Heart Surgery Forum*, **5**(3), E17-E21.

Gibson, I., Cheung, L. K., Chow, S. P., Cheung, W. L., Beh, S. L., Savalani, M. & Lee, S. H. (2006). The use of rapid prototyping to assist medical applications. *Rapid Prototyping Journal*, **12**, 53-58.

Greenleaf, W. & Piantanida, T. (2003). *Medical Applications of Virtual Reality Technology*. In: Biomedical Imaging CRC Press, Taylor&Francis Group London.

Greenleaf, W. J. & Tovar, M. A. (2004). Augmenting reality in rehabilitation medicine. *Artif Intell Med*, **6**, 289-299.

Gutiérrez, M. A., Vexo, F. & Thalmann, D. (2008). *Stepping into Virtual Reality*. Springer Heidelberg NewYork.

Haluck, R. S., Marshall, R. L., Krummel, T. M. & Melkonian, M. G. (2001). Are Surgery Training Programs Ready for Virtual Reality? A Survey of Program Directors in General Surgery. *Journal of The American College of Surgeons*, **193**(6), 660-665.

Hamilton, N. M., Furnace, J., Duguid, K. P., Helms, P. J. & Simpson, J. G. (1999). Development and integration of CAL: a case study in medicine. *Medical Education*, **33**(4), 298-305.

Han, K., Lee, H., Park, J., Cho, S., Kim, I. Y., Ku, J. & Kim, J. J. (2009). Measurement of Expression Characteristics in Emotional Situations using Virtual Reality. **2009** *IEEE Virtual Reality Conference*, 265-266.

Handels, H. (2000). *Medical Image Processing*. B.G. Teubner, Stuttgart, Leipzig.

Hennig, A. (2001). *Die andere Wirklichkeit. Virtual Reality*. Konzepte, Standards, Lösungen. Addison Wesley, München.

Hernes, T., Ommedals, S., Lie, T., Lindseth, F., Lang, T. & Unsgaard, G. (2003). Stereoscopic navigation-controlled display of preoperative MRI and intraoperative 3D ultrasound in planning and guidance of neurosurgery: New technology for minimally invasive image-guided surgery approaches. *Minimally invasive neurosurgery*, **46**(3), 129-137.

Hieu, L. C., Zlatov, N., Vander Sloten, J., Bohez, E., Khanh, L., Binh, P. H., Oris, P. & Tashev, Y. (2005). Medical rapid prototyping applications and methods. *Assembly Automation*, **25**, 284-292.

Hu, Y. (2005). The Role of Three-Dimensional Visualization in Surgical Planning of Treating Lung Cancer. *Proceedings of the 2005 IEEE Engineering in Medicine and Biology*, 646-649.

ISO/IEC 14772-2:2004 (2004) Information technology -- Computer graphics and image processing -- The Virtual Reality Modeling Language (VRML). *International organization for standardization*, http://www.iso.org (last access September 2009)

Kalender, W. A (1995). Thin-section three-dimensional spiral CT: Is isotropic imaging possible? *Radiology*, **197**, 578-580.

Krapichler, C., Haubner, M., Engelbrecht, R. & Englmeier, K. H. (1998). VR interaction techniques for medical imaging applications. *Computer Methods and Programs in Biomedicine*, **56**, 65-74.

Koročsec, D., Holobar, A., Divjak, M. & Zazula, D. (2005). Building interactive virtual environments for simulated training in medicine using VRML and Java/JavaScript. *Computer Methods and Programs in Biomedicine*, **80**(1), 61-70.

Lee, T. J. & Lin, C. H. (2001). Growing-cube isosurface extraction algorithm for medical volume data. *Computerized Medical Imaging and Graphics*, **25**, 405-415.

Lee, T. Y., Lin, C. H. & Lin, H. Y. (2001). Computer-Aided Prototype System for Nose Surgery. *IEEE Transactions on Information Technology in Biomedicine*, **5**(4), 271-278.

Leu, M. C., Niu, Q. & Chi, X. (2008). Virtual Bone Surgery. In: *Virtual Prototyping & Bio Manufacturing in Medical Applications*, B. Bidanda, & P. J. Bártolo, (eds.). Springer Heidelberg NewYork.

Liou, F. W. (2007). Introduction. In: Rapid Prototyping and Engineering Applications: *A Toolbox for Prototype Development*, CRC Press, Taylor&Francis Group London.

Mallepree, T. & Bergers, D. (2009). Accuracy of medical RP models. *Rapid Prototyping Journal*, **15**(5), 325-332.

Mallepree, T. & Bergers, D. (2009). *Advanced Pre-Surgery Planning by Animated Biomodels in Virtual Reality*. IFBME Proceedings 23, Springer Heidelberg NewYork.

Mann, R. (1965). The evaluation and simulation of mobility aids for the blind. In: *Rotterdam Mobility Research Conference*. American Foundation for the blind, New York.

Neugebauer, M., Mühler, K., Thietjen, C. & Preim, B. (2007). Automatische Kamerapositionierung in komplexen medizinischen 3D-Visualisierungen. *Bildverarbeitung für die Medizin*, 318-322, Springer Heidelberg NewYork.

Paloc, C., Kitney, R. I., Bello, F. & Darzi, A. (2001). Virtual reality surgical training and assessment system. *International Congress Series*, **1230**, 210-217.

Parikh, M., Rasmussen, M., Brubaker, L., Salomon, C., Sakamoto, K., Evenhouse, R., Ai, Z. & Damaser, M. S. (2005). Three Dimensional Virtual Reality Model of the Normal Female Pelvic Floor. *Annals of Biomedical Engineering*, **32**(2), 292-296.

Pletcher, T., Bier, K. & von Lubitz, D. (2000). An immersive virtual reality platform for medical education: introduction to the medical readiness trainer. In: *Proceedings of the 33rd Hawaii international conference on system sciences*, *Vol. 5*, 5025, Maui, Hawaii.

Richard, T., Tijou, A., Richard, P. & Ferrier, J. L. (2006). Multi-modal virtual environments for education with haptic and olfactory feedback. *Virtual Reality*, **10**, 207-225.

Rosen, J. M., Laub, R., Pieper, S. D., Mecinski, A., Soltanian, H., McKenna, M., Chen, D., Delp, S., Loan, J. P. & Basdogan, C. (1996). Virtual reality and medicine: from training systems to performance machines. Virtual Reality Ann Int Symp 1996, *Proc IEEE*, 1996, 5-13.

Rubin, G. D., Beaulieu, C. F., Argiro, V., Ringl, H., Norbash, A. M., Feller, J. F., Dake, M. D., Jeffrey, R. B. & Napel, S. (1996). Perspective volume rendering of CT and MR images: applications for endoscopic imaging. *Radiology*, **199**, 321-330.

Schultheis, M. T. & Rizzo, A. A. (2001) The application of virtual reality technology for rehabilitation. *Rehabilitation Psychology*, **46**, 296-311.

Seymour, N. E., Gallagher, A. G., Roman, S. A., Obrien, M. K., Bansal, V. K., Andersen, D. K. & Satava, R. M. (2002). Virtual Reality Training Improves Operating Room Performance: Results of a Randomized, Double-Blinded Study. *Annals of Surgery*, **236**(4), 458-64.

Shahidi, R., Mezrich, R. & Silver, D. (1995). Proposed simulation of volumetric image navigation using a surgical microscope. *J Image Guided Surg*, **1**, 249-265.

Stadie, A. T., Kockro, R. A., Reisch, R., Tropine, A., Boor, S., Stoeter, P. & Perneczky, A. (2008). Virtual reality system for planning minimally invasive neurosurgery. *J Neurosurg*, **108**, 382-394.

Stoyanov, D., ElHelw, M., Lo, B. P., Chung, A., Bello, F., Yang, G. Z. (2003). Current Issues of Photorealistic Rendering for Virtual and Augmented Reality in Minimally Invasive Surgery. *Seventh International Conference on Information Visualization*, (IV'03), **350**.

Szekely, G. & Satava, R. M. (1999). Virtual reality in medicine. *BMJ*, **319**, 1305.

Shi, H., Scarfe, W. C. & Farman, A. G. (2006). Maxillary sinus 3D segmentation and reconstruction from cone beam CT data sets. *Int J CARS*, **1**, 83-89.

Silverstein, J. C., Dec,h, F., Ediso,n, M., Jure,k, P., Helto,n, W. S. & Espa,t, N. J. (2005). Virtual reality: Immersive hepatic surgery educational environment. *Surgery*, **132**(2), 274-277.

Tsuzuki, M. S., Takase, F. K., Gotoh, T., Kagei, S., Asakura, A., Iwasawa, T. & Inoue, T. (2009). Animated solid model of the lung constructed from unsynchronized MR sequential images. *Computer-Aided Design*, **41**, 573-585.

Valvoda, J. T., Hentschel, B., Temur, Y., Hörschler, I., Jesch, A., Mösges, R., Schröder, W., Wein, B., Kuhlen, T. & Bischof, C. (2005). Ein VR-basiertes rhinochirurgisches Softwaresystem für die Analyse der menschlichen Naseninnenströmung. *Bildverarbeitung für die Medizin*, **8**, 470-474.

Verma, D., Wills, D. & Verma, M. (2002). Virtual reality simulator for vitreoretinal surgery. *EYE (Nature)*, **17**, 71-73.

Weiss, P. L., Rand, D., Katz, N. & Kizony, R. (2004). Video capture virtual reality as a flexible and effective rehabilitation tool. *Journal of NeuroEngineering and Rehabilitation*, **1**, 12.

In: Computer Science Research and the Internet
Editor: Jaclyn E. Morris, pp. 221-242

ISBN 978-1-61728-730-5
© 2011 Nova Science Publishers, Inc.

Chapter 11

STP-BASED NETWORKS: ANALYSIS AND DESIGN

P. Medagliani[1,*], *G. Ferrari*[1,†] *G. Germi*[2‡] *and F. Cappelletti*[2,§]

[1] University of Parma, Parma, Italy
[2] Selta spa, Roveleto di Cadeo (PC), Italy

Abstract

In this work we analyze, through simulations, the performance of *Spanning Tree Protocol* (STP)-based Ethernet networks with ring and double ring topologies. In particular, we consider both the presence and the absence of *Virtual Local Area Networks* (VLANs), and we derive the optimized STP parameters which minimize the STP convergence time and maximize the network stability. Two possible techniques for STP internal timers management are evaluated. The presence of failures (either broken links or nodes) is also taken into account, in order to determine the proper STP parameters which guarantee connectivity recovery and convergence in all possible network scenarios. Some of the simulation results are also verified through an experimental testbed. Finally, the use of "transparent" switches is proposed as a solution to (i) accelerate the STP convergence, (ii) increase the reaction capability to failures, and (iii) overcome the limitations, imposed by the STP, on the maximum sustainable number of nodes. In particular, this approach allows to extend the number of nodes in the network, still guaranteeing the possibility of incorporating VLANs. In order to evaluate the impact of failures in a realistic network, the Open Shortest Path First (OSPF) protocol and the Hot Standby Router Protocol (HSRP) are introduced in an STP-based network. This analysis shows that the use of OSPF protocol and the HSRP does not affect the STP performance, even if a longer delay is required in order to start the transmission of ping messages and a reduced reaction capability to node/link failures must be accounted for.

Keywords: Spanning Tree Protocol, Open Shortest Path First, Hot Standby Router Protocol, Virtual Local Area Network, Opnet, simulation, performance, configuration, guidelines.

*E-mail address: paolo.medagliani@unipr.it
†E-mail address: gianluigi.ferrari@unipr.it
‡E-mail address: g.germi@selta.it
§E-mail address: f.cappelletti@selta.it

1. Introduction

Ethernet is a widely used connection technology for Local Area Networks (LANs) [1]. Its simplicity, low cost, and high data transfer capacity have favored its use in several application scenarios. For example, Ethernet is the technology of choice to interconnect racks of servers with low latency and high reliability, or to store data on remote hard disks (i.e., Storage Area Networks, SANs). In all these cases, the ability of the network to react against failures is of paramount importance.

In order to improve the network robustness against failures, a first solution consists in guaranteeing redundancy of paths between a source and its destination. For example, in most process automation plants a long connectivity loss cannot be tolerated. Therefore, exploiting path redundancy to prevent from data loss and react against possible failures is highly desirable. However, the use of redundant paths is not allowed because it leads to the creation of loops in the network, which may quickly saturate its transport capacity. A solution to this problem is given by the adoption of the *Spanning Tree Protocol* (STP) [2], which eliminates the presence of loops in the network and provides alternative paths when the active one fails.

In [3], the author presents a framework for the performance enhancement of Ethernet networks, considering the bandwidth limitations introduced by the STP. Due to the wide diffusion of Ethernet networks in many application fields, the security aspects of this technology must be also taken into account. In [4], the authors analyze the stability of STP and develop a spanning tree port cost-based approach to resist to possible external attacks. In [5], the authors propose the division of an STP-based network into two tiers in order to increase security and hide network infrastructure operations.

Even if STP-based Ethernet networks have a capillary diffusion, in the literature there are a few papers analyzing their performance. Moreover, the choice of the optimized STP parameters, which guarantee network convergence, i.e., absence of loops, is typically left to heuristic trials. In this work, we present a simulation-based performance analysis of STP-based Ethernet networks and, on the basis of the obtained results, we derive some guidelines for optimized configuration of STP parameters. In particular, network behavior is analyzed through the Opnet simulator [6]. Since no suitable models are provided by Opnet, a custom model, through which the convergence of the STP is evaluated and the optimized parameters that allow fastest network convergence are derived, is implemented. The optimized values of the STP parameters are obtained both in the presence and in the absence of VLANs connected to the switches. In addition, the robustness of the STP-based networks against node failures is evaluated and a set of optimized configuration rules for the STP parameters is derived. The use of "transparent" switches is proposed as a possible approach to overcome the limitation, on the maximum sustainable number of nodes, imposed by the STP. Finally, the impact of layer 3 protocols, namely the Open Shortest Path First (OSPF) protocol and the Hot Standby Router Protocol (HSRP), on the performance of STP-based networks is considered.

The structure of this work is the following. In Section 2., an overview of the considered protocols is provided. In Section 3., the performance of STP-based networks is first evaluated in the absence of failures, considering two different internal timer management strategies. In particular, the maximum network dimension (in terms of nodes) is derived as a function of the main STP parameters. Then, this analysis is extended to account for possible failures. In order to overcome the limitations (in terms of network dimension and convergence speed) imposed by the STP, in Section 4. we propose the use of "transparent" switches, which are properly characterized. In Section 5., on the basis of the previous results we summarize simple design guidelines for configuring the STP parameters. Finally, Section 6. concludes the work.

2.   Protocol Overview

2.1.   Spanning Tree Protocol

The segments of a Local Area Network (LAN) are connected through switches, which operate at the Layer 2 of the ISO/OSI stack [7]. These devices forward the packets received from an input port towards one or more output ports. In order to have correct network operation, logical (or layer 2) path loops between the nodes must be avoided, i.e., there must be a unique active path between any pair of switches. In the opposite case, packets would be endlessly forwarded by the nodes, with catastrophic effects on the network performance. These problems are not relevant when transmitted packets have a Medium Access Control (MAC) address field with information known by the switches. In this case, each switch is aware of the devices connected to its ports. On the other hand, a broadcast message or a message directed to a node with an unknown MAC address is forwarded by a switch to all the active ports, except for the input one. In this case, in the presence of a loop, the packets will be replicated by all switches in the network, thus quickly saturating the network.

A possible approach would be physically avoiding loops during the network creation phase. However, this choice can be unreliable in the case of a link failure, after which some areas of the network could become unreachable and isolated. A better approach would exploit the redundancy of paths from a source to a destination. After network start-up, only one of the redundant paths becomes active, whereas the remaining paths are left inactive. In the presence of a failure, the original path is replaced with one of the inactive paths, guaranteeing correct network operations.

The algorithm which manages the activation of the links is known as Spanning Tree Algorithm (STA) and is embedded into the STP, which is a part of the IEEE 802.1D standard [8]. Since the operations, needed to manage the STP, are performed by all the switches in the network, the STA is totally distributed. The goal of the STP is the creation of a tree which allows to route data packets to any segment of the network, avoiding loops and leaving only one active path between any pair of source-destination nodes.

The limitations of this protocol can be summarized as follows: (i) the convergence time increases when the number N of switches in the network increases; (ii) the control traffic introduced by the STP degrades the network performance; (iii) the inactive paths do not increase the overall capacity of the network; and (iv) the maximum number of switches in the network is limited. Solutions to these problems are provided through possible enhancements of the basic STP, such as the Rapid STP [9] and the Multiple STP [10].

The main phases of the convergence process of the STP are: (i) election of a root node (i.e., a root bridge, RB, according to the STP reference names), (ii) determination of the least cost paths, (iii) deactivation of the remaining paths, and (iv) resolution of the paths with equivalent costs. The last phase occurs only when there is more than one path with the same characteristics, whereas the other three steps occur at the network start-up.

Every switch has a unique identifier and an associated priority. In the case of different priorities, the switch with the lowest priority becomes the RB. On the other hand, if all priorities are equal, the node with the lowest identifier will become the RB [11]. Once the tree is created, every node has a minimum-cost path towards the RB. Note that the STP does not guarantee that the path between any source-destination pair is the one with minimum cost, because the minimization of the path cost is not the goal of the STP. The use of minimum-cost paths to the RB is guaranteed by the following rules:

- after the election of the RB, every switch computes the cost of every path from itself to the RB and chooses the one with least cost (the associated port is referred to as root port, RP);

- the switches in the same network segment cooperatively select the switch with least cost (the port which connects a switch to the network segment is referred to as designated port, DP).

Every switch needs to have a complete knowledge of the network (i.e., of the priorities and the identifiers of the other nodes). To this end, a periodical "special" packet, referred to as Bridge Protocol Data Unit (BPDU), is transmitted. A BPDU contains information about the transmitting node, i.e., the states of its ports, its priority, the cost of the path from the switch which originates the BPDU to the RB, and the identifier of the RB. The BPDUs are not forwarded by the receiving switch. According to the STP, there are three kinds of BPDU: (i) Configuration BPDU (CBPDU or simply BPDU), used by the switches to create and maintain the network tree; (ii) Topology Change Notification (TCN), used to notify topology changes in the network or the addition of a new switch; and (iii) Topology Change Acknowledgment (TCA), used to confirm a topology change in the network.

In order to prevent the formation of loops in the network, the STP defines five possible states for the ports of a switch: (i) disabled, (ii) listening, (iii) learning, (iv) forwarding, and (v) blocking. When the network is created, all ports connected to valid links are in listening state, while the others are in disabled state. In the former state, the switches receive the BPDUs from the other nodes. In the presence of a loop, a port of a switch, which becomes aware of the presence of the loop, is turned into the blocking state, in order to prevent the transit of BPDUs. After a time interval, referred to as forward delay (FD), equal to 15 s by default, the ports in listening state switch to learning state [12]. In this phase, the nodes become aware of the surrounding switches. After another FD interval, the ports in learning state are switched into forwarding state and data packets can then circulate throughout the network.

According to the STP, the RB transmits a BPDU with a period denoted as "hello time" (equal to 2 s by default). At the network start-up, each switch elects itself as the RB and transmits a BPDU. If the priority information conveyed by a BPDU from a given switch is higher than the one stored in the receiving switch, the latter updates its status, electing as RB the transmitting switch, and stops transmitting its own BPDUs. In fact, from this moment on it will retransmit only the BPDUs received from the elected RB.

The conditions to be satisfied to guarantee convergence of the STP are the following: (i) all switches elect the same RB; (ii) one of the switches in the loop has a port in blocking state; (iii) the remaining ports of that switch and of all the other switches are in forwarding state; and (iv) the previous three conditions are stable during the time. Once all previous conditions are met, only the RB will broadcast the BPDUs every 2 s and the other switches, upon the reception of a BPDU, will retransmit it and refresh their internal information.

Another important timer of the STP is the max age (denoted as MA) timer, which defines the time interval after which a reset of the switch is required if no refreshing BPDU is received. When a BPDU is retransmitted by a switch, the latter modifies only the cost of the path to the RB and a timer, referred to as message age (denoted as m_{age}), used to measure the "distance" of a node from the RB. In particular, this value is generally increased by 1 s or 2 s, depending on the state of internal timers.[1] This value is used in combination with the MA in order to guarantee the reliability of the information conveyed in a BPDU. More precisely, the RB generates a BPDU with $m_{age} = 0$ s. Then, the switches which receive this BPDU assume that the information transported by the BPDU is valid for a time interval equal to MA. When the BPDU is relayed, m_{age} is incremented and the receiving switch assumes that the information conveyed in the BPDU is valid for $MA - m_{age}$ (dimension: [s]). When the message age of a switch becomes larger than the max age, the switch sends a TCN BPDU to the other switches in order to notify them of the occurred problem. In this case, the STP does not converge.

2.2. Per-VLAN Spanning Tree

VLANs are instrumental to logically segment the network into areas. This solution is less expensive and more flexible than the traditional approach based on the use of dedicated switches. This technology, included into the IEEE 802.1Q standard [13], allows to interconnect the switches which share the same VLAN, even if they belong to geographically separated networks. This operation, referred to as trunking, is based on the use of tags which identify which packets belong to which VLAN. A port which conveys tagged traffic is named trunk port, whereas a port, through which untagged packets enter inside the VLAN, is referred to as access port. In the case of mixed traffic, instead, the port is referred to as hybrid.

There are two possible ways of assigning a device to one or more VLANs: (i) dynamic and (ii) static. In the former case, database-based software packages are used to associate a switch with a specific VLAN. In the latter case, instead, assignments are based on a strict association between a port and the corresponding VLANs. This approach corresponds to the use of port-based VLANs. With this mechanism, all users connected to a port are automatically associated to the assigned VLAN. The STP can be applied to every created VLAN. In this case, the mechanism of the extension of the STP, referred to as per-VLAN Spanning Tree (PVST), remains the same, except for the fact that the tree is computed also for each VLAN (i.e., for the switches belonging to the same VLAN).

---

[1] Generally, a 1 s increment is associated with STP convergence, whereas a 2 s increment denotes no STP convergence in the network.

2.3. Open Shortest Path First Protocol

The OSPF protocol is one of the most used Internet routing protocols nowadays and it operates at the layer 3 of the ISO/OSI stack [14]. The Internet is composed by several routing domains, called Autonomous Systems (ASs) and the data traffic is routed along different paths according to the weights associated to each link by network operators. The OSPF protocol gathers link state information from available routers and constructs a topology map of the network. Therefore, each router has a complete knowledge of the network topology and, using the information associated with the weights at each link, can determine the shortest path to a specific destination. The main advantages of the OSPF protocol with respect to a distance vector-based routing protocol can then be summarized as follows: (i) it converges faster; (ii) the routing update packets are small, as it doesn't send the entire routing table; (iii) it is not prone to routing loops; (iv) it scales very well for large networks; and (v) it recognizes the bandwidth of a link and takes it into account in link selection.

The routers that belong to the same area, i.e., a set of networks and hosts within an AS that have been administratively grouped together, periodically send Hello messages in order to notify surrounding routers of their activity. If a router does not receive Hello messages for a period of time larger than RouterDeadInterval (typically 40 s), it assumes the connectivity with its neighbor is lost and starts generating new Router Link-State Advertisement (LSA) messages to notify to the other routers the topology change. The transmission of the LSA messages forces, in surrounding routers, the recomputation of the shortest path and the following update of the routing tables stored in each node. The duration of the recovery phase is given by the sum of three contributions: (1) the failure detection time, (2) the LSA flooding time, and (3) the time to complete the calculation of the new paths and update the routing tables. Given an Hello interval time equal to 10 s, a failure detection takes between 30 s and 40 s. The LSA flooding time is given by the propagation delay and the delays related to rate limitations on the transmission of a group of LSA messages (denoted as Link-State Update, LSU). Finally, since the computation of the shortest path makes use of the Dijkstra's algorithm [15], which requires significant time in order to complete data processing, an additional time interval, referred to as spfDelay, equal to 5 s, is introduced, in order to collect a large number of LSA message and reduce the number of reprocessing run required by the arrival of a new LSA message.

2.4. Hot Standby Router Protocol

The HSRP is a Layer-3 Cisco proprietary standard for establishing a fault-tolerant gateway [16]. This protocol is designed for use over multi-access, multicast or broadcast capable LANs (e.g., Ethernet), and is based on the use of a single *virtual* IP address for a set of routers which can act as gateways. In order to prevent from network misconfigurations, only one router is active, whereas the remaining nodes are in the standby state. If the active router fails, a priority-based scheme is used in order to determine the router that must switch into the active state and act as network gateway.

In order to notify the neighboring routers of its address and its priority, a router periodically sends an Hello message to a multicast address, i.e., to all routers in the network with HSRP capabilities, in order to notify them of its activity and communicate to them its priority. As soon as a router has become active, the other routers switch into the standby

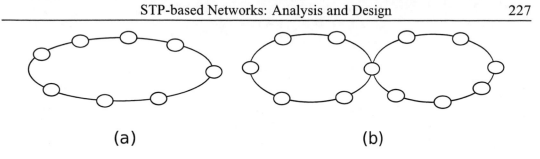

Figure 1. Topologies considered for simulation-based analysis: (a) ring topology and (b) double ring topology.

state and only the active router sends the periodic Hello message. If the active router fails, the other routers can no longer receive the Hello messages. After a time interval, referred to as Hold time and equal to 10 s by default, the second router in the priority list, which was in standby, switches in the active state and replaces the failed router, acquiring the virtual IP address of the active router.

3. Ring and Double Ring Networks

3.1. Scenarios Without Failures

In order to analyze the STP and characterize its performance, a proper Opnet simulator model has been developed. This model, which allows to periodically extract (or log) the states of the ports of each switch, has been derived from the model of a Cisco CS2948 switch and presents 4 layer-2 ports. The links which connect any pair of switches are Ethernet 100 Mbps connections. We first consider (a) ring and (b) double ring topologies, as shown in Fig. 1. In particular, in double ring topologies, the switches are configured so that the RB is the node in the center of the double ring. Since the goal of this work is to provide some guidelines for the configuration of the parameters of the switches in STP-based networks, we derive, for given values of the max age and forward delay, the network convergence time. We point out that a ring topology has been considered as this represents the worst-case scenario for an STP-based network. The double ring topology, instead, is a simple, yet representative, example of a possible extension of the ring topology.

We also validate some of the simulation results through an experimental testbed formed by 9 Cisco 2811 switches[2] equipped with a 4-port HWIC-4ESW interface which operates at 100 Mbps, configured with a VLAN, referred to as VLAN 1, on all the ports.

The first indicator considered for STP convergence analysis, according to the definition provided in Subsection 2.1., is the number of exchanged packets in the network. This number, as a function of time, is shown in Fig. 2. The network parameters are $N = 30$ switches, $MA = 20$ s and $FD = 15$ s. A ring network topology is considered. From the results in Fig. 2, one might be tempted to conclude that the network has converged after approximately 50 s. However, observing the simulator log files and the states of the ports

---

[2]The Cisco switches, i.e., CS2948, used in the simulator have the same functionalities of the switches in the experimental testbed.

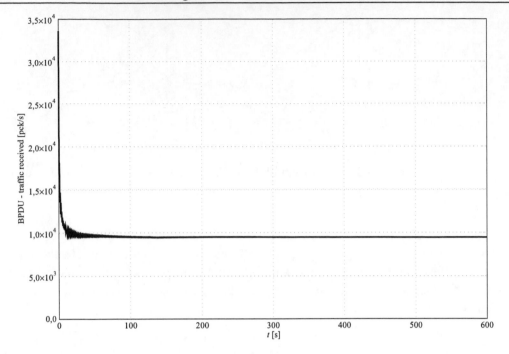

Figure 2. Number of exchanged packets in a scenario with $N = 30$ switches, $MA = 20$ s and $FD = 15$ s.

of each switch—not shown here for lack of space—it can be concluded that the network does not meet the convergence conditions described in Subsection 2.1., even if BPDUs are regularly transmitted. In fact, this analysis technique does not take into account the different types of transmitted BPDUs. In the results presented in Fig. 2, the traffic is due to the presence of TCN BPDUs and not to CBPDUs transmitted after network convergence. In particular, when the value of MA is not correctly selected for the considered network, the most distant nodes receive BPDUs with m_{age} equal to MA. According to the STP, as soon as a switch experiences this situation, it starts sending a TCN message to the other switches, which will eventually reply with TCA messages, upon acknowledgement of the topology change. This means that the chosen values of MA and FD are too small for the considered scenario and the STP does not converge. In this case, the network will be divided into two areas and the RB in the network will not be unique.

The convergence of the network can be verified by careful examination of a properly generated (through our simulator) log file at each node. In particular, we have considered scenarios with different numbers of switches, varying the max age and forward delay, in order to obtain the minimum values of MA and FD which guarantee network convergence. In Fig. 3, the minimum values of MA required for convergence is shown as a function of the number of switches in the network. The FD is not shown, since it can be extracted according to the relation

$$2(FD-1) \geq MA$$

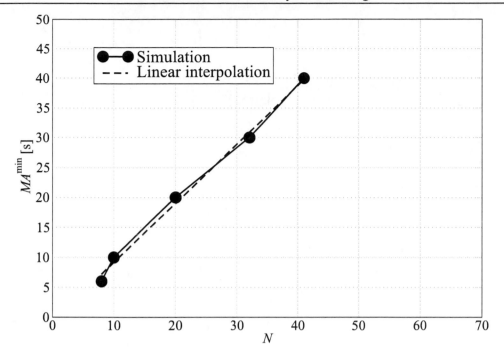

Figure 3. Minimum *MA* considering ring topology with Cisco switches.

required by the IEEE 802. 1D standard. Therefore,

$$FD^{\min} = \frac{MA^{\min}}{2} + 1.$$

By linearly interpolating (as a function of N) the *MA* values in Fig. 3, one finds that

$$MA^{\min} = 0.9876 \cdot N - 0.7242 \simeq N - 0.7. \tag{1}$$

Setting *MA* to the minimum value given by equation (1) guarantees fastest convergence. However, equation (1) is no longer valid when there is a link or node failure since the network topology changes (this case will be explained in Subsection 3.2.). The first point of the curve shown in Fig. 3 has been also verified experimentally (without VLAN 1). Experimental results show that there is convergence with $N = 8$, $MA = 6$ s, and $FD = 4$ s, whereas with $N = 9$ and the same STP parameters the network does not converge.

In Fig. 4, the minimum *MA* required for convergence, in a scenario with the double ring topology in Fig. 1 (b), is shown as a function of N. The considerations carried out for the scenario with ring topology still hold in this scenario. The minimum value of *MA* is given, as a function of N, by the following expression:

$$MA^{\min} = 0.5292 \cdot N - 0.9643 \simeq \frac{N}{2} - 1. \tag{2}$$

Note that expression (2) holds in networks where the RB is the central node of the double ring topology. In other scenarios, this expression is not valid and the convergence is no longer guaranteed.

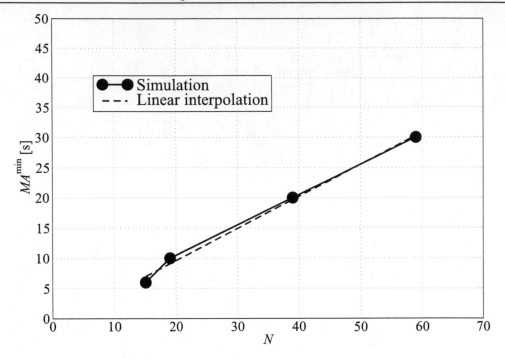

Figure 4. Minimum *MA* considering double ring topology with Cisco switches.

As we have seen, the main limitation to the formation of large STP-based ring and double-ring networks is given by the absence of convergence, caused by the fact that the m_{age} becomes larger than the *MA* at the nodes which are distant from the RB. A possible solution would be the modification of the increment which the m_{age} undergoes when the BPDU crosses a node. In particular, this increment can be expressed as follows:

$$
\begin{aligned}
m_{\mathrm{age}} &= \lfloor BPDU_{\mathrm{cross}} + m_{\mathrm{a-io}} + D_{\mathrm{ma}} \rfloor \\
&= \lfloor BPDU_{\mathrm{cross}} + 1 + 0.5 \rfloor
\end{aligned}
\tag{3}
$$

where $BPDU_{\mathrm{cross}}$ is the BPDU crossing time at switch, $m_{\mathrm{a-io}}$ is the message age increment overestimate, and D_{ma} is the medium access delay. The first term is given by the difference between the transmission instant and the reception instant of the BPDU, i.e., the physical time interval required by the BPDU to cross a switch. The second and third terms, instead, are derived from statistical considerations and are equal to 1 s and 0.5 s, respectively, as indicated by Cisco [12]. In particular, $m_{\mathrm{a-io}}$ is the minimum increment necessary to avoid an underestimation of the BPDU age. D_{ma}, instead, is the time necessary for a device to gain the access to the medium for initial transmission. In other words, D_{ma} corresponds to the time between the instant at which the switch decides to retransmit the BPDU and the instant at which the BPDU effectively begins to leave the switch.

Expression (3) for the message age applies to Cisco switches (i.e., nodes with switching capabilities running the Cisco kernel). A Linux kernel is also publicly available [17]. The Linux kernel neglects the contribution of the message age increment overestimate. There-

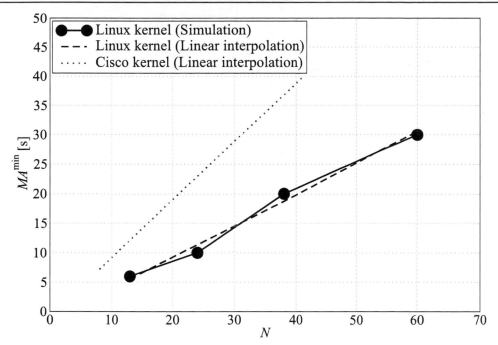

Figure 5. Minimum MA considering ring topology with switches with Linux kernel.

fore, the message age can be given the following expression:

$$m_{\text{age}}^{\text{Linux}} = \lfloor BPDU_{\text{cross}} + D_{\text{ma}} \rfloor = \lfloor BPDU_{\text{cross}} + 0.5 \rfloor.$$

In Fig. 5, the minimum MA of a network is shown, as a function of N, in scenarios with ring topology and switches running the Linux kernel. Since the crossing time is lower in nodes with the Linux kernel, the maximum number of switch, for which convergence is still guaranteed, is larger than in the case with Cisco kernel. In particular, given a value of MA, the number of switches which can be supported using the Linux kernel is twice that supported using the Cisco kernel. More precisely, the minimum message age depends on N as follows:

$$MA^{\min} = 0.5277 \cdot N - 1.309 \simeq \frac{N}{2} - 1.3. \tag{4}$$

In Fig. 5, for comparison purposes, the performance with the Cisco kernel (dotted line) is also shown—this curve is the linear interpolation curve in Fig. 3.

The use of the Linux kernel allows to reduce the convergence time of the STP. In fact, since the convergence occurs after a time interval equal to $2FD$, the possibility of using a lower value of MA and, consequently, a lower value of FD reduces the convergence time. On the other hand, as already mentioned, a switch can detect a link or node failure if it does not receive any refreshing BPDU for a period of time longer than $MA - m_{\text{age}}$. In scenarios with the Linux kernel, since the value of m_{age} increases more slowly (when crossing switches) than in scenarios with the Cisco kernel, the information stored in a node is valid for a longer time interval. Therefore, the failure reaction capability is reduced.

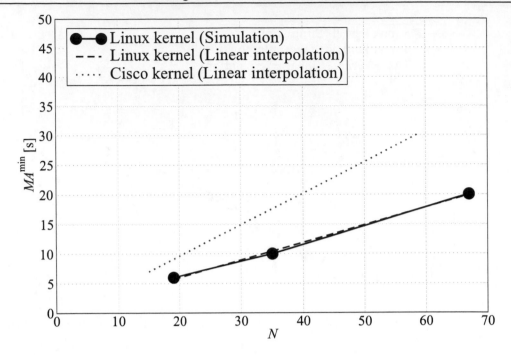

Figure 6. Minimum *MA* considering double ring topology with switches with Linux kernel.

Similar considerations can be made in a scenario with double ring topology and Linux kernel. The minimum required value of message age, as a function of N, is shown in Fig. 6. As assumed in scenarios with Cisco kernel at the switches, the RB is forced to be the switch in the center of the double ring, and the obtained results are valid only for this case. The relation between the number of switches and the minimum max age can be approximated as follows:

$$MA^{\min} = 0.2948 \cdot N - 0.1161 \simeq 0.3N - 0.1. \qquad (5)$$

Similarly to the results presented in Fig. 5, the minimum max age allowed with the Linux kernel is almost twice that allowed with the Cisco kernel.

So far, the convergence has been analyzed in the absence of VLANs connected to the switches. We have then extended our analysis to account for the presence of VLANs, in the case of both single ring and double ring topologies. In particular, we have connected two VLANs (VLAN 1 and VLAN 2) to each node. From the analysis of the log files generated by the switches, it can be concluded that the convergence performance remains the same. In particular, the PVST allows to create both a common tree for all the switches and particular trees for each VLAN. Since in our simulations the VLANs have been connected to each switch using the previously described parameters, the common tree, the tree for VLAN 1, and the tree for VLAN 2 coincide. The convergence instant is still equal to $2FD$.

3.2. Scenarios With Failures

The results presented in the previous subsection have been obtained considering a network without failures. However, in order to test the validity of the STP, one must take into

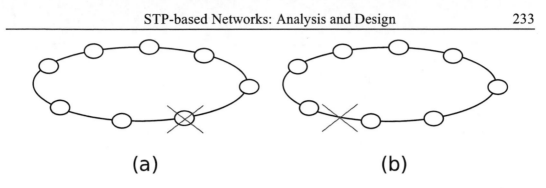

(a)   (b)

Figure 7. Example of network topology in the presence of (a) a node failure or (b) a link failure.

account also the reaction capability in the presence of a failure in the network. In Fig. 7, the illustrative failure configurations considered in this work are shown. In particular, Fig. 7 (a) refers to a *node* failure, whereas Fig. 7 (b) refers to a *link* failure. One can observe that, considering a network with N nodes, after a single node failure, the number of nodes reduces to $N-1$, whereas in the case of a link failure the number of active nodes remains equal to N.

According to the STP, when a switch does not receive a refreshing BPDU for a period of time longer than $MA - m_{age}$, it sends a TCN BPDU in order to notify the neighboring switches of the lack of convergence in the network. After the transmission of the TCN, the switch which has notified the change of topology, starts sending BPDUs assuming to be the RB of the network. If the neighboring nodes have information about a better RB, they start replying with BPDUs in order to notify the node of their information. However, since the node which originates the TCN receives an information which is still "too old," it starts sending another TCN, thus originating the message exchange just described. This exchange of messages is a symptom of the fact that the STP parameters are too small for the considered network. On the other hand, when a neighboring switch accepts the TCN, it sends back a TCA and stores the information about the new RB. In this case, the network separates into two segments with different RBs. In particular, the switch, which originated the TCN, is in an unstable state, since it oscillates between two possible values of the RB.

The latter case is exactly the scenario which occurs when a link or a node fail. More precisely, referring to the scenario with ring topology, a failure creates an open-chain network. If the STP parameters are too small for a network, the switch which verifies that the message age is larger than the max age, will start broadcasting a TCN. Since the nodes after that switch will not receive any other BPDU from the real RB, they will acknowledge the topology change and the new RB in the network. A solution to this problem is given by the use of more "relaxed" STP parameters, which let the BPDUs propagate into the open-chain to the most distant switch from the RB. The determination of the STP parameters through the analysis of an open-chain network with N switches has a peculiar importance in network design. In fact, the STP parameters optimized for this scenario guarantee that every network with loops, where the distance between any couple of (source-destination) nodes is smaller than N hops (i.e., $N-1$ switches must be crossed), converges.

According to the STP, a switch realizes that a reset is required when the value of m_{age} of

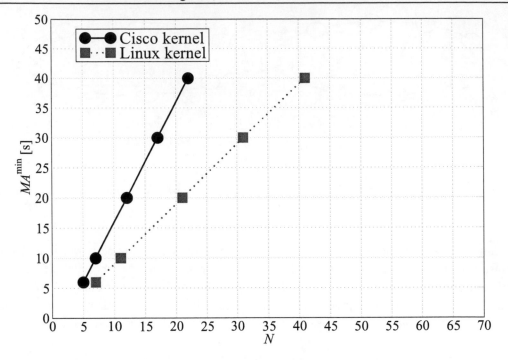

Figure 8. Minimum MA considering an open-chain scenario with a single failure.

a received BPDU is equal to the value of MA. Assume that there is a node or a link failure at a generic instant T^*. After this failure, a switch which does not receive any BPDU for a period of time equal to $MA - m_{\mathrm{age}}$, starts sending a TCN message.[3] After the TCN message has propagated through the network and some switches have reset their information, their ports are first put into listening state. Then, after a time interval equal to FD, these ports are switched into learning state and, after another interval of length FD, into forwarding state. On the other hand, when the failure is recovered and the loop is restored, as soon as a BPDU propagates through the network and updates the information stored in each node, the switch which must put a port in the blocking state, changes its port state and convergence is reached again.

In Fig. 8, the minimum max age required to guarantee convergence in a open-chain network is shown as a function of the number N of switches in the network. Note that an open-chain network, obtained from a ring network with N nodes, upon a single node failure contains $N - 1$ nodes. The performance in scenarios with Cisco and Linux kernels is evaluated. When the Cisco kernel is used, the nodes introduce $m_{\mathrm{a-io}}$ equal to 1 s, and the MA rapidly reaches the value of m_{age}. On the other hand, when the Linux kernel is used, as mentioned above, given a value of MA, the number of admitted switches is larger. This consideration is confirmed by the equations which characterize the minimum values of MA as functions of the number of switches in the network. For the scenario with Cisco kernel

---

[3]Considering $T^* = 30$ s, $MA = 6$ s and a ring-topology with a failure of the switch neighboring the RB, the network becomes aware of the failure at 33 s. In fact, the BPDU at $t = 30$ s is not received by the switch, therefore the last refreshing BPDU was received at $t = 28$ s and the information conveyed is valid for $6 - 1 = 5$ s upon the reception of the last BPDU.

Table 1. Minimum value of *MA* predicted by the experimental testbed with switches with Cisco kernel.

$MA^{\min}$	N
6	4
8	5
14	8

one obtains

$$MA^{\min} = 2N - 4$$

whereas for the scenario with Linux kernel it holds that

$$MA^{\min} = N - 1.$$

This performance analysis can be extended to the case of a link failure, after which there are still N active nodes, unlike the previous scenario, where $N - 1$ switches are active after a node failure. In the case of Cisco kernel, it holds that

$$MA^{\min} = 2N - 2$$

and in the case of Linux kernel one has

$$MA^{\min} = N.$$

The results with Cisco kernel and a link failure have been confirmed through the experimental results presented in Table 1.

According to this configuration rule, the parameters are tighter than those presented in Subsection 3.1.. However, even if this configuration leads to a longer convergence time, the stability of the network is guaranteed in all the scenarios where the paths between any couple of nodes are shorter than N hops. In addition, according to [8, 12], the recommended network diameter (i.e., the maximum number of switches that a packet crosses in order to link any two switches in the network) should be equal to 7. The discrepancy between Cisco recommendations and our results is mainly due to the fact that the Cisco recommendations are conservative. In fact, in order to prevent from possible STP reconfigurations due to delayed transmission of BDPUs in the presence of intense traffic, the specifications given by Cisco force the network to be small, thus guaranteeing convergence even in the presence of traffic congestion. However, our results show that the maximum number of switches which guarantees convergence is 11 in the case of Cisco kernel, and 20 in the case of Linux kernel.

4. Extended Networks

In the previous section, we have presented the performance of the STP both in the absence and in the presence of node or link failures in ring and double ring networks. However, with large networks it is necessary to configure the STP with large values of *MA*

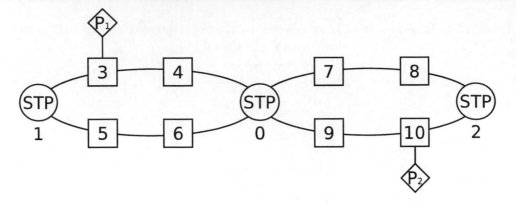

Figure 9. Extended network topology.

and *FD*. This solution, which refers to the configurations presented in Subsection 3.2., is feasible and reliable, but leads to a longer convergence time and a slow reaction to a failure. Therefore, the use of extended networks might be required.

Generally, the network dimension can be extended through hubs, which relay received packets but do not participate to the operations of the STP. This solution is limited, since a hub cannot manage a VLAN. In this work, we propose the use of "transparent" switches with disabled STP. Transparent switches, unlike hubs, can still manage VLANs. In real networks, the transparent switches are implemented by disabling the STP for both VLANs and the common tree. Since the models available in the Opnet simulator do not support this functionality, we have derived a transparent switch model from the model with enabled STP. A transparent switch receives BPDUs from a port and forwards them to all the other active ports. In addition, this switch can manage the VLANs, so that it can act as access port for the VLAN activated on each port and as a trunk for the links which connect the other switches. Since the STP increases the m_{age} as soon as a BPDU crosses a switch, the switches without STP must relay the received BPDU without increasing this value.

We have analyzed a network with double ring topology and three nodes with enabled STP: one is placed in the center of the double ring and the other two at the extremes of the double ring. In the middle of the STP-enabled nodes, a variable number of transparent switches can be placed. In particular, in our simulations a topology with 8 transparent switches, as shown in Fig. 9, is considered. The nodes with STP enabled (e.g., switch 0, 1, and 2) have been configured with $MA = 6$ s and $FD = 4$ s. Recalling the performance presented in Fig. 3, in a scenario with 11 switches, the minimum value of *MA* should be equal to 10 s and, consequently, the minimum value of *FD* should be 6 s. In this scenario, we have also introduced two VLANs, named VLAN 1 and VLAN 2, on every node in the network, both for those with STP enabled and for those with STP disabled. We have then used two nodes, referred to as P_1 and P_2, which periodically send a ping message in order to trace the active path between them. In addition, we have introduce a link failure at $T^* = 30$ s and a link recovery at $T^{**} = 90$ s in order to evaluate the reaction capability of this network. These instants have been chosen to let the network converge and, subsequently, after an alteration of the state of a node or a link, analyze its reaction speed.

The considered network converges at $t = 8$ s, as soon as the ports of the nodes running the STP switch into forwarding state. When the ping messages start to flow, the preferred route from P_1 to P_2 is 3 - 4 - 0 - 9 - 10. When a failure occurs at node 9 (we remark that the BPDU at $t = 30$ s is not delivered), the ping messages do not reach P_2 and BPDUs do not reach switch 2 on that side of the loop for 6 s. Then, at $t = 34$ s switch 2 sends a TCN message.[4] This message forces a change of state in the ports of the switch, so that for a period of time equal to $2FD$ switch 2 is no longer able to relay the received data. As soon as its ports are turned into forwarding state at $t = 42$ s, the new route for the ping message becomes 3 - 4 - 0 - 7 - 8 - 2 - 10. Once the failure is recovered, as soon as a BPDU propagates through the previously failed link, the information stored in the switch 2 is changed and the network converges again since switch 2 turns a port into blocking state. Referring to the failure recovery at $T^{**} = 90$ s (we remark that the BPDU at $t = 90$ s is delivered correctly), the ping message at $t = 91$ s is routed through the path 3 - 4 - 0 - 9 - 10.

Recalling the considerations presented in Subsection 3.2. and equation (3), the convergence is guaranteed when the condition $m_{age} < MA$ holds in each switch in the network, i.e., when the information conveyed by a BDPU and received by a switch is not too old. Considering two switches running STP connected through a set of transparent switches, the m_{age} value conveyed by a BPDU, received by one of the STP-enabled switches, is incremented only by the STP-enabled switches. In particular, since FD is kept small, the STP convergence in a network with "transparent" nodes is faster than in an STP-based network with the same number of switches. In fact, in the latter case, the convergence might be guaranteed using a higher MA and, therefore, a higher FD. In addition, keeping MA small, the network reaction capability is faster, according to the considerations carried out in Subsection 3.2..

The only limitation to the convergence in the considered extended network scenarios is given by the fact that the number of transparent switches crossed by a BPDU introduces a delay on this BPDU such that the information stored by the receiving BPDU is no longer valid. In fact, as mentioned in Subsection 2.1., the information stored in a switch is valid for a time interval equal to $MA - m_{age}$, after which, if no updating BPDUs are received, the switch is reset and the convergence is no longer guaranteed. However, this delay is not critical, especially for realistic networks, where the number of switches ranges between 3 and 30. In fact, the delay introduced by each switch is small, as shown in Fig. 10, where, referring to the topology presented in Fig. 9, we have shown the queueing delay on the links between (i) node 3 and node 4 and (ii) node 9 and node 10, respectively. In particular, we focus on the case of the failure of node 9 after $t = 120$ s and its recovery at $t = 360$ s. Approximatively, the delay is in the order of 10^{-5} s. The links from node 3 to node 4 and from node 10 to node 9 experience a higher delay since node 3 and node 10 have to manage the reception of packets, i.e., BDPUs and ping messages, from a larger number of ports. After the node failure, node 9 stops transmitting packets, so that its queueing delay is 0. On the other hand, the delay on the link from node 10 to node 9 reduces, since node 10 relays only BPDUs to node 9, while the ping messages are routed towards switch number 2. The other observed nodes, instead, basically maintain their delay, but for fluctuations due to transitory traffic following the node failure and recovery. After that node 9 recovers, the

---

[4]In this case, the failure affects a transparent switch, which does not take part to the STP. Therefore, the m_{age} of a BPDU received by the switch 2 is equal to 0 and its stored information are valid for MA seconds.

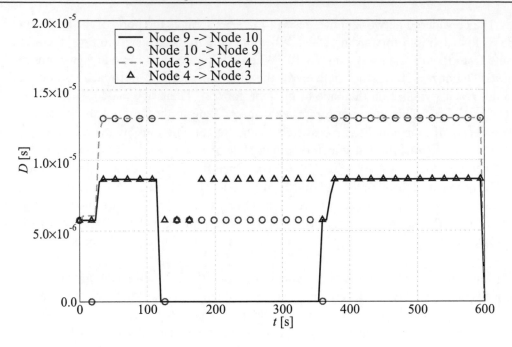

Figure 10. Delay over links between (i) node 3 and node 4 and (ii) node 9 and node 10, both considering the failure of node 9 after $t = 120$ s and its recovery at $t = 360$ s.

Table 2. Fast Ethernet (FE), Switch 100, Switch 10, and DSL ports specifications.

	FE	Switch 100	Switch 10	DSL
Port speed (Kbps)	100,000	100,000	10,000	$N \cdot 64$
Port delay (μs)	0	500	500	300

delay at the nodes return to the initial values.

For sake of completeness, we now present the crossing delay results given by the use of different port speeds. We considered four different scenarios, listed in Table 2: (i) Fast Ethernet (FE) port, (ii) 100 Mbit switch port, (iii) 10 Mbit switch port, and (iv) Digital Subscriber Line (DSL) port. In the latter case, the transmission speed is expressed as a function of the parameter N according to the relation

$$\text{Port speed}_{sDSL} = N \cdot 64 \text{ (dimension: [Kbps])}.$$

In Table 3, the crossing delays results are shown related to the transmission of a ping message at $t = 10$ s. The crossing delay depends on both the port speed and the port delay. However, in all scenarios the crossing delay is low, so that it can be concluded that the use of transparent switches does not affect the convergence of the STP.

We finally introduce the OSPF protocol and the HSRP in the network and evaluate their impact on the STP performance. The reference network topology is shown in Fig. 11. The nodes R0, R1, R2 are routers with both L2 (STP) and L3 (HSRP and OSPF) capabilities.

Table 3. Comparison between transmission instants of FE, Switch 100, Switch 10, and DSL ports.

	FE	Switch 100	Switch 10	DSL ($N = 1$)
Reception instant in 3 (T_{r3}) (s)	10.008692	10.021692	10.022233	10.119993
Reception instant in 4 (T_{r4}) (s)	10.009159	10.023159	10.023817	10.141297
Transit time ($T_4 - T_3$) (s)	0.000467	0.001467	0.001584	0.021304
Difference from the case with FE (s)		0.001000	0.001117	0.020837

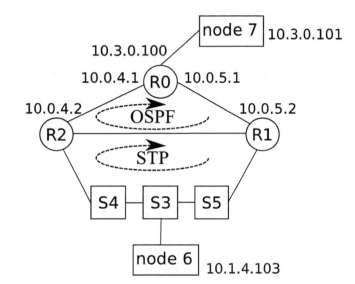

Figure 11. Considered network topology with the use of STP and OSPF.

The layer 3 has been introduced in order to evaluate the performance of an Ethernet network in a realistic scenario. The nodes S3, S4, S5 are nodes which run only the STP, i.e., they are CS2948 switches, whereas the node 6 and 7 are generic workstations used to transmit and receive ping messages—in particular, these messages are expedient to verify correct network functioning. In particular, in the lower part of the figure, i.e., between nodes S3, S4, S5 R0, and R1, the STP is running, whereas in the higher part of the network, the OSPF protocol is running. The HSRP is enabled on both routers R0 and R1: R0 is configured as active router, whereas R1 is the backup router.

The network is able to forward the ping messages to destination only after 65 s. This is due to the sum of two delay contributions: (i) the random delay (uniformly distributed between 5 and 10 s) at the beginning of the set-up phase of the OSPF protocol and (ii) the delay given by the transmissions of Hello messages (every 10 s) which notify the other routers of the active network topology.[5] In particular, since R2 is set as active router according to the HSRP, the ping message flows from node 6 to node 7 through S3-S4-R2-R0.

---

[5]These messages allow to create a forwarding table which contains the "route" from a source to a destination.

Once a failure occurs on the link between R2 and R0, the ping messages are lost for a time interval equal to 40 s, i.e., the router dead interval. However, after R2 realizes that the selected router is no longer active, it starts forwarding the ping messages along an alternative path, i.e., through R1, still guaranteeing the reachability of the destination.

5. Design Guidelines

The performance analysis presented in the previous sections is useful to derive a few design guidelines for STP-based networks. Recalling the results in Figs. 3-6, one can note that the maximum number of switches that a network can tolerate, while implementing STP successfully, is limited. In particular, this number depends on the kernel used by the switches in the network. In fact, the use of the Linux kernel, given a specific value of the MA, allows to create a network with the largest number of switches. For example, considering $MA = 20$ s, the maximum number of nodes using the Linux kernel is 40, whereas the maximum number of nodes using the Cisco kernel is 20. However, the use of the same MA has a different impact on the network reaction capability. In fact, as explained in Section 3.1., the Linux kernel introduces a lower m_{age}, so that the information stored in the switches is valid for a longer period of time from the reception of the last BPDU.

This consideration can be reversed in order to determine the STP parameters that, given a fixed number of nodes N, guarantee fastest convergence and reaction against network failures. For example, given a network with $N = 20$, in the case of the Cisco kernel, the minimum value of the max age is 20 s, whereas in the case of Linux kernel the minimum value is 10 s. In the latter case, the network capability reaction is still under analysis. In fact, with the Linux kernel MA is half of that with the Cisco kernel. However, in the former case the m_{age} increases slowlier than in the latter case, and its impact on the recovery capability needs to be investigated.

In order to have correct network operations, the best solution is configuring the parameters considering an open-chain network with N nodes. In this way, the convergence is guaranteed for every network where the distance between any couple of nodes is lower than N hops. This solution is less efficient in terms of convergence speed, but it assures a high network reliability.

In order to overcome the intrinsic limitations on the number of nodes of the STP, speed the convergence, and increase the failure reaction capability of a network, an appealing solution is the use of "transparent" switches. This solution, in fact, allows to extend the network dimension, still guaranteeing the use of VLAN tagging.

The considerations presented above are still valid when the OSPF protocol and the HSRP are used jointly with the STP. In particular, since the HSRP and OSPF introduce additional delays, the convergence of the network is guaranteed, but for a longer waiting time. In addition, since the routers detect a link or node failure only after some time (for instance, 40 s in the considered illustrative example in Fig. 11), it takes more time to react to the failure and a larger number of data will be lost, with respect to networks which run only STP.

6.   Conclusion

In this work, we have first analyzed, through the Opnet simulator, the performance of an Ethernet network running the STP, with switches equipped with either Cisco or Linux kernels. For each type of device, optimizing rules for setting the STP parameters has been derived, in order to speed network convergence. In addition, the presence of VLANs has been taken into account and the STP parameters have been optimized also in this scenario. Our simulation results have also been confirmed by experimental results. In order to provide a complete set of rules for network configuration, an open-chain network has been considered. From our analysis, it turns out that a proper configuration of STP parameters should guarantee that the STP works with every possible network configuration such that the distance (in terms of number of hops) between any couple of nodes is smaller than N, even if this leads to a longer convergence time and reduced reaction capability. In addition, the extension of the network through "transparent" switches has been considered as a mean to overcome intrinsic limitations of the STP. The use of this type of switches allows to significantly extend the the maximum acceptable dimension (in terms of number of nodes) of an STP-based network. Finally, the impact of failures in a realistic network, running both L2 and L3 protocols, has been evaluated. In this case, it has been shown that STP, OSPF protocol, and HSRP can successfully coexist, even if a reduced reaction capability to failures in layer 3 links and a longer initial delay before the beginning of ping messages transmissions must be taken into account.

Acknowledgments

We acknowledge useful discussions with and continuous support from A. Cavagna and A. Pasino (Selta spa).

References

[1] "IEEE standards for local area networks: supplements to carrier sense multiple access with collision detection (CSMA/CD) access method and physical layer specifications," *ANSI/IEEE Std 802.3a,b,c, and e-1988*, 1987.

[2] Radia Perlman, "An algorithm for distributed computation of a spanning tree in an extended LAN," *SIGCOMM Comput. Commun. Rev.*, vol. 15, no. 4, pp. 44–53, September 1985.

[3] M. Wadekar, "Enhanced Ethernet for Data Center: Reliable, Channelized and Robust," *15th IEEE Workshop on Local & Metropolitan Area Networks* (LANMAN'07)., pp. 65–71, June 2007.

[4] K. Segaric, P. Knezevic, and B. Blaskovic, "An approach to build stable spanning tree topology," *Int. Conf. on Trends in Communications* (EUROCON'01*)*, vol. 2, pp. 400–403, July 2001.

[5] K.H. Yeung, F. Yan, and C. Leung, "Improving Network Infrastructure Security by Partitioning Networks Running Spanning Tree Protocol," *Int. Conf. on Internet Surveillance and Protection (ICISP '06)*, August 2006, 4 pages.

[6] Opnet website, "http://www.opnet.com," .

[7] W. Stallings, "IEEE 802.11: wireless LANs from a to n," *IT Professional*, vol. 6, no. 5, pp. 32–37, 2004.

[8] "IEEE Standard for Information technology- Telecommunications and information exchange between systems- Local and metropolitan area networks- Common specifications Part 3: Media Access Control (MAC) Bridges," *ANSI/IEEE Std 802.1D, 1998 Edition*, pp. i–355, 1998.

[9] "IEEE standard for local and metropolitan area networks - common specification. Part 3: media access control (MAC) bridges - amendment 2: rapid reconfiguration," *IEEE Std 802.1W-2001*, 2001.

[10] "IEEE Standards for Local and metropolitan area networks - Virtual Bridged Local Area Networks - Amendment 3: Multiple Spanning Trees," *IEEE Std 802.1S-2002 (Amendment to IEEE Std 802.1Q, 1998 Edition)*, 2002.

[11] Understanding Spanning tree protocol, Cisco website, "http://www.cisco.com/univercd/cc/td/doc/product/rtrmgmt/sw_ntman/cwsimain/cwsi2/cwsiug2/vlan2/stpapp.htm," .

[12] Understanding and Tuning Spanning tree protocol, Cisco website, "http://www.cisco.com/en/US/tech/tk389/tk621/technologies_tech_note09186a0080094954.shtml," .

[13] "IEEE standards for local and metropolitan area networks. Virtual bridged local area networks," *IEEE Std 802.1Q, 2003 Edition (Incorporates IEEE Std 802.1Q-1998, IEEE Std 802.1u-2001, IEEE Std 802.1v-2001, and IEEE Std 802.1s-2002)*, 2003.

[14] J. Moy, "RFC2328: OSPF Version 2," *RFC Editor United States*, 1998.

[15] E. W. Dijkstra, "A note on two problems in connexion with graphs," *numerische Mathematik*, vol. 1, no. 1, pp. 269–271, 1959.

[16] T. Li, B. Cole, P. Morton, and D. Li, "RFC 2281: Cisco Hot Standby Router Protocol," *RFC Editor United States*, 1998.

[17] The Linux Kernel Archives, http://www.kernel.org.

In: Computer Science Research and the Internet
Editor: Jaclyn E. Morris, pp. 243-286

ISBN 978-1-61728-730-5
© 2011 Nova Science Publishers, Inc.

Chapter 12

ROUTERS AND NETWORKS WITH NEAR-ZERO BUFFERS

Vijay Sivaraman[1,*], *Arun Vishwanath*[1,†], *Marina Thottan*[2‡]
and Constantine Dovrolis[3§]
[1]School of EE&T, University of New South Wales, Sydney, Australia
[2]Networking Research Lab, Bell-Labs Alcatel Lucent, USA
[3]College of Computing, Georgia Institute of Technology, USA

Abstract

All routers have buffers to store packets during periods of congestion. However, as Internet link speeds reach hundreds of Gigabits-per-second and beyond, it is becoming increasingly difficult to equip high-speed routers with large buffers, especially as switching moves into the all-optical domain. In this chapter we first trace the evolution in thinking over recent years on how much buffering is required at Internet routers, focusing specifically on the push towards smaller buffers, from Gigabyte down to Kilobyte sizes, making them amenable for all-optical realisation. We then highlight some of the implications of the move towards such small buffers, such as end-to-end performance for real-time and TCP traffic, the reaction of TCP to reduced buffer availability in the network, and the unexpected interactions between TCP and open-loop traffic. Finally, we propose mechanisms ranging from edge traffic conditioning to packet-level forward error correction within the network as means of overcoming the limitations posed by small buffers in the network, and speculate on the feasibility of a zero-buffer Internet core in the future.

Keywords: Internet routers, buffer sizing, near-bufferless networks, all-optical networks, anomalous loss performance, TCP, UDP

AMS Subject Classification:

---

[*]E-mail address: vijay@unsw.edu.au
[†]E-mail address: arunv@ee.unsw.edu.au
[‡]E-mail address: marinat@alcatel-lucent.com
[§]E-mail address: dovrolis@cc.gatech.edu

1.   Introduction

In today's network routers, buffers are used to reduce packet loss by absorbing transient bursts of traffic. They are also instrumental in keeping output links fully utilised during times of congestion. However, the increasing speed of network interfaces raises an important question concerning the size of these buffers. Under buffered routers lead to packet loss, thus adversely affecting application performance, while an over buffered router entails increased latency, complexity and cost.

We begin this chapter with a brief overview of buffer sizing, focusing on the reduction from Gigabyte to Megabyte to KiloByte buffers. Next, we examine the impact of buffer reduction on TCP traffic performance and characterise an unexpected behaviour that happens when closed-loop TCP interacts with open-loop (real-time) UDP in the KiloByte regime. Subsequently, we outline two novel solutions that are very effective to overcoming buffer limitations, namely, TCP pacing and packet-level Forward Error Correction (FEC). Finally, we summarise our contributions and conclude the chapter by envisioning a zero-buffer Internet core network in the future.

1.1.   Gigabyte Buffers

The widely used *rule-of-thumb*, commonly attributed to [1], suggests that the amount of buffering needed at a router's output interface is given by $B = C \times RTT$, where B is the buffer size, RTT the average round-trip time of a TCP connection flowing through the router, and C the capacity of the router's network interface. This rule-of-thumb is also called the Bandwidth Delay Product (BDP) rule. The motivation behind this rule was to guarantee 100% link utilisation. In other words, the BDP rule ensures that even when a buffer overflows, and TCP reacts by reducing its transmission rate, there are enough packets stored in the buffer to keep the output link busy, thereby ensuring that the link capacity is not wasted when TCP is increasing its transmission rate. This BDP rule was obtained experimentally using at most 8 TCP flows on a 40 Mbps core link in 1994. However, no recommendation was made for sizing buffers when there are a significant number of TCP flows that have different RTTs.

In current electronic routers, for a typical RTT of 250 ms and capacity C of 40 Gbps, the rule-of-thumb mandates a buffer size of 1.25 GigaBytes, which poses a considerable challenge to router design. Further, the use of such large buffers (implemented using a combination of SRAM and DRAM chips) complicates router design, increases its power consumption, and makes them very expensive. The scaling and power consumption requirements for next generation routers can be successfully addressed by building and deploying optical routers in the Internet core. However, one of the primary technological limitations of optical routers is the difficulty in building large optical buffers. All-optical buffers can only be used to delay packets for about 100 ns [2]. In the case of a 40 Gbps link, this optical delay line translates to a buffer size of only a few hundred bits. It is thus worthwhile to revisit the buffer sizing problem and examine if we indeed require the amount of buffering as dictated by the BDP rule.

1.2.   Megabyte Buffers

Researchers from Stanford University showed in 2004 that when a large number N of long-lived TCP flows share a bottleneck link in the core of the Internet, the absence of synchrony among the flows permits a central limit approximation of the buffer occupancy. The combined effect of multiplexing a large number of asynchronous flows leads to a buffer size $B = RTT \times C/\sqrt{N}$ to achieve near-100% link utilisation [3]. This result assumes that there are a sufficiently large number of TCP flows so that they are asynchronous and independent of each other. In addition, it assumes that the buffer size is largely governed by long-lived TCP flows only. Thus, a core router carrying $10,000$ TCP flows needs only 12.5 MB of buffering instead of 1.25 GB as governed by the earlier rule-of-thumb.

1.3.   Kilobyte Buffers

More recently, it has been further argued (see [4–6]) that core router buffers of the order of 20-50 packets suffice for TCP traffic to realise acceptable link capacities. The use of this model however comes at a tradeoff. Reducing buffers to only a few dozen KiloBytes can lead to a 10-20% drop in link utilisation. The model relies on the fact that TCP flows are not synchronised and network traffic is not bursty. Such a traffic scenario can happen in two ways. First, since core links operate at much higher speeds than access links, packets from the source node are automatically spread out and bursts are broken. Second, if the TCP stack running at end-hosts is altered such that it can space out packet transmissions (also called TCP pacing) [7]. The slight drop in link utilisation seems worthwhile since core links are typically overprovisioned, and it pays to sacrifice a bit of link capacity if this permits a move to either an all-optical packet switch or more efficient electronic router design.

1.4.   Sizing Based on Per-Flow Metrics

Researchers from Georgia Tech and Bell-Labs have tackled the buffer sizing problem from a completely different perspective [8]. Rather than assuming that most of the TCP traffic is persistent, i.e., long-lived flows that are mostly in the congestion avoidance mode, they consider the more realistic case of non-persistent flows with flow sizes drawn from a heavy-tailed distribution. This differs from some of the prior work in that non-persistent flows may not saturate the links along their paths, unlike the persistent flows, and can remain in the slow-start phase without entering into the congestion avoidance mode. Also, the number of active flows at any instant is highly time variant. It follows that flows that spend most of their time in the slow-start phase require significantly fewer buffers than flows that spend most of their time in the congestion avoidance mode.

Further, instead of focusing purely on link utilisation, their work focuses on the average per-flow TCP throughput, which is an important metric as far as an end-user is concerned. It can be the case that a link may have sufficient buffers so that it always maintains high utilisation, but the per-flow throughput can be very low. The objective is to find the buffer size that maximises the average per flow TCP throughput. Analytical, simulation and experimental evidence are presented to suggest that the output/input capacity ratio at a router's interface largely governs the amount of buffering needed at that interface. If this ratio is greater than one, then the loss rate falls exponentially, and only a very small amount of buffering is needed. However, if the output/input capacity ratio is less than one, then the loss rate follows a power-law reduction and significant buffering is needed.

Their study concludes by pointing out that it may not be possible to derive a single universal formula to dimension buffers at any router's interface in a network. Instead, a network administrator should decide taking into account several factors such as flow size distribution, nature of TCP traffic, output/input capacity ratios, etc.

For a comprehensive understanding of the router buffer sizing problem, we refer the interested reader to our recent survey paper in [9].

2.   Implications of Small Buffers on TCP Dynamics

There is widespread debate regarding the nature of TCP traffic in today's Internet - while some researchers have shown that it exhibits long-range dependent (LRD) properties, others argue that it can be modelled as a Poisson process due to the high degree of traffic aggregation that exists in the core. In this section, we investigate the nature of TCP traffic as the Internet core moves towards an all-optical packet network with very limited buffering (few tens of KiloBytes) capability.

The publication of the seminal paper in [10] showed empirically that network traffic exhibits long-range dependent characteristics (i.e., bursty traffic over a wide range of time-scales). The heavy-tailed distribution of the file transfer sizes and the duration of active/inactive times of users are the two main reasons why network traffic is thought to be LRD. Since the publication of this result, there has been a keen interest in trying to understand how Internet traffic has evolved. Many have argued that due to the phenomenal growth in Internet traffic [11] (currently in the exabyte (10^{18}) range) and link speeds, there is high degree of statistical multiplexing and traffic aggregation in the core, resulting in the traffic being Poisson in sub-second time-scales [12]. There is further support from stochastic processes theory, which suggests that the superposition of a large number of *independent* flows also converges to a Poisson process [13–15].

Contrary to the above claims, there is still a large body of work showing that despite the growth in the Internet, the traffic is still bursty (LRD) and not smooth (Poisson). Through a combination of wavelet-based analysis and trace data obtained from a OC-48 Internet2 core link, the authors of [16] showed that Internet traffic is bursty in short time-scales because of the self-clocking nature of TCP and queueing at the bottleneck link. Also, as previously argued in [12], the aggregation of many TCP flows does not make the traffic smooth. Further light is shed in the recent paper [17] that uses trace data (spanning seven years) from a trans-Pacific backbone link to show that Internet traffic is indeed LRD and not Poisson.

It must be mentioned that the above measurement studies are pertinent to today's core links that have of the order of delay-bandwidth amount of buffering, since ISPs typically run their networks with such large buffers [1]. Although the recent work advocating the use of small buffers has assumed that TCP traffic at a bottleneck link can be modelled as being Poisson [18], a claim predominantly supported by the theoretical superposition results, to the best of our knowledge, little has been done to justify this assumption using experiments and/or simulations.

The superposition results from stochastic processes are accurate only when the flows are *independent*. This is a critical assumption that easily holds for open-loop traffic (UDP

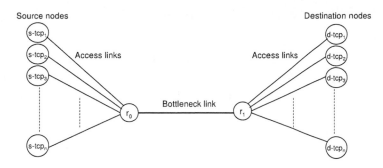

Figure 1. *ns-2* simulation dumbbell topology with TCP traffic.

for example). However, TCP is a closed-loop (i.e., feedback controlled) protocol, and the behaviour of a TCP flow is influenced by the presence of other TCP and/or UDP flows, as well as the buffer occupancy at the bottleneck link. In addition, TCP flows can synchronise their window dynamics behaviour (causing them to be in lock-step), which is a detrimental effect that breaks the independence assumption. As a result it is not very clear if the super-position result is directly applicable to TCP traffic, and as shown in [16], the aggregation of a large number TCP sources does not lend itself to being Poisson.

In the rest of this section, we show that the nature of aggregate TCP traffic is strongly dependent on the size of the bottleneck link buffer. When buffers are small, the aggregate TCP arrival process is well approximated as being Poisson, but when buffers are large (of the order of delay-bandwidth product), TCP flows tend to synchronise their congestion windows, thus creating significant bursty LRD traffic. This seems to indicate that as we move to a core optical network in the future with very limited buffering, approximating the traffic as being Poisson is well justified.

2.1. Simulation Setup

In the context of studying the burstiness of TCP traffic in a small buffer core network, we require a bottleneck link carrying several TCP flows. We use *ns-2* (version 2.33) simulator on the well-known dumbbell topology shown in Fig. 1, which directly captures the bottleneck link, and is commonly used to analyse the performance of various congestion control algorithms, including TCP. We consider TCP-Reno flows corresponding to each source-destination pair $(s\text{-}tcp_i, d\text{-}tcp_i)$, $1 \leq i \leq 2000$, and employ FIFO queue with drop-tail queue management (at the bottleneck router r_0), which is commonly used in most routers today. Each TCP packet is of size 1 KB. The bottleneck link operates at 200 Mbps, while the access link speeds are uniformly distributed between $[8, 12]$ Mbps (mean of 10 Mbps), to reflect a typical home user. The propagation delay on the bottleneck link is 25 ms with the access link delays being uniformly distributed in the interval $[4, 10]$ ms, thus RTT varies between $[58, 70]$ ms. All TCP flows begin their transmission in the interval $[0, 10]$ sec and the simulation is run for 150 sec. Data in the interval $[20, 150]$ sec is used in all our computations so as to capture the steady-state behaviour of the network.

2.2.   Impact of Buffer Size on TCP Burstiness

Our objective is to test if TCP packet arrivals to the bottleneck link buffer are near-Poisson or not. To do so we measure the burstiness of the arrival traffic at various time-scales. Burstiness at time-scale s is quantified by $\beta(s)$, the coefficient of variation (i.e., ratio of standard deviation to mean) of traffic volume measured over time intervals of size s. Log-log plots of $\beta(s)$ versus s are routinely used in the literature to depict traffic burstiness over various time-scales as an indicator of long-range dependency of traffic traces, and to show the influence of the Hurst parameter H. We will use estimates of H obtained from the burstiness plots as a measure of how close the traffic is to being short-range dependent (i.e., Poisson).

Consistent with prior work [16], we are also interested in short time-scales (between $2^{10}\mu s \approx 1$ ms to $2^{20}\mu s \approx 1$ s). Time-scales of sub-1 ms is not very relevant since the average transmission time of a TCP packet on the access link is 0.8 ms (because the TCP packet size is 1 KB and the mean access link rate is 10 Mbps). Further, for a given number of TCP flows, the variation at larger time-scales is due to TCP traffic arriving and departing the network, and not because of the congestion control algorithm of TCP. Therefore, we upper-bound the time-scale of interest to 1 s, which is a few multiples of the average round-trip time.

2.3.   Long-lived TCP Flows

We begin the study by considering the simple case of long-lived TCP flows, i.e., all TCP flows are persistent and have infinite data to send.

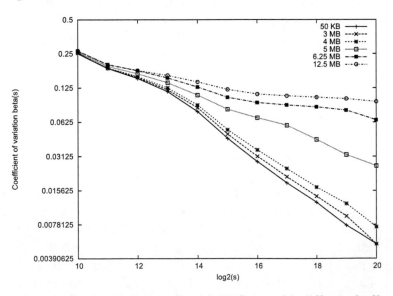

Figure 2. Burstiness for 2000 long-lived TCP flows with different buffer sizes.

Fig. 2 shows the traffic burstiness $\beta(s)$ as a function of the time-scale (s in μs) for six different values of bottleneck link buffer size and 2000 long-lived TCP flows. The bottom curve indicates burstiness when the bottleneck link has very limited buffering - 50 KB, equivalent to 50 packets, since each TCP packet is 1 KB in our simulation. The remaining five curves reflect increasing buffer sizes (ranging from 3 MB to 12.5 MB), with 6.25 MB of buffering corresponding to the delay-bandwidth product (average RTT of 250 ms times 200 Mbps link rate). The curves fairly overlap each other till time-scale of $2^{12}\mu s \approx 4$ ms. However, at time-scales beyond 4 ms, the burstiness curves for large buffers (approaching the delay-bandwidth product) flatten significantly, indicating onset of long-range dependence, with the Hurst parameter estimated at approximately 0.66 (for 5 MB buffers), 0.81 (for 6.25 MB buffers) and 0.88 (for 12.5 MB buffers) respectively. These results show that when buffers are large, TCP traffic is significantly bursty and cannot be modeled as being Poisson. On the contrary, with small buffers, the Poisson approximation seems reasonable.

2.4.   Mix of Short-Lived and Long-Lived TCP Flows

Though results from the previous section indicate that TCP packet arrivals are near-Poisson if we have a large number of long-lived TCP flows and small buffers, the reader may wonder if similar behaviour can be seen when many of the TCP flows are short-lived (or equivalently, the number of TCP flows is time varying). This is an important consideration since measurement studies at the core of the Internet suggest that a large number ($> 80\%$) of TCP flows (e.g. HTTP requests) are short-lived and carry only a small volume of traffic, while a small number of TCP flows (e.g. FTP) are long-lived and carry a large volume of traffic.

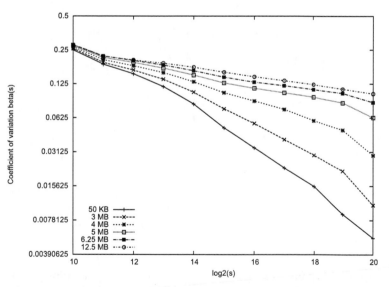

Figure 3. Burstiness for 1600 short-lived and 400 long-lived TCP flows with different buffer sizes.

We simulate such a scenario in *ns-2* using the same dumbbell topology shown in Fig. 1. There are a total of 2000 TCP flows with 1600 of them being short-lived and the rest long-lived. These 1600 users perform successive file transfers to their respective destination nodes, with the size of the file to be transferred following a Pareto distribution with mean 100 KB and shape parameter 1.2. These chosen values are representative of Internet traffic, and comparable with measurement data. After each file transfer, the user transitions into an idle or off state. The duration of the off period is exponentially distributed with mean 1 second. It can be noted that the above traffic generation mechanism, which is a combination of several ON-OFF sources with Pareto-distributed ON periods, is long-range dependent [10].

Fig. 3 shows the resulting burstiness curves for the same set of bottleneck link buffer sizes as before. It is interesting to note from the figure that, although a significant number of TCP flows have LRD properties, when fed into a small buffer (such as 50 KB, the bottom curve), the resulting TCP arrival process becomes near-Poisson (similar to the 50 KB curve in Fig. 2). However, we do note that as buffer size increases, the traffic tends towards LRD, as evidenced by the Hurst parameter values of 0.67 (for 4 MB), 0.79 (for 5 MB) and 0.84 (for 6.25 MB) respectively.

2.5. Burstiness Explained via Queue Occupancy

We are now interested in understanding why the aggregate TCP arrivals in a small buffer network is near-Poisson while it is LRD with large buffers? To do so, we plot the queue (buffer) occupancy (for an arbitrarily chosen interval of 2 sec, consistent with our time-scale of interest) in Fig. 4 with 1600 short- and 400 long-lived TCP flows and two choices of buffer size - 50 KB (small buffers) and 6.25 MB (delay-bandwidth product large buffers).

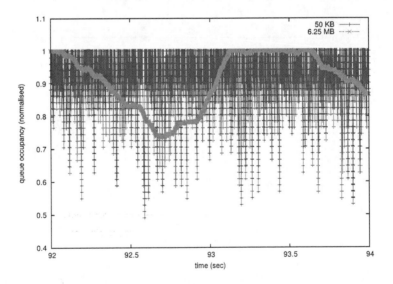

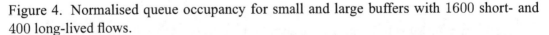

Figure 4. Normalised queue occupancy for small and large buffers with 1600 short- and 400 long-lived flows.

We note from the figure that for large buffers, the queue spends most of its time oscillating continuously between full and ≈ 75% occupancy. The reason for this oscillation is that the TCP flows are not independent, in fact they are synchronised. When the queue is almost full, many flows experience packet drops and simultaneously back-off by reducing their windows in synchrony. This causes the packets already stored in the queue to be drained out, thus providing room for the flows to ramp-up (i.e., expand their windows) again. This periodicity, and hence synchronisation, is primarily because of large buffers as

TCP sources are unable to perceive loss for relatively long periods of time (due to the large queueing delays experienced by the flows). On the contrary, the queue occupancy with small buffers looks like white noise, clearly showing that small buffers are instrumental in mitigating synchronisation effects. The TCP flows can thus be treated as being independent, and the superposition results can be invoked thereby rendering credence to the fact that the aggregation of a large number of TCP flows at a bottleneck link with small buffers is near-Poisson. The synchronisation of TCP flows with large buffers is what causes them to be LRD.

2.6.   Section Summary

In this section, we showed via simulations that if we have a large number of TCP flows and small buffers, then the aggregate TCP arrival process can be well approximated as being Poisson. On the other hand, with larger buffers, the dynamics can be significantly different, and the aggregate arrival process need not converge to the Poisson model.

It would be very interesting to explore via analysis, simulations and experiments the effect of various system parameters - such as the number of TCP flows, core link speed to access link speed ratio, RTT, etc., on the burstiness of TCP. We are currently working on these directions and hope to be able to report the results soon.

3.   Anomalous Loss Performance for Mixed Real-time and TCP Traffic

Most prior studies on buffer sizing focus entirely on TCP traffic performance, and ignore the performance implications for real-time (UDP) traffic. However, multimedia applications such as on-line gaming, interactive audio-video services, VoIP and IPTV are proliferating in the Internet, and becoming part of an ISP's revenue stream. Thus, router buffer sizing studies cannot afford to ignore the performance impact on real-time traffic when it is multiplexed with TCP, which to the best of our knowledge has not been undertaken before in the context of very small buffers. We use the term real-time and UDP interchangeably.

To understand the dynamics of buffer occupancy at a bottleneck link router with very small buffers (up to 50 KiloBytes), we mixed a small fraction of UDP traffic with TCP traffic and measured the UDP packet loss and end-to-end TCP throughput. What we observed was contrary to conventional wisdom. We found that there exists a certain continuous region of buffer sizes (typically starting from 8-10 KB or so) wherein the performance of real-time traffic degrades with increasing buffer size. In other words, packet loss for real-time traffic *increases* as the buffer size *increases* within this region. We call this region of buffer size an "anomalous region" with respect to real-time traffic.

We believe the anomalous phenomenon studied adds a new dimension to the ongoing debate on buffer sizing, including in the context of optical packet switches, and our results aid switch manufacturers and network operators in selecting small buffer sizes that achieve desired performance balance between TCP and real-time traffic.

3.1. The Anomaly

To illustrate the anomalous loss behaviour, we consider a simple dumbbell topology (Fig. 5) that captures packet queueing effects at the bottleneck link, which is the dominant factor in end-to-end loss and delay variation for each flow, while abstracting the rest of the flow path by an access link on either side of the bottleneck link. We use ns-2 [19] (version 2.30) for our simulations and consider 1000 TCP flows, corresponding to each source-destination pair $(s\text{-}tcp_i, d\text{-}tcp_i)$, $1 \le i \le 1000$. Further, we use TCP-Reno in all our simulations, consistent with the TCP version used in previous related work on buffer sizing, and employ FIFO queue with drop-tail queue management, which is commonly used in most routers today.

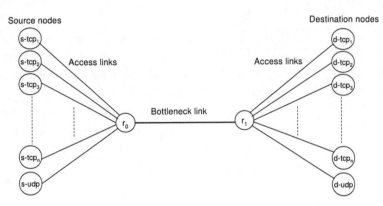

Figure 5. ns-2 simulation dumbbell topology with TCP and UDP traffic.

UDP traffic is generated between nodes $(s\text{-}udp, d\text{-}udp)$. It suffices to have a single UDP flow since open-loop traffic can, without loss of generality, be aggregated. Multiple UDP flows traversing the bottleneck link can thus be modelled as a single UDP flow that represents the aggregate of all individual UDP flows passing through that bottleneck link. However, we need multiple TCP flows since they each react independently to the prevailing network condition and the state of the buffers.

The propagation delay on the UDP access link is chosen at 5 ms, while it is uniformly distributed between $[1, 25]$ ms on the TCP access links. The propagation delay on the bottleneck link (r_0, r_1) is 50 ms; thus round-trip times vary between 102 ms and 150 ms. All TCP sources start at random times between $[0, 10]$ s. UDP source starts at time 0 s. The simulation duration is 800 s and performance measurements are recorded after 200 s, to allow for the stabilisation of all TCP flows.

Buffer size at the bottleneck router r_0 is varied in terms of KiloBytes. To set the packet sizes, we draw on the fact that several real-time applications, for e.g. on-line gaming applications [20] use small UDP packets since they require extremely low latencies. The study showed that almost all packets were under 200 Bytes. Our experiments using Skype and Yahoo Messenger showed that for interactive voice chat, UDP packet sizes were between 150-200 Bytes. Also, traces obtained at a trans-Pacific 150 Mbps link [21] suggests that average UDP packet sizes are smaller than average TCP packet sizes. Therefore, in all our simulations, we fix the TCP packet size at 1000 Bytes and simulate fixed and variable size UDP packets in the range of $[150, 300]$ Bytes.

We first illustrate the phenomenon using the video traffic trace from the movie *Star Wars*, obtained from [22] and references therein. The mean rate is 374.4 Kbps and the peak rate is 4.446 Mbps; the peak rate to mean rate ratio being nearly 12. The packet size is fixed at 200 Bytes. We set the bottleneck link at 10 Mbps and the TCP access links at 1 Mbps, while the UDP access link is kept at 100 Mbps. The bottleneck link was only 10 Mbps because the mean rate of the video trace (UDP) is low (374.4 Kbps), and we want to keep the fraction of UDP traffic feeding into the core to within 3-10% of the bottleneck link rate (to be consistent with the nature of Internet traffic today). In this example, the video traffic constitutes ≈ 3.75% of the bottleneck link rate. We have a high-speed access link for UDP since UDP traffic feeding into the core can be an aggregate of many individual UDP streams. TCP traffic on the 1 Mbps access link models traffic from a typical home user.

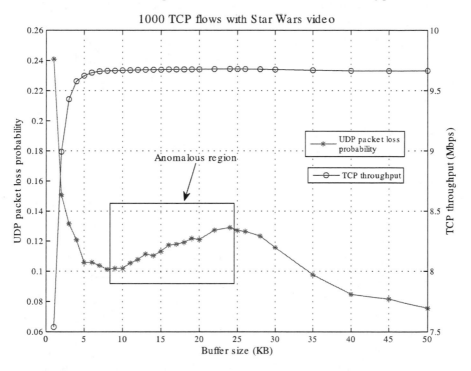

Figure 6. Starwars 200 Byte packets: UDP loss and TCP throughput.

Fig. 6 shows the UDP packet loss and TCP throughput curves as a function of buffer size at the bottleneck router in the range of 1 KB to 50 KB. We see that TCP quickly ramps up to nearly 9.6 Mbps with only about 8 KB of buffering, reaching close to its saturation throughput. Simultaneously, UDP packet loss falls rapidly as well. Up to this point, both TCP and UDP behave as expected. However, as the buffer size increases beyond 8 KB till about 24 KB, UDP performance degrades as its packet loss increases with buffer size in this region. The loss at 24 KB of buffering is approximately 30% more than the loss at 8 KB of buffering. There is however no appreciable increase in TCP throughput.

We also observed this behaviour when UDP traffic is generated from synthetic models (such as Poisson, LRD fractional Brownian motion, etc.), suggesting that the anomaly is fundamental and not just a coincidence. Moreover, in the absence of TCP traffic, UDP loss was observed to drop monotonically with buffer size, confirming that the anomaly arises due to the interaction of open and closed loop traffic at the bottleneck router with very small buffers. In the next subsections, we develop analytical models that captures the anomalous loss behaviour succinctly.

3.2. An Intuitive Analytical Model of the Anomaly

We now provide an intuitive explanation of why we think the anomaly happens, and this helps us develop a simplistic yet effective model that quantifies the buffer sharing dynamics between TCP and real-time traffic.

When buffers at the bottleneck link are extremely small, say in the range 1 KB to about 5 to 8 KB, the congestion window size of each of the TCP flows sharing the bottleneck link will also stay extremely small. TCP's congestion window is not allowed to grow beyond a few packets since several packets sent back-to-back (that would be generated by any TCP version that does not employ pacing) are more likely to be dropped at the very small buffers in the bottleneck link router. The small congestion window size implies that each TCP flow transmits only a few packets in each round-trip time, and is therefore mostly idle. Consequently, the buffers at the bottleneck link are often devoid of TCP packets, allowing UDP packets to enjoy the use of these buffers for the most part. This helps us understand why in this region, wherein TCP and UDP predominantly "time-share" the buffers, UDP loss decreases with buffer size, much like it would if TCP traffic were non-existent.

When buffer size is in the range 10-25 KB (corresponding to the anomaly), a larger fraction of the TCP flows are able to increase their congestion window (equivalently a smaller fraction of the TCP flows remain idle). This leads to higher usage of the buffers at the bottleneck link by TCP traffic, leaving a smaller fraction of the buffers for UDP traffic to use. The aggressive nature of TCP in increasing its congestion window to probe for additional bandwidth, causes the "space-sharing" of bottleneck-link buffers between TCP and UDP in this region to be skewed in favour of TCP, leaving lesser buffers available to UDP traffic even as buffer size increases.

We now try to quantify the above intuition via a simple analytical starting with the following observation. If we have a large number of TCP flows, then TCP's usage of the bottleneck buffers increases exponentially with the size of the buffer. More formally, let B denote the buffer size (in KB) at the bottleneck link, and $P_I(B)$ the probability that at an arbitrary instant of time the buffers at the bottleneck link are devoid of TCP traffic. Then,

$$P_I(B) \approx e^{-B/B^*} \tag{1}$$

where B^* is a constant (with same unit as B) dependent on system parameters such as link capacity, number of TCP flows, round-trip times, ratio of long-lived to short-lived TCP flows, etc. The constant B^* can be inferred from the plot of the natural logarithm of $P_I(B)$ as a function of B, which yields a straight line. The slope of the line corresponds to $-1/B^*$.

This behaviour has been observed in the past by various researchers: by direct measurement of idle buffer probabilities [23, Sec. III], as well as indirectly via measurement of TCP throughput [4, Fig. 1]: the latter has shown roughly exponential rise in TCP throughput with bottleneck buffer size, confirming that TCP's loss in throughput (which arises from an idle buffer) falls exponentially with buffer size. We also validated this via extensive simulations (shown in Fig. 6 and in various other TCP plots in later sections) in *ns-2*. 1000 TCP flows

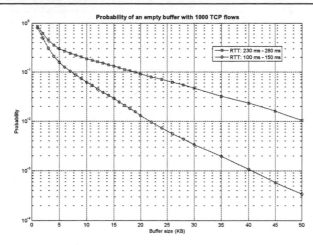

Figure 7. Probability of idle buffer vs. buffer size for TCP traffic.

with random round-trip times from a chosen range were multiplexed at a bottleneck link, and the idle buffer probability was measured as a function of bottleneck link buffer size. The large number of flows, coupled with randomness in their round-trip times, ensures that the TCP flows do not synchronise their congestion windows. Fig. 7 plots on log-scale the idle buffer probability as a function of bottleneck buffer size for two ranges of round-trip times, and show fairly linear behaviour in the range of 5 to 50 packets (each packet was 1 KiloByte), confirming the exponential fall as per Eq. (1).

Having quantified TCP's usage of the bottleneck buffers, we now consider a small fraction f (say 5 to 10%) of real-time (UDP) traffic multiplexed with TCP traffic at the bottleneck link. The small volume of UDP traffic does not alter TCP behaviour significantly; however, TCP's usage of the buffer does significantly impact loss for UDP traffic. If we assume the buffer is very small (a few tens of KiloBytes), we can approximate the buffer as being in one of two states: idle (empty) or busy (full). With the objective of estimating the "effective" buffers space available to UDP traffic, we identify the following two components:

- **Fair-share:** During periods of time when TCP and UDP packets co-exist in the buffer, the buffer capacity B is shared by them in proportion to their respective rates. The first-in-first-out nature of service implies that the average time spent by a packet in the system is independent of whether the packet is UDP or TCP, and Little's law can be invoked to infer that the average number of waiting packets of a class is proportional to the arrival rate of that class. UDP packets therefore have on average access to a "fair share" of the buffers, namely fB, where f denotes the fraction of total traffic that is UDP.

- **Time-share:** Whenever the buffer is devoid of TCP traffic (i.e. with probability $P_I(B)$), UDP packets have access to the remaining buffer space $(1 - f)B$ as well. We call this the "time share" portion, since this portion of the buffer is shared in time between UDP and TCP traffic. The time-share portion of buffers available to UDP is therefore $P_I(B)(1 - f)B$.

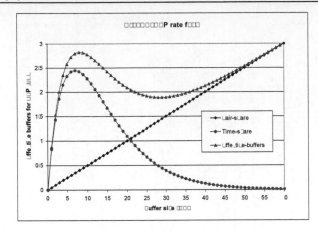

Figure 8. Effective buffers for UDP traffic.

Combining the fair-share and time-share components, and invoking Eq. (1) gives us an estimate of the total "effective" buffers $\bar{B}^{udp}$ available to UDP traffic:

$$\bar{B}^{udp} = fB + (1 - f)Be^{-B/B^*} \tag{2}$$

To illustrate the significance of this equation we plot it for $f = 0.05$ (i.e. 5% UDP traffic) and $B^* = 7$ KB (consistent from Fig. 7). Fig. 8 shows the total effective buffers for UDP, as well as the fair-share and time-share components. The fair-share component fB increases linearly with buffer size, while the time-share component $(1 - f)Be^{-B/B^*}$ rises to a peak and then falls again (readers may notice a shape similar to the Aloha protocol's throughput curve): this happens because smaller buffers are more available for UDP to time-share, but as buffers get larger TCP permits exponentially diminishing opportunity for time-sharing. The total effective buffers for UDP, being the sum of the above two components, can therefore show anomalous behaviour, i.e., a region where larger real buffers can yield smaller effective buffers for UDP. For any realistic UDP traffic model (note that our analytical model does not make any specific assumption about the UDP traffic model), the smaller effective buffers will result in higher loss, which is of serious concern to network designers and operators who operate their router buffer sizes in this region.

The model presented above is highly simplified and ignores several aspects of TCP dynamics as well as real-time traffic characteristics. It nevertheless provides valuable insight into the anomaly, and will be used in later sections for a quantitative understanding of the impact of various parameters on the severity of the anomaly.

3.3. A Markov Model of the Anomaly

It is in general challenging to mathematically analyse finite buffer systems in which several thousand feedback-based adaptive TCP flows interact with stochastic real-time traffic. We now develop a realistic yet rigorous Markov model based on some simplifications:

Assumption: *TCP packet arrivals are Poisson.* Figures 2 and 3 showed that if a large number (potentially thousands) of TCP flows multiplex at a bottleneck link with very small buffers, they do not synchronise their window dynamics behaviour, and can thus be treated

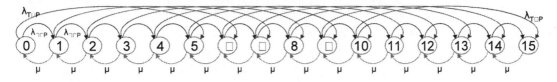

Figure 9. Markov chain state transition diagram for buffer occupancy with buffer size = 3000 Bytes.

as independent flows. Combined with the fact that each TCP flow's window will be quite small (since bottleneck buffers are small), implying that each flow will only generate a small amount of traffic per RTT, the aggregation of a large number of such independent flows can reasonably be assumed to yield Poisson traffic.

Assumption: *UDP packet arrivals are also Poisson.* Stochastic studies such as [14, 15, 24] have shown that the aggregation of traffic from a large number of independent flows (as can be expected at a core link) converges to Poisson. This important result makes the analysis tractable (though the phenomenon of anomalous loss is observed even if UDP arrivals are non-Poisson)

Claim: *UDP packets are on average smaller in size than TCP packets*, as discussed in Section 3.1., and as reported in several measurements of traffic in the Internet core [21]. Consistent with our example presented in Fig. 6, we choose average TCP and UDP packet sizes to be 1000 and 200 Bytes respectively.

Claim: *The aggregate TCP rate increases exponentially with bottleneck link buffer size*, as demonstrated in Fig. 7 and discussed in the previous section. Denoting the bottleneck buffer size as B (in KiloBytes), the TCP throughput λ_{TCP} is given by:

$$\lambda_{TCP} \approx \{1 - (e^{-B/B^*})\} \times \lambda_{TCP}^{sat} \tag{3}$$

where λ_{TCP}^{sat} denotes the saturation throughput of TCP (when buffer size is large).

In order to construct a Markov chain model we make the further assumption that packet transmission times are exponentially distributed (we will relax this assumption in the next subsection). We can then model the FIFO queue at the bottleneck link router as an M/M/1 system with finite buffer B and with two classes of customers:

1. UDP arrivals are Poisson at fixed rate (denoted by λ_{UDP}), and require exponential service time with unit mean (the service rate is normalised to average UDP packet size), and

2. TCP arrivals are Poisson at rate λ_{TCP} derived from Eq. (3), where each TCP packet arrival brings a bulk of 5 customers (corresponding to the packet size ratio $1000/200$), each requiring exponential service time with unit average.

For illustrative purposes, let us consider the buffer size B to be 3 KiloBytes. Then, we can model the state of the system as the number of customers in the FIFO queue. Fig. 9 shows the resulting Markov chain. A transition from state j to state $j + 5$ corresponds to the arrival of a TCP packet, whereas a transition from state j to state $j + 1$ corresponds to the arrival of a UDP packet.

Denoting $B_{bytes} = B \times 1000 = 3000$ to be the corresponding buffer size in Bytes, and N the number of states in the Markov chain, then

$$N = \frac{B_{bytes}}{UDP\,packet\,size} + 1 = \frac{3000}{200} + 1 = 16. \tag{4}$$

If p_j represents the steady state probability of the queue being in state j (i.e., the probability that the queue contains j customers), then we can write the global balance equations as follows:

$$p_0\,(\lambda_{UDP} + \lambda_{TCP}) = p_1\,\mu \tag{5}$$

$$p_i\,(\lambda_{UDP} + \lambda_{TCP} + \mu) = p_{i-1}\,\lambda_{UDP} + p_{i+1}\,\mu$$
$$(1 \le i \le 4) \tag{6}$$

$$p_i\,(\lambda_{UDP} + \lambda_{TCP} + \mu) = p_{i-1}\,\lambda_{UDP} + p_{i+1}\,\mu + p_{i-5}\,\lambda_{TCP}$$
$$(5 \le i \le 10) \tag{7}$$

$$p_i\,(\lambda_{UDP} + \mu) = p_{i-1}\,\lambda_{UDP} + p_{i+1}\,\mu + p_{i-5}\,\lambda_{TCP}$$
$$(11 \le i \le 14) \tag{8}$$

$$p_{15}\,\mu = p_{14}\,\lambda_{UDP} + p_{10}\,\lambda_{TCP} \tag{9}$$

The above equations and the normalising constraint $\sum_{i=0}^{15} p_i = 1$ form a set of linear equations that can be solved to compute the probability that an incoming UDP packet will be dropped, which in this example is p_{15}. Obtaining balance equations as the buffer size B increases is straightforward, and the resulting set of linear equations is easily solvable numerically (in MATLAB) to obtain the UDP packet loss probability.

The analytical result shown in this paper chooses model parameters to match the simulation setting as closely as possible: the normalised UDP rate is set to $\lambda_{UDP} = 0.05$ (i.e. 5% of link capacity), and the TCP saturation throughput $\lambda_{TCP}^{sat} = 0.94/5$ (so that TCP and UDP customers have a combined maximum rate less than the service rate of $\mu = 1$ in order to guarantee stability). The constant $B^* = 7$ KB is chosen consistent with what is obtained from simulations in Fig. 7.

Fig. 10 plots the UDP loss (on log scale) obtained from solving the M/M/1 chain with bulk arrivals and finite buffers, as well as the TCP rate in Eq. (3), as a function of buffer size B. It can be observed that in the region of 1-8 KB of buffering, UDP loss falls monotonically with buffer size. However, in the buffer size region between 9-30 KB, UDP packet loss increases with increasing buffer size, showing that the model is able to predict the anomaly found in simulations.

3.4. Section Summary

Prior work on buffer sizing focus purely on TCP performance. Although real-time (UDP) traffic accounts for only about 5-10% of Internet traffic, we note that its popularity, through the prolific use of on-line gaming, real-time video conferencing, and many other multimedia applications, is growing in the Internet. Consequently, we examined the dynamics of UDP and TCP interaction at a bottleneck link router equipped with very small buffers and observed a curious anomalous loss phenomenon. Further, we developed simple analytical models that gave insights into why the anomaly exists under certain circumstances.

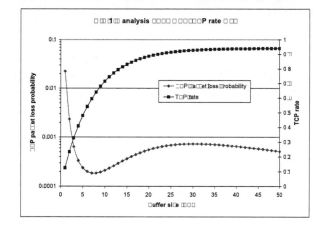

Figure 10. Anomalous UDP loss results from the M/M/1/B analytical model.

We point the interested reader to our papers in [25–27] for a systematic exploration of the impact of various system parameters on the anomaly, and to [28] for a possible way of alleviating it.

4. Realising Small Buffer Networks Using Traffic Pacing

The maturation of Wavelength Division Multiplexing (WDM) technology in recent years has made it possible to harness the enormous bandwidth potential of an optical fibre cost-effectively. As systems supporting hundreds of wavelengths per fibre with transmission rates of 10-40 Gbps per wavelength become available, electronic switching is increasingly challenged in scaling to match these transport capacities. However, due to the absence of a cost-effective technology for storing optical signals, emerging optical packet switched (OPS) networks are expected to have severely limited buffering capability.

A fundamental concern in OPS networks is packet loss due to contention, which occurs at a switching node whenever two or more packets try to leave on the same output link, on the same wavelength, at the same time. Many schemes have been developed to address contention losses - ranging from the use of fibre delay lines (FDLs) to store packets, deflection routing, and wavelength conversion. Unfortunately, these schemes have their own deficiencies: incorporating FDLs into a typical OPS switch design requires larger optical crossbars, which can add significantly to cost as the FDL buffers increase. Deflection routing usually incurs overheads such as packet reordering and implementation complexity, while all-optical wavelength converters are expensive, and often limited in their conversion range. It therefore seems that OPS networks of the foreseeable future will have very limited contention resolution resources.

4.1. Small Buffers: Loss for Real-time Traffic

We first illustrate via simulation the impact of small buffers on losses for real-time traffic. A direct and obvious impact of small network buffers is an increase in packet losses. We begin by observing that not withstanding the high bandwidth available in OPS networks,

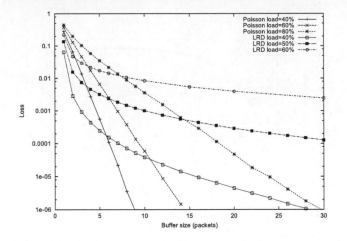

Figure 11. Loss vs. buffer size at a finite-buffer switch.

small buffers at OPS nodes cause significant loss when the traffic exhibits short-time-scale burstiness. As an example we consider a single link with a queue of finite and small capacity. The link rate is set at 10 Gbps, and packets have a constant size of 1250 bytes (this is consistent with earlier studies of slotted OPS systems). Fig. 11 shows the packet losses as a function of buffer size obtained from simulations of short range (Poisson) as well as long range dependent (LRD) input traffic at various system loads. The plots illustrate that an OPS node with very limited buffering (say 10 to 20 packets) can experience significant losses even at low to moderate traffic loads, particularly with the LRD model which is more representative of real-world traffic. This may be unacceptable in a core network supporting real-time applications with stringent loss requirements.

Pacing, also known as smoothing, has been studied before in the context of video traffic transmission. Unlike a shaper, which releases traffic at a given rate, a pacer accepts arbitrary traffic with given delay constraints, and releases traffic that is *smoothest* subject to the time-constraints of the traffic. Here "smoothness" may be measured using the maximum rate, rate variance, etc. The delay tolerance of traffic passing through the pacer is crucial to the efficacy of the pacer – the longer the traffic can be held back at the pacer, the more the window of opportunity the pacer has to smooth traffic and reduce its burstiness.

To the best of our knowledge, there has not been a study on the use of traffic pacing techniques for alleviating contentions in OPS networks with very small buffering resources. Our packet pacer smoothes traffic entering the OPS network, and is therefore employed at the optical edge switches on their egress links connecting to the all-optical packet switching core. Note that the optical edge switches process packets electronically, and are therefore assumed to have ample buffers required to do the pacing. Once a packet enters the OPS core, is it processed all-optically by each OPS core switch, where buffering is limited. The idea of pacing is therefore to modify the traffic profile entering the OPS network so as to use the limited buffers more efficiently and reduce losses, but without adversely affecting end-to-end delay.

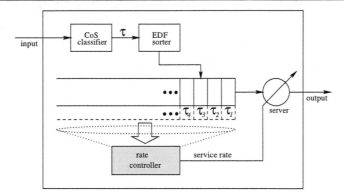

Figure 12. Model of the pacer.

4.2. Pacing Engine and Off-line Optimum

A generic architecture of our pacer is shown in Fig. 12. Incoming packets are classified (according to some criteria) and assigned a deadline by which they are to be released by the pacer. The objective of the pacer is to produce the smoothest output traffic such that each packet is released by its deadline. It is natural for the pacer therefore to release packets in order of deadline, namely to implement Earliest Deadline First (EDF) service.

Our pacing strategy derives from studies of video traffic smoothing, which we summarise next. Let $[0, T]$ denote the time interval during which the pacing system is considered, chosen such that the system is devoid of traffic at 0 and T. Denote by $A(t), 0 \leq t \leq T$ the *arrival curve*, namely the cumulative workload (say in units of bytes) arriving in $[0, t)$. Denote by $D(t), 0 \leq t \leq T$ the *deadline curve*, namely the cumulative workload that has to be served in $[0, t)$ so as not to violate any deadlines (thus any traffic with deadline earlier than t contributes to $D(t)$). Fig. 13 depicts an example $A(t)$ and $D(t)$ for the case where all arriving traffic has identical delay requirements. Note that by definition $D(t)$ can never lie above $A(t)$. Any service schedule implemented by the pacer can be represented by an *exit curve* $S(t), 0 \leq t \leq T$, corresponding to the cumulative traffic released by the pacer in $[0, t)$. A feasible exit curve, namely one which is causal and satisfies the delay constraint, must lie in the region bounded above by the arrival curve $A(t)$, and below by the deadline curve $D(t)$.

Amongst all feasible exit curves, the one which corresponds to the smoothest output traffic, measured by various metrics such as transmission rate variance, has been shown in [29] to be the *shortest path* between the origin $(0, 0)$ and the point $(T, D(T))$, as shown in Fig. 13. This curve always comprises a sequence of straight-line segments joining points on the arrival and deadline curves, each segment representing a period during which the service rate is a constant. Computation of this curve requires knowledge of the complete traffic arrival curve, which restricts the approach to off-line applications like the transmission of stored video files.

Unlike the video transmission context, smoothing or pacing in OPS networks will have to operate under much more demanding conditions. Current mechanisms for smoothing consider one or a few video streams at end-hosts or video server; by contrast OPS edge nodes will have to perform the pacing on large traffic aggregates at extremely high data

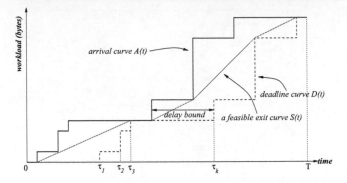

Figure 13. Arrival, deadline, and exit curves for an example workload process.

rates. The time-constraints for computing the optimal pacing patterns are also much more stringent – unlike video smoothing where a few frames (tens to hundreds of milliseconds) of delay is acceptable, OPS edge nodes will have to buffer traffic for shorter time lest the buffering requirement becomes prohibitively expensive (at 10 Gbps, 1 msec of buffering needs 10 Mbits of RAM). The next subsection therefore develops algorithms that are amenable to efficient implementation at OPS edge nodes.

4.3.   Efficient Real-time Pacing

It is shown in [29] that an off-line pacer yields the smoothest output traffic satisfying the delay constraints if its service rate follows the shortest path lying between the arrival and deadline curves. In the on-line case, however, the packet arrival process is non-deterministic, and the arrival curve is not known beforehand. In the absence of any assumptions about future packet arrivals, our on-line algorithm determines the smoothest output for the packets *currently* in the pacer. Thus at time t, the arrival curve considered to the right of t is a horizontal line (since future arrivals are not known yet), and the shortest-path exit curve degenerates to the convex hull of the deadline curve [30]. Upon each packet arrival, the deadline curve is augmented, and this may require a recomputation of the convex hull which defines the optimal exit curve. This section develops algorithms for the efficient update of the convex hull of the deadline curve upon each packet arrival.

4.3.1.   Single Delay Class – Constant Amortised Cost Algorithm

We first consider the case where all packets entering the pacer have identical delay constraints. This simplifies the hull update algorithm since each packet arrival augments the deadline curve at the end. Our first algorithm computes the convex hull in $O(1)$ amortised time per packet arrival.

Fig. 14 depicts this update algorithm performed upon each packet arrival, and Fig. 15 illustrates the operations with an example. Recalling that the convex hull is piecewise-linear, we store it as a doubly linked list, where each element of the list corresponds to a linear segment whose start/end times and slope are maintained. In step 1 of the algorithm, the length of the incoming packet is determined, along with its deadline. The arrival of this new packet causes the deadline curve to be amended, which results in a new segment being

```
      // determine length and deadline of new packet p
1.   L = length(p); T = currtime; T_p = T + d
      // append new hull piece
2.   h = new hullPiece
3.   h.startT = ((hullList.empty()?) T : hullList.tail().endT);
4.   h.endT = T_p;
5.   h.slope = L/(T_p-h.startT)
6.   hullList.append(h)
      // scan backwards to restore hull convexity
7.   h = hullList.tail()
8.   while ((hPrev=h.prev)≠NULL ∧ hPrev.slope ≤ h.slope)
9.        h.slope = [h.slope * (h.endT − h.startT)
                    + hPrev.slope *
                    (hPrev.endT − max(T, hPrev.startT))]
                 / (h.endT − max(T, hPrev.startT))
10.       hullList.delete(hPrev)
11. end while // the hull is now convex
```

Figure 14. On-line algorithm for hull update upon packet arrival.

appended to the hull. Steps 2-6 therefore create a new linear segment with the appropriate slope and append it to the end of the hull (shown by operation $\boxed{a}$ in Fig. 15). The new piece may cause the hull to lose convexity, since the newly added piece may have slope larger than its preceding piece(s). Steps 7-11 therefore scan the hull backwards and restore convexity. If a hull piece has slope larger than its preceding piece, the two can be combined into a single piece which joins the end-points of the two pieces (as depicted by operations $\boxed{b}$ and $\boxed{c}$ in Fig. 15). The backward scan repeatedly fuses hull pieces until the slope of the last piece is smaller than the preceding piece (operation $\boxed{d}$ in Fig. 15). At this stage the hull is convex and the backward scan can stop, resulting in the new hull.

4.3.2. General Poly-Logarithmic Cost Algorithm

We now consider the general case where arriving packets may have arbitrary delay constraints. Handling packets with different delay times is complicated by the fact that the arrival of a new packet causes significant changes to the deadline curve. Recalling that the deadline curve is a piecewise-linear curve, where the start/end times of its individual segments correspond to deadlines of packets already in the system, we represent it as a planar polygonal line whose vertices $v_0, v_1, \ldots v_n$ form a sequence in increasing order with respect to both axes. The arrival of the new packet with a deadline between two existing vertices, say v_i and v_{i+1}, changes the deadline curve through the insertion of a new vertex u between them in the sequence and raising each of the vertices in the sub-sequence $v_{i+1}, v_{i+2}, \ldots, v_n$ by a value corresponding to the size of the new packet. As a result some vertices of the deadline curve, which were not part of the hull prior to arrival of the new packet, may appear as convex hull vertices as illustrated in Fig. 16. The number of such new points can be

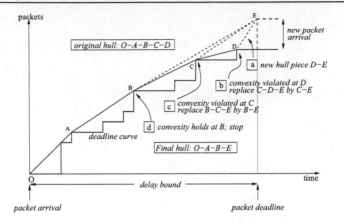

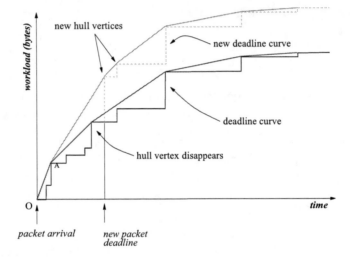

Figure 15. Example showing single-class hull update in amortised $O(1)$ time.

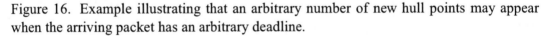

Figure 16. Example illustrating that an arbitrary number of new hull points may appear when the arriving packet has an arbitrary deadline.

as high as the number of packets in the system, and the process of re-computing the convex hull is not as simple as searching a binary tree as we did in the single-class case above.

The idea behind the algorithm is that for an incoming packet with arbitrary deadline, the original deadline curve is split into two parts, corresponding to the left and right of the new arrival's deadline. The convex hulls for each of the parts is independently computed, after the deadline curve to the right has been shifted up to account for the new packet arrival. The two hulls are then merged back to get the complete convex hull. The goal is to perform this process as efficiently as possible.

Fig. 17 depicts our algorithm for determining the convex hull upon each packet arrival. Our vertices are stored in the leaves of a search tree T structure which is capable of supporting concatenable-queue operations with the value of time used as the search key. Each internal node of T stores the convex hull of its leaves in a secondary tree structure that is also capable of supporting concatenable-queue operations. A linear size of the tree T and

1. *Determine size and deadline of newly arrived packet and create new vertex u.*

2. *Insert u into the 2-3 tree and divide it into trees T_L and T_R. T_L holds keys $\leq$ that of u, and T_R the remaining. Store size of new packet in root of T_R.*

3. *Merge T_L and T_R into a single tree.*

Figure 17. Multi-class hull update algorithm.

all its secondary structures is achieved by storing a vertex in the convex hull of an internal node only if it is not stored in any of its ancestor nodes [31].

In step 1 of the algorithm, the size of the incoming packet is determined, along with its deadline, and a new vertex u is created. The arrival of the new packet, which causes the deadline curve to be altered, triggers re-computation of the convex hull. Step 2 therefore searches the tree T along the root-to-leaf path and inserts the new vertex u as a new leaf according to its deadline value. The tree T is then *divided* about u so that all the leaves to the left of u and u itself are in one 2-3 tree T_L and all the leaves to the right of u are in a second 2-3 tree T_R. The division is a recursive process. For each internal node visited during the search process that will be deleted in the divide process, we use the convex hull stored in its secondary structure to compute a complete hull for each of its children, as described in [31]. At the end of the divide process, values of all vertices in T_R need to be incremented by the size of the incoming packet (i.e. shift the deadline curve up); this is achieved by storing the size of the new packet in the root of T_R. In step 3, the two trees T_L and T_R are again concatenated into a single tree, which yields the final convex hull of the new deadline curve. The complexity of the entire convex hull update operation that need to be performed upon each packet arrival is $O(\log^2 n)$, where n is the number of queued packets [31].

As in the single-class case, a hull segment needs to be deleted once packets corresponding to the segment have been released. The complexity of deleting a vertex of the convex hull and restructuring the tree T again has an $O(\log^2 n)$ cost, where n is the number of queued packets, as shown in [31].

4.4. Performance Evaluation for a Single Flow

Having addressed the *feasibility* of pacing at high data rates, we demonstrate the *utility* of pacing in OPS systems with small buffers. This section evaluates via simulation the impact of pacing on traffic burstiness and loss for a single flow, while the next section evaluates via simulation loss performance for several flows in realistic network topologies.

We apply our pacing technique to Poisson and long range dependent (LRD) traffic models (both of which were introduced in section 4.1.); the Poisson model is selected for its simplicity and ease of illustration of the central ideas, while the LRD model is chosen since it is believed to be more reflective of traffic in real networks.

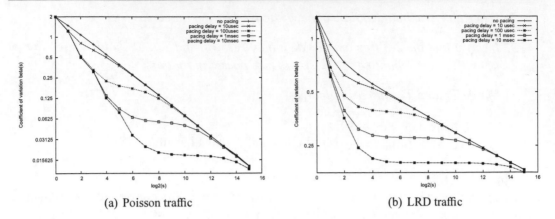

(a) Poisson traffic   (b) LRD traffic

Figure 18. Burstiness vs. time-scale for various pacing delays from simulation of Poisson and LRD traffic.

4.4.1. Impact of Pacing on Traffic Burstiness

We now study using simulation and analysis how pacing changes the burstiness of a traffic stream at various time-scales. Burstiness at time-sale s is quantified by $\beta(s)$, the coefficient of variation (i.e. ratio of standard deviation to mean) of traffic volume measured over time intervals of size s. Log-log plots of $\beta(s)$ versus s are routinely used in the literature to depict traffic burstiness over various time-scales as an indicator of self-similarity of traffic traces and to show the influence of the Hurst parameter H. Our simulations in this section fix the link rate at 10 Gbps and packet sizes at 1250 bytes (such that each packet requires exactly $1\mu s$ for transmission).

Fig. 18 shows for Poisson and LRD traffic the burstiness $\beta(s)$ versus time-scale s (in μsec) on log-log scale observed in simulation for pacing delay d of 0 (i.e. no pacing), $10\mu sec$, $100\mu sec$, 1msec, and 10msec. We first note that the unpaced Poisson stream (at 8 Gbps or 80% load) in Fig. 18(a) and the unpaced LRD stream (at 4 Gbps or 40% load) both exhibit straight lines with respective slopes -0.5 and -0.15; this validates the expected slope $-(1 - H)$ for Hurst parameter settings $H = 0.5$ and $H = 0.85$ of the short and long range dependent traffic respectively (the different slope at very short time-scales for LRD traffic arises from the packetisation of the ideal fluid model).

We next note that pacing reduces burstiness only within a range of time-scales, explained as follows. At *very short* time-scales (e.g. $s = 2^0 = 1\mu sec$ in our example), burstiness is invariant to pacing due to the discrete nature of packet release. Specifically, if $p_i(\Delta t)$ denotes the probability that an interval of size Δt has i packets, then for $i \geq 2$: $\lim_{\Delta t \to 0} p_i(\Delta t) = o(\Delta t)$ is vanishingly small when the traffic model does not permit batch arrivals. The burstiness $\beta(\Delta t)$ at very short time-scales therefore depends only on $p_0(\Delta t)$ and $p_1(\Delta t)$, which in turn are determined by the mean traffic rate and are invariant to pacing. At *very long* time-scales (beyond the delay budget d of the pacer), burstiness is again invariant to pacing. This is because the pacer does not hold any packet back beyond its deadline, and so pacing cannot alter the characteristics of the traffic at time scales that are much longer than the pacing delay budget.

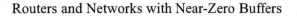

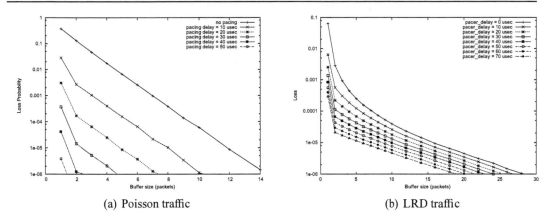

(a) Poisson traffic   (b) LRD traffic

Figure 19. Loss versus buffer size at various pacing delays from simulation of Poisson and LRD traffic.

Pacing is most effective in the range of time-scales within the pacer's delay budget. Barring the very-short time-scale region (that is dominated by the discrete nature of the packet pacing process), we observe that for both Poisson and LRD traffic, and for any fixed pacer delay budget d, the burstiness of the paced traffic remains nearly constant at $\beta(d)$ with time-scale, till it converges with the burstiness of the input traffic. This demonstrates the efficacy of pacing in reducing short time-scale burstiness, without altering longer time-scale traffic characteristics.

4.4.2. Impact of Pacing on Packet Loss

Having quantified the impact of pacing on the burstiness of Poisson and LRD traffic, we now feed the paced traffic into a constant rate server (OPS link) and observe how losses are affected by pacing. For analytical and conceptual simplicity we consider only a single flow with fixed size packets in this section; realistic network topologies with multiple flows and variable packet sizes are considered in the subsequent section.

In our simulation we feed the paced traffic stream into an OPS link with fixed capacity and small buffers, and observe the packet loss probability as a function of buffer size for various pacing delays. Fig. 19(a) plots for Poisson traffic (at 60% link load) the observed loss (on log scale) as a function of buffer size (in packets) for pacing delays of 0 (corresponding to no pacing), 10, 20, 30, 40, and 50 μsec (recall that 1μsec corresponds to the transmission time of a packet). Pacing is seen to be extremely effective in reducing loss: at the cost of a few tens of μsec of increase in end-to-end delay, the packet loss probability can be reduced by multiple orders of magnitude, which is a very attractive cost-benefit trade-off. Fig. 19(b) plots the losses for an LRD traffic stream (at 40% load) when pacing delay of 0 to 70μsec is employed. Once again pacing is seen to be effective: for example, a 70μsec pacing delay (which contributes to a very small increase in end-to-end delay), reduces losses at the link by more than an order of magnitude.

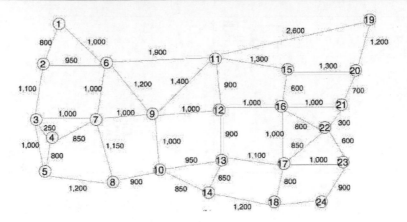

Figure 20. Core Network Simulation Topology.

4.4.3. Simulation Study of Networks

Our second set of experiments simulate the core network topology shown in Fig. 20 comprising of 24 core OPS nodes. Each core node is connected to four edge nodes (not shown in the figure), and the network thus has 96 edge nodes. Each edge node generates traffic to one other randomly chosen edge node, giving us a total of 96 flows in the network. Each flow is routed along the shortest path (computed using the shown fibre lengths) from origin to destination. All flows generate Poisson traffic (we did not have sufficiently long traces of LRD traffic to generate sufficient packets for this large topology), and the maximum core link load in the network is maintained between 64% and 80% of link capacity. In the next subsection, we discuss another scheme to alleviate contention losses in a bufferless core network.

Fig. 21 shows the aggregate packet loss probability in the network as a function of buffer size (in bytes) when optical buffering is employed for contention resolution. Each curve in the figure corresponds to a different pacing delay. Once again pacing is seen to be very effective in reducing core loss for a very small penalty in end-to-end delay: for 10-20 packets (4200-8400 bytes) of buffering, a pacing delay of $100\mu s$ reduced loss by as much as three orders of magnitude, which would be a very attractive loss-delay trade-off in a core OPS network.

For in-depth analytical and simulation results, we encourage the reader to refer our papers in [32, 33].

4.5. Section Summary

Emerging optical packet switched (OPS) networks will likely have very limited contention resolution resources usually implemented in the form of packet buffers or wavelength converters. This can cause high packet losses and adversely impact end-to-end performance. We identify short-time-scale burstiness as the major contributor to the performance degradation, and proposed to mitigate the problem by "pacing" traffic at the optical edge prior to injection into the OPS core. Pacing dramatically reduces traffic burstiness for a bounded and controllable penalty in end-to-end delay. We presented algorithms of poly-

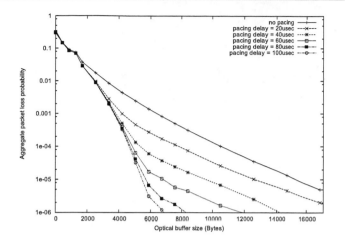

Figure 21. Loss versus buffer size.

logarithmic complexity that can efficiently implement optimal real-time pacing of traffic aggregates with arbitrary delay requirements. We showed via simulation of realistic OPS network topologies that pacing can reduce losses by orders of magnitude, at the expense of a small and bounded increase in end-to-end delay. This ability to trade-off delay for loss makes pacing a very attractive way of realising acceptable performance from OPS networks with small buffers.

5. Realising Bufferless Networks Using Packet-level FEC

From the discussions in the previous sections it is clear that as router line card rates continue to increase, we are approaching the limits of semiconductor (SRAM and DRAM) technology in terms of switching speeds, power savings and heat dissipation. This observation has forced high capacity router/switch designers, and network providers to consider leveraging the use of optics for switching and transmission in core routers.

However, incorporating even a few packets of buffering using an all-optical on-chip memory is a formidable challenge due to the inherent complexity associated with maintaining the quality of the optical signal and the physical size limitations of the chip [34]. At the moment, our IRIS router is capable of buffering 100 nanosec worth of data. At 40 Gbps line rate, this translates to 500 Bytes, which is not sufficient to buffer a typical 1500 Byte Internet packet.

Given these challenges and limitations associated with all-optical buffering, we investigate if we can enable a high-speed wide-area bufferless (or near-zero buffer) core optical network capable of delivering acceptable end-to-end performance. The concern in a bufferless network is that packet losses can be unacceptably high. We propose the use of packet-level forward error correction (FEC) coding by the electronic edge routers as a method for recovering from packet loss in the bufferless core.

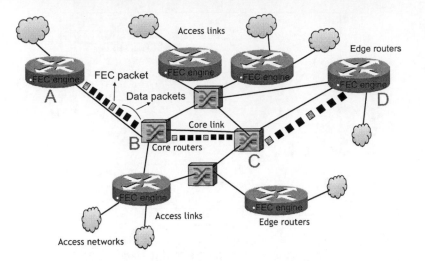

Figure 22. Topology to illustrate the edge-to-edge FEC framework.

5.1. Motivation for Choosing FEC

An interesting question that we ask in the context of a bufferless core network is: do we expect that the losses in the core will be bursty? Losses in packet networks are known to be bursty [16], but that is in the case of drop-tail queues and also when the lossy links are the flows' bottlenecks. In practice, the capacity of the core links is orders of magnitude higher than the access/edge links [8], thus ensuring that the bandwidth bottleneck for a flow is either at the access/edge link, and not at any core link. Thus, losses will occur in the core, not because a single flow can saturate the core link with a burst of back-to-back packets, but because we can have the simultaneous arrival of two or more packets from different edge/core links in a given time-slot. Thus, loss at core links is due to *contention*, not congestion.

It is well-known that FEC works best when losses are random, and hence our choice of using FEC is primarily inspired by this fact that packet losses in a bufferless core will occur randomly (due to contention) and not in a bursty manner (due to congestion).

Other reasons for choosing FEC are that it is a well established technique, cost-effective, and can be easily implemented in hardware. FEC can introduce some bandwidth overhead, but this is a small price to pay for building scalable and power efficient bufferless core nodes, and also because ISPs typically operate their core networks at relatively low loads ($\approx$ 20-30%) [35]. In addition, packet-level FEC has, to the best of our knowledge, not been studied before in the context of a bufferless network. Finally, it also complements other techniques outlined above to minimise loss, namely that it is possible to combine FEC with traffic shaping/pacing etc.

5.2. The Edge-to-Edge Packet-Level FEC Framework

Fig. 22 shows a small segment of a typical ISP network comprising of electronic edge routers and optical core routers. The distinguishing feature between the core and edge routers is that the core router links are bufferless (near-zero buffer) while the electronic router links have large buffers. The FEC framework presented in this paper is implemented at the electronic edge routers across the aggregate packet flow between an edge router (ingress) to another edge router (egress), and not for flows between any two end-hosts. Hence our implementation is an *edge-to-edge* based FEC implementation. As an example, all traffic that enters the core network from an ingress router say in New York city and exits at an egress router say in Los Angeles is viewed as an edge-to-edge flow, and it is protected by the FEC redundancy. It is important to note that the FEC scheme is scalable since if an ISP network has N edge routers, then each electronic edge router will compute FEC packets for just $N - 1$ edge-to-edge flows. Further, the proposed FEC framework has the advantage of being completely transparent to the end-hosts with control purely with the ISP.

The ingress edge routers receive traffic from applications running at various end-hosts on the access network via access links (DSL, cable modem, etc.), classifies the traffic on an edge-to-edge basis, and computes the FEC packets per egress edge router. The FEC framework discussed in this work uses the well-known and simple XOR scheme. The strength of FEC is the number of data packets over which the XOR operation is performed, henceforth referred to as block-size. The scheme has a unique property, namely that if in addition to a block of k data packets the ingress router also transmits the XOR of the k data packets (thereby transmitting $k + 1$ packets for every k packets), the corresponding egress router will be able to recover from loss provided there is only one missing data packet.

For ease of illustration, the figure shows traffic flowing from edge router A to edge router D along the path A-B-C-D. Assuming the block-size is three, A keeps a running XOR of the data packets destined to D. After every third packet, the FEC packet comprising the XOR value is transmitted and the XOR is cleared. D also maintains a running XOR of the packets it receives from A. If it detects exactly one lost data packet in the window of $k + 1$ packets, the running XOR is XOR'd with the FEC packet to recover the lost data packet, which is then forwarded on. In the case of zero (or > 1) loss, recovery is not possible and the running XOR is cleared.

To deal with variable-size packets, we assume that the size of each FEC packet equals the MTU size in the optical core. For XOR purposes, smaller packets are treated as being padded with zeros. The egress router must have sufficient information to recover a missing data packet correctly. Therefore, the FEC packet constructed by the ingress router takes into account the header information and the payload of each data packet. This ensures that the reconstructed packet will be identical to the original (missing) data packet.

The edge routers do not introduce much overhead in computing the FEC packet (since the XOR computation can be performed in real-time), nor do they require significant additional memory for the XOR process. The extra memory required is for storing one FEC packet per edge router in the network. This is however not a concern because FEC is performed at the edge routers that have large electronic memory. Insertion of one FEC packet for every k data packets increases the bandwidth requirement by a fraction $1/k$, which may be acceptable in a typical optical core that has abundant bandwidth but limited buffering.

The recovery operation can introduce a delay that in the worse case is the time to receive all k subsequent packets in a window of $k + 1$ packets (assuming the first data packet is lost). The delay will be very small in practice because we have eliminated the large buffers

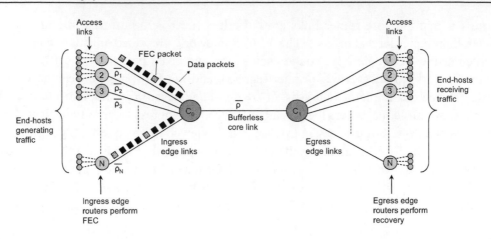

Figure 23. Example dumbbell topology with a single core link.

that exist in today's core routers (millions of packets), and we consider edge-to-edge flows with possibly thousands/millions of packets per second.

5.3. Role of FEC on Single Link Goodput and Loss

We implemented the above edge-to-edge FEC framework in *ns-2* (version 2.33), and apply it to the single core-link dumbbell topology shown in Fig. 23. Ten edge links feed traffic into the bufferless core link at router C_0, with each edge link in turn fed by three access links. The 30 end-hosts each have 5 TCP (Reno) agents, and the network therefore simulates 150 long-lived TCP flows. Similarly the TCP flows are sinked by the 30 end-hosts on the right. The propagation delays on the access and edge links are uniformly distributed between $[1, 5]$ ms and $[5, 15]$ ms respectively, while the core link C_0-C_1 has delay 30 ms. In line with the prevalent situation in today's networks, we ensure that the TCP flows are bottlenecked at access links, rather than the core which typically has much higher capacity. Our access link speeds are uniformly distributed in $[3, 5]$ Mbps, all edge links operate at 40 Mbps, and the core link at 400 Mbps. For these link speeds, it can be seen that the access link is the bottleneck since each flow's fair-share of the bandwidth on the access links varies between 0.6-1 Mbps, while on the edges and the core it is 2.67 Mbps. The start time of the TCP flows is uniformly distributed in the interval $[0, 10]$ sec and the simulation is run for 35 sec. Data in the interval $[20, 35]$ sec is used in all our computations so as to capture the steady-state behaviour of the network.

We measure the average per-flow TCP goodput for each setting of the FEC block-size k in simulation. We use goodput as a metric since it has been argued to be the most important measure for end-users [36], who want their transactions to complete as fast as possible. It should be mentioned that *ns-2* does not permit setting buffer size to zero as it simulates store-and-forward rather than cut-through switches. Thus, our simulations use a buffer size of 1 KB (the closest we can come to zero buffer) to accommodate a single TCP packet (TCP packets in our simulation are of size 1 KB) that is stored and forwarded by the switch.

Fig. 24 shows the per-flow TCP goodput as a function of block-size k. For comparison, it also depicts, via horizontal lines, the average goodput without FEC (the bottom line) and

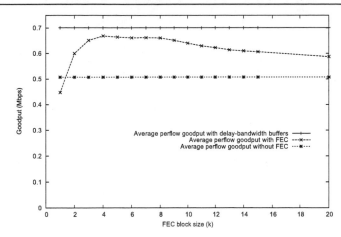

Figure 24. Average perflow goodput for 150 TCP flows on dumbbell topology.

the average goodput if the core link were to have sufficient (delay-bandwidth) buffering of around 12.5 MB (top line). Large buffers yield a per-flow goodput of 0.7 Mbps, while eliminating buffers reduces this goodput to 0.5 Mbps, a sacrifice in goodput of nearly 30%. Employing edge-to-edge FEC over the bufferless link can improve per-flow goodput substantially, peaking at nearly 0.68 Mbps when the FEC block-size k is in the range of 3-6, and bringing the per-flow TCP goodput for the bufferless link to within 3% of a fully-buffered link. This small sacrifice in goodput is a worthy price to pay for eliminating buffering at router C_0.

Another interesting aspect to note from Fig. 24 is that TCP goodput initially increases with FEC block-size k, reaches a peak, and then falls as k increases. Qualitatively, this is because stronger FEC (i.e., smaller block-size k) in general improves the ability to recover from loss, but is also a contributor to loss since it increases the load on the link by introducing redundant packets. In the next subsection, we capture this effect via a simple analytical model to determine the optimal setting of FEC block-size that minimises loss on a bufferless link.

5.3.1. Analysis

We develop a simple analytical model to quantitatively understand the impact of FEC strength on edge-to-edge loss, and to identify the block-size settings that achieve low loss and consequently larger goodput. Our analysis makes several simplifying assumptions:

1) The end-hosts that generate traffic are independent of each other. Consequently, traffic coming into the core links from the various edge links are also independent of one another. This is a reasonable assumption, even for TCP traffic when the number of flows is large enough [3]. Moreover, we assume that the contribution to the load on the core link from each of the edge links is similar.

2) We assume a time-slotted cut-through link, with loss happening if and only if two or more packets arrive to the link for transmission in the same slot (since the core is bufferless).

3) We do not model feedback, i.e., TCP's adjustment of rate in response to loss. Instead, we will assume that the steady-state load on the link is known aforehand.

Denote by ρ_i the original load (i.e., load without FEC) on each of the edge links (i, C_0), $i \in \{1, N\}$ (see Fig. 23). The offered load at the core link C_0-C_1 is then $\rho = \sum_{i=1}^{N} \rho_i$. Now, if each edge link performs FEC using block-size k, then the new load $\overline{\rho_i}$ on each of these edge links is

$$\overline{\rho_i} = \left(\frac{k+1}{k}\right) \rho_i \tag{10}$$

since FEC inserts one additional packet for every k data packets. Correspondingly, the offered load $\overline{\rho}$ post-FEC at the core link is

$$\overline{\rho} = \sum_{i=1}^{N} \overline{\rho_i} = \sum_{i=1}^{N} \left(\frac{k+1}{k}\right) \rho_i = \left(\frac{k+1}{k}\right) \rho \tag{11}$$

Assuming that each edge link contributes equally to the load $\overline{\rho}$ on the core link, the probability that in a given time-slot a packet arrives from any chosen edge link is $\overline{\rho}/N$ where N denotes the number of edge links. The loss probability $\mathbb{L}_c$ at the core link in a chosen slot is then the probability that packets arrive from two or more edge links:

$$\mathbb{L}_c = \sum_{i=2}^{N} \binom{N}{i} \left(\frac{\overline{\rho}}{N}\right)^i \left(1 - \frac{\overline{\rho}}{N}\right)^{N-i} \tag{12}$$

It is worthwhile mentioning that for large N, the binomial distribution above converges to the Poisson distribution with the same mean. The number of input links (N) interfacing with a core router is called fan-in, and is fairly large in practice. For example, the mean number of working ports in a core network with 60 nodes and uniform full mesh of demands is about 354 [37]. Therefore, Eq. (12) can be approximated by

$$\mathbb{L}_c = 1 - e^{-\overline{\rho}}(1 + \overline{\rho}) \tag{13}$$

Knowing the probability of packet loss in the core, we can now estimate the edge-to-edge packet loss probability $\mathbb{L}_e$ by computing the expected number of irrecoverably lost packets in a window of $k + 1$ packets (comprising k data packets and one FEC packet) as follows:

$$\mathbb{L}_e = \mathbb{L}_c \sum_{j=1}^{k} \binom{k}{j} (\mathbb{L}_c)^j (1 - \mathbb{L}_c)^{k-j} \frac{j}{k} + $$
$$(1 - \mathbb{L}_c) \sum_{j=2}^{k} \binom{k}{j} (\mathbb{L}_c)^j (1 - \mathbb{L}_c)^{k-j} \frac{j}{k} \tag{14}$$

The first term on the right in Eq. (14) captures the case when the FEC packet is lost along with j data packets, in which all j data packets are irrecoverable, while the second term captures the case when the FEC packet arrives and $j \geq 2$ data packets are lost, in which case the j packet losses are irrecoverable. Eq. (14) can be simplified yielding

$$\mathbb{L}_e = \mathbb{L}_c \left[1 - (1 - \mathbb{L}_c)^k \right] \tag{15}$$

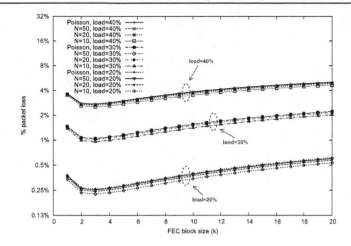

Figure 25. % edge-to-edge packet loss for different loads and fan-in.

Eq. (15) states that a data packet is irrecoverably lost only if it is lost in the core (with probability $\mathbb{L}_c$) **and** not all other k packets in the window (this includes the FEC packet) are successfully received (otherwise the lost data packet can be reconstructed).

Eq. (15), in conjunction with Eq. (12) (or Eq. (13)) and Eq. (11), can be used to directly estimate edge-to-edge loss $\mathbb{L}_e$ as a function of FEC block-size k. In Fig. 25 we plot on log-scale the edge-to-edge packet loss probability as a function of the block-size k for different values of load ρ (20%, 30%, 40%) and fan-in N. We first observe that for a given load, loss is not very sensitive to the fan-in N at the core link, and further that the Poisson limit seems to be a good approximation that frees us from having to consider the fan-in parameter N explicitly in the model. The most important observation to emerge from this plot is that for a given load, the loss decreases with block-size k, reaches a minimum, and then starts increasing as the block-size gets larger. This provides some explanation as to why the simulation plot in Fig. 24 shows TCP goodput to first increase and then fall with block-size k, as TCP throughput is inversely related to the square root of end-to-end packet loss [38]. The figure also gives us some estimate of the strength of FEC required ($k = 3$ in this case) for minimising loss: the recovery benefit of stronger FEC (i.e., lower k) is outweighed by the overhead it introduces in terms of load, while weaker FEC (i.e., larger k) does not sufficiently recover lost data packets. In the next subsection we explore if similar observations extend to a more complex multi-hop topology.

5.3.2.   FEC Performance in a Multi-HOP Network

Having seen the benefits offered by FEC for a single link, we now evaluate its performance on a more general wide-area network topology. To this end, we choose the NSFNet topology shown in Fig. 26 as our representative core network, which is made up of core routers (numbered 0 to 13) and the bufferless optical links interconnecting them. The numbers along the core links indicate the propagation delay in milliseconds. For the sake of clarity, the figure shows only two edge routers connected to every core node and each edge router receives traffic from only two end-hosts (via access links). However, in all our simulations, we consider larger number of edge/access links, as described next.

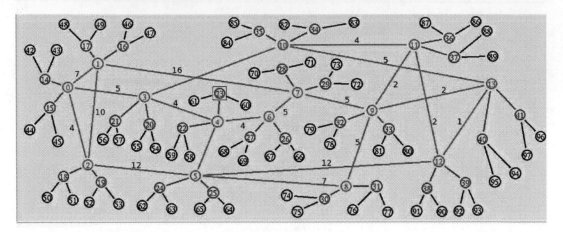

Figure 26. Example NSFNet topology with 2 access links per edge node and 2 edge links per core node from *ns-2* network animator.

We consider ten edge links feeding traffic into every core router, and each edge router in turn is fed by five access links. All core links operate at 1 Gbps, all edge links at 100 Mbps, and the access link rates are uniformly distributed between [7, 10] Mbps, to reflect a typical home user. These numbers ensure that the core is not the bottleneck for any TCP flow. The destination end-hosts are chosen randomly such that every flow traverses at least one hop on the core network; in all there are 3480 TCP flows in the network comprising of 784 one-hop flows, 1376 two-hop flows and 1320 three-hop flows. We assume all flows to be long-lived (Section V describes results when both short-lived and long-lived TCP flows coexist). Data in the interval [20, 35] sec is used for the computations in order to capture the network's steady state behaviour.

Fig. 27 plots the ratio (average goodput with FEC to the corresponding average goodput with delay-bandwidth buffers) for 1-, 2- and 3-hop TCP flows as a function of the block-size (the maximum number of hops along the shortest path between any two core nodes on the NSFNet is three). It makes sense to use the goodput obtained with delay-bandwidth buffers in the core as the benchmark because core routers today have large buffers [1], and the performance witnessed by ISPs is typically under such large buffering. We note from the simulation results that with delay-bandwidth buffers, the load on the core links varies between 7% to 38% with the average load being ≈ 24%. These numbers are realistic and fall in the regime in which most ISPs operate their networks today. The figure also indicates, via horizontal lines, the corresponding goodput ratios in the non-FEC case.

A fundamental point that we can infer from the figure is that the bufferless core network (with and without FEC) is very unfair towards multi-hop flows when compared to single-hop flows. On average, 1-hop flows with FEC (at $k = 3$) achieve nearly 1.5 times the goodput (1.05 times in the non-FEC case) when compared to what they achieve when all core routers have delay-bandwidth buffers. This means that 1-hop flows perform better in a bufferless network than in a fully-buffered network! The ratio reduces to 0.56 for 2-hop flows and further to just 0.3 for 3-hop flows, indicating heavy skewing in favour of short-hop flows.

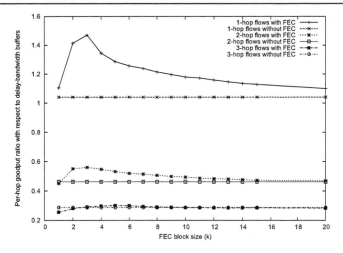

Figure 27. Ratio (average goodput with FEC to average goodput with delay-bandwidth buffers) for 1-, 2-, 3-hop TCP flows on NSFNet topology.

To explain why multi-hop TCP flows perform so poorly, we plot in Fig. 28 the histogram of edge-to-edge packet loss (for the non-FEC case) for flows with different hop-lengths. We can observe that while over 95% of 1-hop flows experience loss only in the range 0.5-3%, it increases to 1.5-4.5% for 2-hop flows, and further to 2.5-6% for 3-hop flows. To appreciate the impact these numbers have on the edge-to-edge performance, if we assume, for example, that the loss rate doubles from 1% to 2%, then the throughput of open-loop UDP traffic reduces by roughly 1%, whereas for closed-loop TCP traffic, it reduces by nearly 30%, since the average throughput of a TCP flow in the congestion avoidance mode is inversely proportional to the square root of packet loss. TCP goodput, however, can be much lower, as seen by Fig. 27. The relatively higher loss rates for 2- and 3-hop flows result in their fair-share of the bandwidth being unfairly utilised by 1-hop flows (since TCP is inherently greedy and is designed to exploit as much of the bandwidth as available), leading to unfairness. These results motivate us to devise a scheme that provides fairness to both single- and multi-hop flows, which will be the focus of the next section.

5.4. FEC for a Bufferless Network and Fairness

We observed from the results in the previous section that in a bufferless network, multi-hop TCP flows can experience significantly lower end-to-end goodput than single-hop flows, leading to unfairness. In this section, we address this deficiency by developing a framework that ensures fairness to both single- and multi-hop flows.

5.4.1. Analysis

We denote $\lambda_{i,j}$ to be the offered load to the core network by the edge-to-edge flow between ingress router i and egress router j, henceforth represented as (i, j), under the assumption that they are not using FEC. Let $\overline{\lambda_{i,j}}$ be the new load to the core network when

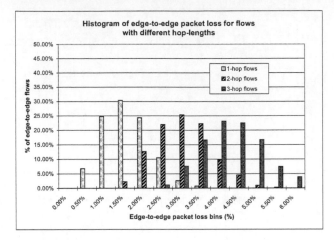

Figure 28. Histogram of edge-to-edge packet loss for TCP flows with different hop lengths (and no FEC) on the NSFNet.

the flow employs FEC using $k_{i,j}$ as its block-size. Consequently,

$$\overline{\lambda_{i,j}} = \left(\frac{k_{i,j} + 1}{k_{i,j}} \right) \lambda_{i,j} \tag{16}$$

Under the assumption that packet arrivals at a core link (u, v) in every time-slot is Poisson with mean $\overline{\lambda_{i,j}}$, we can compute the packet loss probability $L_c^{u,v}$ at the link as the probability of two or more simultaneous packet arrivals from all flows that traverse (u, v). Thus,

$$
\begin{aligned}
L_c^{u,v} &= 1 - \left(e^{- \sum_{(u,v) \in r(i,j)} \overline{\lambda_{i,j}}} \right) - \\
&\quad \left(\sum_{(u,v) \in r(i,j)} \overline{\lambda_{i,j}} \times e^{- \sum_{(u,v) \in r(i,j)} \overline{\lambda_{i,j}}} \right) \\
&= 1 - e^{- \sum_{(u,v) \in r(i,j)} \overline{\lambda_{i,j}}} \left(1 + \sum_{(u,v) \in r(i,j)} \overline{\lambda_{i,j}} \right)
\end{aligned} \tag{17}
$$

where $r(i, j)$ is the routing path of edge-to-edge flow (i, j). In general, a flow can traverse multiple hops on the core network before reaching the egress edge router. If loss rates on core links are sufficiently small (say 10^{-2} or lower), it is reasonable to assume that edge-to-edge losses are independent and additive over the links the flow traverses. Therefore, denoting $\mathbb{L}_c^{i,j}$ to be the aggregate core path loss probability for the flow (i, j),

$$\mathbb{L}_c^{i,j} = \sum_{(u,v) \in r(i,j)} L_c^{u,v} \tag{18}$$

We can now compute $\mathbb{L}_e^{i,j}$, the edge-to-edge packet loss probability for flow (i, j) by substituting in Eq. (15) the core path loss probability for the flow derived from Eq. (18). Thus,

$$\mathbb{L}_e^{i,j} = \mathbb{L}_c^{i,j} \left[1 - \left(1 - \mathbb{L}_c^{i,j} \right)^{k_{i,j}} \right] \tag{19}$$

Simulation results in the previous section show that bufferless core networks can be unfair towards multi-hop TCP flows. Thus, to achieve fairness, multi-hop flows need more aggressive FEC than single-hop flows. We now capture this notion of fairness by formulating an optimisation problem as follows.

Inputs:

- Offered load $\lambda_{i,j}$ by every edge-to-edge flow (i, j).

- $r(i, j)$ the routing path of the flow (i, j).

Objective function:

$$\min_{k_{i,j}} \left(\max_{i,j} \ \mathbb{L}_e^{i,j} \right) \tag{20}$$

Subject to: $k_{i,j} \in \{1, 2, 3, \ldots\}$

Output: The set $\{k_{i,j}\}$, which denotes the optimum FEC block-size for every edge-to-edge flow.

The optimisation objective in Eq. (20) is a min-max objective expressed in terms of the edge-to-edge loss rate (conversely, it can be viewed as a max-min objective in terms of edge-to-edge goodput). It seems reasonable to consider the above objective since it ensures that the network bandwidth is assigned to the various (single- and multi-hop) flows in a fair manner, thus preventing the 1-hop flows from exploiting the available bandwidth and penalising the multi-hop flows (assuming that an ISP is equally concerned about multi-hop flows as single-hop flows).

It can be noted that the formulation has a non-linear objective function since the block-size $k_{i,j}$ that we are interested in is in the exponent of Eq. (19). In addition, we also have the constraint that each $k_{i,j}$ must be an integer. Although an optimal solution set exists for the formulation, the above two constraints render the problem intractable to large size networks. Indeed, the problem is NP-Hard since integer linear programming is itself NP-Hard. Thus in what follows, we propose a sub-optimal but practical heuristic that treats flows differently based on their hop-length.

5.4.2. Hop-Length Based Simple Heuristic

In general, the best block-size to use for an edge-to-edge flow depends on the load on each of the links it goes through, which in turn depends on the FEC strength of the other flows traversing those links. To simplify these interdependencies and reduce the solution space, we consider a heuristic scheme in which flows of identical hop-length h use identical block-size k_h. For this assumption to be reasonable, two flows of similar hop-length should see similar link loads along their paths. One way this could hold is when all links in the network are roughly equally loaded, and further that the relative contribution to load by flows of different hop-lengths is similar across links. If loads vary significantly across links, one could generate a worst case bound in which all links are as heavily loaded as the maximum loaded link in the network. In this section, for purely illustrative purposes, we will assume that all links have the same average load λ and flows of different hop-lengths contribute equally to the load on each link. Specifically, for the NSFNet topology considered, flows are of 1-, 2- or 3-hops, and have offered load $\{\lambda_1, \lambda_2, \lambda_3\}$ given by

$$\lambda_1 = \lambda_2 = \lambda_3 = \frac{\lambda}{3} \tag{21}$$

Denoting $\overline{\lambda_c}$ to be the load on any core link c post FEC, then considering the 1-, 2- and 3-hop flows, $\overline{\lambda_c}$ is given by

$$\overline{\lambda_c} = \left(\frac{k_1 + 1}{k_1}\right)\lambda_1 + \left(\frac{k_2 + 1}{k_2}\right)\lambda_2 + \left(\frac{k_3 + 1}{k_3}\right)\lambda_3 \tag{22}$$

Employing the Poisson assumption, the probability of loss $\mathbb{L}_c$ at a core link c can be expressed as

$$\mathbb{L}_c = 1 - e^{\overline{\lambda_c}}\left(1 + \overline{\lambda_c}\right) \tag{23}$$

Since we are assuming that all core links have the same average load, and hence the same loss rate, the core path loss probability $\mathbb{L}_{c,h}$ for a h-hop flow can be expressed as

$$\mathbb{L}_{c,h} = \mathbb{L}_c h \tag{24}$$

Now, from Eq. (15) the edge-to-edge packet loss probability $\mathbb{L}_{e,h}$ for a h-flow is

$$\mathbb{L}_{e,h} = \mathbb{L}_{c,h}\left[1 - \left(1 - \mathbb{L}_{c,h}\right)^{k_h}\right] \tag{25}$$

We are now interested in finding the sub-optimal set $\{k_1, k_2, k_3\}$ that minimises the maximum edge-to-edge loss $\mathbb{L}_{e,h}$. Assuming that each k_h can take a value between 1 and 100 (since larger block-sizes are generally not beneficial, as we observed earlier), it is easy to use a simple brute-force approach to determine this set, and using MATLAB, we are able to obtain the result in just a couple of seconds since we only have a million combinations to choose from. For the same simulation setting described in Section 5.3.2. (the average NSFNet link load λ for a bufferless network being $\approx 11\%$), the resulting solution is $k_1 = 19$, $k_2 = 4$ and $k_3 = 2$. These results clearly suggest that we need to have different block-sizes for flows with different hop-lengths, and indeed multi-hop flows require a much more aggressive FEC scheme than single-hop flows (since $k_3 < k_1$).

5.4.3. Simulation Results and Fairness on the Nsfnet Network

Using $k_1 = 19$, $k_2 = 4$ and $k_3 = 2$ (obtained from our heuristic in the previous subsection), we repeated the simulation with identical settings as before (having the same number of TCP flows on the NSFNet topology). Recall that our objective is to minimise the maximum edge-to-edge loss, or equivalently, maximise the minimum edge-to-edge goodput so as to achieve fairness across all flows. We employ the widely used Jain's fairness index [39] as an indicator of the heuristic's performance. It is extremely difficult to determine analytically what the optimum average goodput will be for the various 1-, 2- and 3-hop TCP flows from an overall network perspective, since analysing a single TCP flow is by itself very notorious, and we consider several thousand TCP flows with heterogeneous RTTs flowing through the network. Therefore as our benchmark, we again choose the goodput numbers

Network setting	Average goodput (Mbps)			Fairness Index
	1-hop flows	2-hop flows	3-hop flows	
No FEC	1.571	0.667	0.391	0.78
k = 3 for all flows	2.219	0.807	0.397	0.70
k_1 = 19, k_2 = 4, k_3 = 2	1.090	0.760	0.596	0.96
delay - bandwidth buffers	1.509	1.440	1.359	1

Figure 29. Relative fairness indices.

obtained when all core links have delay-bandwidth buffers. If λ_1', λ_2' and λ_3' are the good-puts of 1-, 2- and 3-hop flows with large buffers, then the Jain's fairness index FI can be expressed as

$$FI = \frac{\left(\sum_{i=1}^{3} \frac{\lambda_i}{\lambda_i'}\right)^2}{3\left[\sum_{i=1}^{3} \left(\frac{\lambda_i}{\lambda_i'}\right)^2\right]} \qquad (26)$$

The fairness index is a real number between 0 and 1, with a higher value indicating better fairness. Fig. 29 shows the fairness index for four pertinent cases - no FEC, FEC with $k = 3$ for all flows, FEC with $k_1 = 19$, $k_2 = 4$ and $k_3 = 2$, and with delay-bandwidth core buffers.

Following are the salient observations we can draw from the figure. Firstly, the non-FEC case has a rather low fairness index of 0.78, and although setting the block-size to $k = 3$ improves the performance of 1- and 2-hop flows quite significantly, it fails to lift the goodput of 3-hop flows, and surprisingly performs poorly on the fairness scale when compared to the non-FEC case (0.70 compared to 0.78). Secondly, tuning the block-size according to our heuristic, corresponding to $k_1 = 19$, $k_2 = 4$ and $k_3 = 2$, results in a good fairness index of 0.96, confirming that the network bandwidth is indeed used by the various 1-, 2- and 3-hop flows efficiently. These results provide valuable insight on how a future bufferless core network can be envisaged using the edge-to-edge FEC scheme.

5.4.4. Sensitivity Analysis of the Block-sizes

We now undertake a sensitivity analysis to ascertain how a slight perturbation to the values of k_1, k_2 and k_3 affects the fairness index. Our heuristic suggests using $k_1 = 19$, $k_2 = 4$ and $k_3 = 2$. We vary each k_h such that k_1 takes on values between 17 and 21, k_2 is in the range $\{3, 4, 5\}$, and k_3 is either 2 or 3. The simulation is repeated for each combination of the respective block-size. We note from the results that the fairness index varies between 0.924 (lower by 3.75%) and 0.962 (higher by 0.21%) when compared to 0.96 that was obtained by the heuristic, suggesting that the block-sizes derived by our heuristic algorithm is stable.

Before concluding this section, we wish to highlight that we performed many simulations by varying the distribution of the number of 1-, 2- and 3-hop TCP flows. The results we obtained follow closely the ones we have reported, omitted for brevity.

5.4.5.   Performance of the Fairness Heuristic at Different Loads

The objective of this subsection is to provide some insights for when the proposed FEC fairness heuristic performs best. In Fig. 30, the Y axis on the left (note the log-scale) shows the average edge-to-edge packet loss (of 1-, 2- and 3-hops) as a function of the average offered link load for two scenarios, namely, without FEC and when we use the fairness heuristic. The Y axis on the right shows the overhead (in terms of load) that FEC introduces for a given average offered load. The non-FEC loss rates are obtained from Eq. (24), where the value of $\mathbb{L}_c$ for a given load is derived from Eq. (13). The loss rates with FEC are as a result of the heuristic.

There are essentially two main points that we want to make regarding the figure. First, if the ISP wishes to operate the network such that the edge-to-edge loss is below a certain acceptable threshold (say 10^{-3}), then we note that without FEC, the load can be pushed to at most 10%. On the other hand, employing the FEC heuristic allows the network to be run at 30% load, thus contributing significantly to the ISPs revenue stream. Second, operating the network at high load restrains FEC because there is not much room to introduce additional redundancy (as the total load cannot exceed the available capacity). Thus the benefit offered by the heuristic seems to diminish at higher loads ($> 60\%$). If the network is very lightly loaded ($< 10\%$), then loss rates are significantly low to begin with that there really is no incentive to use FEC. Since ISPs typically operate their networks at 20-30% load [35], the use of FEC in a future bufferless core network seems valuable.

These numbers must only be viewed in light of the proposed heuristic (that does not model TCP feedback and uses static block-sizes) since we could design more efficient TCP aware adaptive FEC schemes that adjust the block-sizes dynamically based on the loss rate that an edge-to-edge flow observes in its path. In general, FEC seems beneficial only under certain load regimes and not across the entire spectrum.

5.5.   Section Summary

As buffering of packets in the optical domain is a complex and expensive operation and we are soon approaching the limitations of electronics, we addressed the feasibility of enabling a wide-area bufferless (near-zero buffer) core optical network. We proposed a novel edge-to-edge based packet-level FEC architecture as a means of battling high core losses. We also considered a realistic core network (NSFNet), developed an optimisation framework, and proposed a simple heuristic to improve fairness between single- and multi-hop flows. The technique we have developed is a first step towards understanding the potential of FEC in envisioning a future bufferless core network.

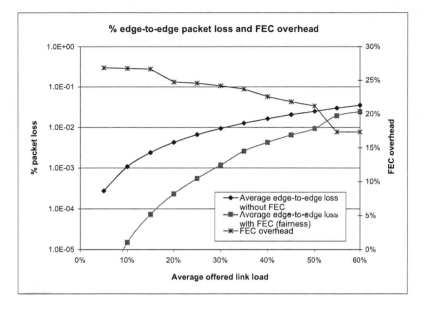

Figure 30. % edge-to-edge packet loss and FEC overhead for different average offered link loads obtained from analysis.

6.   Conclusion

In this chapter we first traced the evolution in thinking over the past few years on how much buffering is required at Internet routers. We then highlighted some of the implications of the move towards (potentially all-optical) KiloByte buffers, such as the reaction of TCP to reduced buffer availability in the network, and the unexpected interactions between TCP and real-time (UDP) traffic. Finally, we proposed mechanisms ranging from edge traffic pacing to packet-level forward error correction as means of overcoming the limitations posed by small buffers in the network.

We believe that through our ongoing work, we have only scratched the surface of what could well be a clean-and-green Internet architecture with near-zero buffers. "Green networking" has gained significant attention from ISPs and router manufacturers alike. There is scope for breaking new ground towards this goal. First, in terms of developing analytical and experimental models to understand TCP's reaction to very small buffers. If there is further insight into the Poisson convergence, then its implications on the design of a future all-optical packet switched network can be huge. Second, extending the edge pacing and FEC frameworks to incorporate traffic grooming and load-balanced switching can aid ISPs in tuning and optimising their networks effectively. Finally, new service models appropriate to near-bufferless networks can be developed taking into account economics, power consumption and other user requirements.

References

[1] C. Villamizar and C. Song, "High Performance TCP in ANSNet," *ACM SIGCOMM Computer Communication Review*, vol. 24, no. 5, pp. 45–60, Oct 1994.

[2] P. Bernasconi et al., "Architecture of an Integrated Router Interconnected Spectrally (IRIS)," in *Proc. IEEE High Performance Switching and Routing*, Poland, 2006.

[3] G. Appenzeller, I. Keslassy, and N. McKeown, "Sizing Router Buffers," in *Proc. ACM SIGCOMM*, USA, 2004.

[4] M. Enachescu, Y. Ganjali, A. Goel, N. McKeown, and T. Roughgarden, "Routers with Very Small Buffers," in *Proc. IEEE INFOCOM*, Spain, 2006.

[5] N. Beheshti et al., "Buffer Sizing in All-Optical Packet Switches," in *Proc. IEEE/OSA OFC/NFOEC*, USA, 2006.

[6] D. Wischik and N. McKeown, "Part I: Buffer Sizes for Core Routers," *ACM SIG-COMM Computer Communication Review*, vol. 35, no. 2, pp. 75–78, Jul 2005.

[7] A. Aggarwal, S. Savage, and T. Anderson, "Understanding the Performance of TCP Pacing," in *Proc. IEEE INFOCOM*, Israel, 2000.

[8] R. S. Prasad, C. Dovrolis, and M. Thottan, "Router Buffer Sizing Revisited: The Role of the Output/Input Capacity Ratio," in *Proc. ACM CoNEXT*, USA, 2007.

[9] A. Vishwanath and V. Sivaraman and M. Thottan, "Perspectives on Router Buffer Sizing: Recent Results and Open Problems," *ACM SIGCOMM Computer Communication Review*, vol. 39, no. 2, pp. 34–39, Apr 2009.

[10] W. Willinger, M. S. Taqqu, R. Sherman, and D. V. Wilson, "Self-Similarity Through High-Variability: Statistical Analysis of Ethernet LAN Traffic at the Source Level," in *Proc. ACM SIGCOMM*, USA, 1995.

[11] "Cisco white paper: Approaching the zettabyte era http://www.cisco.com/en/US/solutions/collateral/ns341/ns525/ns537/ns705/ns827/white_paper_c11-481374.pdf, jun 2008."

[12] T. Karagiannis et al., "A Nonstationary Poisson View of Internet Traffic," in *Proc. IEEE INFOCOM*, Hong Kong, Mar 2004.

[13] D. R. Cox and V. Isham, "Point Processes," Chapman and Hall, 1980.

[14] J. Cao and K. Ramanan, "A Poisson Limit for Buffer Overflow Probabilities," in *Proc. IEEE INFOCOM*, USA, 2002.

[15] J. Cruise, "Poisson Convergence, in Large Deviations, for the Superposition of Independent Point Processes," *Submitted to Annals of Operations Research*, 2009.

[16] H. Jiang and C. Dovrolis, "Why is the Internet Traffic Bursty in Short Time Scales?" in *Proc. ACM SIGMETRICS*, Canada, Jun 2005.

[17] P. Borgnat et al., "Seven Years and One Day: Sketching the Evolution of Internet Traffic," in *Proc. IEEE INFOCOM*, Brazil, Apr 2009.

[18] A. Lakshmikantha, R. Srikant, and C. Beck, "Impact of File Arrivals and Departures on Buffer Sizing in Core Routers," in *Proc. IEEE INFOCOM*, USA, 2008.

[19] "ns-2 network simulator - http://www.isi.edu/nsnam/ns/."

[20] W. Feng, F. Chang, W. Feng, and J. Walpole, "A Traffic Characterization of Popular On-Line Games," *IEEE/ACM Transactions on Networking*, vol. 13, no. 3, pp. 488–500, Jun 2005.

[21] "Packet traces from measurement and analysis on the WIDE Internet backbone. http://tracer.csl.sony.co.jp/mawi."

[22] V. Markovski, F. Xue, and L. Trajkovic, "Simulation and Analysis of Packet Loss in Video Transfers Using User Datagram Protocol," *The Journal of Supercomputing*, vol. 20, no. 2, pp. 175–196, 2001.

[23] L. Andrew et al., "Buffer Sizing for Nonhomogeneous TCP Sources," *IEEE Communications Letters*, vol. 9, no. 6, pp. 567–569, Jun 2005.

[24] G. Raina and D. Wischik, "Buffer Sizes for Large Multiplexers: TCP Queueing Theory and Instability Analysis," in *Proc. EuroNGI*, Italy, 2005.

[25] A. Vishwanath and V. Sivaraman, "Routers with Very Small Buffers: Anomalous Loss Performance for Mixed Real-Time and TCP Traffic," in *Proc. IEEE International Workshop on Quality of Service (IWQoS)*, Netherlands, 2008.

[26] A. Vishwanath and V. Sivaraman and G. N. Rouskas, "Considerations for Sizing Buffers in Optical Packet Switched Networks," in *Proc. IEEE INFOCOM*, Brazil, 2009.

[27] ——, "Anomalous Loss Performance for Mixed Real-Time and TCP Traffic in Routers with Very Small Buffers," *IEEE/ACM Transactions on Networking (pending minor revision)*, 2010.

[28] A. Vishwanath and V. Sivaraman, "Sharing Small Optical Buffers Between Real-Time and TCP Traffic," *Elsevier Optical Switching and Networking*, vol. 6, no. 4, pp. 289–296, Dec 2009.

[29] J. D. Salehi, Z.-L. Zhang, J. Kurose, and D. Towsley, "Supporting Stored Video: Reducing Rate Variability and End-to-End Resource Requirements Through Optimal Smoothing," *IEEE/ACM Transactions on Networking*, vol. 6, no. 4, pp. 397–410, Aug 1998.

[30] V. Sivaraman and D. Moreland, and D. Ostry, "A Novel Delay-Bounded Traffic Conditioner for Optical Edge Switches," in *Proc. IEEE High Performance Switching and Routing*, Hong Kong, May 2005.

[31] M. H. Overmars and J. van Leeuwan, "Maintenance of Configuration in the Plane," *Journal of Computer and System Sciences*, 1981.

[32] V. Sivaraman and H. Elgindy and D. Moreland and D. Ostry, "Packet Pacing in Short Buffer Optical Packet Switched Networks," in *Proc. IEEE INFOCOM*, Spain, 2006.

[33] ——, "Packet Pacing in Small Buffer Optical Packet Switched Networks," *IEEE/ACM Transactions on Networking*, vol. 17, no. 4, pp. 1066–1079, Aug 2009.

[34] J. D. LeGrange et al., "Demonstration of an Integrated Buffer for an All-Optical Packet Router," *IEEE Photonic Technology Letters*, vol. 21, no. 2, pp. 781–783, Jun 2009.

[35] A. Odlyzko, "Data Networks are Mostly Empty and for Good Reason," *IT Pro*, vol. 1, no. 2, pp. 67–69, Mar/Apr 1999.

[36] N. Dukkipati and N. McKeown, "Why Flow-Completion Time is the Right Metric for Congestion Control," *ACM SIGCOMM Computer Communication Review*, vol. 36, no. 1, pp. 59–62, Jan 2006.

[37] S. K. Korotky, "Network global expectation model: A Statistical Formalism for Quickly Quantifying Network Needs and Costs," *IEEE/OSA Journal of Lightwave Technology*, vol. 22, no. 3, pp. 703–722, Mar 2004.

[38] M. Mathis and J. Semke and J. Madhavi and T. Ott, "The Macroscopic Behavior of the TCP Congestion Avoidance Algorithm," *ACM SIGCOMM Computer Communication Review*, vol. 27, no. 3, pp. 67–82, Jul 1997.

[39] R. Jain and D. Chiu and W. Hawe, "A Quantitative Measure of Fairness and Discrimination for Resource Allocation in Shared Computer System," *DEC Technical Report*, 1984.

In: Computer Science Research and the Internet   ISBN 978-1-61728-730-5
Editor: Jaclyn E. Morris, pp. 287-300   © 2011 Nova Science Publishers, Inc.

Chapter 13

A DISTRIBUTED AUGMENTED REALITY SYSTEM USING 3D FIDUCIAL OBJECTS

Qishi Wu, Yi Gu† and Brad Montgomery ‡*
Department of Computer Science University of Memphis
Memphis, TN 38152

Abstract

Augmented reality (AR) often makes use of a 2D fiducial marker to render computer graphics onto a video frame so that the computer-generated object appears aligned with the scene. We extend this idea to 3D where real-world objects are used as fiducial markers and propose a distributed AR system that utilizes geographically located resources to meet high computing demand, enable sustained remote operations, and support collaborative efforts. Within the distributed AR system, we present technical solutions to several key modules in AR that form a linear computing pipeline. We generalize and formulate the pipeline network mapping as optimization problems under different mapping constraints and develop heuristic algorithms that maximize the frame rate to achieve smooth data flow. Extensive simulation-based results show that the proposed mapping heuristics outperform the existing methods.

Keywords: Augmented reality, 3D fiducial, object detection, frame rate

1.   Introduction

Augmented Reality (AR) uses live video imagery that is digitally processed and "augmented" by the addition of computer-generated graphics. Although it is a relatively new paradigm in Human-Computer Interaction, AR has found successful applications in many fields as diverse as entertainment, education, medical diagnostics or surgery, military and emergency services, and scientific collaboration of distributed teams.

Many conventional AR systems make use of a 2D fiducial consisting of a black-and-white marker on a flat surface. In these systems, computer vision techniques are used to

---

*E-mail address: qishiwu@memphis.edu

†E-mail address: yigu@memphis.edu

‡E-mail address: Brad.Montgomery@memphis.edu

identify the marker and its position in the scene. Once identified, the marker's position and orientation are then used to calculate the pose of a virtual 3D object with which the marker is associated, and as such, the virtual object can be drawn on top of the video frame relative to the position of the marker. Such systems often perform this set of operations for each frame in a video stream before displaying it, thus giving the illusion that the virtual object is "attached" to the marker. While popular with many AR researchers, the use of 2D fiducial has the following drawbacks.

- Impractical for hand-held virtual objects: In many AR applications, fiducial markers are often affixed to a flat surface such as a wall. However, it is conceivable that there could be a wide variety of cases in which the virtual objects in an AR application are hand-held by the user. For instance, many of the demo applications built using ARToolKit [3] include a 3D virtual object which a user may choose to inspect. However, when attempting to view the "back" of the virtual object (the side "facing" the fiducial marker), the object disappears. This is due to the fact that the 3D object is affixed to a 2D plane. Many of the sample applications using ARTag [17] attempt to overcome this problem by using multiple 2D markers affixed tangentially to a 3D object. However, this technique could be viewed as a crux for which the credibility of immersive AR applications begins to falter. In essence, the 2D marker offers a non-intuitive and peculiar interface for hand-held or worn virtual objects.

- Vulnerable to occlusion: While many alternative techniques for identifying 2D fiducial markers have been proposed, they all exhibit less-than-ideal performance under occlusion. This is primarily the case when the entire outline, or the entire border of the marker must be visible to the camera in order to differentiate the marker from the rest of the scene. In order to overcome this, we must be able to identify an object without "seeing" a connected contour of the entire object.

- Unnatural addition to the scene: 2D fiducial markers are an unnatural addition to real-world scenes. By "unnatural", we mean that a typical 2D fiducial marker is not something that the majority of people see in their day-to-day environment. Additionally, the placement of markers in the world may be a time-consuming activity, and for some applications these markers may lead to a less-believable experience.

To overcome the above limitations of 2D fiducial, we propose to use 3D fiducial where real-world objects are conceived as fiducial markers and develop a distributed AR system using such 3D fiducial objects based on the following considerations: (i) The data volumes and computing demands are significantly increased for larger graphics or objects with more complex structures, which might go far beyond the capabilities of traditional computing solutions based on standalone PCs. (ii) The data source (live video imagery), computer-generated graphics, and end user may reside at different sites. Particularly, in recent years, a wide variety of system resources including supercomputers, data repositories, computing facilities, network infrastructures, storage systems and display devices have been rapidly developed and deployed around the globe. Such resources are typically shared over the Internet or dedicated connections, and must be properly scheduled and utilized based on their location, availability, capacity, and capability. (iii) Various AR operations such as video extraction, feature detection, descriptor matching, pose estimation, image rendering, and final frame display must be done remotely to support collaboration efforts of geographically distributed teams. Within the proposed distributed AR system, we present technical solutions to key modules in AR that form a linear computing pipeline. We generalize and formulate the pipeline network mapping as optimization problems under different mapping constraints and develop heuristic algorithms that maximize the frame rate to achieve smooth data flow. We conduct extensive simulations to illustrate the efficacy of the proposed mapping heuristics.

The rest of the paper is organized as follows. We provide a summary of related work in Section 2.. In Section 3., we construct a distributed framework of the AR system and analytical cost models for computing modules and communication links, based on which, we formulate the AR network mapping as a set of optimization problems and propose heuristic algorithms to maximize the frame rate. In Section 4., we present the technical solutions to various computing components in the proposed AR system. The simulation and performance evaluations for the network mapping heuristics are presented in Section 5.. We conclude our work and discuss future research directions in Section 6..

2.   Related Work

Many AR applications are categorized as being either marker-based or markerless. Marker-based applications use some sort of fiducial marker to estimate the pose of the camera. A great deal of research efforts have been devoted to constructing hand-held or movable virtual objects based on 2D fiducial markers. Popular software packages for developing AR applications using marker-based techniques include ARToolkit [3] and ARTag [1], whose technical details are given in [21] and [17], respectively.

Not all AR applications make use of fiducial markers. There are numerous publications in which features (such as parallel lines) are detected in the scene and are used to compute the location and scale of a virtual object. However, many of these features are located on static, or unmoving objects such as walls or statues. These types of applications are not applicable to a system where a user would interact with a hand-held virtual object. As such, many of those techniques focus on an area of AR which is beyond the scope of this paper.

There also exists much work exploring vision-based techniques for markerless AR applications. In [25], Simon *et al.* detect planar structures in the scene with which virtual objects are aligned. In [7], Bradley *et al.* describe a way to control the view into 3D applications by manipulating a sphere. Shahrokni *et al.* propose a method where objects can be detected, tracked, and from which pose can be estimated based on facet detection [23]. In [14], Comport *et al.* propose a real-time visual tracking system for markerless applications based on virtual visual servoing; while in [15], a comparison and analysis of two techniques based on non-linear optimizations is provided. In [20], Jiang *et al.* present a hybrid method that uses fiducial markers as well as natural features from the scene. Camera pose has also long been studied in the fields of computer vision and pattern analysis with significant contributions in [22] and [16].

The mapping and scheduling problems have been extensively studied by many researchers in various disciplines [4, 11, 18, 24, 12] and continue to be the focus of attention of the distributed computing community due to their theoretical significance and practical importance, especially as the grid computing technology prevails [9, 8, 10]. In [6], Benoit *et al.* discussed the mapping of computing pipelines onto different types of networks with identical processors and links (fully homogeneous platform), with identical links but different processors (communication homogeneous platform), or with different processors and links (fully heterogeneous platform). They also showed that three versions of the mapping problems, i.e. one-to-one, interval, and general mappings, are NP-complete in fully heterogenous platforms. A grid scheduling algorithm, called *Streamline* [2], is developed for placing a coarse-grain dataflow graph on available grid resources. This scheduling heuristic is specifically designed to improve the performance of streaming applications with various demands in grid environments. Chen *et al.* proposed and evaluated a runtime algorithm for supporting adaptive execution of distributed data mining on streaming data [13].

Our work is mainly focused on the development of a distributed AR system that uses real-world objects as fiducial markers for virtual object generation. The key component modules in such an AR system are strategically distributed in heterogeneous network environments to support sustained remote operations in collaborative AR applications.

3. A Distributed AR System

3.1. System Framework

We are faced with a growing challenge to support increasingly complex AR systems over wide-area networks with heterogeneous computing nodes and communication links for collaboration of distributed teams. As shown in Fig. 1, an AR system using 3D fiducial objects typically contains a number of computing modules (subtasks or stages) that form a linear computing pipeline.

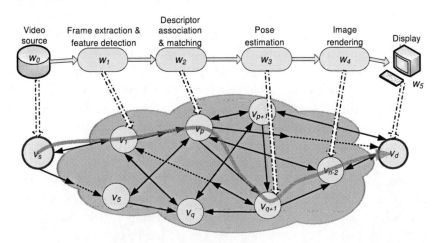

Figure 1. A distributed framework of AR system using 3D fiducial objects.

The AR computing pipeline usually starts with a module that acquires a video stream as data source. For each frame extracted from the video, the system runs certain algorithms to detect a set of feature points for an object of interest. These feature points define a descriptor or signature for the object under study. In other words, a descriptor is always associated with a particular object. Such a descriptor is then matched against a large number of object templates stored and managed in a descriptor library, which is typically generated off-line in a similar way. Based on the orientation of a successfully matched real-world 3D object, we are able to estimate the camera's pose and then generate the virtual objects or artificial graphics based on the camera's pose information. The virtual objects are rendered and composited with the original video frame to form a final frame, which is sent to the remote client for display. These key modules in AR may be executed on different computing nodes located at different places. However, the performance of the distributed AR system critically depends on how these modules are mapped to the computing nodes in a real network.

3.2. Mathematical Models and Objective Function

We construct cost models for pipeline and network components to facilitate mathematical formulations of mapping objective functions. The computational complexity of a computing module w_i is denoted as a function $f_{w_i}(\cdot)$ of the incoming data size $z_{i-1,i}$ sent from its preceding module w_{i-1}, which determines the number of instructions needed to complete the subtask defined in the module. Note that the actual execution time of a computing module also depends on the availability and capacity of the system resources on the selected network node. The processing capability of a network node is a complex notion that combines a variety of host factors such as processor frequency, bus speed, memory size, storage performance, and presence of co-processors. For simplicity, we use a normalized quantity p_i to represent the overall computing power of a network node v_i without specifying its detailed system resources. The communication link $e_{i,j}$ between two neighbor nodes v_i and v_j is characterized by bandwidth (BW) $b_{i,j}$ and minimum link delay (MLD) $d_{i,j}$. We estimate the computing time of module w_i running on network node v_j as $T_{\text{comp}}(w_i, v_j) = \frac{f_{w_i}(z_{i-1,i})}{p_j}$ and the transfer time of message size z over communication link $e_{i,j}$ as $T_{\text{tran}}(z, e_{i,j}) = \frac{z}{b_{i,j}} + d_{i,j}$.

We consider a pipeline that consists of m sequential modules, $w_0, w_1, \ldots, w_{m-1}$, and a network that is represented as a graph $G = (V, E), |V| = n$, where V denotes the set of network nodes and E denotes the set of communication links. The contiguous modules mapped onto the same node can be considered as a group once we have a mapping scheme. A general mapping scheme divides the pipeline into q groups of modules denoted by $g_0, g_1, \ldots, g_{q-1}$ $(1 \le q \le m)$, and maps them onto a selected path P of not necessarily distinct q nodes (depending on mapping constraints), $v_{P[0]} = v_s, v_{P[1]}, \ldots, v_{P[q-1]} = v_d$, between a given pair of source node v_s to destination node v_d in the computer network. We assume that the first module w_0 only transfers data from the source node v_s and the last module w_{m-1} only performs computation on the destination node v_d.

We wish to maximize the frame rate of the pipeline to produce the smoothest data flow for AR applications where video frames are continuously generated and fed into the system. This goal is achieved by identifying and minimizing the time incurred on a bottleneck (BN) link or node, which is defined as:

$$
\begin{aligned}
&T_{\mathrm{BN}}(\text{Path } P \text{ of } q \text{ nodes}) \\
&= \max_{\substack{\text{Path } P \text{ of } q \text{ nodes} \\ i=0,1,\ldots,q-2}}
\begin{pmatrix}
T_{\mathrm{comp}}(g_i), \\
T_{\mathrm{tran}}(e_{P[i],P[i+1]}), \\
T_{\mathrm{comp}}(g_{q-1}), \\
\frac{\alpha_{P[i]}}{p_{P[i]}} \max_{j \in g_i, j \geq 1} (f_{w_j}(z_{j-1,j})), \\
\frac{\beta_{P[i],P[i+1]} \cdot z(g_i)}{b_{P[i],P[i+1]}} + d_{P[i],P[i+1]}, \\
\frac{\alpha_{P[q-1]}}{p_{P[q-1]}} \max_{j \in g_{q-1}, j \geq 1} (f_{w_j}(z_{j-1,j})),
\end{pmatrix} \\
&= \max_{\substack{\text{Path } P \text{ of } q \text{ nodes} \\ i=0,1,\ldots,q-2}}
\end{aligned}
\tag{1}
$$

where $\alpha_{P[i]}$ is the number of modules assigned to node $v_{P[i]}$, and $\beta_{P[i],P[i+1]}$ is the number of datasets transferred over link $e_{P[i],P[i+1]}$ between nodes $v_{P[i]}$ and $v_{P[i+1]}$. We assume equal share of node computing power and link BW among concurrent module executions and data transfers, respectively.

3.3. Dynamic Programming-based Mapping Solution

We formulate the AR pipeline network mapping for Maximum Frame Rate (MFR) in distributed environments as optimization problems, which have been proved NP-complete [19]. We propose heuristic algorithms based on dynamic programming (DP) to solve these problems. We use $1/T_{\mathrm{BN}}^{j-1}(v_i)$ to denote the MFR with the first j modules mapped to a path from source node v_s to node v_i in a computer network, and the following recursion leads to the final solution $T_{\mathrm{BN}}^{m-1}(v_d)$:

$$
T_{\mathrm{BN}}^{j-1}(v_i) \underset{j=2 \text{ to } m, v_i \in V}{=} \min
\left(
\begin{array}{l}
\max \left(
\begin{array}{l}
T_{\mathrm{BN}}^{j-2}(v_i), \\
\frac{\alpha_i f_{w_{j-1}}(z_{j-2,j-1})}{p_i}
\end{array}
\right), \\
\min_{v_u \in adj(v_i)} \left(
\max \left(
\begin{array}{l}
T_{\mathrm{BN}}^{j-2}(v_u), \\
\frac{\alpha_i f_{w_{j-1}}(z_{j-2,j-1})}{p_i}, \\
\frac{\beta_{u,i} z_{j-2,j-1}}{b_{u,i}} + d_{u,i}
\end{array}
\right)
\right)
\end{array}
\right)
\tag{2}
$$

with the base condition computed as:

$$
T_{\mathrm{BN}}^{1}(v_i) \underset{v_i \in V, \text{ and } v_i \neq v_s}{=}
\begin{cases}
\max\left(\frac{f_{w_1}(z_{0,1})}{p_i}, \frac{z_{0,1}}{b_{s,i}} + d_{s,i}\right), & \forall e_{s,i} \in E \\
+\infty, & \text{otherwise}
\end{cases}
\tag{3}
$$

In the above recursive procedure, we consider three different types of mapping constraints: (i) no node reuse, i.e. a node on the selected path P executes exactly one module; (ii) contiguous node reuse, i.e. two or more contiguous modules in the pipeline are allowed to run on the same node; and (iii) arbitrary node reuse, i.e. two or more modules, either contiguous or non-contiguous in the pipeline, are allowed to run on the same node. Note that node reuse will cause resources sharing by a successor module allocated to a used node and affect the optimality of module mapping carried out in the previous steps. Hence, in no node reuse we have $\alpha = 1$ and $\beta = 1$.

4. Technical Solutions to AR Computing Modules Using 3D Fiducial Objects

In order to address some of the limitations in using 2D fiducial markers, we aim to identify fundamental techniques to use real-world objects as a replacement for 2D markers. For simplicity, we implemented a prototype application using a toy block with which we associate a virtual cube. To integrate 3D fiducial objects in our system, we need to address the following three main problems that are directly related to AR operations: fiducial designation, fiducial identification, and pose estimation. We will present our technical solutions to these problems as follows.

4.1. Fiducial Designation

A fundamental challenge to this work involves the association of real-world objects with a 3D model to be used as a virtual overlay. We call this the problem of *Fiducial Designation*, which deals with the detection and storage of features corresponding solely to the object (or objects) used as a fiducial. Not only must these features be easily reproducible, but there must also be some technique for which these features can be computed, saved, and used to identify the object in arbitrary images.

Since the foundation of this problem lies in the realm of object detection, we chose to build upon the work of Bay *et al.* using SURF[5]. SURF, an acronym for Speeded Up Robust Features, describes a feature point detector and a feature point descriptor that can be used to match objects in arbitrary images. SURF's notable features include the use of integral images in order to speed up calculations, a feature detector based on the determinant of the Hessian matrix, and a scale and rotation-invariant descriptor. Additionally, SURF gains speed over other schemes through the use of approximations, such as the use of box filters to approximate the Laplacian of Gaussian and scaled filters rather than re-sampled images to analyze scale space. Interestingly, these approximations do not cause a reduction in robustness or accuracy, and, as such, SURF lends itself to possible use in real-time applications.

Using points and their corresponding descriptors (as given by SURF), we can build a library containing the "best" descriptors associated with an object. In addition to the information provided by the feature point detection and description algorithm, this *Descriptor Library* also contains manually assigned values which link each point descriptor to a particular face of the cube. In general, the Descriptor Library can be computed through the following steps:

- Capture video for the object that is to be used as a fiducial, and extract the frames from this video. This should be done in a "clean" environment so that the only feature points that are detected in each frame correspond to the object.[1] Additionally, all sides of the object should be included in the video.[2]

---

[1] We used a simple off-the-shelf USB webcam to capture video of an object sitting on a white sheet of paper, with another white sheet of paper taped to the wall as a background.

[2] If it is not possible to fill the entire object in one shot, the object can be repositioned and refilmed in multiple shots.

- Once all frames have been extracted from the video, calculate feature points and descriptors for each frame.

- Match features across adjacent frames, keeping descriptors for features that match and discarding descriptors for features that do not.[3]

4.2. Fiducial Identification

The next step in our process involves the identification of feature points corresponding to the object which we are using as an AR fiducial. The success of this step relies on the ability to uniquely and consistently identify the object in an arbitrary scene. To accomplish this, we again use the feature point detection and description algorithm used in the *Fiducial Designation* step.

Given a frame captured from some video input, we calculate all feature points and descriptors for that frame. Once these feature points have been identified, their corresponding descriptors can be matched to those in our Descriptor Library. The result of this step produces a set of pixel coordinates in the input image frame that correspond to points on the fiducial object. Additionally, we have the face of the cube to which each point belongs. While the accuracy of SURF compares well to similar feature detectors [5], it may produce false positives.

In order to contend with the possibility of falsely identified points, we attempt to find a weighted center of all feature points that lie on the same face of the cube. We create a vector, $\vec{v}$ from the image frame origin[4] to each feature point that belongs to a particular face on the cube. We then find the mean horizontal and vertical components for each of these vectors, from which we create a new vector whose base is at the origin. The endpoint of this resulting vector is then used as the center for a face. For n vectors $\vec{v} = \langle p_i, p_j \rangle$, where p_i is a horizontal distance from the origin and p_j is a vertical distance from the origin, the center is given by the vector $\vec{z} = \langle \bar{x}, \bar{y} \rangle$, where:

$$\bar{x} = \frac{1}{n} \sum_{k=1}^{n} p_{ik}, \tag{4}$$

$$\bar{y} = \frac{1}{n} \sum_{k=1}^{n} p_{jk}. \tag{5}$$

This process is continued for each face from which points were detected.

4.3. Pose Estimation

Once we have identified the center for each visible face, we can use the same technique to find the center of all visible faces. This will be the point to which we translate the origin of our virtual cube.

---

[3]We have found experimentally that descriptors matching across three adjacent frames provide a "good" descriptor of that object, and subsequently reduce the size of the library of descriptors

[4]The origin of an image is typically positioned at the top left corner.

Since we know *a priori* that we are drawing a cube, and we also know the visible faces of the cube, we can determine how to rotate a unit cube so that one of the visible faces of the cube are pointed toward the user. For example, in Fig. 2, we would rotate the cube 90° about the x-axis in order for the top of the cube to face out of the screen.

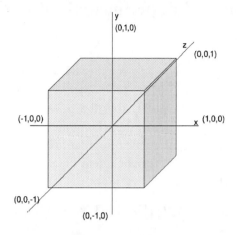

Figure 2. A unit cube.

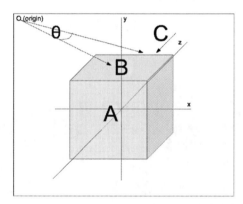

Figure 3. Rotation of a cube based on visible faces.

Once we have one face of the virtual cube directed outward from the screen, we can calculate the angles between the vectors from the image origin to the center of the visible faces. This should be done for all visible faces, and the resulting angle can be used to rotate the cube around the axis for which the two faces do not intersect.

We can find the angle, θ, between two vectors $\vec{a}$ and $\vec{b}$ as follows:

$$\theta = \cos^{-1} \frac{\vec{a} \cdot \vec{b}}{\|\vec{a}\|\|\vec{b}\|}. \tag{6}$$

For example, in Fig. 3, face A is orthogonal to face B, so the cube can be rotated 90° about the x-axis in order to position face B so that its normal would be directed outward from the computer screen. Additionally, if vectors to the center of face B and face C result in an angle of θ, the cube would be rotated an additional $\theta°$ about the x-axis so that both face B and face C would be visible to the user.

5.   Implementation and Experimental Results

5.1.   3D Fiducial Objects

In our prototype AR system, we used a number of sample clips containing various 3D objects to build the descriptor library. One such object is displayed in Fig. 4, where white points indicate the detected feature points, but the lines indicated the points that match across all three frames. The feature vector describing these points are kept as a template in the library for later matching. A real application that uses this object as a fiducial marker is illustrated: a test image in Fig. 5(a) is matched to the descriptor library and the matched points are labeled in Fig. 5(b).

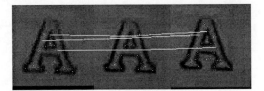

Figure 4. A 3D fiducial object.

(a)   (b)

Figure 5. (a) a test image, (b) a matched test image.

5.2.   Evaluation of Mapping Heuristics

The proposed mapping heuristics are implemented in C++ and run on a Windows XP desktop equipped with a 3.0 GHz CPU and 2 Gbytes memory. For comparison purposes, the *Streamline* [2] algorithm adapted to linearly pipelined workflow and a *Greedy* algorithm are also implemented and tested with the same simulation datasets on the same computing platform. We generate these simulation datasets by randomly varying the following pipeline and network attributes within a suitably selected range of values: (i) the number of modules and complexity and input and output data sizes of each module; (ii) the number of nodes and processing power of each node; (iii) the number of links and link bandwidth and minimum link delay of each link. The extensive simulation results illustrate the efficacy of our algorithms based on the performance comparisons with Streamline and Greedy algorithms.

For a visual performance comparison, we plot the performance measurements of MFR under different constraints in Fig. 8, Fig. 7 and Fig. 6, respectively. We observed that our algorithm DP exhibits comparable or superior performances in maximizing frame rate over the other two algorithms in all the cases we studied. We did not compare with Streamline in the case of contiguous node reuse because Streamline does not allocate the resources by the stages' (modules') sequence number so we may not know the previous node when the current one is being allocated. The MFR, the reciprocal of the bottleneck in a selected path, is not particularly related to the path length, and hence the performance curves in Fig. 8, Fig. 7 and Fig. 6 lack an obvious increasing or decreasing trend in response to varying problem sizes.

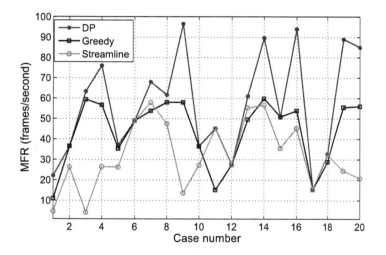

Figure 6. Performance comparison of MFR with arbitrary node reuse among DP, Greedy and Streamline.

6. Conclusion

We identified a basic set of steps that can lead toward the use of a 3D fiducial for augmented reality. We extended the AR system to distributed environments by mapping these steps onto selected computing nodes and optimizing the mapping to achieve maximal frame rate for the smoothest dataflow.

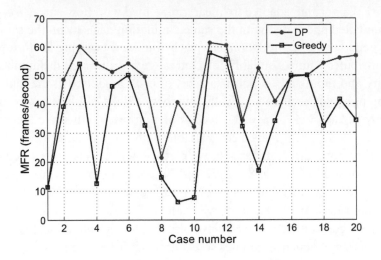

Figure 7. Performance comparison of MFR with contiguous node reuse between DP and Greedy.

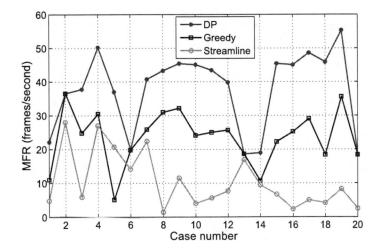

Figure 8. Performance comparison of MFR with no node reuse among DP, Greedy and Streamline.

It is our future interest to investigate methods to produce a more definitive *Descriptor Library* so that the object can be recognized in the image with fewer falsely identified points. Additionally, we would like to provide a quantitative analysis for the number of points necessary for accurate detection and pose estimation for the fiducial. Along this line, we also plan to construct accurate cost models for various AR computing modules to estimate their runtime performance. Lastly, we would like to identify techniques where the fiducial designation process could be automated, optionally giving feedback regarding the possible accuracy of detecting the chosen object.

References

[1] http://www.artag.net/.

[2] B. Agarwalla, N. Ahmed, D. Hilley, and U. Ramachandran. Streamline: a scheduling heuristic for streaming application on the grid. In *Proc. of the 13th Multimedia Comp. and Net. Conf.*, San Jose, CA, 2006.

[3] ARToolKit. http://www.hitl.washington.edu/artoolkit/.

[4] A.F. Bashir, V. Susarla, and K. Vairavan. A statistical study of the performance of a task scheduling algorithm. *IEEE Trans. on Computers*, 32(12):774–777, Dec. 1975.

[5] H. Bay, T. Tuytelaars, and L.V. Gool. Surf: Speeded up robust features. In *Proc. of the 9th European Conference on Computer Vision*, 2006.

[6] A. Benoit and Y. Robert. Mapping pipeline skeletons onto heterogeneous platforms. *J. Parallel and Distributed Computing*, 68(6):790–808, 2008.

[7] D. Bradley and G. Roth. Natural interaction with virtual objects using vision-based six dof sphere tracking. In *Proc. of the 2005 ACM SIGCHI Int. Conf. on Advances in computer entertainment technology*, 2005.

[8] R. Buyya. *Economic-based distributed resource management and scheduling for grid computing*. PhD thesis, Monash University, Melbourne, Australia, Apr. 2002.

[9] R. Buyya, D. Abramson, and J. Giddy. Nimrod/G: an architecture for a resource management and scheduling system in a global computational grid. In *Proc. of the 4th Int. Conf./Exhibition on the High Performance Computing in the Asia-Pacific Region*, volume 1, pages 283–289, 2000.

[10] J. Cao, S.A. Jarvis, S. Saini, and G.R. Nudd. GridFlow: workflow management for grid computing. In *Proc. of the 3rd IEEE/ACM Int. Symp. on Cluster Computing and the Grid*, pages 198–205, May 2003.

[11] V. Chaudhary and J.K. Aggarwal. A generalized scheme for mapping parallel algorithms. *IEEE Trans. on Parallel and Distributed Systems*, 4(3):328–346, May 1993.

[12] L. Chen and G. Agrawal. Resource allocation in a middleware for streaming data. In *Proc. of the 2nd Workshop on Middleware for Grid Comp.*, Toronto, Canada, Oct. 2004.

[13] L. Chen and G. Agrawal. Supporting self-adaptation in streaming data mining applications. In *Proc. of IEEE Int. Parallel and Distributed Processing Symp.*, 2006.

[14] A. Comport, E. Marchand, and F. Chaumette. A real-time tracker for markerless augmented reality. In *ACM/IEEE Int. Symp. on Mixed and Augmented Reality, ISMAR'03*, pages 36–45, 2003.

[15] A.I. Comport, D. Kragic, E. Marchand, and F. Chaumette. Robust real-time visual tracking: Comparison, theoretical analysis and performance evaluation. In *Proc. of the 2005 IEEE Int. Conf. on Robotics and Automation*, pages 2841–2846, 2005.

[16] D. DeMenthon and L.S. Davis. Model-based object pose in 25 lines of code. In *European Conference on Computer Vision*, pages 335–343, 1992.

[17] M. Fiala. Artag revision 1. a fiducial marker system using digital techniques. NRC-CNRC, November 2004.

[18] A. Gerasoulis and T. Yang. A comparison of clustering heuristics for scheduling DAGs on multiprocessors. *JPDC*, 16(4):276–291, Dec. 1992.

[19] Y. Gu, Q. Wu, A. Benoit, and Y. Robert. Optimizing end-to-end performance of distributed applications with linear computing pipelines. In *Proc. of the 15th Int. Conf. on Para. and Dist. Sys.*, Shenzhen, China, Dec. 8-11 2009.

[20] B. Jiang, S. You, and U. Neumann. Camera tracking for augmented reality media. In *IEEE Int. Conf. on Multimedia and Expo.*, volume 3, pages 1637–1640, 2000.

[21] H. Kato and M. Billinghurst. Marker tracking and hmd calibration for a video-based augmented reality conferencing system. In *Int. Workshop on Augmented Reality*, 1999.

[22] L. Quan and Z. Lan. Linear n-point camera pose determination. In *IEEE Transactions on Pattern Analysis and Machine Intelligence*, 1999.

[23] A. Shahrokni, L. Vacchetti, V. Lepetit, and P. Fua. Polyhedral object detection and pose estimation for augmented reality applications. In *Proc. of Computer Animation*, 2002.

[24] B. Shirazi, M. Wang, and G. Pathak. Analysis and evaluation of heuristic methods for static scheduling. *J. of Parallel and Distributed Computing*, (10):222–232, 1990.

[25] G. Simon, A. Fitzgibbon, and A. Zisserman. Markerless tracking using planar structures in the scene. In *Proc. of ISAR*, 2000.

In: Computer Science Research and the Internet
Editor: Jaclyn E. Morris, pp. 301-339

ISBN 978-1-61728-730-5
© 2011 Nova Science Publishers, Inc.

Chapter 14

HYBRID SWITCHING TECHNIQUES FOR HETEROGENEOUS TRAFFIC SUPPORT IN MULTI-PROCESSORS SYSTEM ON CHIP AND MASSIVELY PARALLEL PROCESSORS

Francesca Palumbo, Danilo Pani and Luigi Raffo *
DIEE - Dept. of Electrical and Electronic Engineering
University of Cagliari, 09123 Cagliari - Italy

Abstract

Multi-Processors System on Chip (MPSoCs) and Massively Parallel Processors (MPPs) architectures are conceived to efficiently implement Thread Level Parallelism, a common characteristic of modern software applications targeted by embedded systems. Each core in a MPP environment is designed to execute a particular instructions flow, known as thread, in a completely self-sufficient manner, being able to communicate with the other cores in order to exchange shared data. The demand of parallelism in MPPs and MPSoCs entails the design of an efficient communication layer able to sustain it. This means that the interconnection medium has to be both scalable, to allow multiple accesses of the different cores to the shared resources, and optimized in terms of wiring. These are all native characteristics of Networks on Chip (NoCs).

In MPSoCs and MPPs, it is necessary to provide:

- a quick resolution of the interdependencies among different threads, single scalar data or even vectors. Interdependencies are responsible of completion time delay because it prevents a thread from completion when not resolved;

- load balancing support techniques to avoid hot spots and to efficiently exploit all the cores available on chip. When threads migration occurs, a regular and continuous traffic is generated, made up of long streams of data;

- management of end-to-end small control data.

Circuit Switching (CS) technique is the method by which a dedicated path, or circuit, is established prior the sending of the sensitive data. Circuit switched networks are

---

*E-mail address: francesca.palumbo@diee.unica.it, danilo.pani@diee.unica.it, luigi@diee.unica.it

suitable for guaranteed throughput applications, especially in case of real time communications. In Packet Switching (PS) methodologies the intermediate routers are responsible for routing the individual packets through the network, neither following a predefined nor a reserved path. Packet switched networks are suitable for best-effort services or for soft-timing constrained communications.

In this chapter, we will look at the possibility of combining CS and PS in order to support the heterogeneous traffic patterns coexisting in a MPP environment. Hybrid switching networks are designed to guarantee the benefits of both CS and PS consisting in a better usage of the available bandwidth and in a global increase of the overall throughput, at the price of a more complex hardware implementation. In this scope, the latest approaches in literature are presented, together with a particular NoC model able to provide dual-mode hybrid switching in a non-exclusive way, intended as the possibility of co-sharing the amount of available bandwidth between CS and PS communications.

Keywords: Hybrid Switching, Packet Switching, Circuit Switching, Heterogeneous Traffic, NoC, MPSoC, MPP.

1.   Introduction

Electronic systems are all around us in everyday environments: people are surrounded by digital devices and embedded systems. The number and varieties of these devices is amazing, and all the more so for the applications requiring them (see Figure 1), from transportation (small embedded systems aiming at aiding an controlling) to medical devices (from digital hearing aids to complex diagnostics supplies), from military applications (e.g., radar and smart targeting systems) to home and consumer electronics (e.g., domotic systems, mobile phones, and entertainment devices).

This trend has been guided by the continuous improvements in VLSI technologies but it had also an impact on the computational power requirements, which started to represent a limit for traditional hardware platforms. Therefore in the last decade, new attitudes in the conception and design of processors took place. It is possible to embed more and more complex functionalities on the same device and, at the same time, to design smaller and more compact devices with the same functionalities. Together with the scaling in size, which according to the well known Moore's Law brought to a doubling of available processing resources on a single chip every second year; frequency has improved as well, allowing higher computational rates. Nevertheless, this seems to be not enough to cope with the market requirements: applications are not only computational hungry but also characterized by unpredictable workload fluctuations, so that hardware has to provide an adequate computational support and a good level of flexibility. The scientific and industrial community, in spite of the privilege of scaling the operating frequency to achieve better systems performance, also explored the possibility of exploiting different kinds of parallelism at architectural level to address this issue.

These two approaches, i.e., exploiting parallelism and improving the single core performance, eventhough these may not sound correlated, they are surely not in contrast; rather they can be considered as complementary. Obviously, as anybody knows there is no free lunch, therefore an important drawback has to be faced: the management of this growing

Figure 1. Typical application fields of digital devices.

complexity has become a critical issue. In this field complexity can be intended as:

- increased design complexity, due to the growing number of different functional units to be integrated, in order to handle:

  1. the design of the cores, either homogeneous or heterogeneous,

  2. the resource mapping,

  3. the choice of programmability model

- increased complexity of communication infrastructures to be implemented, in order to support:

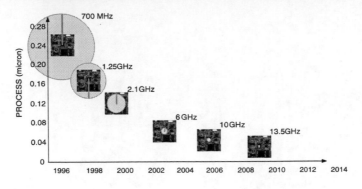

Figure 2. Evolution of the reachable range of a wire in one clock cycle [10].

1. heterogeneous traffic characteristics and/or heterogeneous protocols,

2. massive data sets,

3. data integrity in the field of deep submicron technology

- increased complexity of the simulation strategies, to find a compromise between time to market and accuracy.

A very promising approach dealing with the complexity of the design is to try to exploit as much as possible the concept of design for re-use, migrating towards architectures such as the tile-based ones. These architectures are composed of several, periodically replicated in space, identical elements, called *tiles*, which typically form a regular grid. Tile-based architectures with a large number of processing elements are often called Massively Parallel Processors (MPPs). It is not strictly necessary for the tiles to be homogeneous, but it is very common to keep the heterogeneity level very low, in order to benefit as much as possible from re-usability and to ensure an adequate orthogonality. Examples of this trend are: the RAW processor [1], the AmBric processor [2, 3, 4], the picoArray by picoChip [5], the Teraflops Research Chip [6, 7] by Intel and the Tile64 pioneer chip of a family of multi-core processors by Tilera [8, 9]. The large number of cores per die in the prevoiusly mentioned commercial and academic MPP examples exposes a considerably high level of resources parallelism, which represents the basis to withstand the thread level parallelism proper of modern software and adopted both to speed up computation and to achieve multi-tasking.

This new generation of architectures has also different requirements in terms of inter-connection medium. Communication backbone has:

- to allow parallel accesses to the communication medium with an effectively large bandwidth, in order to properly support the large number of integrated cores,

- to be scalable and modular, in order to avoid limiting the intrinsic scalability and regularity of the tile-based architectures,

- to provide communication flexibility and traffic/protocol heterogeneity support, in order to deal with multi-threaded and multi-vendors environments.

Chip communication infrastructures that are better than others are able to sustain all these demands for the Networks on Chip (NoCs). As the International Technology Roadmap for Semiconductors of the Semiconductor Industry Association (SIA) has reported along the years ([11, 12, 13]), one of the drawbacks of frequency scaling along with technology scaling is the impossibility of conceiving long wires able to connect the various elements on chip without affecting synchronization. Figure 2 gives an idea of the reduction that affected the wires range per cycle along the last decades. That is why, at the communication level, solution based on shared mediums or full crossbars turn out to be impractical and the migration towards NoC architectures, as shown in Figure 3, quite straightforward. NoCs are modular, able to connect the cores adopting shorter wires and to provide the appropriate parallel accesses and bandwidth to the cor es of MPP chips. When Systems on Chip (SoCs) were introduced in the 90s, custom designed ad-hoc mixes of buses and point-to-point links [14] were more than enough to satisfy communication requirements. Shared bus communication infrastructures and their evolution, the hierarchical busses, for a long time were leader in the on chip communication field. Nevertheless, as the number of connected cores increased there became a bottleneck due to wiring and power dissipation issues. In such systems, bandwidth does not increase with the number of attached cores whereas, on the contrary, the power dissipation per communication event does. Fully connected crossbars can guarantee as much parallelism as needed, but they are not able to scale with the number of connected cores, as well as dedicated point-to-point infrastructures, and suffer from wiring related issues.

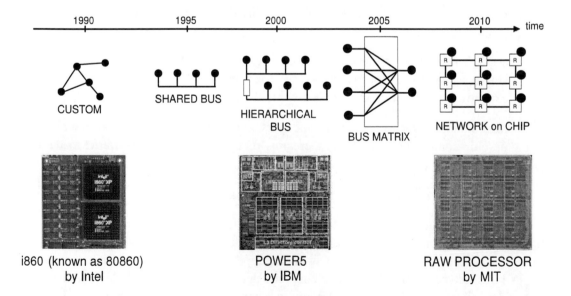

Figure 3. On chip communication evolution.

Even if NoCs are probably the best interconnection backbone for MPP devices, dealing with them has a counterbalance relatively to their higher design complexity compared to other solutions. Several design issues have to be considered and various design trade-offs have to be explored, in order to meet the overall design constraints. NoCs in fact, with respect to shared mediums or full crossbars, expose several more degrees of freedom to the developers such as: topology, switching type, routing strategy, mapping algorithm and so on. Such complex and highly parameterizable systems impose to manage wider design spaces. The explorations to search the best trade-offs in cost-performance will require a considerably large amount of time. In fact, the bigger are hardware designs and the more complex are the implemented functionalities to cope with software requirements, the more the validation of the system is difficult. This should be intended both in terms of deeply exploring the complete design space and in terms of providing a large variety of simulation scenarios in order to detect, as early as possible, any potential bug prior prototyping.

1.1. Chapter Focus

This chapter focuses on one of the aspects related to communication complexity in NoC design: the heterogeneity support for multi-threaded applications in MPPs. Each core in a MPP is assigned to a particular segment of code, known as *thread*, in a completely self-sufficient manner. At the same time, since threads could not be independent from each others, communication backbone has to provide them an efficient way to exchange shared data. Therefore NoCs, due to their native characteristics, have emerged to the academic and industrial scenario as a possible solution to efficiently support communications in these scenarios. Nevertheless, a unique optimal choice does not exist and normally, depending on the reference architecture and its requirements, different types of NoC can be adopted. Some studies demonstrated that having classical packed switched NoC implementations, depending on the considered workloads, can be inefficient [15].

In order to tackle multi-threaded applications in MPP environments, the communication backbone has to cope with:

- a quick resolution of the interdependencies among different threads, ranging from single scalar data to long vectors, which are responsible for their suspension from execution and therefore can delay completion time;

- load balancing support, to avoid hot spots and to efficiently exploit all the available on-chip computational resources, creating regular and continuous traffic, made up of long streams of data;

- end-to-end small control data exchanged among the tiles.

All of these communication applications are summarized in Table 1. This table, besides the list of all the communication transactions that can take place, offers also a classification of these transactions in terms of the best switching type.

All of these considerations lead to conclude that, in such multi-threaded and heterogeneous scenarios, it would be very effective to support the communication not adopting a unique switching technique, but allowing to serve each different transaction type with the appropriate one. The key idea behind the approach we have developed [16] (presented in paragraph 3.) to manage hybrid switching is to allow packets and circuits to flow in parallel, in a way that we define *non-exclusive*.

To make a step further towards the integration of a complete MPP on a single chip, another investigation is proposed in this chapter. NoCs performance is usually explored stand-alone, overlooking the impact of the higher communication levels in the ISO OSI

Table 1. MPPAs Typical Heterogeneous Traffic Patterns.

Traffic Type	Data Type	Switching
Thread Interdependencies	Scalar Data	Packet
	Short Vectors (length $< T$)	Packet
	Long Vectors (length $> T$)	Circuit
High Level Control Packets	Scalar Data	Packet
Tasks Migration	Long Vectors (length $> T$)	Circuit

micronetwork stack representation of the communication flow. Nevertheless, since CPUs have to be relieved of communication management, higher communication levels such as DMA engines necessarily influence communication. This chapter discusses the bias on hybrid switching communication infrastructure these higher levels can have by exploring the impact of two different DMA implementations, full-duplex and half-duplex, on the NoC that is going to be proposed.

The remainder of this chapter is organized as follow.

Paragraph 2. gives an overview of the state of the art of NoC architectures, providing a little bit of history, generalities and issues regarding the interconnection networks design.

Paragraph 3. goes into the details of a particular hybrid switching NoC model, which challenges this issue differently from other state of the art solutions. This NoC [16] approaches hybrid switching in a non-exclusive way meaning that, at the price of having a slightly more complex router design, allows the flowing of packets and circuits in parallel.

Paragraph 4., through the integration of two different DMA models with the hybrid switching NoC presented in paragraph 3., discusses the bias of the higher communication levels on NoC performance.

Finally, prior to conclude (paragraph 6.), paragraph 5. demonstrates adopting a top-down approach that some effort should also be put in the definition of the higher level communication modules functionality in the system, beyond the optimization and tuning effort at the NoC level. Then, once chosen a full-duplex approach at this level, the effectiveness of the non-exclusive approach is presented, by highlighting its benefits with respect to an *exclusive* hybrid switching NoC through a series of common NoC metrics (latency, average queuing time, injection delay and so on).

2. State of the Art and Generalities of Network on Chip Architectures

The possibility of developing quite complex architectures, such as Multi-Processors System on Chip (MPSoCs) and Massively Parallel Processors (MPPs), allows to deal with today's applications that, as already said, require massively parallel processing and interdependent executions support, together with more stringent real-time constraints. These demands impact on the characteristics that the underlying communication infrastructure has to provide.

From an historical perspective, design costs were mainly related to computation rather than communication, but technology scaling [12, 13, ?] has altered this trend. Several new physical and functional limitations impact on communication backbone development and scientific literature has reported as a real cost gap between communication and computation the fact that wires do not scale as well as transistors do [12, 13, ?].

Here is a short list of communication design issues, well addressed by NoC, as stated earlier, represent an interesting choice for the communication infrastructure of MPSpCs and MPPs..

- *Wire Delay*. Technology scaling has different impacts on wire resistance and capacitance [11]: the wire resistance per-mm is increasing whereas the wire capacitance does not change much. Therefore wire delays are now comparable to gate delays and, as the computational performance gows (local processing cycle time improvements), global wire lengths get worse becoming a performance limiter. Breaking long wires with registers to address this issue allows to keep high frequencies at the expenses of an increased latency, also adding synchronization problems. Obviously this has been taken into account by interconnection developers by avoiding long communication wires [18] and preferring to route packets instead of wires, as the NoCs do.

- *Signal Integrity*. As technologies proceed in the modern deep submicron (DSM) era, signals are more and more affected by integrity problems and consequently reliability issues arise. Below 90 nm, manufacturing defects start to affect yield. Yield loss is no longer dominated by random defects since printability problems and systematic defects give their significant contribution (source: IBS Report). Long wires exacerbate these problems, together with crosstalk (due to the higher integration capabilities) and noise sensitivity. Avoiding long wires is a good design strategy and also with packetized information it is easier to apply error detection/recovery strategies to restore correctness.

- *Synchronization*. In DSM it is quite difficult to achieve global synchronization on chip. It is more likely to have different clock regions on the same chip, therefore the conception of Globally Asynchronous Locally Synchronous (GALS) systems in gaining interest [19, 20, 21]. Moreover, multi-vendor environments, imposed by reusability issues, natively work at different operating frequencies. A common shared communication medium could represent a limitation in these senses.

- *Power Dissipation*. Power dissipation goes with a power of two with respect to frequency. Thus, as frequency has increased, the problem of lowering power consumption has become fundamental [22]. In fact, it normally represents one of the design constraints hardware architects have to deal with, being not feasible to design portable objects without limiting the power dissipation (which directly means battery lifetime). In modular communication infrastructures, such as NoCs, it is possible to conceive power management strategies, e.g., switching off some unused resources, not feasible with shared mediums.

- *Design Productivity Gap*. As already discussed integration has fostered design complexity, which is totally in contrast with the demands of time to market shrinking to

maintain products competitiveness. This is the reason, besides complexity management, to go for Intellectual Properties (IP) re-use. This fact leads also to plug IPs
of different vendors on the same chip. Therefore, it arises the problem of protocol
heterogeneity: a common shared communication medium could limit sockets standardization with respect to modular communication infrastructures such as NoCs.

- *Verification*. Multi-million gates MPSoC designs are extremely complex to be verified, different architectural configurations have to be explored, as well as several
  stimulation patterns have to be used to stress the design under test in order to discover functional bugs or potential bottlenecks. System verification is not a design
  flow phase anymore, rather it runs in parallel along the whole design process from
  specification to implementation [23]. Verification effort has reached more or less
  70% of engineering efforts. It is clear then how simple modular and re-usable structures such as NoCs can help in achieving quicker and struggle less with verification
  in respect to monolithic and ad-hoc mediums.

If the number of cores is not so high (less than 20) it is still viable to adopt ad-hoc or
shared medium backbones (e.g., the Cell processor [24, 25] adopts a token ring bus) but as
the systems grow shared, segmented and distributed communication structures are preferred
(e.g., picoArray [5], Teraflops Research Chip [6, 7] and Tile64[8, 9] all adopt NoCs). The
term NoC was used for the first time by Hemani et al. [26] in 2000, dealing with the problem
of defining an efficient communication layer for platform belonging to the billion transistor
era. In 2001, Dally and Towles [18] addressed wiring related issues by formulating the
proposal of routing packets instead of wires on a NoC infrastructure. Contemporarily, quite
the same approach has been proposed by the GigaScale Research Center (GSRC) [27]. At
the end of the same year the Philips Research came out with a complete router architecture
[28]. Finally in 2002, Benini and De Micheli formalized the concept of NoC, adopting the
fairly well known SoC paradigm [29, 30].

Chip networks inherited a lot of concepts from macro-networks and it seemed very
straightforward to describe their characteristics and composition adopting the ISO OSI description as Benini and De Micheli did. The ISO OSI stack is shown on the right-hand
side of Figure 4, where the complete flow of data from source to destination (passing or
not through intermediate nodes) in a MPSoC environment is depicted. The ISO OSI reference model is a hierarchical structure defining the requirements for communication among
processing elements. Each layer offers a set of services to the upper layer, using functions
available in the same layer and in the lower ones (by requiring services to them). This
model offered an effective way to handle complexity management regarding communication, making possible to exploit standardization, modularity and re-usability as much as
possible.

Figure 4 is also useful to introduce the main components of a generic NoC infrastructure, listed hereafter.

- *Network Interface* (NI): it represents a bridge between the cores (IP blocks) and the
  network. The NI is responsible of decoupling computation from communication and,
  when needed, it handles frequency and protocol conversions.

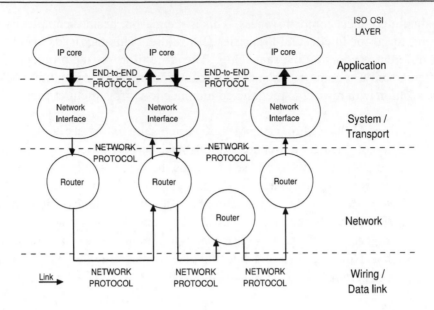

Figure 4. On chip communication dataflow and relative ISO OSI stack layers.

- *Router*: it simply routes the data, according to the defined protocols, from their source to their destination. Routers normally ignore the content of the carried messages and simply deliver them to the downstream item (whether it is another router or the destination NI).

- *Link*: it is responsible of the physical connections among the nodes and can implement one or more logical or physical channels.

In the rest of this paragraph the layers of the ISO OSI stack referable to the micronetwork stack are going to be detailed [29, 30, 31].

2.1. NoC as a Micronetwork: Physical Layer

Problems affecting wires have been already discussed at the beginning of this paragraph, the most important thing to recall is that they represent the physical realization of communication channels. The two major problems affecting them are delay and reliability. The latter is caused by signal integrity and attenuation, more evident for long and thin wires with technology scaling. Four different areas of interest can be identified as research fields in NoCs at this level of abstraction [31]: synchronization [19, 20, 21], implementation [32, 33, 34, 35, 36], reliability [37], and encoding [38, 39, 40, 41].

No further details are provided here about the physical layer, since it is out of the scope of this chapter.

2.2. NoC as a Micronetwork: Architecture and Control Layer

The second layer in the ISO OSI stack is related to architecture and control. The former specifies mainly the topology and the physical organization of the NoC, while the latter defines protocols and algorithms adopted to specify the NoC behavior and to manage the NoC resources. The topology defines the physical NoC structure, meaning how the different resources are connected, whereas protocols and algorithms specify how these resources have to be used.

The definition of the network topology implies to choose between *generality* and *customization*. The more general is the topology the more the NoC is re-usable and scalable, two key features in MPP designs. The price to pay for generality is an optimization lack, which is on the contrary the main strength of customized NoCs.

From the topology point of view, NoCs can be divided [42] in *direct networks* and *indirect networks*. In the former case, each router is connected to a core, whereas in the latter this is not the case.

It is also common to classify NoCs in terms of *regularity* of their topology and obviously scalability benefits from regularity. That is the reason why all the mentioned MPP architectures ([5, 6, 7, 8, ?]) adopt regular topologies to interconnect their resources, being easier to place them on a 2-D layout. Regular topologies ensure higher predictability both in area occupation and power consumption. Predictability in the field of complex systems design is a desirable feature as well as scalability. Figure 5 shows some examples of regular topologies. The *k-ary n-cube* (grid-type) (*k* dimensions degree, *n* number of dimensions) is a common example of regular topology ([43, 44]), as well as the *k-ary tree*, the *k-ary n-dimensional fat tree* and the *torus* [45]. Irregular topologies as shown in Figure 6 are applicati on specific, since they are able to provide more flexibility and optimization. However, it would be impractical to predict area and power consumption in such cases, therefore they are typically not adopted in MPP architectures. Nevertheless, it is also possible to enhance regular topologies introducing, with a small area penalty, application specific long-links to improve their performance [46].

The Architecture and Control layer can be divided into: Data Link, Network, and Transport Sections.

2.2.1. Data Link Section

Data Link is used to improve the reliability of the underlying Physical layer. Furthermore, it rules on the access to a shared-medium network (when it is the case), in which contention for a communication channel can take place. According to these responsibilities, it is composed of the media access control (MAC) and the data link control (DLC). As stated at the beginning of this paragraph, NoCs benefit from packetization to deal with channel reliability issues, making error containment, therefore error recovery is an easier possiblity:

- to limit errors to the packets boundaries,

- to apply a recovery strategy in a packet-wise fashion,

- to achieve correction using standard error-correcting codes,

- to adopt several packet-based error detection and recovery protocols developed for wide-area networks (such as the go-back-N), which are parameterizable in terms of

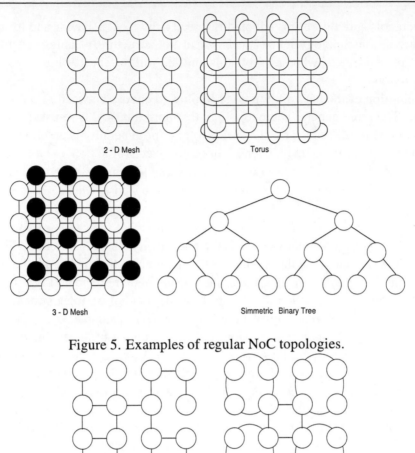

Figure 5. Examples of regular NoC topologies.

Figure 6. Examples of irregular NoC topologies [31].

packet size, number of outstanding packets, and so on, making them very suitable to MPSoC and MPP scalability and reusability requirements.

2.2.2. Network

While Data Link copes with improving the reliability of the underlying layer, Network implements the end-to-end delivery control and is more involved with protocols defining switching and routing.

Switching policies [42] are fundamental for the topic addressed in this chapter. Switching can be classified as:

- *Circuit switching* - This technique implies to reserve a complete path, named circuit, from source to destination, where all the data will be blindly sent. This circuit is defined using the routing information stored in a so-called *request packet*, which is the first item of the communication. As the entire communication along the reserved path terminates, the reserved resources can be released tearing down the established circuit. This technique is suitable to transmit streaming infrequent messages since, as soon as the circuit is defined, latency and throughput become very predictable on the fixed path. The drawback for having these benefits is that circuits setup and teardown represent an overhead, avoided in packet based networks. The possibility of determining in advance latency and throughput makes this policy ideal for guaranteed throughput communications, especially when real time constraints have to be met.

- *Packet switching* - This technique does not imply to reserve any path in advance, meaning that each packet travels across the network possibly competing with other packets for shared network resources. Therefore to implement this switching strategy it is necessary to have intermediate buffering elements, in order to prevent any loss due to congestion. This policy leads to non-deterministic and unpredictable amount of delay due to congestion and consequent queuing. Anyway, it allows to get rid of setup and tear down overheads and bandwidth wasting (due to under-utilized already reserved resources). This kind of switching is very suitable to provide best-effort services or soft-timing constrained communications, when the number of transactions is unpredictable and the their length is small or medium.

Unfortunately, as already discussed in paragraph 1.1., a strict classification in terms of traffic is becoming unfeasible and mixed approaches have already been experienced in literature [47, 48, 49, 50, 51, 15, 52, 53, 16].
Dealing with packet switching, it is possible to define different techniques of packet management, which are hereafter explained.

- *Store and Forward Switching* - As its' name says, according to this approach the entire packet has to be completely stored in an intermediate node before starting to route it downstream. Until the packet is not completely received and/or the downstream item (another router or the destination NI) is not able to receive it (meaning that it has enough room for it), packets items are stacked in the current node adding a certain amount of saturation to the occupied buffer. Therefore the main drawback of this technique is that, in order to stall as less as possible communications and not to experience high latency values per communication, it requires a considerably high amount of buffering. CLICHE [54] is an example of a store-and forward NoC.

- *Virtual Cut-Through switching* - This approach, similar to the previous one, aims at reducing possible latency penalties by adding pipelining. In this case, it is not necessary for packets to be completely received in an intermediate node prior to be forwarded downstream. The counterbalance of having better intermediate memory usage and packets latency reduction is possible message blocking: a packet can be stacked between two routers, preventing any other resource to access the intermediate link (if logic channels exceed physical channels), due to a locations lack in the downstream item. This drawback has a severe impact on NoC predictability, especially under heavy and heterogeneous traffic conditions.

- *Wormhole switching* - According to this technique packets flow segmented in smaller units, named *flits* (flow control units). These flits are created by the source NI and are typically classified as Header (H), is the first flit, Body (B), the intermediate flits, and Tail (T), the last one. The destination NI recovers the packets from the received flits. This policy aims at combining the benefits of packet switching (small overheads and limited bandwidth wasting) with the data streaming quality achievable by circuit switching network with respect to latency and throughput. The idea is to reserve the routing channels along the path to destination according to the control information stored in H, allowing then B and T to follow blindly the reserved path without competing at all with other packets. The benefit with respect to circuit switching is that as soon as T leaves an intermediate node, the reserved resources can be re-allocated to an eventually queued H. This strategy, with respect to the two mentioned earlier, does not require to wait anywhere along the path. This means that as soon as H gains the access to a resource it can proceed on its way to destination. This has a positive effect on buffering and latency, which are minimized, but if eventually congestion or any other reasons prevent packets to reach their destinations, the overall network will be extremely congested since flits of the same packets might occupy (a s a worm) more than one router each [55]. Nevertheless, it is the most adopted packet switching strategy for on chip communication networks.

Switching is tightly coupled to routing, which defines the path that a message has to follow to go from source to destination. First of all, routing can be classified as *deterministic* or *adaptive*. Determinism provides always the same predictable path for each source/destination pair and it is more suitable for uniform and regular traffic characteristics. Adaptive routing schemes, by taking into account the NoC status, are able to define at run time the direction to be followed and are more suitable for irregular traffic patterns. Moreover, they are necessary when dealing with highly unreliable nodes and links or in possibly fault-subjected environments. Obviously it is always possible to derive hybrid approaches, represented in this case by semi-deterministic algorithms: the source/destination pair does not fix a unique path (as in the deterministic case) but a series of paths, to be chosen randomly or in a cyclic way (to add a little bit of non-determinism in or der to reduce congestion). Anyway, they still do not take into account any traffic information.
Routing can be also classified in terms of where the path to be followed by packets is decided.

- *Source routing* - the path is established at the source. Obviously if the path is determined at the source it is impossible for this type of routing to be adaptive as well. In fact, no decisions can be taken along the path and each intermediate node simply reads from the incoming packet the output port it is destined to. No local intelligence has to be added to the routers, therefore their hardware complexity is kept low. The drawback is that packets dimension suffer of the overhead of the path encoding, which is at least $Nlog_2K$ bits (N is the number hops and K the outputs per router).

- *Distributed routing* - the path is determined along the way, according to the destination address and the local address. Distributed routing schemes can be whether deterministic or adaptive, but are much more suitable for regular topologies. In fact, some local intelligence has to be added to intermediate routers and hardware complexity, in this case, is as much affected for irregular topologies. A very common example of Distributed Routing is the X-Y routing scheme typically implemented in grid-based topologies.

- *Hybrid routing* - at the source node packets are routed towards preferential directions, but each intermediate node decides locally the output port to be used to forward downstream the incoming packet.

- *Centralized routing* - all the routing operation are left to a centralized controller.

Routing policies are tightly related to a very important NoC property, which is the possibility of providing *deadlock free transactions*. *Deadlock* implies that one or more packets cannot be forwarded towards destination being stacked somewhere along their path. Such a situation can take place, for example, if the destination consumer is not able to process the already received packets. The *consumption assumption* [56] states that all the messages forwarded through the routers can be accepted and delivered if the destination node is able to consume them. Since it is generally assumed by hypothesis, in case of *deadlock* routing is typically fully responsible for it. Two similar issues are: *livelock* and *starvation*. *Livelock* implies that a packet keeps traveling around the network without reaching its destination. *Starvation* implies that a packet remains blocked, due to the heavy traffic, because the requested resources are always assigned to other packets.

2.2.3. Transport

Transport layer mainly responsible of end-to-end tasks, e.g., (i) decomposing messages into packets at the source, (ii) decomposing packets into flits (when it is the case) at the source, (iii) reordering and reassembling packets and flits at the destination, (iv) controlling the flow of data into the network, (v) allocating network resources, and (vi) negotiating a certain Quality of Service (QoS). These tasks are typical responsibilities of the NI, which is the NoC item placed in the Transport section of the Architecture and Control layer in the ISO OSI stack. An important NoC feature fixed in this section is packets granularity, which strongly impacts on the control algorithms.

Largely used in NoC infrastructures to ensure flow control are the so calld Virtual Channels (VCs) [57]. VCs are buffers that allow for sharing a physical channel by several logically separate channels, implemented by individual and independent queues. Obviously their presence impacts on the overall area of the NoC and, due to the additional driving logics they require, on power dissipation too. Nevertheless, they provide several advantages [31] in:

- avoiding deadlocks - breaking possible cycles in the resource dependency graph [42] since they are completely independent;

- optimizing wire utilization - limiting the usage of physical wires favoring logical connections;

- improving performance - relaxing the inter-resource dependencies in the network and minimizing stalls [42, 58];

- QoS - allowing for storing different priority packets in different physical buffers ([59, 60, 61]) and/or providing guaranteed service levels on dedicated connections [52].

Some recent works [62, 46] try to adopt VCs to close the gap between the state of the art packet switched network and ideal interconnect by proposing the concept of express virtual channels (EVCs). EVCs are adopted to allow packets to virtually bypass intermediate routers along their path to destination in a completely non-speculative fashion, thereby lowering the energy/delay towards that of a dedicated wire while simultaneously approaching ideal throughput.

QoS negotiation involves [31]: correctness of the result, completion of the transaction and bounds on the performance.

In terms of bandwidth utilization NoC can be classified as follow.

- *Best-Effort (BE)* - It is normally a connection-less packet switched network, delivering packets as fast as possible depending on congestion of the NoC. On average operating conditions, NoC performance is good but it is not possible to provide guarantees regarding behaviors under worst-case operating conditions.

- *Guaranteed Throughput (GT)* - It is normally a connection-oriented circuit switched network, being able always to guarantee the required performance constraints, but normally underutilizing the available resources during average operating conditions.

As already stated before, relatively to packet switched and circuit switched NoCs, it is not unusual to try to combine GT and BE services [47, 48, 49, 50, 51, 15, 52, 53, 16] in order to provide the appropriate support to traffic heterogeneity in modern MPSoC and MPP architectures. In [63, 59, 61, 60] NoCs providing prioritized BE traffic classes are presented. SoCBUS [64] provides soft guaranteed services implementing GT using a BE NoC to reserve and tear down circuits. Æthereal [49, 65, 66], NOSTRUM [45], MANGO [52], SONICS [67], aSOC [68, 69, 70], the interconnection network presented in [36] and the one adopted for the RAW processor [1] implement GT adopting connection-oriented network or VCs to establish end-to-end connection.

2.3.   NoC as a Micronetwork: Software Layer

Programmability is one of the most important features of both modern end nodes (e.g., general-purpose and application-specific microprocessors or reconfigurable logic) and I/O peripherals and memories. Therefore, at this level of the ISO OSI stack, it is necessary to determine the appropriate programming model and software services to allow properly exploiting the computational power and the flexibility provided by the MPSoC architectures. It is normally composed of two sections: system and application software. The former has to deal with choosing the IPs and the operating systems, whereas the latter is tightly related to the services the architecture has to provide to accomplish the required tasks.

No further details are provided here about the Software layer, since it is out of the scope of this chapter.

2.4.   Academic and Industrial Hybrid Switching NoC Examples

This paragraph lists a series of interesting hybrid circuit switching approaches at the state of the art, prior the introduction of our own approach.

2.4.1. NOSTRUM

NOSTRUM has been developed at KTH in Stockholm starting from a system-level chip design approach [54, 71, 45]. The basic assumption of NOSTRUM and NOSTRUM NoC Simulation Environment (NNSE) developers is that communication-centric design is the correct design paradigm to withstand the needs of modern applications. NOSTRUM is able to provide QoS through looped containers, implemented by virtual circuits using an explicit time division multiplexing mechanism called Temporally Disjoint Networks (TDN). This architecture implements both BE using single message passing between resources (datagram based communication) and Guaranteed Bandwidth (GB) using stream oriented data distribution (Virtual Channels based). BE and GB are packet based and the destination NI is responsible of ordering and de-segmentation.

These last issues are completely avoided in the network we have designed (see paragraph 3.), which is able to guarantee in-order communications.

2.4.2. MANGO

The MANGO network (Message-passing Asynchronous Network-on-chip providing Guaranteed services over OCP interfaces) [52] is a clockless NoC, which provides both BE and GT (Virtual Channels based) on a packet switched network. VCs are adopted to guarantee a fixed level of QoS, as explained in paragraph 2.2.3.. The routers provide output buffering adopting eight VCs and internally can be subdivided in BE and GT. The BE router section occupies a single VC and is responsible of configuring the connection for the other seven VCs, dedicated to GT management. To create a GT connection between two tiles, multiple BE packets have to be injected into the network to configure all the VCs along the path to be reserved to implement the GT communication. The MANGO NI is Open Core Protocol (OCP) compliant; it is capable of supporting interrupts based on virtual wires and is responsible of synchronizing the clocked OCP interfaces to the clockless network.

For our approach, MANGO handles circuit switching in a completely different way: it is based on VCs and the BE section is used to send just requests for circuits establishment.

2.4.3. SoCBUS

SoCBUS is a NoC architecture [72, 64] that uses optimistic circuit switching to send the packets between two processing cores. It provides soft GT, using a BE NoC both to reserve circuits and to tear them down, but allows only circuit switching communications. This is in fact the main drawback of this NoC: small packets suffer an extremely high overhead due to circuit establishment. Circuits reservation (distributed minimum path adaptive routing algorithm), usage and tear down is quite standard but, in case of negative acknowledgement for the requested path, the setup request is dropped to prevent deadlock. Obviously being a circuit switched network, as the circuit is acknowledged, latency and throughput are guaranteed.

The hybrid switching non-exclusive NoC that we are about to present is able to mix circuit switching and packet switching, in order to gain from GT when long data streams have to be transmitted and from BE when small packets have to be sent.

2.4.4. Æthereal

Philips Research Lab [28, 49, 73, 48, 74, 75, 66] implemented a dual-mode switch named Æthereal that provides GT along with BE services. In the Æthereal, GT traffic is served by circuit switching. In the earlier releases of this architecture, circuits did not have any header and the path was determined by local slot tables. In more recent implementations, slot tables have been removed to save area and a header has been introduced to set up the path. BE traffic makes use of non-reserved or un-used slots and it is mainly exploited to program the GT slots of the routers. Allocation of slots can be either static or dynamic during run-time. When regarding buffering, input queuing is implemented.

It has to be underlined that in this approach hybrid switching is handled in the most classical exclusive way, just one physical link connects two different nodes and GT or BE transactions are multiplexed on it. GT data have a higher priority with respect to the BE ones and this implies that:

- packet switched data, if a circuit has been already established, will have to wait in intermediate nodes until the GT path is torn down;

- tasks completion time will be delayed, since scalar data interdependences can flow as packet switched data.

These drawbacks are completely avoided exploiting a non-exclusive approach.

2.4.5. Hybrid Circuit Switching

Another interesting approach to dual mode switching is the hybrid circuit switching (HCS) proposed in [15]. In this case the aim is removing circuits setup time overhead by intermingling packet and circuit switched flits. The NoC relies on a traditional setup approach, that handles construction and reconfiguration of circuits and stores the switches configuration for active circuits. Moreover, circuit switched data do not wait for any acknowledge to traverse the network, since they are piggybacked immediately behind the circuits setup request. The problem is that, in case of contention, circuit switched communications can be tagged as packet switched ones, flowing in this way until they reach their destination.

In our non-exclusive approach, all the circuit switched communications have to wait for an acknowledgment prior to start but, when started, their throughput is guaranteed since they will never be interrupted nor downgraded to packet switched transactions.

Other architectures targeting the problem of hybrid switching have been proposed by Hsu et al. [50] and by Ahmad et. al [51] too. These approaches are based on traditional exclusive hybrid switching management (circuit switching and packet switching are not served in parallel) and, moreover, BE is normally used just to handle and program GT.

3. Non-exclusive Hybrid Switching NoC Model

In this paragraph, the architecture we have developed in order to combine the benefits of circuits and packets switching is presented. As already said in paragraph 1.1., we can define our approach *non-exclusive* [16], meaning that GT and BE services are implemented in parallel along separated links, avoiding packet switching communications to stall for long time intervals due to circuit switched transactions. Therefore, non-exclusivity allows for a quicker interdependencies solving, even during tasks migration. Moreover, with respect to exclusive approaches, implementing non-exclusivity it is possible to achieve more robustness and predictability, even under heavily heterogeneous traffic injections. The overhead of splitting a wider link into two different parallel links (16+16 bits) driven by two different crossbars is the price to be paid in order to provide both types of switching in parallel.

This architecture supports all the typical NoC features [76]: data integrity, deadlock free communications, lossless data delivery, in-order data delivery and a certain level of QoS relatively to throughput and latency. From a structural point of view the possibility of avoiding deadlock is guaranteed by fulfilling the *consumption assumption* paradigm [56] and by having separated buffers per message type (necessary but not sufficient condition [56] to avoid deadlock). Moreover, a fair arbitration scheme (round-robin) guarantees to avoid any form of starvation and a minimal path X-Y routing scheme (deadlock free by construction) has been used to avoid deadlocks and livelocks at the routing level. To handle packet switching, a standard wormhole switching strategy combined with a credit-based control flow technique (if no slots are available in the selected output channel no more packet items are requested to the upstream node) is impleme nted, in order to guarantee lossless and in-order data delivery. Finally, throughput and latency depend merely on the transaction to be initiated: circuit switching or packet switching are appropriately selected at the Transport layer by the NI. This means that from the point of view of the higher communication layers and of the attached IPs, the decision of implementing packet switching or circuit switching is completely transparent.

3.1. Hybrid Switching Router

In the NoC model, we are presenting in this paragraph the traditional view of a typical packet switching router [42] has been enriched by the presence of a circuit handling section. Figure 7 depicts a general block diagram of our architecture. Since this NoC has been designed for MPP environments the chosen topology is a 2-D mesh and each router has then 5 I/O connections (4 neighbors plus the NI). It is clear from Figure 7 that each router can be sub-divided into two parallel sections, named *Packet Handling* (PH) section and *Circuit Handling* (CH) section, sharing some common control logics. These two sections are not conceived to implement two separated couples of datapath/control paths that separately serve packets and circuits. On the contrary, they cooperate and exchange control signals in order to allow the establishment of circuits (CH section) and packets (PH section) flows.

The PH section is quite standard [42], with respect to packets management. Packets are routed according to the wormhole switching technique and the flits are stored, along the path to destination, into output buffers. Input buffering has not been implemented, even though each incoming flit is stored in a register prior to be sent to the proper output channel, in order to avoid any loss in case of congestion. In order to guarantee also some QoS end-to-end, we have decided to fix two different packets priorities therefore output channels embeds two different VCs multiplexed on the same physical output link. Priorities are assigned by the source NI and reside in the header flit of each packet, together with all the

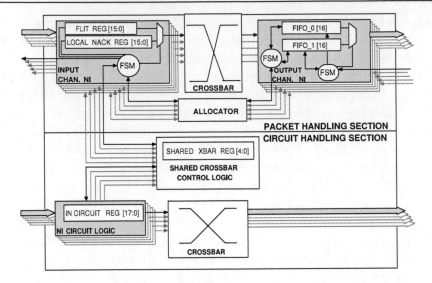

Figure 7. Non-Exclusive Hybrid Switching Router General Overview.

other control information.

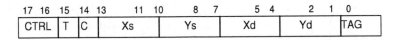

Figure 8. Header flit.

The Header flit, depicted in Figure 8, is composed of the following fields:

- TAG: specifies the type of the flit [$TAG=00$ Header, $TAG=01$ Body, $TAG=10$ Tail] and is included in all the flits;

- Y_d: indicates the Y coordinate of the destination, three bits (configurable) are used since it is assumed to deal with an 8×8 processing array;

- X_d: indicates the X coordinate of the destination, three bits (configurable) are used since it is assumed to deal with an 8×8 processing array;

- Y_s: indicates the Y coordinate of the source, three bits (configurable) are used since it is assumed to deal with an 8×8 processing array;

- X_s: indicates the X coordinate of the source, three bits (configurable) are used since it is assumed to deal with an 8×8 processing array;

- $CTRL$: defines the type of the circuit management flit [$CTRL=00$ for REQ packets, $CTRL=01$ for ACK packets, $CTRL=10$ for NACK packets];

The two Header fields responsible of QoS management are C and T.

- $C = 0$ stands for packet switching transactions and is used to:

- send scalar data to solve an interdependency among tasks in a multi-threading environment ($T = 0$),

- notify to the other interested tiles a task migration, when load balancing techniques are implemented ($T = 1$).

- $C = 1$ stands for circuit switching transactions establishment. In this case a higher priority packet is sent to reserve the path to destination when:

  - a vectorial data has to be transmitted to solve an interdependency among tasks in a multi-threading environment ($T = 0$),

  - a task has to be moved from a tile to another, when load balancing techniques are implemented ($T = 1$).

Contentions for VCs are solved in a round-robin fashion and a credit based flow technique is implemented to manage nodes interactions.

As already stated, by having implemented a 2-D mesh being the most straightforward choice for tile-based architectures, the X-Y routing scheme has been adopted. Nevertheless, in this sense the proposed architecture differs with respect to a standard packet switched router. In fact, we have decided to introduce a certain level of adaptability in the control of the input channel when a circuit setup packet is received. For circuit establishment request Header (*TAG=00*, *CTRL=00*, *C=1* and *T=1/T=0*), the X-Y routing scheme can be changed to a Y-X one (and vice versa if necessary) if the originally requested output link in the CH section has been already reserved for another circuit (either is just reserved or already in use). Each input channel exchanges control signals with the shared crossbar control logic in the CH section, to check if the requested link can be reserved or not. If not, it tries the complementary routing scheme and, if eve n in this case the link is already booked, the setup packet will be turned in a NACK packet (*TAG=00*, *CTRL=10*, *C=1* and *T=1/T=0*) and sent back to the source. This mechanism does not lead to any form of deadlock because the module responsible to select the proper VCs, which is placed in each input channel, is allowed to choose just VCs leading to minimal path for the packets. Therefore the worst case is when at each node the request packet is forced to change from X-Y to Y-X and vice-versa, leading to a stairwise routing path.

The CH section has its own 18 bits crossbar:

- 16 for the data;

- 1 validity bit;

- 1 release bit (to manage circuits tear down).

In order to cut any possible long critical path in the datapath of the CH section, 5 different input registers are used to store these previously mentioned values prior to send them to the crossbar to be forwarded downstream.

In most of the hybrid switching routers in literature, circuit switching has been handled mainly using time division multiplexing [49, 51], but those solutions typically implied to exploit recording tables [50], slot tables [48], or routing tables [51]. In order to save any extra area overhead, besides the one necessary to implement the logic driving the second

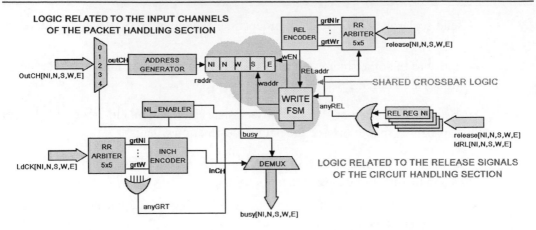

Figure 9. Shared logic for circuit crossbar control.

crossbar in the CH section, we decided to get rid of any sort of table adopting a simple shared 5 bits register for circuit switching management. Figure 9 shows all the logic necessary to implement our run-time programmable circuit switching approach. The shared 5 bits register is accessible by all the input channels that need to check for the availability of a certain output port in the CH section. A round-robin based arbitration avoids collisions and write hazards. This register is initialized to zero by default. It is synchronously written and asynchronously read. When an input channel receives a circuit setup packet and evaluates which output link has to be reserved, the correspondent bit of the shared 5 bits register is accessed. If the link is already reserved, the evaluated bit will be found to be one, whereas if not the correspondent bit of the register is zero and it will be possible for the input channel to reserve it turning the read bit to one. At the end of the communication over the established circuit, the source NI raises a release signal which follows blindly the circuit and is used to tear it down by switching back to zero the proper bit in the shared 5 bits register.

4.   Higher Communication Level Bias

It is common opinion that communication infrastructure performance impacts on the overall system behavior. In fact we have argued several times that to address the heterogeneity of traffic in MPP architectures it is better to try to exploit hybrid switching techniques. Besides targeting multi-threaded applications, it is necessary to relieve processing elements and CPUs of communication management, to fully exploit the available time for computations. Therefore, high-level communication modules, such as Direct Memory Access (DMA) engines, can be adopted to handle memory accesses and communications over the interconnection infrastructure, without any CPU intervention. Thus, in the ISO OSI representation depicted in Figure 4 and extensively described in paragraph 2., it is necessary to add DMAs interposing them between CPUs and NIs, as shown in the center of Figure 10.

It is possible to demonstrate [77] that not only the NoC can influence the overall system behavior, but it is also true that higher level communication modules, such as DMA engines, must be carefully taken into account since stand-alone NoC testing overlooks their actual impact on the system performance. The more is necessary to guarantee a certain behavior of the communication backbone (such as in [66, 15, 16]) the more the bias of these higher levels has to be considered.

In this paragraph, as Figure 10 suggests, we are going to discuss the impact of two different DMA implementations, respectively half-duplex and full-duplex, on the performance of the NoC described in the previous paragraph.

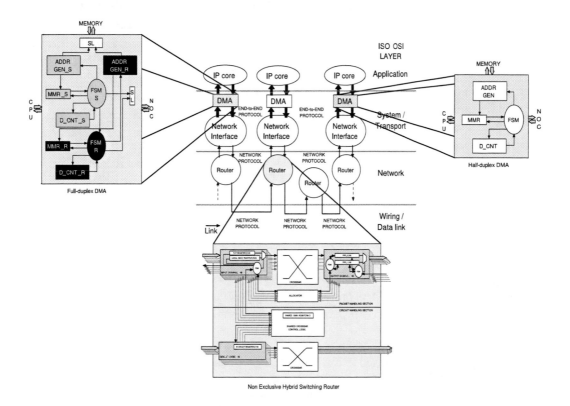

Figure 10. On chip communication dataflow completed with the insertion of DMA engines.

4.1. Half-Duplex and Full-Duplex DMA Models

Considering the ISO OSI stack to describe communication data flow, it should be clear that the performance of the modules in the Network layer can be influenced by those of the components in the System/Transport layer. Even though this is well known from the scientific literature for the NI, it is less obvious for the DMA. The DMA in this case acts as a communication manager and, to determine if it has an impact on the underlying communication backbone, we have simply explored the hybrid switching NoC performance interfacing it with two different DMA engines. Half-duplex refers to the possibility of transmitting data in just one direction at a time, whereas a full-duplex DMA is able to deal with communications in both directions in parallel.

4.1.1. Half-Duplex DMA

The datapath of the half-duplex DMA is depicted on the right-hand side of Figure 10. It is composed of a state machine (*FSM*) handling all the control and dispatching/receiving data, extracted/written from/to a unique Memory Mapped Register (*MMR*) bank, to/from the NoC. Data are read/written from/to the Memory, according to the address generated by an Address Generator (*ADDR_GEN*) controlled by the *FSM*. A down counter (*D_CNT*), programmed as soon as a transaction occurs, is used to access the proper location of the *MMR* bank, since all the registers are sequentially written in order to trigger any data transfer.

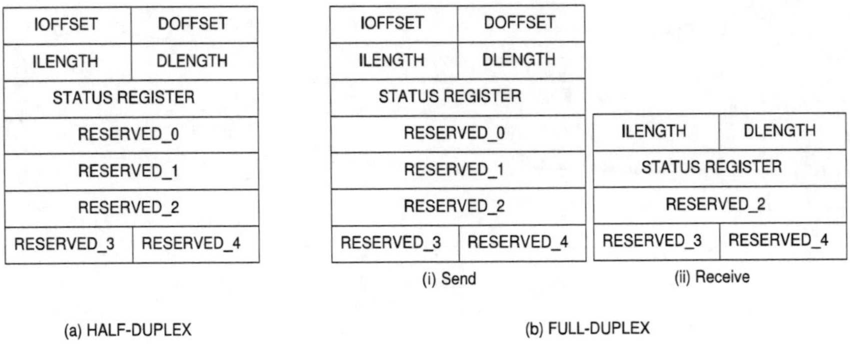

IOFFSET	DOFFSET
ILENGTH	DLENGTH
STATUS REGISTER	
RESERVED_0	
RESERVED_1	
RESERVED_2	
RESERVED_3	RESERVED_4

(a) HALF-DUPLEX

IOFFSET	DOFFSET
ILENGTH	DLENGTH
STATUS REGISTER	
RESERVED_0	
RESERVED_1	
RESERVED_2	
RESERVED_3	RESERVED_4

(i) Send

ILENGTH	DLENGTH
STATUS REGISTER	
RESERVED_2	
RESERVED_3	RESERVED_4

(ii) Receive

(b) FULL-DUPLEX

Figure 11. Half-duplex and Full-duplex *MRR* bank.

Both the implemented DMAs are memory mapped and the information stored in their *MMR* banks (see Figure 11), composed of 32-bit registers, are:

- the first memory address occupied by a long stream of data to be transmitted (*IOFFSET* and *DOFFSET*), used in the transmission phase only;

- the size of the data stream to be transmitted/received (*ILENGHT* and *DLENGTH*);

- the *STATUS REGISTER*, conveying all the control information exchanged between DMA and NI in order to setup/receive a transaction, i.e.,

    1. the *C* bit and *T* bit to be embedded in any transaction Header,
    2. the *(X,Y) COORDINATE* of the destination tile,
    3. the *TASK ID* that identifies a specific *task*,
    4. the *THREAD ID* that identifies a specific *thread* of a *task*.

- some end-to-end reserved registers.

4.1.2. Full-Duplex DMA

The full-duplex DMA engine is similar to the half-duplex one, thus we are not going to explain its implementation in details, but we just shortly highlight the differences between the two. Two separated channels manage the sending and the receiving phases. Therefore two different *MMR* banks will be exploited to implement a non-blocking full-duplex DMA, as depicted in Figure 11. The Send *MMR* bank is identical to the half-duplex *MMR* bank, whereas the Receive one implements only a subset of registers. The possibility of sending and receiving transactions in parallel it is very helpful to support the underlying hybrid switching communication backbone. It is possible in fact to receive packets and circuits while a request for a circuit switching communication is pending. On the contrary, in the half-duplex engine a request for circuit establishment is blocking. In fact, even if the NI would start a communication with the DMA, it will not be possible to serve it without losing the information stored in its *MMR* bank. The counterbalance is that, having two separated channels operating in parallel, makes the control more complicated: two different *FSMs* exchanging control signals are necessary to support the full-duplex behavior and the overall logic is somehow duplicated, as the datapath on the left-hand side of Figure 10 shows.

We have also demonstrated [77] that full-duplex DMAs, avoiding by definition to stall the receiving section due to a pending request in the sending section, offers a good support also to deadlock avoidance. Obviously this is not the only possible way of dealing with this problem. Having implemented a half-duplex DMA:

- one could define strategies of deadlock prevention or recovery at the operating system level;

- the NI can be instrumented with watchdog timers and end-to-end control logic, in order to flush a request and to recover the correct system status.

Nevertheless, the area overhead of a full-duplex DMA is not so much (11 32-bits registers instead of 7 in the *MMR* banks and a slightly more complex datapath) to represent a limit to its adoption in MPP environments, especially considering that they offer also some very interesting performance benefits as it will be soon detailed.

5.   Hybrid Switching NoC Performance

The NoC architecture proposed in this chapter is composed of a homogeneous tile-based system such as the one presented in Figure 12. An 8×8 2-D mesh has been assembled using in each tile:

- a simple traffic generator, which is responsible of initiating and receiving data transactions of different lengths;

- a DMA, such as the ones described in paragraph 4.;

- a very simple NI, which converts the data received from the DMAs in NoC compliant packets and vice versa;

- the hybrid switching router presented in paragraph 3..

This MPPs-like environment, described in SystemC at RTL level, has been stressed using different traffic patterns exploiting a parallel simulation framework which allowed us to perform parallel multi-parametric simulations [78]. The injected traffic has been characterized both temporally and spatially. Spatial distribution regards the possible mapping of different tasks to the tiles. A static mapping of seven different clusters of tiles on a mesh

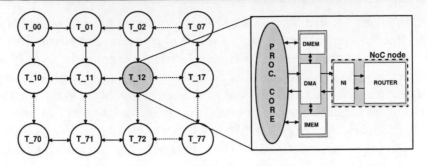

Figure 12. Experimental NoC environment: 8×8 tile-based 2D mesh of homogeneous tiles.

of 64 tiles is adopted, using three different allocation algorithms in literature: Buddy [79], LeapFrog [80] and a Custom [81] one. Temporal traffic characterization highly depends on the type of simulation performed. Basically the default traffic injection time distribution (for both packets and circuits) is Gaussian, but the developed framework allows also to choose two other possible distributions at run-time: Uniform and Poisson. Each distribution can be properly customized in ter ms of the characteristic parameters. It is also allowed to combine the aforementioned distributions to differentiate packets and circuits transactions injection. Moreover, the framework enables to perform different kinds of simulations, where the effect of changing a single traffic or architectural parameter is explored. In particular, it is possible to run multi-parametric simulation sets changing:

- architectural parameters such as the FIFO depth in every router;

- the shape of the injection time traffic distribution;

- the density of the population of the injected transactions.

5.1. Impact of the Higher Level Communication Layer

In this paragraph, we present some of the benefits deriving from the adoption of a full-duplex DMA engine instead of a half-duplex one at the higher level communication layer, dealing with an underlying hybrid switching communication infrastructures. Generally speaking, having a full-duplex engine accounts for the experience of less stalls; thanks to its non-blocking behavior while waiting for circuits establishments. This feature has a benefit influence on several typical NoCs metrics, such as the injection delay, the average queuing time and the transmission time.

Figure 13 is representative of the delay that packets experience during execution with respect to the theoretical scheduled injection time. In this figure the results of this metrics are plotted for two different multi-parametric sets, linearly varying the number of injected packets (on the top) or the number of injected circuits (on the bottom). With respect to packets injection, besides the fact that full-duplex is able to provide better absolute values, it is also possible to notice that the half-duplex plot is more disturbed, whereas the full-duplex one presents a linear increment of the delay with the number of packets. The linearity of the delay in the half-duplex case is affected by a less efficient support to traffic heterogeneity;

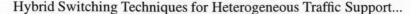

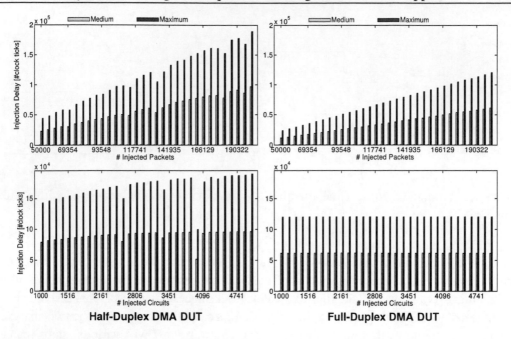

Figure 13. Injection Delay affecting a hybrid switching NoC equipped with a Half-duplex (left) and a Full-duplex (right) DMA engine.

this behavior suggests that the half-duplex DMA poorly reacts also to circuits injection. In fact, as the two bottom plots in Figure 13 demonstrate, the NoC exploiting the full-duplex DMA is quite in sensitive to the variation of the population of the injected circuits while this is not the case for the system adopting the half-duplex DMA, whose delay is not constant at all as the number of injected circuits increases.

A very interesting situation can be observed by looking at the plots in Figure 14. This figure depicts the average queuing time affecting the described half-duplex (on the left) and full-duplex (on the right) systems. These plots are obtained for: (i) the Buddy allocation scheme, (ii) a constant number of injected transactions (5000 circuits and 200000 packets), (iii) a Uniform circuits injection time distribution and (iv) the variation of the packets injec-

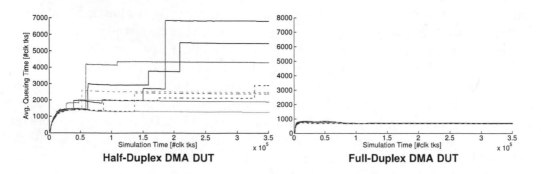

Figure 14. Average Queuing Time affecting a hybrid switching NoC equipped with a Half-duplex (left) and a Full-duplex (right) DMA engine.

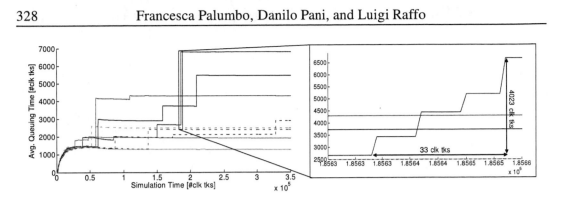

Figure 15. Average Queuing Time affecting a hybrid switching NoC equipped with a Half-duplex DMA.

tion time distribution (always Gaussian with fixed mean but different standard deviations). The average queuing time gives an idea of the NoC congestion, being representative of the incremental average over all the tiles of the clock ticks necessary to each packet to leave the encountered queues in the path to destination. In this case, the behavior of the two analyzed systems is completely different. In fact, adopting a half-duplex DMA various "steps" can be observed in its average queuing time plot. These steps, as it can be noticed in the zoom (Figure 15), are not instantaneous. The motivation of this behavior can be explained throughout the example of Figure 16. Let us consider the DMA of the Tile_00 busy in a circuit switched communication with the DMA of the Tile_10. If some other DMAs are sending packets to Tile_00, sooner or later, they saturate the shaded FIFOs in the output channels of the routers encountered in the paths towards the Tile_00 since half-duplex DMAs are not able to send and receive data at the same time. When the circuit will be released and the DMA of the Tile_00 will be finally able to receive again, all the queued packets saturating the FIFOs will be able to proceed towards the Tile_00 and their contribute to the average queuing time will be summed up. Their contribution can be considerably high since in our simulations circuits length varies in the range 170-700 elements and furthermore a DMA is considered busy even if still waiting for the answer of the receiver availability to receive data. Clearly, having full-duplex DMA engines in the system avoids completely this saturation situation, since they are non-blocking.

Some final remarks should be spent about the total transmission time of the two versions of the NoC. This matrix is defined as the sum of the injection delay and the latency affecting each packet while crossing the network. Figure 17 represents the box plots of this matrix obtained using the full-duplex engine (on the right) and the half-duplex one (on the left) for the same multi-parametric simulation sets of Figure 13. As it can be noticed, even in this case, the full-duplex solution provides better results. Generally speaking, the absolute values are reduced with respect to the half-duplex case and, moreover, it is able to achieve more regularity, meaning more predictability, with respect to packets volume variations (on the top of Figure 17) and more robustness with respect to circuits volume variation (on the bottom of Figure 17).

Keeping in mind all the results presented, it should be quite clear that the adoption of a half-duplex DMA engine when dealing with a hybrid switching communication layer as a substrate could lead to a limitation of the potential performance of the underlying com-

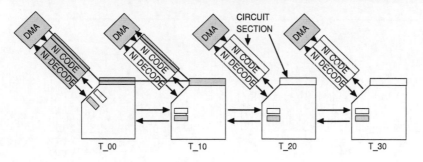

Figure 16. Half-duplex DMA: FIFOs saturation example during a circuit switching communication.

munication medium. Therefore, the performance of the non-exclusive hybrid switching NoC presented in this chapter (see paragraph 3.) will be discussed utilizing the full-duplex DMA engine. It should be noted that, even if it could be predictable a better result of the full-duplex solution, this short dissertation demonstrates how such high level modules can influence the NoC functionality: overlooking these aspects can lead to misleading conclusions about the NoC performance.

5.2. Proposed Non-exclusive Hybrid Switching NoC Performance

In this paragraph, a selection of some interesting results demonstrating the benefits of implementing the non-exclusivity feature in hybrid switching NoCs are presented.

Figure 18 is representative of the influence on the injection delay that the variation of packets (on the top) and circuits (on the bottom) volume have both dealing with the exclusive and the non-exclusive hybrid switching NoCs. Non-exclusivity guarantees better absolute values. Furthermore, it seems that exclusivity acts somehow like the half-duplex feature at the higher level. In fact, it does not allow to obtain circuit-insensitive characteristics.

Figure 19 attempts to give an idea of the intrinsic NoC latency of both the exclusive and the non-exclusive NoCs. The latency is defined as the time required for each packet to cross the network (routers only) and it is retrieved by the adopted simulation framework as a summary of statistics comprehensive of the mean, the standard deviation, the minimum, the lower quartile (25th percentile), the median (50th percentile) and the upper quartile (75th percentile) for all the injected packets. Plots in Figure 19 have been derived running 64 simulations where: (i) the injected circuits population is kept constant in sub-groups of 8 simulations and (ii) the injected packets population is linearly varied in the range [50000-200000] within each sub-group. These plots demonstrate that despite the overall trend the latency is the same, the non-exclusive NoC (on the right) is able to provide better results; considering that, even in the last sub-group (5000 circuits) for the highest packet volume (200000 packets), the median of the achieved latency is better than in any combination of traffic adopting the exclusive approach to hybrid switching.

Finally, Figure 20 shows the performance that can be achieved when an architectural parameter, such as the FIFO depth, is varied. This figure plots the average queuing time and the total transmission time when 5000 circuits and 200000 packets are injected in both the

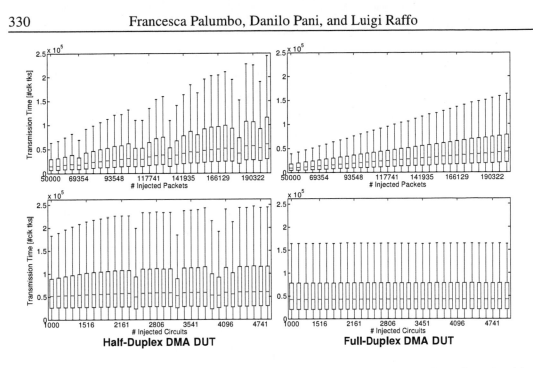

Figure 17. Transmission Time characterizing a hybrid switching NoC equipped with a Half-duplex (left) and a Full-duplex (right) DMA engine.

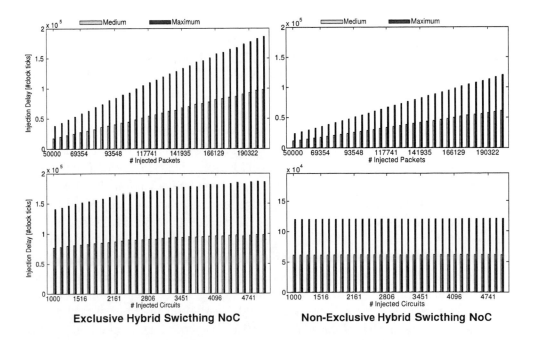

Figure 18. Injection Delay affecting the Exclusive (left) and the Non-Exclusive (right) Hybrid Switching NoC.

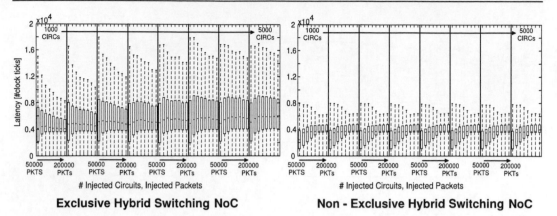

Figure 19. Latency characterizing the Exclusive (left) and the Non-Exclusive (right) Hybrid Switching NoC.

hybrid switching NoCs. Considering the depicted matrix, absolute values are better for the non-exclusive NoC. Moreover, by looking at the average queuing time, the non-exclusive NoC succeeds better in following the traffic injection distribution, which in this case is Poissonian. The reason is that, due to the non-exclusivity feature, packets can be scheduled and sent across the NoC sooner. Conversely, implementing an exclusive approach, since packets are subjected to stalls due to the established circuits, the average queuing time curve is smoothed and it is not able to follow the peak of the injection time distribution. Regarding transmission time, the non-exclusive NoC is able to provide considerably mor e robustness. In fact, despite the increase of the available slots, the total transmission time distribution median does not appreciably decrease, meaning that the adoption of deeper FIFOs does not produce any significant benefits in this sense.

6.   Conclusion

The problem addressed by this chapter was the definition of a proper optimal communication medium to be adopted in multi-core architectures. Modern applications, sustained by the improvements of CMOS technologies, have led multi-core and massively parallel processors to emerge on the scene of digital systems. The complexity in the design of such architectures has reached considerably high levels, therefore the possibility of designing for re-use has become a fairly widespread concept. Tile-based architectures represent a way of addressing this complexity. Being typically composed of regular replicated structures of simple elements connected by short wires, they turned out to be very suitable: (a) to sustain time to market pressure and system complexity management by exploiting as much as possible the paradigm of re-use; (b) to effectively face modern applications requirements by providing a huge computational power having a large number of simple processing elements embedded on th e same die rather than a smaller number of cores singularly providing better performance.

Such complex systems have complex communication requirements. This topic has been challenged in this chapter by discussing the possibility of providing the most appropri-

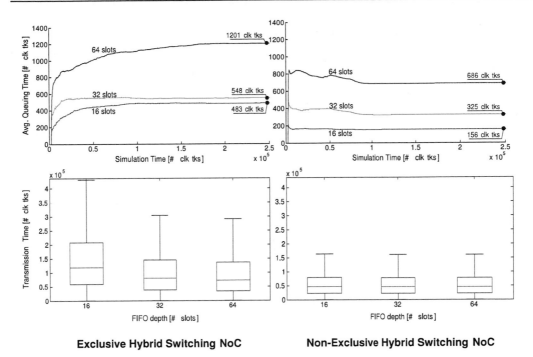

Figure 20. Impact of FIFOs Depth Variation on the Average Queuing Time and the Transmission Time of the Exclusive (left) and the Non-Exclusive (right) Hybrid Switching NoC.

ate communication features at the different levels of the communication medium explored through an ISO OSI stack representation. Shared buses and simple rings do not have the features and the capabilities to sustain such systems with the appropriate scalability degree and demanded bandwidth and, at the same time, full crossbars are impractical as the number of cores grows. Therefore Networks on Chip have emerged as common interconnection backbone for tile-based architectures.

Common packet switched NoC models seem to fail in providing the efficient communication for tile-based MPPs, taking into account their heterogeneous traffic characteristic, typical of multi-threaded applications. To tackle these issues we have demonstrated that it is better to adopt hybrid switching NoCs, combining the benefits of both packet switched and circuit switched interconnects.

To this aim, we have presented in this chapter a particular model of hybrid switching NoC, able to support this dual mode switching with non-exclusive links usage. This architecture is able to provide: (a) soft guaranteed throughput by ensuring, as soon as a circuit switching communication is established, completely deterministic throughput and bandwidth; (b) best effort communications with prioritized Quality of Service support. These features make this NoC particularly suitable for MPSoCs and MPPs, as deeply demonstrated comparing its performance with the ones of an equivalent exclusive hybrid switching strategy. A detailed comparison demonstrated that, with this non-exclusivity feature implemented, it is possible to provide better performance in terms of the absolute values obtained but also in terms of more predictable and robust behaviors.

Sticking to the problem of defining a suitable communication architecture model to be

embedded in a multi-tile chip, this chapter has also discussed the fact that the higher level communication layers in an ISO OSI stack representation of the data flow plays an important role. In fact, they have a certain bias on the performance of the underlying communication infrastructure, typically overseen when optimizing and exploring the interconnection medium. In this sense, the outcome of the presented analysis is that, even if normally the impact of the communication medium on the overall system performance is considered, it is misleading to try to design and test it stand-alone. Severe limitations on its performance by means of other higher level modules can easily be ignored in this way. In particular, in the case of hybrid switching NoCs for highly heterogeneous traffic support, the adoption of a half-duplex higher level communication layer modules (as DMAs) or software techniques cou ld lead to severe performance limitations.

Acknowledgments

The research leading to these results has received funding from the European Community's Seventh Framework Programme (FP7/2007-2013) under grant agreement n. 248424, MADNESS Project.

References

[1] E. W. Michael, M. Taylor, V. Sarkar, W. Lee, V. Lee, J. Kim, M. Frank, P. Finch, S. Devabhaktuni, R. Barua, J. Babb, S. Amarasinghe, and A. Agarwal, "Baring it all to software: The raw machine," *IEEE Computer*, vol. 30, pp. 86–93, 1997.

[2] M. Butts, A. M. Jones, and P. Wasson, "A structural object programming model, architecture, chip and tools for reconfigurable computing," in *FCCM07: Proceedings of the 15th Annual IEEE Symposium on Field-Programmable Custom Computing Machines*. Washington, DC, USA: IEEE Computer Society, 2007, pp. 55–64.

[3] M. Butts, "Synchronization through communication in a massively parallel processor array," *IEEE Micro*, vol. 27, no. 5, pp. 32–40, 2007.

[4] A. M. Jones and M. Butts, "Teraops hardware: A new massively-parallel mimd computing fabric," in *IEEE Hot Chips Symposium*, August 2006, pp. 59–66.

[5] picoArray. picochip company. [Online]. Available: http://www.picochip.com/

[6] Intel. The teraflops research chip. [Online]. Available: http://techresearch.intel.com/articles/Tera-Scale/1421.htm

[7] S. Vangal, J. Howard, G. Ruhl, S. Dighe, H. Wilson, J. Tschanz, D. Finan, P. Iyer, A. Singh, A. Singh, T. Jacob, S. Jain, S. Venkataraman, Y. Hoskote, and N. Borkar, "An 80-tile 1.28tflops network-on-chip in 65nm cmos," in *Solid-State Circuits Conference, 2007. ISSCC 2007. Digest of Technical Papers. IEEE International*, 2007, pp. 98–589.

[8] T. Corporation. The tile64 chip. [Online]. Available: http://www.tilera.com/

[9] S. Bell, B. Edwards, J. Amann, R. Conlin, K. Joyce, V. Leung, J. MacKay, M. Reif, L. Bao, J. Brown, and M. Mattina, "Tile64tm processor: A 64-core soc with mesh interconnect," in *International Solid-State Circuits Conference, 2008 (ISSCC 2008)*.

[10] S. Amarasinghe, "6.189 IAP 2007 Lecture 18," MIT, Boston, 2007

[11] "International Technology Roadmap for Semiconductors,Technical Report 1997 Edition," Semiconductor Industry Association, Tech. Rep., 1997.

[12] "International Technology Roadmap for Semiconductors, Technical Report 2003 Edition," Semiconductor Industry Association, Tech. Rep., 2003.

[13] "International Technology Roadmap for Semiconductors, Technical Report 2005 Edition," Semiconductor Industry Association, Tech. Rep., 2005.

[14] K. Lahiri, A. Raghunathan, G. Lakshminarayana, and S. Dey, "Communication architecture tuners: A methodology for the design of high-performance communication architectures for systems-on-chips," in *DAC*, 2000, pp. 513–518.

[15] N. D. E. Jerger, L.-S. Peh, and M. H. Lipasti, "Circuit-switched coherence," in *NOCS '08: Proc. of the Second International Symposium on Networks-on-Chip*, 2008, pp. 193–202.

[16] F. Palumbo, S. Secchi, D. Pani, and L. Raffo, "A novel non-exclusive dual-mode architecture for mpsocs-oriented network on chip designs," in *SAMOS08: Proc. of the 8th international workshop on Embedded Computer Systems*. Berlin, Heidelberg: Springer-Verlag, 2008, pp. 96–105.

[17] "International Technology Roadmap for Semiconductors, Technical Report 2007 Edition," Semiconductor Industry Association, Tech. Rep., 2007.

[18] W. J. Dally and B. Towles, "Route packets, not wires: On-chip inteconnection networks," in *DAC'01: Proceedings of the 38th Annual Design Automation Conference*. New York, NY, USA: ACM, 2001, pp. 684–689.

[19] D. M. Chapiro, "Globally-asynchronous locally-synchronous systems (performance, reliability, digital)," Ph.D. dissertation, Stanford, CA, USA, 1985.

[20] T. Meincke, A. Hemani, S. Kumar, P. Ellervee, J. Oberg, T. Olsson, P. Nilsson, D. Lindqvist, and H. Tenhunen, "Globally asynchronous locally synchronous architecture for large high-performance asics," in *ISCAS*, 1999, pp. 512–515.

[21] J. Muttersbach, T. Villiger, and W. Fichtner, "Practical design of globally-asynchronous locally-synchronous systems," in *ASYNC '00: Proceedings of the 6th International Symposium on Advanced Research in Asynchronous Circuits and Systems*, 2000, p. 52.

[22] T. Mudge, "Power: A first-class architectural design constraint," *Computer*, vol. 34, no. 4, pp. 52–58, 2001.

[23] P. Rashinkar, P. Paterson, and L. Singh, *System-on-a-chip verification: Methodology and techniques*. Norwell, MA, USA: Kluwer Academic Publishers, 2000.

[24] T. Chen, R. Raghavan, J. N. Dale, and E. Iwata, "Cell broadband engine architecture and its first implementation: A performance view," *IBM J. Res. Dev.*, vol. 51, no. 5, pp. 559–572, 2007.

[25] SONY-IBM-TOSHIBA. The cell project. [Online]. Available: http://www.research.ibm.com/cell/home.html

[26] A. Hemani, A. Postula, A. Jantsch, J. Oberg, M. Millberg, D. Lindqvist, and S. Kumar, "Network on a chip: An architecture for billion transistor era," in *Proc. of the IEEE NorChip Conference*.

[27] M. Sgroi, M. Sheets, A. Mihal, K. Keutzer, S. Malik, J. Rabaey, and A. Sangiovanni-Vincentelli, "Addressing the system-on-a-chip interconnect woes through communication-based design," in *Design Automation Conference, DAC'01*, 2001.

[28] E. R. Kees, K. Goossens, and P. Wielage, "A router architecture for networks on silicon," in *In Proceedings of Progress 2001, 2nd Workshop on Embedded Systems*, 2001, pp. 181–188.

[29] L. Benini and G. De Micheli, "Powering networks on chips: Energy-efficient and reliable interconnect design for socs," in *ISSS01: Proc. of the 14th international symposium on Systems synthesis*. New York, NY, USA: ACM, 2001, pp. 33–38.

[30] L. Benini and G. D. Micheli, "Networks on chips: A new SoC paradigm," *Computer*, vol. 35, no. 1, pp. 70–78, 2002.

[31] T. Bjerregaard and S. Mahadevan, "A survey of research and practices of network-on-chip," *ACM Comput. Surv.*, vol. 38, no. 1, p. 1, 2006.

[32] R. Ho, K. W. Mai, and M. A. Horowitz, "The future of wires," in *Proceedings of the IEEE*, 2001, pp. 490–504.

[33] K. Lee, "On-chip interconnects-gigahertz and beyond," *Solid State Technology*, vol. 41, pp. 85–89, Sept. 2004.

[34] R. Havemann and J. Hutchby, "High-performance interconnects: An integration overview," vol. 89, no. 5, May 2001, pp. 586–601.

[35] D. Sylvester and K. Keutzer, "A global wiring paradigm for deep submicron design," in *IEEE Transaction on Computer Aided Design Integrated Circuits Systems*. New York, NY, USA: ACM, 1998, pp. 521–532.

[36] J. Liu, L.-R. Zheng, and H. Tenhunen, "Interconnect intellectual property for network-on-chip (noc)," *J. Syst. Archit.*, vol. 50, no. 2-3, pp. 65–79, 2004.

[37] A. Jantsch and H. Tenhunen, Eds., *Networks on chip*. Hingham, MA, USA: Kluwer Academic Publishers, 2003.

[38] K. Nakamura and M. Horowitz, "A 50% noise reduction interface using low-weight coding," in *Symposium on VLSI Circuits*, 1996, pp. 144–145.

[39] A. Bogliolo, "Encodings for high-performance for energy-efficient signaling," in *ISLPED01: Proceedings of the 2001 International Symposium on Low Power Electronics and Design*. New York, NY, USA: ACM, 2001, pp. 170–175.

[40] J. Bainbridge and S. Furber, "Chain: A delay-insensitive chip area interconnect," *IEEE Micro*, vol. 22, no. 5, pp. 16–23, 2002.

[41] M. Dall'Osso, G. Biccari, L. Giovannini, D. Bertozzi, and L. Benini, "xpipes: a latency insensitive parameterized network-on-chip architecture for multi-processor socs," in *ICCD '03: Proceedings of the 21st International Conference on Computer Design*. Washington, DC, USA: IEEE Computer Society, 2003, pp. 536–539.

[42] W. Dally and B. Towles, *Principles and Practices of Interconnection Networks*. San Francisco, CA, USA: Morgan Kaufmann Publishers Inc., 2003.

[43] W. J. Dally, "Performance analysis of k-ary n-cube interconnection networks," *IEEE Trans. Comput.*, vol. 39, no. 6, pp. 775–785, 1990.

[44] H. Sarbazi-Azad, L. Mackenzie, and M. Ould-Khaoua, "Performance analysis of k-ary n-cubes with fully adaptive routing," *Parallel and Distributed Systems, International Conference* , vol. 0, p. 249, 2000.

[45] M. Millberg, E. Nilsson, R. Thid, and A. Jantsch, "Guaranteed bandwidth using looped containers in temporally disjoint networks within the nostrum network on chip," in *DATE '04: Proceedings of the conference on Design, automation and test in Europe*. Washington, DC, USA: IEEE Computer Society, 2004, p. 20890.

[46] T. Krishna, A. Kumar, P. Chiang, M. Erez, and L.-S. Peh, "Noc with near-ideal express virtual channels using global-line communication," in *Hot Interconnects*, 2008, pp. 11–20.

[47] K. G. Shin and S. Daniel, "Analysis and implementation of hybrid switching," *IEEE Transaction on Computers*, pp. 211–219, 1996.

[48] E. Rijpkema, K. Goossens, A. Radulescu, J. Dielissen, J. V. Meerbergen, P. Wielage, and E. Waterlander, "Trade-offs in the design of a router with both guaranteed and best-effort services for network on chip," in *Proc. of the conference on Design, Automation and Test in Europe*, vol. 1, 2003, pp. 294–302.

[49] K. Goossens, J. V. Meerbergen, A. Peeters, and P. Wielage, "Network on silicon: Combining best-effort and guaranteed services," in *Proc. of the Design, Automation and Test in Europe Conference and Exhibition, DATE*, 2002, pp. 423–425.

[50] S. Hsu, Y. Lin, and J. Jou, "Design of a dual-mode noc router integrated with network interface for amba-based ips," in *Proc. IEEE Asian Solid-State Circuits Conf.*, 2006, pp. 211–214.

[51] B. Ahamad, A. Erdogan, and S. Khawarm, "Architecture of a dynamically reconfigurable NoC for adaptive reconfigurable MPSoC," in *Proc. of the first NASA/ESA Conf. on Adaptive Hardware and Systems (AHS'06)*, 2006.

[52] T. Bjerregaard and J. Sparsø, "A router architecture for connection-oriented service guarantees in the MANGO clockless network-on-chip," in *Proceedings of Design, Automation and Testing in Europe Conference 2005 (DATE05)*. IEEE, 2005.

[53] S. Secchi, F. Palumbo, D. Pani, and L. Raffo, "A network on chip architecture for heterogeneous traffic support with non-exclusive dual-mode switching," *Euromicro Symposium on Digital Systems Design*, pp. 141–148, 2008.

[54] S. Kumar, A. Jantsch, M. Millberg, J. berg, J.-P. Soininen, M. Forsell, K. Tiensyrj, and A. Hemani, "A network on chip architecture and design methodology," *VLSI, IEEE Computer Society Annual Symposium on*, pp. 117–124, 2002.

[55] K. Al-Tawil, M. Abd-El-Barr, and F. Ashraf, "A survey and comparison of wormhole routing techniques in a meshnetworks," *Network, IEEE*, vol. 11, no. 2, pp. 38–45, 1997.

[56] Y. H. Song and T. M. Pinkston, "A progressive approach to handling message-dependent deadlock in parallel computer systems," *IEEE Transactions on Parallel and Distributed Systems*, vol. 14, no. 3, pp. 259–275, 2003.

[57] W. J. Dally, "Virtual-Channel Flow Control," in *Proc. of the 17th Annual International Symposium on Computer Architecture (ISCA)*, Seattle, Washington, 1990, pp. 60–68.

[58] J. Duato, S. Yalamanchili, and N. Lionel, *Interconnection Networks: An Engineering Approach*. San Francisco, CA, USA: Morgan Kaufmann Publishers Inc., 2002.

[59] T. Felicijan and S. B. Furber, "An asynchronous on-chip network router with quality-of-service (QoS) support," in *Proceedings IEEE International SOC Conference*, 2004, pp. 274–277.

[60] D. Rostislav, V. Vishnyakov, E. Friedman, and R. Ginosar, "An Asynchronous Router for Multiple Service Levels Network on Chip," in *Proceedings of the 11th IEEE International Symposium on Asynchronous Circuits and Systems*, 2005.

[61] E. Beigne, F. Clermidy, P. Vivet, A. Clouard, and M. Renaudin, "An Asynchronous NOC Architecture Providing Low Latency Service and its Multi-Level Design Framework," in *Proceedings of the 11th IEEE International Symposium on Asynchronous Circuits and Systems*, 2005.

[62] A. Kumar, L.-S. Peh, P. Kundu, and N. K. Jha, "Express virtual-channels: towards the ideal interconnection fabric," in *Proc. of the 34th Intl. Symp. on Computer Architecture (ISCA-34)*, 2007.

[63] E. Bolotin, I. Cidon, R. Ginosar, and A. Kolodny, "QNoC: QoS architecture and design process for network on chip," *Journal of Systems Architecture, special issue on Network on Chip*, vol. 50, pp. 105–128, 2004.

[64] S. Sathe, D. Wiklund, and D. Liu, "Design of a switching node (router) for on-chip networks," *Proceedings of the 5th International Conference on ASIC*, pp. 75–78.

[65] K. Goossens, J. Dielissen, O. P. Gangwal, S. G. Pestana, A. Radulescu, and E. Rijpkema, "A design flow for application-specific networks on chip with guaranteed performance to accelerate SOC design and verification," in *Proc. Design, Automation and Test in Europe Conference and Exhibition (DATE)*, 2005, pp. 1182–1187.

[66] K. Goossens, J. Dielissen, and A. Radulescu, "The Æthereal network on chip: Concepts, architectures, and implementations," *IEEE Design and Test of Computers*, vol. 22, no. 5, pp. 21–31, 2005.

[67] W.-D. Weber, J. Chou, I. Swarbrick, and D. Wingard, "A quality-of-service mechanism for interconnection networks in system-on-chips," in *DATE*, 2005, pp. 1232–1237.

[68] J. Liang, S. Swaminathan, and R. Tessier, "aSOC: A Scalable, Single-Chip Communications Architecture," in *the IEEE International Conference on Parallel Architectures and Compilation Techniques*, 2000, pp. 524–529.

[69] A. Laffely, J. Liang, P. Jain, N. Weng, W. Burleson, and R. Tessier, "Adaptive system on a chip (aSoC) for low-power signal processing," in *Thirty-Fifth Asilomar Conference on Signals, Systems, and Computers*, 2001.

[70] A. Laffely, J. Liang, R. Tessier, and W. Burleson, "Adaptive system on a chip: A backbone for power-aware signal processing cores," in *Proc. of the IEEE Conference on Image Processing*, Barcelona, Spain, 2003.

[71] S. Kumar, "On packet switched networks for on-chip communication," in *Networks on Chip*, A. Jantsch and H. Tenhunen, Eds. Kluwer Academic Publishers, 2003, ch. 5, pp. 85–106.

[72] D. Wiklund and D. Liu, "Socbus: Switched network on chip for hard real time embedded systems," in *IPDPS '03: Proceedings of the 17th International Symposium on Parallel and Distributed Processing*. Washington, DC, USA: IEEE Computer Society, 2003, p. 78.1.

[73] P. Wielage and K. Goossens, "Networks on silicon: Blessing or nightmare?" in *DSD '02: Proceedings of the Euromicro Symposium on Digital Systems Design*. Washington, DC, USA: IEEE Computer Society, 2002, p. 196.

[74] J. Dielissen, A. Rădulescu, K. Goossens, and E. Rijpkema, "Concepts and implementation of the Philips network-on-chip," in *Workshop on IP-Based System-on-Chip Design*, 2003.

[75] A. Radulescu, J. Dielissen, K. G. W. Goossens, E. Rijpkema, and P. Wielage, "An efficient on-chip network interface offering guaranteed services, shared-memory abstraction, and flexible network configuration," in *DATE*, 2004, pp. 878–883.

[76] A. Radulescu and K. Goossens, "Communication services for networks on chip," in *Domain-Specific Processors: Systems, Architectures, Modeling, and Simulation.* Marcel Dekker, 2004, pp. 193–213.

[77] F. Palumbo, D. Pani, A. Pilia, and L. Raffo, "Impact of half-duplex and full-duplex dma implementations on noc performance," 2010.

[78] D. Pani, F. Palumbo, and L. Raffo, "A fast mpi-based parallel framework for cycle-accurate hdl multi-parametric simulations," *To Appear in International Journal of High Performance Systems Architecture, Special Issue on Power Efficient, High Performance General Purpose and Application Specific Computing Architectures.*

[79] M. Livingston and Q. Stout, "Parallel allocation algorithms for hypercubes and meshes," in *Proc. 4th Conf. Hypercube Concurrent Comput. Applications*, 1989, pp. 59–66.

[80] F. Wu, C.-C. Hsu, and L.-P. Chou, "Processor allocation in the mesh multiprocessors using the leapfrog method," *IEEE Trans. Parallel Distrib. Syst.*, vol. 14, no. 3, pp. 276–289, 2003.

[81] F. Palumbo, D. Pani, L. Raffo, and S. Secchi, "A surface tension and coalescence model for dynamic distributed resources allocation in massively parallel processors on-chip," in *NICSO '07: Proc of the International Workshop on Nature Inspired Cooperative Strategies for Optimization*, 2007, pp. 335–345.

INDEX

U

T

V

W

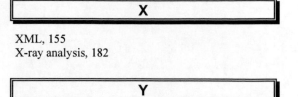

Y